THE AGE OF AIRPOWER

THE AGE OF AIRPOWER

MARTIN VAN CREVELD

PUBLICAFFAIRS
New York

Published in the United States by PublicAffairs™, a member of the Perseus Books Group.

Printed in the United States of America.

PublicAffairs books are available at special discounts for bulk purchases in the U.S. by corporations, institutions, and other organizations. For more information, please contact the Special Markets Department at the Perseus Books Group, 2300 Chestnut Street, Suite 200, Philadelphia, PA 19103, call (800) 810-4145, ext. 5000, or e-mail special.markets@perseusbooks.com.

Book Design by Timm Bryson

Library of Congress Cataloging-in-Publication Data
Van Creveld, Martin, 1946-
The age of airpower / Martin van Creveld.—1st ed.
p. cm.
Includes bibliographical references and index.
ISBN 978-1-58648-981-6 (hardcover)
1. Air power—History. I. Title.
UG630.V285 2011
358.4'03—dc22

2010042365

First Edition
10 9 8 7 6 5 4 3 2 1

FOR STEVEN CANBY

In thirty years, no cloud has ever darkened *our* sky.

CONTENTS

PART IV
LITTLE WARS, 1945–2010

PART V
WAR AMONGST THE PEOPLE, 1898–2010

PREFACE

In the end, perhaps the most revealing witnesses are the pictures. An unknown World War I machine gunner standing up in the nose of his aircraft, ready to fire at any enemy who came too close. His contemporary, the British ace Captain Albert Ball, proudly holding in one arm the engine cowling of a German opponent he has shot down and in the other the propeller. A Zeppelin on its way to drop a load of bombs on some British city. A World War II German Me-109 fighter with its ground crew on a French stubble field, and another aircraft of the same type taxiing in the Russian mud. An endless line of B-24 Liberator medium bombers being assembled at a Consolidated plant in Fort Worth, Texas, in 1943. Twenty thousand Allied paratroopers floating down on their way to be massacred by the Germans at Arnhem even as another 15,000 men were landing by glider. The first "atomic" bomb, dropped from a B-29 bomber, exploding over Hiroshima on August 6, 1945.

Better than a thousand words, pictures show where air warfare has come from and how it has changed over time. But this is not just a book about the past; it seeks to peer into the future as well. We know, or think we know, where we are. But where are we going? Is airpower destined to go from success to success, as many observers believe? Or has it already reached what the great nineteenth-century military theoretician Carl von Clausewitz in *On War* called the "culminating point"? If it has a future, what might that future look like? Or is it in its final days? And if so, what, if anything, could take its place?

When I say "air" I include both naval aviation and space. About the former, I have never understood why many books exclude it merely because the aircraft on which it relies are based aboard ship and/or often carry out a somewhat different kind of mission. After all, land-based aviation has often been used against targets at sea, and vice versa. Should one exclude Pearl Harbor from discussion just because the Japanese aircraft operated from carriers? Should one exclude Midway, Leyte Gulf, the Falklands war? Speaking of space, it is useful to recall that, until the last years of World War II, when the first ballistic missiles started traveling through space from launching point to target, it played no part in warfare. Since then its role has vastly expanded. This is partly because space operations supplement and assist those that take place in the air and partly because they are steadily taking the latter's place. Needless to say, it is only by way of the air that space can be reached at all. Not for nothing does NASA stand for National Aeronautics *and* [my emphasis] Space Administration. In a word, space and air operations have become inseparable, and this fact is reflected in the way they are treated in this book.

When I use the term "air warfare," I do not mean just the campaigns and the battles. Nor am I referring merely to the machines that did the fighting and to the men (there were hardly any women, but those who did participate will not be ignored) who flew them. Rather, I include the organizations that designed and developed and produced the machines as well as those that assembled and trained and commanded the men. In other words, I have tried to look at things from as many different points of view as possible. If an account does not do all this, it cannot be anything close to complete, and indeed passing over these matters could lead to serious misreadings of the history. Clausewitz said that "fighting is to war what cash payment is to business life";[1] yet any account of business life consisting solely of a list of cash transactions would not just fail to capture what took place but in fact be quite meaningless.

The outline of the volume is as follows. Part I, "Into the Blue," provides a brief introduction to the rise and evolution of air warfare until the outbreak of World War II. Part II, "The Greatest War of All," examines air campaigns and operations during World War II. Part III, "The War That Never Was," looks at the Cold War confrontation when another world war always seemed to be just around the corner but somehow never broke out. Part IV, "Little Wars" (compliments to H. G. Wells, who published a book with that title in 1905), deals with air warfare as it was conducted against, or by, all kinds of countries other than the superpowers during the period 1945–2010. Part V, "War Amongst the People" (compliments to my friend, General [ret.] Rupert Smith), examines the century-long history of attempts to use airpower in all its numerous forms against uprisings, guerrilla forces, terrorism, and similar forms of "non-trinitarian" warfare. Finally, the title of the concluding chapter, "Going Down," speaks for itself.

I am obliged to many people for their help as I wrote this book. In fact, Lieutenant Colonel John Olsen, Royal Norwegian Air Force, provided the stimulus when he asked me to write an article on the history of airpower for a collection he was editing. John has also read and commented on the manuscript of this book; so did Wing Commander (ret.) Alan Stephens, of the Royal Australian Air Force, and Dr. Grant Hammond, formerly of the NATO Defense College in Rome and the author of a book on John Boyd. Both Alan and Grant also gave me some of their excellent writings on airpower for research.

Gregory Alegi kindly allowed me to read his paper on aerial combat during the Italo-Turkish War of 1911. My former student, Colonel (ret.) Dr. Moshe Ben David lent me some of the hard-to-get early works on the law of air warfare he had collected for his dissertation. Werner Froelich, of the Heeresgeschichtliches Museum, Vienna, explained some early Austrian attempts to use balloons in war. Monica Malgarini, also of the NATO Defense College, helped me find material concerning the 1911 Italo-Turkish War. Hava Noventern, who runs the Edelstein Library at the Hebrew University, helped me locate some esoteric publications on the origins of flight. Eva Reineke, formerly of the Deutsches Museum, Munich, kindly helped me find material about the flight pioneer Wilhelm Bauer. My longtime friend Robert Tomes, in Washington, D.C., provided me with encouragement and books at a moment when I was almost about to throw in the sponge. Dr. Rivka Yermiash, who in addition to her many other virtues holds a pilot's license and is an expert on airfield operations, has kindly allowed me to make extensive use of the dissertation she wrote under my supervision. So did Yagil Henkin, whose dissertation is probably the best account of the Rhodesian war of independence. Two other former students, Zeev Elron and Liran Ofek, helped me find mountains of material that, but for them, I would almost certainly have overlooked.

Though some of my requests for information must have seemed weird to those whose job it was to try to meet them, not once did I encounter a single refusal. To the contrary, most people went out of their way to help and even volunteered to read the text. Without any doubt, for those who have lost their faith in humanity, this is the way to go.

PART I

INTO THE BLUE

1900–1939

How did military aviation originate, how did it affect World War I, and how did it develop during the "twenty years' armistice"? The answers to some of these questions are well-known, whereas many others have been lost in time or all but disappeared into dusty archives. Here we shall answer them in brief, starting at the beginning and reaching all the way to the last years before World War II.

CHAPTER I

ANTECEDENTS AND BEGINNINGS

For practical purposes, manned flight may be said to have started with the French brothers Joseph and Étienne Montgolfier, who, in 1783, held the first public demonstrations of hot air balloons. Benjamin Franklin, the American minister to France, witnessed one of the Montgolfiers' manned balloon flights that year and would later express the hope that this new technology could be used in the cause of peace. A century later, the astronomer Camille Flammarion wrote of those first flights: "In the whole of human history, no invention was greeted by greater applause. Never did human genius achieve a greater triumph. The mathematical and physical sciences received a most striking affirmation. . . . Man achieved mastery over nature. . . . triumphantly, he took possession of the celestial realms."[1]

The year 1783 also saw Jacques Charles invent the hydrogen balloon, which almost immediately replaced the less efficient hot air balloon. Hydrogen had been recently discovered by the British scientist Henry Cavendish; known to weigh only 7 percent of a corresponding volume of air, it was called "flammable air." Over the next decades, adventurous spirits, mostly from France, flew longer and further missions in the hydrogen balloons, dubbed "Charliers" after their inventor. In 1803, Étienne-Gaspard Robert, a professional stuntman of Belgian origins, and a German physician named Lhoest took off in a balloon from Hamburg and ascended to an altitude of 23,000 feet. Later they described the experience: "the pain we felt was of the kind one feels when diving with one's head underwater. It was as if our breasts had expanded. . . . All arteries were tense and showed themselves in relief. So much did the blood flow into my head that I felt as if my hat had grown too small for me. . . . When the barometer showed 4/100 [that is, two-fifths of normal at sea level] we felt even worse. . . . Both physically and emotionally I sank into a kind of torpor in which we thought we could recognize the approach of death."[2]

However, it soon turned out that the Charliers had all but exhausted the technical possibilities of lighter-than-air flight for the next century. Balloons could neither be steered nor go up and down freely, and many balloonists tried to correct these shortcomings. One added flapping wings, and a tail for steerage.[3] Thomas Jefferson wrote of some kind of "screw which takes hold of the air and draws itself along by it" and expressed the hope that "perhaps it may be used . . . for the balloon."[4] Others hoped to use oars or sails, and one planned to propel the balloons by harnessing eagles that would be directed by means of tasty morsels held out to them at the end of a pole. As English expressions like "gasbags" and "hot air merchants" show, by 1870 balloonists had acquired a reputation as charlatans.

Only after the invention of the internal combustion engine in the 1880s did the technical problems appear on their way to being solved, with the introduction of the dirigible, so named because it could be steered. Again, it was the French who took the lead in this new field, and in 1886 a French dirigible flew from Boulogne to Yarmouth in England. But today, the name indelibly associated with dirigibles is not French but rather that of a Prussian count, Ferdinand von Zeppelin. The count's interest in aviation dated to the American Civil War, which he witnessed as his country's official observer.[5] Yet it was not until 1890, after his retirement from the military, that he took up the matter full-time, and it was only in July 1900 that the first Luftschiff Zeppelin, the LZ 1, had its maiden flight. The machines, which soon grew to gigantic dimensions, were built around a frame of triangular lattice girders covered with fabric. For reasons of safety, control, and maintenance, the gas was contained in separate gas cells. A catwalk gave the crew access to every part of the ship. Power was provided by gasoline engines, and steering was carried out by means of fins.

Meanwhile, what of heavier-than-air flight? The fact that it was possible in principle could hardly be denied. Birds apart, one only had to watch children playing with kites or with top-like devices that, equipped with a propeller that was rotated rapidly by pulling a string, could lift into the air; indeed, if there was anything unnatural about flight it was lighter-than-air devices, not heavier ones. The nineteenth century was obsessed with achieving heavier-than-air flight. As one contemporary wrote: "If there be a domineering tyrant thought, it is the conception that the problem of flight may be solved by man. When once this idea has invaded the brain it possesses it exclusively."[6] Until 1860, the British Patent Office received on average one application a year connected with aviation, but soon the figure increased sevenfold. Almost every feature later incorporated into aircraft was foreshadowed during this time. Meanwhile, starting in 1891, Otto Lilienthal became the first person to make successful flights with gliders, sailing off a hill not far from Neuruppin in Brandenburg. There a rather neglected monument marks the place where he experimented and, in the end, fell to his death.

It was up to another pair of brothers, this time not French but American, to make the next great breakthrough. Both Wilbur and Orville Wright attended high school for a time, but neither graduated. They had read about Lilienthal's experiments and knew about their own countryman, Samuel Langley, who in 1896 succeeded in flying an unmanned steam-powered model aircraft. The Wright brothers' machine was a double-decker made of wood, wire, and fabric. It had a custom-built gasoline engine that drove two "pusher" propellers in opposite directions. To minimize weight and drag, the undercarriage used a rail instead of wheels. The Wrights' decisive contribution consisted of the controls: horizontal ones mounted in front, vertical rudders in the rear, and a third set, made up first of wings that could be "warped" and then of ailerons, that provided roll. All this allowed them to control their craft as no previous experimenter had done. The contraption took off at Kitty Hawk, North Carolina, on December 17, 1903, and covered 120 feet in 12 seconds.

Right from the beginning, the Wrights tried to sell their invention to various armies around the world. This was nothing new. No sooner had the first Charliers gone up in 1783 than their inventor wrote in a letter to the daily newspaper *Journal de Paris* that they "could be made very useful to an army for discovering the positions of its enemy, his movements, his advances, and his dispositions."[7] Indeed the year had not yet ended before a 20-page tract was published in Amsterdam and Paris advocating the use of balloons to capture Gibraltar from the British.

Balloons could also be enlisted to impress a country's enemies. An interesting attempt to do just that was made by Napoleon—General Bonaparte, as he then was—in Egypt in 1798. He had occupied the country, and now had a guerrilla war on his hands. He tried to intimidate the population by arranging a balloon flight. The Muslim scholar Abdl Rahman al Jabarti witnessed the event and described it as follows: "their claim that this apparatus is like a vessel in which people sit and travel to other countries in order to discover news and other falsifications did not appear to be true. On the contrary, it turned out that it is like kites which household servants build for festivals and happy occasions."[8]

Following the balloons' disappointing performance in Egypt, Napoleon ordered the unit that operated them disbanded. A big mistake, that: had he possessed them at the Battle of Waterloo in June 1815, he might have discovered Field Marshal Bluecher's approaching columns before they arrived and took him in the flank. He might also have located Marshal Grouchy's "lost" cavalry corps and sent it against those very columns. Probably the emperor would still not have won the battle, but he might very well have avoided defeat. Others were more open-minded; throughout the first half of the nineteenth century, inventors in various countries continued their experiments.

Considered as military instruments, balloons suffered from many disadvantages. On pain of drifting off in God knows what direction, they had to be tethered to the ground. This limited the altitude to which they could rise and thus enabled ground troops to take potshots at them. In addition they were awkward to transport, took a long time to inflate, and had difficulties communicating with the troops on the ground. During periods of bad weather they could not carry out their observations or even take off at all. None of this prevented the Austrians in 1849 from trying to use them to bring rebellious Venice back under their control.[9] The city being protected by its lagoons, which made it hard to attack with artillery, the idea was born to do so from the air. Two hundred hot air balloons were manufactured, each carrying a small bomb. They were launched from a ship, the *Vulcano*, in the hope that, coming down into the town, they would cause both damage and panic. As it happened, contrary winds turned the attempt into a near-complete failure. Only one bomb actually exploded inside the town, and even it did no damage.

By the middle of the nineteenth century, no futuristic novel was complete without some more or less fantastic reference to flying devices, and many of these were meant to be used in warfare of some sort. Particularly interesting was Albert Robida's *War in the Twentieth Century* (1887).[10] His Great War, which was supposed to take place in 1945, made use of many inventions to come, including submarines, flamethrowers, chemical and biological warfare, and tanks. Robida, who has been called "the most gifted and original artist in the history of science fiction,"[11] even anticipated the debate between those who wanted to use flying machines against military targets and those who thought they would be most effective against civilian ones.

During the American Civil War, both sides, but the North in particular, extensively used balloons largely because of the advent of two new technologies: telegraphic communications and photography. The former permitted communications between the ground and the air, and the latter allowed a more accurate and comprehensive record of reconnaissance. The most important American pioneer in the use of balloons was Thaddeus S. C. Lowe.[12] Just as the Civil War got under way, his experiments attracted the attention of Lincoln. At the First Battle of Bull Run during the following month, Lowe was attached to the Army of Northeastern Virginia. He took off successfully and performed impressively but had the misfortune of landing behind enemy lines. Unable to walk because of an injury, he had to be rescued by his wife, who with the help of others, carried him to safety. Convinced that a balloon corps could play a useful role in the war, the president established it and appointed Lowe its commander, the Chief Aeronaut of the Union Army Balloon Corps. With some of his four, and later seven, balloons Lowe participated in the Peninsular Campaign. On at least one occasion, the battle of Fair Oaks in Virginia in May 1862, he provided critical intelligence that saved part of the Union Army. He was also present at Sharpsburg and Fredericksburg. If nothing else, the balloons proved a nuisance to the enemy, who felt exposed and were forced to take countermeasures, for example, by moving at night. As the Confederate general E. P. Alexander wrote, "even if the observer never saw anything, his balloons would have been worth all they cost, trying to keep our movements out of sight."[13] The Confederate Army also formed a smaller version of the balloon corps. However, since initially it did not have the equipment needed to generate hydrogen gas, it was forced to rely on hot air balloons, now called Montgolfières for their inventors.

In 1870–71, the French famously used balloons during the siege of Paris. First intelligence-gathering flights were mounted. Next, the city having been cut off from the world, a balloon post was formally established. Over a period of four months 66 flights took off.[14] Thus some sort of communication between the capital and the government, established first at Tours and then at Poitiers, was maintained. However, all attempts to pass news *into* Paris by this means failed. Another use to which the balloons were put was to fly out prominent persons, including Léon Gambetta, who later became prime minister for a short time. Though the system proved itself, it always remained rather uncertain. Not only was the equipment extremely primitive, but the Germans took potshots at the balloons. To this were added the hazards of the weather. Once a balloon had taken off, there was no knowing where it might come down again.

Though still limited to lighter-than-air devices, military aviation slowly began turning from a somewhat outlandish enterprise directed by adventurers into a more serious concern. By 1884 the armies of France, Britain, Russia, Italy, Spain, and Germany all had balloon units with facilities to match. In 1892 the U.S. Army followed their example. The French took balloons to Indochina and the Italians, to Ethiopia, where they were soundly defeated. The British used them in South Africa. They served at the sieges of Ladysmith and Mafeking as well as the battles of Spion Kop and Paardeberg where they helped their owners spot artillery. One Boer prisoner even said that, if he and his comrades ever laid their hands on the balloonist who forced them to "creep" from shelter to shelter, they would kill him.[15]

In 1898 the U.S. Signal Corps took its only balloon to Cuba. Decades later, the historian of the U.S. Army credited it with finding a trail up San Juan Hill and directing artillery fire on Spanish positions there. This feat, she claimed, "may have been the determining factor" in the victory.[16] Theodore Roosevelt, who famously commanded the Rough Riders during the battle, had thought otherwise. In his memoirs he wrote that the "captive balloon [which] was up in the air at that moment . . . was worse than useless."[17] Another author explained that, by approaching too near the front line, the "untrained" balloon crew attracted enemy fire and that "this aroused an unfriendly feeling towards aeronautics on the part of the ground troops."[18] The War Department sided with Roosevelt. It disbanded the balloon detachment, reactivating it only in 1907.

As the nineteenth century ended, the prospect of inflicting death, even large-scale death, from the air also began to attract the attention of lawyers and diplomats. When the first international disarmament conference met at The Hague in 1899 to consider limits on air war, the objective was to preserve military "efficacy" while minimizing human suffering. The principal supporter of limitations on air war of all kinds was Russia, which hoped to compensate for its technological backwardness. Its appeal was seconded by the smaller states, such as Portugal, Belgium, and the Netherlands. By contrast, France, Germany, Britain, Italy, and the United States were all keenly interested in the emerging military possibilities of lighter-than-air devices and instructed their delegates to oppose the proposed ban.

Later the Americans changed their mind, allowing their representative, Captain William Crozier, to make a speech that set new standards in hypocrisy:

> It seems to me difficult to justify by a humanitarian motive the prohibition of the use of balloons for the hurling of projectiles or other explosive materials. We are without experience in the use of arms whose employment we propose to prohibit forever. Granting that practical means of using balloons can be invented, who can say that such an invention will not . . . decide the victory and thus . . . diminish the evils of war and to support the humanitarian considerations which we have in view?[19]

In other words, dropping ordnance from the air could safely be banned precisely because the existing technical means for doing so had *not* yet reached the point where it was very powerful or very accurate. As better air weapons made their appearance, though, the prohibition on their use would have to be reconsidered. By no means should it be allowed to prevent one side or another from winning a rapid victory and, by so doing, bestowing the blessings of peace. This Alice in Wonderland logic was well received by the delegates. A resolution was passed to prohibit "for a term of five years, the launching of projectiles and explosives from balloons, or by other new methods of a similar nature."

In reality, the declaration amounted to a mere moratorium. To quote Crozier again, in the future, weapons might well be "perfected." They might become capable of "localizing at important points the destruction of life and property"; what nation would be prepared to forgo such wonderful arms? When the Second Disarmament Conference met in 1907, things went even worse for those who had hoped to ban or limit bombardment from the air. The prohibition was renewed with only a slight change in the wording. Much of the credit for this must go to Britain, which at that time felt itself lagging behind the rest in the development of military aviation and was beginning to worry about the so-called air peril. Even so, the ban was to remain in force only until such a time as the next conference gathered. That conference never materialized. As British air marshal Arthur Harris, who in 1939–45 contributed as much to the indiscriminate bombardment of cities and the killing of civilians as anyone else, later commented: "In this matter of the use of aircraft in war there is, it so happens, no international law at all."[20]

Meanwhile art was anticipating life. In 1907 the famous British writer H. G. Wells published the novel *The War in the Air*. In it, sometime in the following decade, the Kaiser launches a surprise attack on the United States using a fleet of Zeppelins. The largest, the *Vaterland,* is 2,000 feet long and can reach a speed of 90 miles per hour. "A huge herd of airships rising one after another had an effect of strange, portentous monsters breaking into an altogether unfamiliar world."[21] The armada sinks much of the U.S. Navy and bombs New York, forcing it to surrender, but the "spirited" American people refuse to give up. Fleets of American airplanes, secretly "developed after the Wright model," appear out of nowhere. They attack the Zeppelins, which, designed mainly for bombing, are all but unable to defend themselves and are brought down. But now Japan and China form an alliance and join the war against America. The remaining European powers also get involved. Even "down in South America" people start fighting among themselves. Mighty fleets of flying machines—lighter-than-air ones, airplanes, and, on the Japanese side, swarms of small, agile "swordsmen" with celluloid wings—take to the air and clash.

Wells describes the effects of a single bomb—"a flash of fire . . . preposterous clumsy leaps . . . a faint screaming . . . a falling mass of brickwork . . . dust and black smoke":

> In this manner the massacre of New York began. She was the first of the great cities . . . to suffer by the enormous powers . . . of aerial warfare. She was wrecked as in the previous centuries endless barbaric cities had been bombarded. . . . As the airships sailed along they

> smashed up the city as a child will shatter its cities of brick and card. Below, they left ruins and blazing conflagrations, and heaped and scattered dead; men, women and children mixed together. . . . Lower New York was soon a furnace of crimson flames from which there was no escape. Cars, railways, ferries, all had ceased and never a light led the way of the distracted fugitives in that dusky confusion but the light of burning.[22]

London, Paris, Hamburg, and Berlin are also bombed and destroyed. The "flimsy fabric of credit"[23] that holds the modern world together having been disrupted, the outcome is global chaos.

With the benefit of hindsight, perhaps the most astonishing aspect of Wells's vision was the enormous exaggeration of the damage that even "thousands" of airships, armed with conventional explosives, can inflict; at one point he says that "with a few hand grenades they [the Germans] made short work of every villa within a mile."[24] Like many others after him Wells seems to have completely misjudged the way civilian populations coming under air attack might react. He had no idea of the remarkable recuperative powers that cities such as Hamburg would turn out to possess, let alone of the social discipline that, contrary to his expectations,[25] would make that recuperation possible.

Around this time, the problem of making lighter-than-air devices independent of the wind was finally on its way to being solved. Accordingly, in 1905 the French Army bought its first semi-rigid dirigible, which could cover 60 miles in a single flight at a speed of 25 miles per hour. In 1905, the Italian Army also purchased its first dirigible.[26] In the same year, the first experiments in using dirigibles to bombard targets from the air were made. Spurred by French efforts in this direction, the armies of Russia, Austria, and Spain also purchased dirigibles. Still, the most spectacular progress was being made in Germany, and specifically by Count Zeppelin, whom we have already met. In 1908 he succeeded in convincing the army to buy his third airship, the LZ 3. By August 1914 a total of 14 had been sold to the army and the navy. However, several of them crashed or were decommissioned, so that the number of those actually in service at the outbreak of hostilities was five, plus another three that were requisitioned from their civilian owners. At the time this represented the largest number of dirigibles operated by any power.

The greatest advantage of airships was always their ability to make extremely long voyages without having to land, refuel, or change crews. Once airborne, they were simpler and safer to operate than aircraft. On the ground, the situation was exactly the opposite. The largest Zeppelins had a volume of over 2,500,000 cubic feet. They needed enormous hangars, inside which, weighing as much as 50 tons when emptied of gas, they were suspended between missions. Taken outside, tethered Zeppelins were very vulnerable to side-winds. Early on, more came to grief trying to take off or land than during flight itself. Hence some hangars were mounted on huge revolving platforms like those used to repair locomotives. Near Cuxhaven, the German Navy built an installation known as Nobel. It consisted of twin hangars capable of turning 360 degrees in tandem. Each was 596 feet long, later extended to 655 feet; their width was 98 feet, their height 229 feet. Total weight amounted to 4,200 tons, all supported by eight enormous carriages.[27] To fly a mission, it was first necessary to produce, store, and pump vast volumes of gas—all procedures that required extensive and fairly complex equipment. Inflating a typical Zeppelin took about one and a half to two days. To operate its fleet of five, the German Navy required an organization of no fewer than 4,000 men.[28] To make things worse, the hydrogen gas that provided the necessary lift presented a very serious hazard so that any accidental spark might turn the entire contraption into a blazing inferno.

Meanwhile, what about the use in war of heavier-than-air flying machines? From the moment the Wright brothers made their first powered flight to the one when they first tried to sell their "flyer" to the U.S. Army, which declined, little more than a year had passed. Convinced that the only possible buyers for their machines would be the military,[29] the Wrights developed contacts in Europe, where, according to Hiram Maxim, the inventor of the machine gun, people were ready to buy anything that would help them cut each other's throats.[30] The brothers tried Britain, where both the navy and the army refused their advances. Next, arriving in France, they were at first denounced as hoaxers and liars—since they were not French, how could they be anything else? Yet the wind soon changed. In 1909, following a series of very successful flights in which Wilbur demonstrated the by now much-improved capabilities of the family machine, the War Ministry purchased no fewer than seven aircraft. During the subsequent maneuvers pilots flying Blériot and Antoinette monoplanes not only showed that they could control their machines but took aerial photographs and used wireless to transmit the results of air reconnaissance to the commanders below. This demonstration of Gallic prowess convinced other countries to follow suit. However, the organization was decidedly amateurish, and many pilots were not even members of the armed forces but rich civilians who volunteered along with their crates. Employed to perform reconnaissance, liaison, and communication tasks, so much did aircraft and pilots suffer from the weather and from engine failure as to almost eliminate any advantage that might have been gained from their use.[31]

Still, some people must have been impressed. Shortly after the French maneuvers, the British changed their mind. Besides buying aircraft, they established the Aerial Navigation Committee. It was the first-ever government body specifically charged with military-aeronautic research; later it gave birth to the Royal Aeronautics Factory at Farnborough. Abroad, too, the "air forces" of the various powers continued to expand. By 1910 Germany had five military aircraft, England four, and Russia three. Italy, Austria, Japan, Belgium, and the United States had two each. With no fewer than 36 machines, France had more than all the rest put together.[32] Still, the debate as to which type was more suitable for military purposes continued. As one German officer wrote in 1908, "the performance of the apparatus developed by the Wrights will always remain very far behind that of Balloons."[33]

As so often happens when a new technology is introduced, a bewildering number of constantly changing models made their appearance. Each was built in very small numbers. Most were antiquated almost before they could be distributed to the units. From then to the present, the saying that the best is the enemy of the good has remained one of the salient problems of airpower as a whole. An excellent example is the French Blériot XI. There were 132 produced, an unusually large number for the time, but these machines came in 12 different versions. They differed in their configuration, their carrying capacity (there were one-, two-, and three-seaters), and the power of their engines. During the aircraft's years of service the latter went up from 25 through 50 to 140 horsepower. There was a "military" version, an "artillery" version, an "engineering" version (designed for easy assembly and disassembly so it could be transported), a hydroplane, and a clipped-wing training version known as the Blériot roulant.[34] Probably this last-named contraption, though unable to fly, has the right to be called the first aircraft simulator.

By August 1914, the order of battle of the various powers looked as follows:

COUNTRY	AIRCRAFT	AIRSHIPS	BALLOONS
Germany	232	5	16
Austria-Hungary	48	3	12
France	165	10	10
Russia	263	4	46
Britain	63	–	–
Belgium	16	2	2

As important as numbers are organization, command and control, every kind of facility such as bases, as well as training. Most countries divided their nascent "air forces" between their armies and their navies, but apart from that the organizations they built up had little in common. In some countries they were appended to the cavalry as the arm that had traditionally been responsible for reconnaissance. In others they formed part of the artillery, the "learned arm" whose guns they were supposed to help direct. Alternatively they might form part of the corps of engineers, another learned arm (in France, there was a time when responsibility was divided between the two), or else of the transportation corps as in the German Army; in the United States they constituted a branch of the signal corps.

Usually there was some system of dual command. An inspectorate, established within any one of the above arms, looked after the bases and the various flying devices. It also assumed responsibility for procurement, technical development, the training of personnel of every kind, and the like. In wartime, though, the various flying devices came under the orders of the formations to which they were attached and which they served. The general commanding an army might have a squadron of aircraft assigned to him; a corps commander might have a balloon or two, and the rear admiral in command of a squadron of warships a small dirigible or else a hydroplane. Only in Britain was an army air corps, forerunner of the Royal Air Force, established even before World War I broke out.

Building bases for aircraft was much easier than for lighter-than-air flying devices. Though they too had to take account of the weather, they were able to take off from, and land on, almost any level field with a reasonably consistent, reasonably smooth, surface. Little special preparation was needed; if the craft broke a wheel or a strut, the damage could often be repaired on the spot. Small craft and low speeds meant that, compared with what was to come later on, takeoff and landing distances were very short. Still, operating a fleet, even a fairly small fleet, of military aircraft required something more. At a minimum, hangars had to be constructed and maintenance and repair facilities provided. Fuel tanks had to be installed, ammunition dumps established, and quarters for the personnel found. It was also necessary to have some meteorological equipment, however rudimentary. To prevent the bases from turning into targets in wartime, they had to be camouflaged. The whole complex had to be provided with a communications network. Finally, a logistic system capable of keeping the bases supplied had to be called into being.

Inevitably the earliest pilots were self-trained, and inevitably this "training" led to accidents, many of them fatal. The first schools for military balloon operators opened during the mid-1880s. Besides teaching students how to fly, they instructed them in meteorology and the use of the telegraph.[35] Two decades later, the first flying schools proper opened their doors. The first air units were small and experimental, with the result that the selection process was often haphazard.[36] While all armies relied on volunteers there was no agreement as to who would make the best pilots. Some tried to get former cavalrymen. Others looked for qualities such as good motor coordination and the physical condition needed to fly at high altitudes in open, unheated nacelles without oxygen; others still, for the ability to carry out what were inevitably very lonely missions, which required a suitable temperament. One British observer found pilots "curiously alike in type—quiet keen, interested faces, foreheads narrow rather than wide, eyes set somewhat close together . . . as unlike the old bullet face as possible, tenacious and determined rather than aggressive and obtrusive."[37] Perhaps the most problematic quality, required by the Germans in particular, was "pugnacity." Not only was devising objective tests for it difficult, but it was often possible to put different interpretations on the same results.

To get a sense of how training was carried out, take the case of Duncan Grinnell-Milne.[38] In 1915, when he was just over 18, he volunteered for flight training at Shoreham. The airfield consisted of open fields and a few sheds. The first days were spent looking over the machines, watching instructors take off and land, and talking shop in the mess. Only after two weeks did Grinnell-Milne make his first flight. Next he went up several times a day, getting used to the sensation of flying and learning to operate the controls. After three hours and 20 minutes' worth of flying he was allowed to fly solo. Over the next few weeks he often flew various machines. On one occasion the engine conked out and he had to carry out an emergency landing in an open field, but escaped without injury. On the ground, during all this time, instruction in rigging and engine fitting went on. Occasionally he and his fellow trainees were given "vaguely scientific lectures upon aerodynamics."[39] The final examination was an oral one. Some questions about aeronautics, some about engines, and a Morse test—and the ordeal was over.

At the time Grinnell-Milne and his comrades received their wings in 1915, the world's first air war was already four years in the past. Today, all that remains of the Italo-Turkish War of 1911–12 are some vague memories. At the time, it aroused much interest. Here I shall rely primarily on a 1913 volume by Commodore William H. Beehler, who introduces himself as "formerly attaché to the United States Embassies in Berlin, Rome and Vienna," as well as some recent works.[40] The origins of the war must be seen in great power politics—at the time it broke out, many choice Mediterranean morsels formerly under Ottoman rule had already been taken away by Britain and France, and Italy wanted its share.[41] Libya at the time was defended by a ragtag Ottoman force numbering some 7,000 men. Later another 20,000 Arab volunteers joined in and soon proved to be excellent, if ill-organized, fighters, intimately familiar with the country, abstemious, crafty, and very cruel. The main ports were fortified, but their fortifications and artillery were antiquated. Commanded by Lieutenant General Carlo Caneva, the Italians had 40,000 men, as well as 11 "flying machines of the French type."[42] With the Ottoman armed forces famous for their weakness, the campaign was supposed to be short and decisive—what aggressive war isn't? Hostilities opened on September 28, 1911, when the Italian Navy blockaded Libya and demanded that Tripoli surrender. Early in October, after no reply had been received, the town was bombarded and occupied. However, the fall of Tripoli and other coastal towns simply caused the Ottoman forces to retreat into the interior of the vast country. It did nothing to bring the war to an end.

Preparing for the war, the Italians hastily put together a contingent of nine aircraft, all single-seaters. They had engines capable of developing around 50 horsepower and cost some $6,000 each. This force left Naples aboard two ships on October 12 and 13 and arrived on October 16. Operations started on the 22nd. Later during the war, smaller contingents of aircraft, numbering two or three each, were distributed among the remote, and much smaller, towns of Benghazi, Derna, and Tobruk. As the number of aircraft slowly increased, so did that of pilots, officers, and men. Ground facilities consisted of a rough quadrangle of flat terrain that had been cleared of all obstacles and, sometimes, fenced in. To combat the soft desert sand, some bases had wooden planks laid end to end to form runways 300 feet long by 75 wide. Later some of the runways were illuminated at night. Scattered all around were tents that served as hangars for the various flying machines—huge, metal-framed ones for the dirigibles and smaller ones for the aircraft. The picture was completed by a hospital, a guard company, and the inevitable radiotelegraphic apparatus crowned by a tall antenna. Though there were some experiments in the use of wireless for air-to-ground and ground-to-air communication, it was too cumbersome to be so routinely employed.

Over the next few months the Italian pilots recorded a long list of firsts. These included the first recorded flight by a military aircraft over enemy territory (October 22), the first use of aircraft to lay naval gunfire (October 28), the first wartime use of wireless for air-to-ground and ground-to-air communication, the first wartime attempt at aerial bombing (November 1), the first wartime use of aerial photography (November 23), the first wartime mission flown by night (March 4, 1912), and the first, rather unsuccessful, experiment with nighttime bombing (June 11). By this time, weather and serviceability permitting, Italian columns making their way across the desert were regularly escorted by aircraft. Their mission was to reconnoiter the flanks and spot ambushes ahead of time. Some pilots flew what were considered very long distances—as much as 75 miles from base and back.

Though the Italians enjoyed complete control of the air, they did not have it all their own way. In part, this was because of technical limitations. Flying without radio over uncharted terrain, pilots suffered from isolation and experienced great difficulty in navigation. Wind and dust often proved too strong for the primitive equipment and/or limited the pilots' visibility. The Cipelli grenades that were used as bombs turned out to be far from ideal for the purpose. Weighing about five pounds, they had to be held between the knees of the pilot who had to control the aircraft with one hand and use the other to remove the safety pin. Most of the grenades missed their targets, exploding harmlessly in the sand. Others hit noncombatants. This not only proved counterproductive, helping drive people into the insurgents' arms, but led to lively condemnations in the international press.

The latter, the Italians claimed, was motivated by "pseudo-humanitarian ideologies."[43]

Though taken by surprise, the enemy quickly started fighting back. On October 25, a Captain Moizo became the first heavier-than-air aviator to have his aircraft shot at while he was in the air, reporting three hits on his Nieuport. This anti-aircraft fire, though primitive and uncoordinated, forced the Italians to climb higher and higher. On the other hand, the Italian officers in charge of the air battalion could console themselves with the fact that casualties were very light. Only on August 25, 1912, did Lieutenant Pietro Manzini become the first pilot to be killed in the war, and even so his death was the result not of enemy action but of a flying accident. Two weeks later, Moizo, having been forced to land owing to engine trouble, had the dubious honor of becoming the first aviator in history to be taken prisoner. Operations in Libya dragged on; as long as they remained within 40 miles of the coast, the Italians had little difficulty occupying any place they set their eyes on. However, each time they did so the elusive, but highly motivated, enemy retreated in front of their cumbersome columns, escaping into the desert. As the Italians, affected by a dearth of provisions as well as water, began to retreat, the Arab irregulars would emerge from their hiding places and launch surprise attacks. Each attack brought a fresh wave of casualties, including not just the usual crop of dead and wounded but men who had been impaled, crucified, and emasculated.

If anything, the use of airships proved even more problematic. The Italians had two of them, and they arrived at Tripoli on December 3 and 16, respectively. However, whereas aircraft could be housed in simple tents, dirigibles needed much larger hangars; besides, the ships had been damaged while en route. As a result, they could only start operations at the beginning of March 1912, long after the war had turned into a struggle of attrition. Airships could carry heavier bombs, and their endurance also made them more suitable for accompanying columns on the march. On the other hand, they proved much more vulnerable to enemy fire than aircraft—a portent, as it turned out, of things to come. The most important single operation carried out by airships took place on April 12, 1912, when they helped their owners reconnoiter the Ottoman positions at the little settlement of Zuara, far to the west. However, the land attack aimed at capturing the place failed. After an operation that lasted 12 hours, the two airships barely made it back to Tripoli, 75 miles away.

In October 1912, Italian forces in Libya amounted to 100,000 men. Of them perhaps a few hundred were airmen, ground crews included. During the war as a whole, they are said to have flown exactly 712 sorties and dropped a few hundred bombs.[44] Their role in the eventual victory was negligible; that victory, in fact, was brought about not in Libya but by the outbreak of the Balkan War, which diverted the attention of the Ottomans and sapped their resources in Libya. A handful of aircraft were used during the Balkan Wars of 1912–13 and also during the Mexican Revolution, which began in 1910. Most were flown by foreign volunteers, or mercenaries, who brought along their own aircraft, rather than by military pilots of the belligerents. Consequently operations tended to be sporadic and haphazard. Whatever the shortcomings of the Italian armed forces that the struggle in Libya helped reveal, it put the nascent Italian Air Force into a position where it was the most experienced of its kind in the world. Yet the conflict did little to bring the debate as to the respective merits of lighter- and heavier-than-air devices to an end. Writing in his capacity as an official observer, Beehler felt that "Italy is the first nation to use aeroplanes in war, and they were operated by Italian naval aviation with considerable success, but they did not prove as formidable as weapons as was expected." The Cipelli hand grenades in particular had proven all but useless, and the longer the war, the more the Italians themselves tended to replace them with leaflets that called upon the enemy to surrender.

The field where flying devices *did* excel was reconnaissance. Not only did they bring in enemy intelligence, but they also enabled the Italians to map parts of Libya from the air. As Caneva, commenting on the various sources of intelligence at his disposal, wrote, "our only certain knowledge derives from what our aviators have seen with their own eyes."[45] In this they were much assisted by the use of photography. Perhaps the most important lesson was that the single-seaters in use were not really more suitable for that kind of mission than for air bombardment. But whereas the task of throwing bombs from aircraft could be simplified by installing a bomb-release mechanism, reconnaissance flights were best carried out with the aid of a separate observer. The problem was that the use of observers required two-seater aircraft with more powerful engines. Too, aircraft, though unopposed in the air, did not prove invulnerable to ground fire. In the future it would be necessary to armor the most vulnerable parts.

A point that seems to have escaped most contemporary observers, but which assumed very great importance later on, was that airpower did not play an equal role in every stage of the conflict. As we saw, both the Italian aircraft and, even more so, their airships only reached Libya after Tripoli and the remaining coastal towns had fallen. Once there, at first they proved quite useful in the fighting that followed, providing intelligence on enemy concentrations and helping naval gunners aim their guns. As the Ottomans dispersed and resorted to guerrilla warfare, though, the effectiveness not only of the Italian forces as a whole but of their flying contingent declined. For one thing, the Italians simply did not have enough craft to cover even a small part of the huge country. As time went on, the Turkish-Arab enemy, technologically very backward though he was, learned to cope with Italian airpower. Either he fired back, scoring the occasional hit and forcing the Italians to fly higher where their ability to see objects on the ground and hit them with their grenades was reduced, or he camouflaged his bases or switched to nighttime operations. Italian attempts to bomb these bases—in reality, they usually consisted of a few tents with, perhaps, some camels tethered to pegs in the ground—from the air were often ineffective. On other occasions their aircraft hit the wrong targets, thus contributing to the growing number of atrocities committed by both sides.

One British observer, Ernest Bennett, wrote that "the Arabs show no sign of perturbation when they see the air-ships."[46] The Italian airplanes, he thought, had often brought back useful intelligence. However, most of their efforts at bombing were inaccurate and "singularly futile."[47] Nevertheless, to Beehler's mind, the war forcefully "demonstrated the indispensable necessity of aeroplanes and dirigible airships in war." In London the *Times,* which was probably the most important newspaper of the age, concluded that, in the future, no country should presume to go to war without "sufficient" aerial forces.[48]

Though losses turned out to be negligible, operating under the primitive conditions that prevailed in Libya and flying the fragile machines of the day took tenacity, courage, and resourcefulness. Above all, it demanded an ability to improvise that would have astonished subsequent air forces with their ultrasophisticated equipment, minute division of labor, strict procedures, and split-second timetables in which every aspect of every mission is laid down in the smallest detail. On the other hand the war also showed the limitations of the nascent airpower and the possibility that people's expectations of it were considerably exaggerated.

CHAPTER 2

TEST PASSED

When the first shots were fired in the Great War, the number of uniformed men immediately available for being butchered was around 15 million. At the same time, advances in firepower, mainly quick-firing artillery and machine guns, forced troops to take cover and disperse, and so, instead of being concentrated at a single battlefield, they spread over fronts hundreds of miles long. A very few senior commanders apart, hardly anybody had an overall view of where friendly forces were, what they were doing, in what direction they were moving, and what their intentions were. Intelligence about the enemy tended to be even more fragmented. In other words, never in history had so many marched into battle knowing so little about themselves and their enemies.

In this situation, aviation came to the rescue. Compared to what came later, the flying machines of the time were primitive and fragile and their capabilities very limited. Their use for reconnaissance gave rise to many problems; especially important were the impact of the weather and the difficulty of making out details when flying over complex terrain. Another problem was the difficulty of distinguishing enemy forces from friendly ones. Yet aircraft had the advantage of being able to cover large spaces very fast regardless of topographical obstacles. One estimate was that they could do in four hours what it took a cavalry patrol 24 to accomplish.[1] Furthermore, rather than being confined more or less to the front line, they were able to gather intelligence far into the enemy's rear.

The most dramatic incident took place on September 3. As the Germans decided to abandon the Schlieffen Plan for defeating France and turned their forces toward the southeast, thus presenting their right flank to Paris, it was aviation that brought the decisive news. As early as August 31, the day the Germans started their maneuver, a French captain of cavalry, Lepic, reconnoitering west of Compiègne, saw a German column advancing toward that city rather than south toward the capital. That night, another piece of information arrived, this time based on a bloodstained map taken from a dead German officer attached to the headquarters of the German First Army. It showed that, on the next day, its four corps were supposed to march not toward Paris but away from it. On the morning of September 3, the news concerning the enemy's change of direction was substantiated by a certain French aviator, Lieutenant Watteau. Flying north of Paris, he had observed the German columns "gliding" east, as he put it. Another aircraft was sent up and confirmed the news.[2]

This kind of mission was typical of the times. Day by day dozens of aircraft with their pilots and observers took off trying to observe the movements of the armies below. Still, claims like Field Marshal Paul von Hindenburg's about why the Germans beat the Russians at the battle of Tannenberg—"without the airmen, no Tannenberg"[3]—should be treated with caution. Here as elsewhere, aircraft represented only one out of many sources of intelligence. Their reports were not always considered reliable; the principal German staff officer involved, Max von Hoffman, insists that interception of Russian radio messages was critical whereas air reconnaissance sometimes led to confusion.[4] As with all sources, even the most sensational news brought by the aviators was sometimes out-of-date. Even when it arrived on time it had to be arranged in suitable form, assessed for reliability, and fitted into the gigantic puzzle. Often, doing so proved harder than obtaining it in the first place.

As trench warfare replaced maneuver, things changed. Artillery came into its own, but it was not the artillery of 50 years before. Except on rare occasions, its range having grown to between six and 18 miles, artillery relied on indirect fire at targets the gunners could not see. To correct the fall of shot, flying observers armed with binoculars were used. However, the disadvantages of aircraft quickly made themselves felt. At a time when barrages sometimes lasted for days and even weeks on end, aircraft had limited endurance. To stay in the air they had to keep moving, which meant that the observers' perspective kept changing. Communication with the ground was also problematic. Against this background, balloons began to be regarded in a new light. Not only were they better suited for observation, but being tethered they could be linked to the ground by telephone. Quite soon no army was willing to do without these useful devices.

Fragile and often anything but easy to handle, early World War I aircraft presented about the worst possible platforms for launching aimed rifle fire. In any case rifles were too long and heavy to be comfortably handled in the cramped space available aboard. Handguns did not suffer from this disadvantage, but their range was limited and their accuracy poor. After a few months when opposing aviators took potshots at one another, all sides realized that the solution was one or more machine guns. The first to solve the problem of firing a machine gun straight ahead was the French flier Roland Garros, whose answer consisted of armor-plating the propeller so it would resist the bullets streaming through it. After his aircraft had been shot down and captured by the Germans, this primitive system was improved upon by the Dutch aircraft manufacturer Anthony Fokker, who found a way of synchronizing the propeller blades with the machine gun firing through them.[5] The result was the emergence of a new type of aircraft, the fighter. It differed from the reconnaissance aircraft in use in that it carried only one man, not two. As the first fighters reached the battlefield late in 1915, they opened the era of air-to-air combat, which has now all but ended.[6] The appearance of true fighters soon led to their being grouped in the appropriate units; the first of these were created by the Germans in August of the next year and took part in the later stages of the Battle of the Somme.

Normally pilots encountered one another by forming visual contact during patrols. At that point the aircraft's qualities would come into play. The most important ones were speed, range, altitude (and the ability to gain it quickly), maneuverability, and firepower. Speed and range enabled a pilot to start and end a fight at will. Altitude enabled him to fly higher than his opponent and swoop down on him from some unexpected direction—if possible, out of a cloud, or from the direction of the sun. Maneuverability was required to get into an advantageous position behind an enemy's tail, inside his turning circle, or under his belly (the way to hit two-seaters in particular). It was also useful for pilots trying to make their escape. Firepower was provided first by one, later by two, machine guns. All these capabilities were determined very largely by engine power as the most important variant of all. From 1914 to 1918, fighter aircraft more than doubled the power of their engines. Weight went up by about 45 percent, maximum speed by about 30.[7]

Since engine power was always limited, the remaining qualities tended to come at each other's expense. Since each designer had his own preferences, it was often hard to say which aircraft were superior. Among aircraft produced roughly in the same year, probably none was superior in every respect. There were limits to what could be done, and not even the best pilots were able to overcome the shortcomings of an inferior machine. On the other hand, where overall quality was approximately equal, the pilot who best understood the qualities of his own *and* the enemy's aircraft and knew how to make the best of them usually won. So exhausting was air combat that pilots, though they had fought in subzero temperatures, often returned bathed in sweat. Losses were horrendous—in April 1917, the life expectancy of British pilots stood at eight days from their first combat flight. While aces lived a little longer, theirs was hardly a safe existence; by the time he was killed, at 23, with 53 victories to his credit, French ace Georges Guynemer had been wounded twice and shot down eight times. Until the spring of 1917, when the Germans started issuing them, pilots were not even given parachutes.

Unlike ground warfare, the air war was waged by small numbers of volunteers; even in the last year of the war no country produced more than 8,000 of them. Combat took place at high speed as both parties approached one another at as much as 220 miles per hour. The fighting was short and wild, with aircraft diving, turning, and maneuvering crazily in all directions. Sometimes they collided with each other, and indeed some German pilots believed that the Russians deliberately resorted to ramming.[8] Here is one entirely typical description of what it was like:

> A pilot, in the second between his own engagements, might see a Hun diving vertically, an SE 5 on his tail, the tail of the SE 5 another Hun, and above him, again, another British scout. These four, plunging headlong at two hundred miles an hour, guns crackling, tracers streaming, suddenly break up. The lowest Hun plunges flaming to his death, if death has not taken him already. His victor seems to stagger, suddenly pulls out in a great leap, as a trout leaps at the end of a line, and then, turning over on his belly, swoops and spins in a dizzy falling spiral with the earth to end it. The third German zooms, veering, and the last of that meteoric quartet follows bursting. . . . But such a glimpse, lasting perhaps ten seconds, is broken by the sharp rattle of another attack.[9]

The character of air combat, plus the fact that the pilots tended to be young, upper-crust volunteers, turned aircrew into heroes. Their pictures were published, their exploits endlessly narrated by the press. They acted as guests of honor at all kinds of festive occasions, were decorated, interviewed by the press, and received by dignitaries. For example, Manfred von Richthofen, the Red Baron, as the best-known German ace of all, once had a talk with the Kaiser. Obviously unimpressed, later he wrote that "the conversation was very one sided. The principal topic was anti-aircraft defenses."[10] Aces received mountains of fan mail—much of it including all kinds of proposals, from making a child to marriage, though not necessarily in that order. When Major James McCudden (1895–1918), one of five British aviators to hold a Victoria Cross, walked into a London restaurant, "the women . . . fought to get at him just like they do at a bargain counter [and] the girl with him thought she was the Queen of Sheba."[11]

Much has been written about the "chivalry of the air" that supposedly did something to make war a little less terrible. Certainly pilots on both sides sometimes dropped messages on each other's bases, challenging their enemies to take off and fight in the manner of medieval knights. Certainly captured aviators usually got decent treatment, and those who had been killed behind enemy lines, a decent burial. On occasion captors would protect captives from attacks by the local population. The warring sides would ask for, and receive, information concerning missing airmen. They might also ask for, and receive, their prisoners' kits. Enemies who happened to land close together might greet one another courteously enough.[12]

But there was a darker side to all this. Much air combat was based on surprise. If anything distinguished outstanding pilots from the rest, it was their ability to take an enemy unaware and kill him before he had even realized what was going on; it is told that, when an old woman whom Guynemer had almost killed in a traffic accident called him a "murderer," his response was, "Madame, you don't know how right you are." Speed and the almost total lack of communication between opponents made it hard to give quarter "without betraying the interests of your country," as another French ace, René Fonck, put it.[13] Furthermore, to prevent false claims, accidental or deliberate, all sides soon adopted the system whereby kills had to be confirmed. Many pilots loved to see their opponents crash. All in all, chivalry may have made air warfare a little less terrible than it would otherwise have been. Perhaps, too, the belief that "with us every battle is personal, man against man, with equal weapons and equal chance,"[14] helped airmen come to terms with their murderous work.

Since Britain, France, and Germany together produced over three-quarters of all the relevant aircraft, air warfare focused on the Western Front. Now one side, now the other, gained a slight advantage; but normally such an advantage only lasted for months, if that. Tactically, perhaps the most outstanding characteristic of the Western Front was that the winds usually blew from west to east, reducing the range of German aircraft.[15] On the other hand it gave them an advantage on the return journey and also in case of an emergency landing behind their own lines. The fact that the country in the east was flat and had few landmarks made navigation more difficult than it was in the west. A much lower aircraft-to-space ratio also meant that air operations played a smaller role; less than one-half of 1 percent of the victories the Germans claimed were won in the east.[16] Another characteristic of the Eastern Front was that there were fewer modern transportation arteries such as railways. Thus, when a yard or station *was* hit, the effect on the front was immediate and the damage considerable. Huge spaces and the paucity of major cities and industrial centers also meant that anti-aircraft defenses were weak.[17] Down in the south the Italians enjoyed a decisive numerical advantage (they outproduced the Austrian-Hungarians by almost four to one, and unlike their enemies they only had one front to fight on).[18] Yet the mountainous terrain made reconnaissance, as the most important way by which aircraft were made to support major ground operations, more difficult than usual. Other theaters of war, such as the ones in Albania, Macedonia, Gallipoli, Palestine, and Iraq, had their own peculiarities.

From early 1918 on, the balance in the air tended to swing toward the Allies. Until then, notwithstanding shortages of raw material that sometimes forced them to cut corners, the Germans seem to have maintained a slight technical edge. Another German response to their enemies' numerical superiority was careful training. German pilots received 65 flying hours before they entered specialized combat training.[19] By contrast, there were moments in the war when British pilots were sent to their units with as little as 17 hours' flying time behind them. This difference was accentuated by the fact that, whereas most German pilots were shot down over their own territory and, if they survived, went back into combat almost immediately, Allied ones, having crossed the front to the east, were much more likely to be captured. All this may explain why the Germans managed to shoot down between two and three aircraft for each one they lost.[20] Taking the war as a whole, they lost a smaller percentage of their total force than did either the French or the British.[21]

From very early on in the war, aviators sometimes used their carbines to take potshots at the enemy below. William Bishop, a Canadian pilot who with 72 confirmed kills was the Allies' second highest-scoring fighter pilot, described how "with hate in my heart . . . I fired every bullet I could" into the "frightened faces" of the "Huns" 30 feet underneath.[22] However, as General (as he then was) Hugh Trenchard, commander of the Royal Flying Corps in France who later became the first commander of the Royal Air Force (RAF), wrote, there was no attempt to select targets systematically or to coordinate air operations with those on the ground.[23] Things began to change in the spring of 1917 when the German retreat to the Hindenburg (Siegfried) line created a situation where the Allies needed fewer aircraft for artillery observation and more could be allocated to ground attack. Furthermore, moving columns of men, machines, and horses proved a lot easier to hit than infantry in their shelters. In the words of a subsequent British air marshal, Sholto Douglas, "these low flying attacks . . . were a wretched and dangerous business, and also quite useless."[24] Even before the war, some observers understood that ground attack aircraft should have their most vulnerable parts covered with armor. By the middle of the war, engines had grown sufficiently powerful for the process to begin. "Battle aircraft," as they were known, were designed both for strafing and for dropping small bombs, though accuracy was always a problem. Unlike the British, who apparently believed that any fighter pilot could engage in ground attack, the Germans provided their pilots with specialized training. Hence they played an important role in the March 1918 offensive with which the German High Command sought, but ultimately did not succeed, to end the war.[25]

Later the boot was on the other foot. During the great battles of May–July 1918, Allied aircraft, including American ones, proved equally effective first in halting the German second-echelon troops and then in harassing them as they in turn tried to retreat. The historian of the Bavarian List Regiment, the same in which Adolf Hitler served as a runner, described its experiences in late July 1918 when it was retreating across the Marne:

> Aviators . . . reconnoiter our positions and bomb them. They machine gun infantry, artillery and marching columns. Sporadically they fly high behind our lines and fire at a barrage balloon, which

> falls to the ground in flames. . . . The most frightening, however, are aircraft armed with anti-personnel bombs. . . . Twenty-five, thirty and more aircraft suddenly appear [and] each drops forty bombs. We do not worry anymore about infantry fire [and] we have become used to artillery, but these pilots drive the troops to distraction. We literally climb up the trees, in order to avoid fearsome low trajectory projectiles from the exploding bombs.[26]

To defend themselves against ground attack at the front as well as the zone of communications, armies developed some of the earliest anti-aircraft defenses. Some of the guns in use, mostly of about 76-millimeter caliber, were capable of firing as many as 25 rounds a minute, filling the air with lead. Contemporaries varied in their assessment of the defenses, rating them from almost useless to very effective indeed. By one account, the most famous air ace of them all, Richthofen, the Red Baron, was killed not in air combat but by an Australian machine gun firing from the ground.[27] At the very least, the need to cope with such opposition made it much harder for pilots to aim their own weapons.

During the years before the war, many writers and journalists examined the possibility of so-called strategic bombardment aimed at centers of population and industry. Tapping into the same mindset as Wells did in *The War in the Air,* many assumed that, in such a case, destruction would be vast and that the population, mad with fear, would force governments to make peace.[28] Yet much of this remained in never-never land; at the time hostilities broke out, only the German Zeppelins were capable of staying in the air for long periods, covering considerable distances, and carrying more than a token load of ordnance. Heavier-than-air machines were too small, and their range too limited, for them to present a serious threat. Assessing the situation in mid-1915, Trenchard concluded that "the results [were] in no way commensurate with the efforts made, the risks incurred and the number of bombs dropped."[29]

It was, however, a conclusion that was not followed up on. As the Germans also resorted to strategic bombing, the call for revenge was hard to resist. In 1916, Allied fliers raided Germany 41 times. They killed 151 people and injured another 237. The number of raids rose to 81 in 1917, and the figure for 1918 was larger still. By the summer of that year hardly a night passed without Allied squadrons launching an attack; between June and November, the British alone dropped over 500 tons. Impressive as this growth was, it was as nothing compared to the millions of tons of artillery ammunition being fired at the front.[30] Targets were meant to consist of installations producing, storing, or transporting war materials and troops.

The heaviest bomber of all was the British Handley Page V/1500 known as the "Berlin bomber." Thirty-two were built, but they came too late to take an active part in operations. The machine was 62 feet long and had a wingspan of 126 feet. Four Rolls-Royce engines rated at 375 horsepower each enabled a crew, plus four or five machine guns, to be carried. While ceiling and speed (a maximum of 97 miles per hour) were only slightly greater than those of previous models, the bomb load went up to 7,500 pounds, almost twice as much as any other aircraft of the time. Though the weight of bombs increased—by the end of the war, the British were experimenting with devices weighing 1,650 pounds—finding targets and hitting them was very difficult. Even in 1917 a bomb dropped from 10,000 feet might easily miss by 3,000 feet. In practice it was entire districts, not individual towns, that suffered; the result was harassment, not serious operations of war.

Except for the airships, about which more in a moment, developments on the German side ran roughly parallel to those on the Allied one. Like their enemies, the Germans entered the war without any aircraft suitable for bombing missions. Like their enemies, this fact did not stop them from trying. Owing to the military targets they contained, towns such as Dunkirk, Nancy, Luneville, Belfort, Besançon, Toul, and Verdun often came under attack. However, two-engine machines capable of bombing London became operational only in mid-1916. Still not satisfied, the army turned to four-engine machines in the form of the Staaken R-VI. It could lift a load of a little over two tons of bombs to a distance of about 500 miles. By the end of the war, 18 had been built. They were used first on the Eastern Front and then against Britain, on which they dropped a total of 30 tons of bombs. Yet losses of the planes were heavy, and in May 1918 the raids were suspended.

Much more than the Western Allies, the Germans had invested in airships.[31] Used mainly for reconnaissance, those operating over land proved a complete failure, but the story of the navy's airships was very different. On January 19, 1915, the Navy High Command launched the first three Zeppelins against the small port of Yarmouth on the East Anglia coast. As it turned out, one of the three developed engine trouble and had to abort its mission. The second succeeded in killing exactly one man and one woman; the third drifted way off course but was ultimately able to repeat the same feat as the second in another town over which it had flown by mistake. Yet the navy was not discouraged. As more and better ships became available, the raids were mounted at a rate of about one every fortnight on the average. By the time they were discontinued in August 1918, some 275 tons of bombs had been dropped.[32]

Compared to bombers, the airships' greatest advantage was the size of their payload, which increased from three tons in 1915 to well over twice that three years later. They also had an extremely long range; some German commanders even dreamed of bombing New York. On the other hand, the airships' large size and low speed made them easier to discover and destroy. The obvious solution was to fly higher. Yet as the Zeppelins rose to 17,000–20,000 feet they began suffering from mechanical problems. Engines lost power, windows (made of celluloid) cracked, and control cables froze and refused to budge. To make things worse, not having helium, the Germans were forced to fill their airships with hydrogen instead. Once incendiaries started to be used in 1916, the crew's chances to avoid a horrendous death were minimal. But even when the ships escaped the fighters, things did not always go right for them. Out of 11 that embarked on the so-called silent raids (silent because the Zeppelins flew so high they were barely noticed, let alone countered) in October 1917, only seven returned to base. By the end of the war, out of 82 Zeppelins that had seen service, only nine were left.

The anti-aircraft defenses used at or closely behind the front did not work well against high-flying bombers and airships. What was needed was some kind of forewarning concerning the approach of the enemy, his altitude, and his course. Normally such warning was provided by an observation post employing optical and acoustical means; the British even tried using blind people on the assumption that they were better able to hear sounds and identify them than those who could see.[33] Some of the defenses were deployed in lines, protecting or at least seeking to protect entire countries much in the way trenches did on the ground. Both the Germans and the French had lines covering the border between them in Alsace-Lorraine. Alternatively, they were focused around particularly important points such as cities. Since more and more bombing attacks took place at night, electric searchlights were used. Anti-aircraft defenses represented one of the most important growth areas in the whole of World War I. The Germans put the total number of Allied craft that flak brought down at 1,590.[34] Later, too, anti-aircraft defenses were always a factor that the proponents of airpower, often much against their will, had to take into account.

Civil defense apart,[35] the other way to counter strategic bombing was to scramble up fighters. For example, late in the war the British were operating a system intended to protect London as the most important target of all.[36] News of an enemy attack could be telephoned to a central operations room within 30 seconds of the first sighting. In the room, the attackers, represented by small colored wooden blocks called counters, were marked on a map; next, orders went to the anti-aircraft batteries as well as the fighter squadrons. Repeated drill ultimately enabled fighters to take off within two and a half minutes of receiving their orders. From this point on, everything depended on how fast they could reach the attackers' altitude; unfortunately this was a field where Allied aircraft designers lagged.[37] Success rates varied from very high to very low. General Edward Ashmore, the officer in charge of the London Air Defence Area, estimated that out of every eight fighters he got into the air one would contact the raiders.[38] Fighting back with their machine guns, the latter sometimes succeeded in driving off or destroying the fighters. Yet the need to avoid or fight off the defenders forced the attackers to break formation and scatter. Early in 1918, one out of ten German bombers participating in any given raid was shot down and another was lost to some kind of accident. Though true figures are hard to get, clearly the bombing operations involved heavy attrition of aircraft and personnel. Pressed by a shortage of raw materials as well as labor, ultimately the Germans found them unsustainable.

The best indicator of the increasing emphasis on strategic bombing was the growing amount of resources committed to it. Still remaining with the British, who as an island nation were more intent on bombers than anyone else, in 1918 they had 86 air squadrons on the Western Front. Of those, 12 percent were suitable for long-range operations, a figure very similar to the corresponding German one.[39] Had the plans for 1919 been realized, the RAF, founded in 1918, would have grown to 179 squadrons, of which just over one-third were to consist of bombers. Excluding reserves, the total number of machines would have risen to a little over 1,000, far more than that of bombers still left in service in all air forces *combined* in the twenty-first century.[40] Since each bomber required far more men and resources than a fighter, the above figures actually underestimate the effort that building Britain's new bomber arm required.

At sea, as on land, some prewar officers saw aircraft as mere toys and vowed they would never be of any great use.[41] However, especially among young officers, expectations were very high. Particular attention was paid to the use of anti-submarine warfare.[42] In February 1914, Winston Churchill, who was serving as the Lord of the Admiralty, wrote:

> The objectives of land aeroplanes can never be so definite or important as the objectives of seaplanes, which when they carry torpedoes, may prove capable of playing a decisive part in operations against capital ships. The facilities of reconnaissance at sea, where hostile vessels can be sighted at enormous distances while the seaplanes remain out of possible range, offer a far wider prospect even in the domain of information to seaplanes than to land aeroplanes, which would be continually brought under rifle and artillery fire

> from concealed positions on the ground, among trees, behind hedges, etc.[43]

Accordingly he did everything in his power to build up naval aviation, requisitioning funds, setting up an Air Department within the admiralty, establishing bases along the east and south coasts, and purchasing aircraft left and right. By the summer of 1914 he had about 50 of them, mostly based on land not far from the shore. They were meant to defend the navy's vital installations, particularly the terminals on which it depended for its oil as well as the ports along the eastern and southern coasts. Others were earmarked to act as the fleet's eyes, locating any approaching German warships and bringing them to battle.

Developments in other countries were quite similar. For example, as early as 1909 the Austrian-Hungarians, not otherwise known for their prominence in the field of aviation, set up a naval air arm. In 1914 it consisted of 22 seaplanes, among them the Lohner flying boat, which was considered the best of its kind in the world. Just one day after Italy entered the war in May 1915, some of them bombed the arsenal at Venice. By contrast, the German Navy only entered the field of heavier-than-air aviation in 1913. Later it built airfields both along the Baltic and along the English Channel, where they were used to assist submarines going on patrol or returning to port. Among the main belligerents, the laggard in developing maritime aviation was France. Only in 1912 did the French Navy begin to create an aeronautical service. It entered World War I with just eight naval planes.

The earliest hydroplanes, equipped with floats instead of skids or wheels, as well as flying boats were built even before the first decade of the twentieth century was out. However, their performance was almost always inferior to that of their land-based counterparts. Besides, the operations of these aircraft were hampered by the fact that they could only take off and come down when the sea was relatively calm. The obvious solution was to base aircraft aboard ship. Several navies converted merchantmen into floating hangars, equipping them with cranes to lower the aircraft into the water and retrieve them after they had returned from their mission. On December 25, 1914, three British ships of this kind launched nine aircraft against the Zeppelin base at Cuxhaven. Owing partly to the weather and partly to mechanical problems, only seven reached their target. They dropped some small bombs, doing no damage. On the way back all but one had to ditch in the sea, though their crews were rescued. Later a second attempt was no more successful.

In February 1915, aircraft from the British *Ark Royal* directed naval gunfire against the Ottoman fortifications in the Dardanelles; however, her low speed made her a good target for submarines and she had to be withdrawn.[44] On August 12, her replacement launched an aircraft that in turn launched the first torpedo at sea. Operating in narrow seas or close to the shore, aircraft reconnoitered, spotted for gunners both from the sea to the land and from the land to the sea, and occasionally launched more or less effective bombing and torpedo attacks. Still, when the German High Sea Fleet left port for a cruise that was to lead to the Battle of Jutland in May 1916, the news reached the British Admiralty not from an aircraft or a dirigible but from an intercepted German radio transmission.[45] From this point on, as one author later wrote, both fleets, with over 200 warships between them, approached one another "like blind men driving cars"[46] at a combined speed of 56 miles per hour. In theory, aircraft or airships flying at 3,000 feet should have been able to spot the enemy when he was still 60 miles away. In reality, as is often the case in that part of the world, visibility was much better at sea level than further aloft. Early in the action an aircraft from the seaplane carrier *Engadine* was able to warn Admiral David Beatty, whose battle cruisers formed the British vanguard, of the presence of some light German cruisers. Yet the pilot missed the main German body under Admiral Reinhardt Scheer and thus did more to mislead Beatty (who, thinking he was facing an easy prey, rushed forward into what turned out to be a losing encounter) than to help him.[47] The lookouts in their precarious crows' nests remained as vital as they had ever been. They were able to spot Scheer's force only when the range had closed to a dozen miles or less.

The Germans on their part had been planning the sortie for months past. However, repeatedly they were foiled by the weather, which prevented their airships from taking off.[48] When they finally set sail on May 30, adverse winds kept four of the five available airships on the ground; the one that went with the fleet was blinded by fog. When the Germans sent out a seaplane on another scouting mission, low clouds forced it to return.[49] Ultimately it was a torpedo boat sailing ahead of the main body that discovered the Home Fleet.[50] Zeppelin or no Zeppelin, so unaware was Scheer of the British moves that twice within a little more than an hour—this was the early evening of May 31—he ran head-on into the assembled Grand Fleet. As he later described these unpleasant surprises, "suddenly the entire horizon, from north to east, leapt into a vast sea of flame." Twice, Scheer was only saved by a rapid turning maneuver. Fortunately for him, shifting mists prevented any British aircraft that may have been present from following him. Less than an hour after the two fleets had separated for the second time, darkness fell, causing the British to lose track of their opponents. It was only on the next day that the Germans were finally able to put four of their Zeppelins in the air at the same time. However, so variable was the weather that only two of them, the L-11 and the L-24, sighted any parts of the Grand Fleet. Even so, they kept losing touch with it in the swirling mists so that identifying the ships and providing reliable information on the course they were taking were impossible.[51]

In the absence of other major engagements, the most important contribution airpower made was probably in anti-submarine warfare. Starting late in 1914, both sides, the one seeking to assist its submarines' missions and the other trying to obstruct them as much as possible, often clashed in air combat over the Channel. Royal Navy aircraft also did their best to reduce the submarine menace by bombing the bases at Zeebrugge and Ostend. Further to the west the picture was different. Since German aircraft did not have the range to fly so far, and even Zeppelins only rarely showed up, British naval pilots had the air to themselves. They spent countless hours escorting convoys and watching the approaches to their home islands. By one set of figures, on average, every 6,000 miles flown yielded one submarine sighted.[52] Even so, not every submarine that had a few small bombs dropped at it was hit, let alone sunk. One difficulty was that the bombs used were too small for the purpose. Since increasing weight inevitably meant reducing range and endurance, this was a problem that not even more powerful engines could always correct. Though balloons and airships did not suffer from this problem, their larger size sometimes made it easier for submarines to locate them than the other way around. Postwar German figures show that, out of 146 submarines sunk, just seven were lost to either airships or aircraft.

Still, by forcing submarines to dive, airships and aircraft could greatly reduce their speed, their endurance (submarines could only stay underwater for about ten hours before being forced to surface to recharge their batteries), and, most of all, their ability to look for and spot targets. A submarine cruising at periscope depth was half blind, one sheltering at greater depth completely so. Thus the contribution naval aviation made to anti-submarine warfare and to the safety of convoys, though not great in terms of losses inflicted, was substantial. By the final months of the war, so confident were the commanders of the Royal Naval Air Service (RNAS) that harassment alone was achieving their objective that it was common for aircraft engaged on this mission to take off without any bombs that would have reduced their range and the time they spent in the air. As long as convoys were accompanied by aircraft, they were all but immune to submarine attack.[53]

The remaining Allied powers followed a similar path, although the scale of their operations was smaller. For example, the air arm of the Italian Navy entered the war with just 86 men, 25 aircraft, and two dirigibles left over from the war of 1911–12. An organization capable of operating even these modest devices barely existed.[54] Greatly expanded during the war, the force joined the navy's surface ships and submarines in an effort, which proved successful in the end, to keep the Austrian-Hungarian surface fleet bottled up in the Adriatic. The last to enter the field were the Americans. In November 1917, over the Bay of Biscay, a U.S. crew for the first time flew an anti-submarine mission. Four months later an American naval aircraft dropped depth charges, resulting in a "probably damaged" evaluation; by the end of the war the Americans were operating from a string of bases both along the French coast and in the British Isles, making the seas northwest of Ireland in particular very unsafe for the Kaiser's submarines.

Yet anti-submarine patrol work and escort duty only represented one part of the extremely varied missions carried out by naval aviation. By the time the armistice was finally signed on November 11, 1918, they included shore-to-sea and sea-to-shore liaison (sea-to-sea liaison was possible in principle, but I have not found any actual cases of aircraft being used on this mission); various kinds of anti-aircraft work; mine-laying and its opposite, searching for mines, marking their locations, and destroying them; fleet reconnaissance; spotting for ship-to-ship, ship-to-shore, and shore-to-ship artillery action; support for amphibious landings (both at Gallipoli and in the Baltic); bombing enemy ships and naval bases; and the first experimental torpedo attacks on enemy surface ships.[55] For all the enormous technical progress that they brought, future decades were to add very little to this list.

Here and there individual operations, notably the attack by aircraft from the British carrier *Furious* on the base near Cuxhaven in July 1918, led to spectacular successes. Two Zeppelins were destroyed in their hangar; though the cost was heavy—out of nine aircraft only two made it back—those responsible could draw satisfaction from the fact that the fire of burning hydrogen was visible dozens of miles away.[56] Meanwhile, detractors of naval airpower could point to the adventures of the German battle cruiser *Goeben*. When the war broke out she was caught in the Mediterranean, where the British and French navies enjoyed a four-to-one advantage over the Austrian-Hungarian one. She was nevertheless able to escape to Constantinople from where she later made sorties into the Dardanelles, the Black Sea, and the Aegean. Repeatedly attacked by Allied aircraft, over time she had several hundred "wretched little bombs" aimed at her but only suffered two hits.[57] In fact she remained almost unscathed until, in the end, it was mines that disabled her. Similarly it was argued that, out of 80 torpedoes launched at the Grand Fleet at Jutland (by submarines, not aircraft),

79 missed their targets, and that therefore the aircraft carrying them did not really pose a grave threat, either.[58]

Then as now, such debates had something Talmudist about them. To counter the "lesson" drawn from the *Goeben* episode, it could equally well be said that, had the Royal Navy in the Mediterranean disposed of just a few reconnaissance aircraft at the beginning of the war, the ship would never have reached Constantinople. Arguments as to whether naval air-power could have developed even faster if only the admirals (and generals) had been less conservative are also futile; in fact, perhaps the most impressive thing about it during these years was precisely the speed with which it *did* develop. Possibly the best indication of this is the fact that, whereas the French naval air service entered the war with eight aircraft and 32 pilots, at the end it had 1,264 aircraft, 37 airships, 702 pilots, and 6,470 men. Across the Channel, the RNAS entered the war with 93 aircraft, 58 officers, and 589 men. Three and a half years later the numbers had increased to 2,949, 5,378, and 49,688 respectively. By September 1917 it had no fewer than seven specialized carriers with a full complement of 31 aircraft, and it was expected that, within the next few months, the numbers would increase to 12 and 67, respectively.[59]

Such figures testify to another very important aspect of the air war, namely the role that economic factors played in it. Before 1914 civilian demand for flying devices of every kind was limited very largely to wealthy amateurs, on the one hand, and professional sports fliers and stuntmen, on the other. However, the outbreak of war caused this situation to change. First, owing to the vast demands of total war, the military market came to overshadow the civilian one to an even greater extent than before. Second, though performance improved by leaps and bounds, it was no longer simply a question of setting records and carrying out stunts. Instead, the various armed forces developed a strong interest in aircraft that could be mass-produced and flown by mass-produced pilots. Mass production also entailed greater capital outlays and greater productivity per worker employed. To illustrate these developments at the hand of a few figures, in 1914 the French aircraft industry, as the world's largest, employed 3,000 workers. The corresponding German and British figures were 2,500 and 1,000, whereas the American one—in the United States, a military market for aircraft hardly existed—just 168. Two years later France had 63,000 aviation workers and Britain 42,000. By 1918 the U.S. industry employed 175,000 people. At the outbreak of the war, the German military estimated that the country's manufacturers might be able to provide 100 machines a month. Four years later, French and British ones were each producing 2,300 to 3,000 of them within a similar period. The growth of industry explains why the belligerents could take the tremendous losses they did. In 1914, Britain had to replace 33 percent of its aircraft each month just to cover wastage.

Since the aircraft of the time could often be whipped from the drawing board onto the production lines within a matter of months, any machine more than a year old was likely to be obsolescent. Engines took considerably longer to develop. They required not only precision engineering and specialized machine tools but a number of precious raw materials, mainly nonferrous metals, that were not always readily available to the various belligerents. Consequently the Kaiser's aircraft sometimes had to wait for weeks and even months before engines could be found for them.[60] At the other end of the scale was France. Though many of its most industrialized provinces had been overrun, it succeeded in producing more engines and aircraft than anybody else. Part of the miracle is explained by the fact that the French, focusing on the front as opposed to the deep rear, produced no four-engine aircraft and relatively few twin-engine ones. Another factor was what they used to call *rusticité*, rusticity. They preferred simple, even crude, but easy-to-manufacture designs to more sophisticated ones that required more labor and a better finish; this may help explain why, of the three main belligerents, proportionally they lost the most aircraft. At the other end of the scale were the Germans. They always tended to put quality first, even though, by the last year of the war, their efforts were limited by a shortage of raw materials such as rubber and copper. Their emphasis on Zeppelins also diverted resources away from aircraft. One way or another, during the war, both France (67,987 aircraft) and Britain (58,144) outproduced Germany (48,537).[61] This was true even though, in terms of its industrial potential, Germany was stronger than either.[62]

Other differences also separated the belligerents. For example, the Austrian-Hungarians had a number of talented innovators and designers. The best known was Ferdinand Porsche, later famous as the creator of the Volkswagen Beetle. However good some of its aircraft, the Danube Empire did not have a highly developed industry. Producing only 5,431 aircraft during the war, it required support on every theater where its forces operated. Russia resembled Austria-Hungary in that some of its engineers made a name for themselves, especially in the field of heavy bombers. Yet Russia too did not have the industrial base to manufacture large numbers of them; like all the remaining Allies, it imported some of its engines from France. Even so, it had difficulty in keeping its forces in flying condition due to the lack of adequate supply and maintenance facilities. Italy, which did much better in the First World War than in the Second, is said to have produced twice as many aircraft as Austria-Hungary and Russia combined. The total number is estimated at 20,000, and some of them were even exported. Then as later, the outstanding characteristic of America's aviation industry was its preference for enormous engines; the best-known one, manufactured by Packard, could not be run at full throttle for fear that the vibration would tear the airframes apart. Yet the short time the United States spent in the war only enabled it to build some 15,000 aircraft. During the conflict as a whole, France, Britain, Italy, Russia, and the United States outproduced the Central Powers by more than three to one.[63]

Quite as important as the quantity and quality of the aircraft that were coming out of the factories was the question of organization. In particular, it was necessary to distribute aviation between the army and the navy. To start with Britain as the largest naval power of all, at first the Ministry of War and the Admiralty each proceeded entirely on their own. There was no attempt to coordinate doctrine, equipment, training, operations, or even communications; nor were things helped by the fact that, within the navy, Churchill came close to treating aviation as his private hobby. When hostilities broke out, the army immediately moved as many of its aircraft and its personnel as it could to France. As a result, as early as September 1914, the navy was asked to assume responsibility for dealing with Zeppelin raids if and when they would materialize. From then until 1917, when a reorganization took place, the only army pilots who participated in this mission had not yet completed their training. When the time came for Britain to start building its own strategic bombing force, the geographical separation between the home country and the front also caused that task to be entrusted to the navy.

Against the background of constant struggles over money, men, and aircraft, the British government formed the Smuts Committee, named for the South African leader Jan Smuts. In August 1917 it issued its report, which many now call the Magna Carta of military aviation. It noted that "an air fleet can conduct extensive operations far from, and independently of, both Army and Navy" and that, "as far as can at present be foreseen, there is absolutely no limit to the scale of its future independent war use." It therefore recommended the creation of "one unified air service, which will absorb both the existing services under arrangements which will fully safeguard the efficiency and secure the closest intimacy between the Army and the Navy and the portions of the air service allotted or seconded to them." This was duly done, and in April 1918 the new service, the RAF, as well as the new ministry to which it answered, saw the light of day. Yet conflicts between the generals and admirals went on. No other government succeeded in knocking the heads of the generals and admirals together and forcing them to follow the British example. Instead, the status of aviation within each service was gradually upgraded.

To take the German Feldflugwesen (Field Aviation Service) as our example, its principal task was to provide the front with suitable aircraft, and so it sent its officers to supervise every factory around the country. Others were setting up a comprehensive system of selecting, training, and administering personnel; building and maintaining ground facilities; developing tactics and writing doctrine; as well as running the specialized weather-forecasting and navigation services without which airpower can neither exist nor operate. The Feldflugwesen also appointed its own representatives at the headquarters of each field army, and conflicts sometimes arose as to the exact division of authority between those representatives and the commanders they were supposed to advise and assist. Yet all this only applied to the imperial army. All the time, acting parallel with the Feldflugwesen, was the corresponding naval organization, including, of course, the famous Zeppelins. Failing to put army and navy aviation under a single command, the United States was no worse than most other countries. However, it differed from them in that it did not even set up a unified air command within the army but kept aviation as part of the signal corps.

Finally, how successful was airpower and to what extent could the vast resources invested in it be justified? The question is most easily answered in respect to those symbols of World War I airpower, the Zeppelins. As one British source put it in late 1918, at best they were of some value in assisting the High Seas Fleet; that apart, "it seems unlikely that they have come up to the expectations of the German people as instruments of destruction, or justified the enormous expenditure lavished upon them."[64] The same is only slightly less true of the long-range heavier than air machines that the German Army used for strategic bombing. We know that, during the war as a whole, strategic bombardment killed 1,414 Britons; by way of comparison, about 2,000 Britons were killed by traffic accidents in 1913 alone.[65] Even as the war went on, Chancellor Theobald von Bethmann-Hollweg told Hindenburg that the psychological effect of bombing, instead of weakening British morale as expected, might cause it to strengthen. The chief of the British General Staff, Field Marshal William Robertson, thought the same.[66]

The raids, whether by Zeppelins or by aircraft, did tie down considerable British resources—by the end of the war they amounted to 20,000 men and 290 guns.[67] Calculating both Zeppelins and bombers, the ratio of attackers to defending aircraft was approximately one to one. Yet it must be remembered that the machines on both sides were not equal. Each Zeppelin and each bomber cost much more than a fighter, especially in terms of the number of engines they needed. Each one also carried several times as many highly trained crew members, who, in case their machines were shot down or wrecked by accident, were much more likely to be killed or taken prisoner. When everything is said and done, compared to the overall war effort the resources committed to homeland defense only represented a drop in the bucket. Shifting to the production of fighters in 1918, the Germans themselves concluded that the game was not worth the candle.

Though the Allies never used airships to bomb cities, probably on their side the balance was not too different. By the end of the war Britain's strategic bombers, comprising five squadrons of night bombers and four of day bombers, had flown a total of 650 missions. Between them they lost 302 aircraft and 287 aircrew killed or missing. They dropped 585 tons of bombs; together with French ones, these raids killed 729 people. To have several highly trained crew members lift a ton of explosive into the air, fly it to a distance of what was often several hundred miles, and use it to kill a little over one enemy civilian—729 divided by 585 equals 1.25—hardly makes military sense.

Attempting to justify the effort, the British official history says that air attacks on steelworks at Volkingen, in the Saar, during the last two years of the war resulted in the loss of precisely 30,680 tons of steel.[68] Yet in 1913, German output of this critical raw material had stood at 17,600,000 tons.[69] In the 1920s a German inquiry put the damage caused by Allied bombing at 23.5 million marks. Compared with the 180 million marks *per day* that the war effort cost in 1918, this was small potatoes indeed.[70] A quick calculation will show that, in terms of lost bombers alone, the offensive cost much more than the damage it inflicted.[71]

The size of the German anti-aircraft defense organization was comparable to the British one. At peak, near the end of the war, it employed 20,000 men. As in Britain, many of them were elderly or invalids; the number of active-list officers was just 200. These men—in contrast to World War II, there were very few women—operated 900 guns, 454 searchlights, and 500 balloons. Anti-aircraft headquarters also commanded 330 aircraft; since the British bomber force never numbered more than 120 machines, each bomber kept almost three fighters busy.[72] Again, the figures are misleading. First, as already noted, bombers cost much more than fighters, and their crews stood a considerably lower chance of returning from a mission to fly another one. Second, many German fighters, stationed along the front and not on an island far behind it, were also available for other duties.

Closer to the front, the situation was different. Throughout the war, the methods used by both sides to gain intelligence about each other were extremely numerous and varied. Still, as long as the weather was clear, airpower was uniquely able to reach deep into the enemy's rear and, even more so, cover large spaces in a short time. Its role in artillery spotting was also extremely important, although, as the Germans showed during their 1918 offensive, not absolutely essential. The importance of reconnaissance is brought out by the fact that, by the middle of the war, five fighters were sometimes detailed to protect a single aircraft engaged in this task. Conversely, in the French service reconnaissance aircraft outnumbered all the rest combined. Airpower also played a large role in artillery spotting. This is not to say that it was always successful in carrying out these tasks; not merely the Germans in March 1918, but the British at Cambrai four months earlier, were able to conceal their offensive preparations and achieve surprise in spite of the sharp eyes of the other side's aviators. They did so by assembling their forces at night while using road transport instead of railways; as so often, the weather helped. Furthermore, much of the time the striking power of airpower, by which is meant its ability to inflict death and destruction, remained almost as limited on land as it was at sea. At no time was this fact demonstrated more clearly than at the Somme in 1916. Though the British had near-complete command of the air, they were repulsed. Used against a well-entrenched enemy, airpower was certainly no more effective than artillery and infantry were and may well have been less so.

Only if and when one side or another left their trenches and a battle of movement ensued was ground support able to play a greater role. Good examples are provided by the great German spring offensive of 1918, the German retreat later in that year, and also the last stage in Field Marshal Edmund Allenby's 1918 Palestine campaign. The trouble with close air support (CAS) was that, since it required that aircraft fly very low in the face of the enemy, of all forms of air warfare it was the most expensive;

mission for mission, CAS claimed more aircraft wrecked and more pilots killed, captured, or missing even than air combat did. Faute de mieux, many air commanders turned to interdiction behind the front, attacking bases, lines of communications, and so on; the French in particular specialized in this kind of operation.

This brings us to air-to-air combat as the best-known form of air warfare. Originally such combat came about almost by accident; yet once the roles aircraft could play in reconnaissance and artillery spotting were recognized, it became inevitable that machines flown by the pilots of both sides would meet and do whatever they could to shoot one another out of the sky. The spectacular nature of air combat, machine against machine and man against man with many others straining necks and eyes to watch, tended to enhance the importance many people attributed to it even further. The fact that the results were much more easily quantifiable than in other fields undoubtedly helped. The outcome was to surround the fighter jock, as he was later called, with an aura that often came at the expense of other, no less important, kinds of personnel. Too often the outcome was that the role of such combat was overemphasized in relation to other types of missions. In quite a number of places, this remains true even today.

CHAPTER 3

VISIONS, ORGANIZATIONS, AND MACHINES

In theory, air warfare, like warfare as a whole, is merely a means to an end, a rational, if very brutal, activity rationally directed toward achieving some rational end. In reality, however, nothing could be further from the truth.[1] War is a product of the human mind and subject to all kinds of social, cultural, and psychological influences. At no time was this more the case than during the so-called golden age of aviation. Races and meetings were held, trophies were offered, and records seemed to be broken almost daily, all to the eager acclaim of the media. Interest in the subject was very intense. Charles Lindbergh's reception after his return from his 1927 transatlantic flight was among the most lavish ever given to any human being in history.[2] So great was the interest that even seemingly innocuous activities such as flying the mail—which, at the time could be quite dangerous—became the subject of a large body of literature.

The trend was evident even in France, a country that during these years was more pacifist, some would say defeatist, than any other.[3] In his 1923 best seller, *L'Équipage* (The Crew), Joseph Kessel depicted aircrews' adventures, with an emphasis on their disorderly life between missions—heavy drinking, smoking, gambling, visits to prostitutes, both amateur and professional. Kessel was particularly skillful in describing the tender feelings that, underneath their devil-may-care exterior, bound the men to each other as they faced a rotten world made up of clueless civilians and pompous military bureaucrats. *L'Équipage* went through 82 editions and earned the author a place in the French Academy. In Germany the best-known representative of the genre was Ernst Jünger, a holder of the Pour le Mérite who, in his memoir *In Stahlgewittern* (Storm of Steel), repeatedly expressed his envy of the aviators' life. He was only one of many writers who competed in their attempts to endow their people with what, at the time, was called *Luftbewustsein* (air-consciousness). Yet the country that put the greatest emphasis on military aviation not just as an instrument for war and conquest but as a means for bringing about the spiritual regeneration of an entire nation was, predictably, Fascist Italy. Benito Mussolini himself set the example, taking out his license in 1920 and later often piloting his own aircraft. In 1923 he said that, though not all Italians could learn to fly, all should envy those who did so and follow the development of their country's wings.[4] Two of his sons, Bruno and Vittorio, also became military aviators. Still Il Duce was not content. In June 1940, when he launched Italy into World War II, one of his first orders went out to his son-in-law, Galeazzo Ciano, to leave his desk as foreign minister and start flying combat missions instead.[5]

To be sure, the mystic association with supermen and suffering was much less pronounced in the democracies where heroes are seldom allowed to be very different from the rest of us. Yet in Britain and, above all, the United States, countless novels were written and movies produced that described the use of airpower against various nefarious enemies of democracy, capitalism, and progress in general.[6] There were also movies that celebrated the heroic exploits of men and the beautiful women who, after many twists and turns, agreed to become their trophies. Howard Hughes's *Hell's Angels*, released in 1930, was the most expensive movie made up to that time. Further east, the Soviet Union was as eager to create a new type of man as any fascist regime was. What better specimen of the new breed of Bolshevik supermen than military pilots, most of them male but including a few women, who had mastered modern technology and were always ready to sacrifice their lives for the socialist motherland? The greatest and mightiest of the land saw the benefit of having a pilot in the family; among them were Anastas Mikoyan's son, Stepan; Nikita Khrushchev's son, Leonid; and Stalin's own son, Vassily.[7] Collectively, they had the honor of being called Stalin's Falcons. They accomplished their "daily heroics" in quest of "human progress" under the benign supervision of the Father of Nations.[8] A typical piece of propaganda, written by (or for) a record-setting pilot, ran as follows:

> He is our father. The aviators of the Soviet Union call Soviet aviation Stalinist aviation. He teaches us, nurtures us, warns us about risks like children who are close to his heart; he puts us on the right path, takes joy in our successes. We Soviet pilots feel his loving, attentive, fatherly eyes on us every day. He is our father. Proud parents find affectionate, heartfelt, encouraging words for each of their sons. . . . He sends his falcons into flight and wherever they wander keeps track of them and when they return he presses them close to his loving heart.[9]

This, then, was the cultural setting in which the "prophets of airpower" made their voices heard. All agreed that airpower was the most revolutionary, most far-reaching innovation in history; as one officer-writer put it, it had introduced "that sort of change in the tide of human affairs occasioned by the recession of the ice cap, which would result were the Gulf Stream to change its course."[10] The question was how to put it to the best possible use. Perhaps we should start our account with Hugh Trenchard, whom we have already met.[11] Essentially Trenchard was a practitioner rather than a theoretician. As he told a subordinate, "I can't write what I mean, I can't say what I mean. But I expect you to know what I mean!"[12] Yet he was the first commander of the world's largest and first independent air force, so his views carried weight.

Already during the war, Trenchard had emphasized the importance of strategic bombing and pushed for a vast expansion of the bomber force. Later he continued to pursue the same line. In Trenchard's favor it must be said that, unlike some of the more extreme visionaries, he never believed that the RAF would replace the other services and go on to win "the next great war with a European nation" on its own;[13] rather, the objective was to enable the army to occupy the enemy country, not to create a situation where it would no longer be needed.

On the other side of the Atlantic the most prominent advocate of airpower was General Billy Mitchell. Like Trenchard, whom he visited several times and whom he greatly admired, Mitchell was a bona fide war hero. In 1918, during the St. Mihiel offensive, he commanded no fewer than 1,500 British, French, and American aircraft.[14] His main work, *Winged Defense*, was published in 1925. The world, we learn, was standing on the threshold of a new epoch. In it, "the destinies of all people will be controlled through the air" just as, in the past, it was determined first by those who developed their communications on land and, following "the era of the great navigators," at sea. Aircraft, having "set aside all ideas of frontiers," can carry "the most powerful weapons deep into "the heart of an [enemy] country" without any need for the armies protecting that country to be defeated first. Using gas, they will cause "the complete evacuation of and cessation of industry" in any place they choose to attack. "This would deprive armies, air forces, and navies even, of their means of maintenance . . . in the future, the mere threat of bombing a town by an air force will cause it to be evacuated, and all work in munitions and supply factories to be stopped."[15]

As time went on the leaders of the U.S. Army Air Corps, which succeeded the Air Service in July 1926, came to agree with him. Their chief vehicle for spreading the gospel was the Tactical School, which opened its doors at Maxwell Air Force Base, Montgomery, Alabama, in 1931.[16] It acted as a kind of funnel through which all commissioned personnel had to pass if they were to stand a chance of attaining high rank. During the 1930s, going out to bomb objectives deep in the enemy's rear was presented as almost the only way the army air corps could contribute to victory. Even so, there was a catch. During World War I, British strategic warfare aimed at Germany's cities and industries had not, to put it mildly, been very effective. Indeed it was precisely this fact that made Trenchard claim that, in this kind of war, the psychological damage inflicted on the enemy's population would exceed the physical 20 to one. Yet Americans never liked the idea that the instrument at their disposal would be used for mounting indiscriminate attacks on civilians.[17] Some other method had to be discovered, and, on paper at any rate, another method was duly found. Devising its doctrine for waging strategic warfare far behind the front, the air corps decided it would go for industrial plant. Yet two problems immediately presented themselves. First, even the largest factories presented pinpoint targets and were hard to hit. Second, it was anything but certain that a large industrial country with countless factories and other installations dispersed all over its territory could really be knocked out by such means. At best, the outcome would be a prolonged struggle of attrition.

To cope with the former objection the air corps decided that, in contrast to the normal practice that both sides eventually adopted during World War I, it would send in its bombers by daylight. To cope with the latter, it developed the idea that the enemy's economy did not consist simply of numerous independent plants but of an intricate system. All were linked to each other; the more numerous the links any of them had, the more critical it was. Thus the trick consisted of identifying the most important ones and knocking them out, whereupon the rest would be paralyzed and general collapse would follow.[18]

The last, and in many ways most important, prophet of airpower was the Italian Giulio Douhet, whose masterpiece, *Il dominio dell'aria* (The Command of the Air), was published in 1921. Douhet noted the rapidly growing importance of airpower and called for it to be entrusted with "independent offensive missions"—in other words, for the establishment of an independent air force no longer part of, but equal to, the two older services.[19] The development of air technology happened to coincide with advances in other fields of science, resulting in unprecedentedly powerful explosives, gases, and germs. As a result it was becoming possible to "ravage [the enemy's] whole country" not only with ordinary bombs but also with chemical and bacteriological warfare.

Air warfare, however, differed from that waged on land and at sea. "The airplane has complete freedom of action and direction; it can fly to and from any point of the compass in the shortest time—in a straight line—by any route deemed expedient. Nothing man can do on the surface of the earth can interfere with a plane in flight, moving freely in the third dimension." Hostilities, instead of being limited to artillery range, will extend over "hundreds and hundreds of miles over all the lands and seas of nations at war. No longer can areas exist in which life can be lived in safety and tranquility, nor can that battlefield any longer be limited to actual combatants." For Italy this meant that, in case of another conflict, not even "the strongest army we can deploy in the Alps" would be of much avail. On the other hand, it also opened up unprecedented possibilities.

Another factor had to be taken into account. Recent decades had witnessed the development of firepower, "and the truth is that *every improvement in firearms favors the defensive*" [emphasis in the original]. Yet the "indisputable principle that wars can only be won by offensive force" remained in force. This was where airpower came in, for thanks to the aircraft's unparalleled range, speed, freedom of action, and ability to concentrate against selected targets, 20 defenders would be needed to counter every attacker, which was a clear impossibility. By its very nature, airpower was an offensive instrument and a violent offense, the best and indeed almost the only way in which it should be used. The first task in any offensive would be to achieve "command of the air," by which Douhet meant "to be in a position to prevent the enemy from flying while retaining the ability to fly oneself." Once that had been done, the rest would be relatively easy.

The air force, then, would have to consist primarily of bombers, though Douhet did concede the need for "combat power [i.e. fighters] proportionate to the enemy's possible strength." It would open hostilities with a mighty blow aimed at "destroying the mobilization, maintenance and production centers" supporting the enemy's aviation. Attacks on "railroad junctions and depots, population centers at road junctions, military depots and other vital objectives" would follow, handicapping the enemy's mobilization. Bombing "the most vital civilian centers [would] spread terror through the nation and quickly break down [the enemy's] material and moral resistance." Most important would be attacks on the centers of large cities; in every country, civilian morale was the weak link in the war effort. "Here is what would be likely to happen to the center of the city within a radius of about 250 meters: Within a few minutes some 20 tons of high explosive, incendiary, and gas bombs would rain down. First would come explosions, then fires, then deadly gases. . . . As the hours passed and night advanced, the fires would spread while the poison gas paralyzed all life. By the following day the life of the city would be suspended."

As early as the 1920s several Soviet air commanders supported the idea of an independent air force, though none of them seems to have gone quite as far as Douhet did in actively calling for the destruction of cities. In 1931 Yakov Ivanovich Alksnis was put in charge of the air component of the Red Army. A close associate of the chief of staff, Field Marshal Mikhail Tukhachevsky, who himself advocated the use of airpower in "deep operations" behind the front, Alksnis saw himself as Douhet's disciple.[20] In 1936, reporting to the Communist Party's Eighth Congress, he boasted that the Red Army's air component—there was no independent air force—was the strongest in the world and that 60 percent of it consisted of bombers. However, in 1938 Alksnis was arrested and shot in the usual Stalinist fashion. His demise, along with that of Tukhachevsky in whose court-martial he had been forced to participate, marked a long shift toward close air support (CAS) and so-called flying artillery; throughout World War II, the Red Air Force remained the most tactically oriented of all.[21]

The other important country that hesitated to accept Douhet's theories was Germany. It is true that Hitler's Luftwaffe was built as an independent service equal to the army and the navy. Still this does not mean that they followed closely in Douhet's footsteps. They agreed that airpower, thanks to its speed, flexibility, and ability to concentrate, was essentially an offensive instrument and that its first task should be to obtain command of the air,[22] but they did not accept his emphasis on bombing civilian targets; to them it was but one of several options and not necessarily the one they liked best. Instead they preferred CAS (which they called "direct support") and, above all, interdiction ("indirect support") against military ones located in the zone of communications. Such targets were likely to be much smaller and harder to hit than factories and cities in the rear; to that extent, the implication was a focus on daylight operation.

The decision to avoid morale bombing grew out of the fact that, starting under Moltke the Elder, the Prussian-German Army had developed a strong reliance on combined arms warfare. The objective was to defeat the enemy's army, if possible by means of large-scale "operational" movements culminating in a battle of annihilation.[23] The implication was that the enemy's cities would be taken care of after that battle—not, as Trenchard had suggested, before it, and not, as Douhet had done, as a substitute for it. Also important in all this was the fact that Germany was a continental country with long land frontiers and continental enemies to fight. In this respect it resembled the Soviet Union but differed strongly from Britain and the United States or, insofar as Italy forms an elongated peninsula and is separated from Europe by the Alps, even from Douhet's own country.

Amidst all this, the one really novel method of air warfare that was developed during those years was airborne assault. The pioneers in the field were the Soviet Union and Germany. The first Soviet airborne formations were created during the mid-1930s. The intent was to have them operate deep behind the enemy front where they could attack headquarters and bases, seize communication centers, and sow panic and confusion. In 1936 foreign military visitors, among them the future British field marshal Archibald Wavell, were treated to the spectacle of an entire Soviet airborne battalion being dropped.[24] Reaching the ground, they assembled, seized, and secured an "enemy" airfield. Other aircraft then arrived, flying in two additional battalions complete with light artillery and trucks. The Soviets also experimented in the use of gliders to reach their objectives. While the German airborne forces were much smaller than the Soviet ones,[25] they too went back to the mid-1930s, when suitable transport aircraft, in the form of the Ju-52, became available. The first division consisted of paratroopers who were also trained to reach their targets by gliders. Later another one was configured for transport in Ju-52s. Like their Soviet counterparts, the commanders of these forces conducted numerous experiments aimed at enabling them to conduct sustained operations by resolving such issues as keeping them supplied and providing them with transport and some heavy weapons. However, those objectives were never completely achieved either in Germany or anywhere else.

While many people celebrated airpower as the means to rejuvenate humanity and others considered how best to use it for war and conquest, probably the largest number trembled in view of what they thought it could do. To H. G. Wells's fears, as expressed in *The War in the Air,* was added the possibility that gas might be used. "In future warfare," wrote an anonymous author in the 1923 issue of the *Naval Review,* "great cities such as London will be attacked from the air and . . . a fleet of 500 aeroplanes each carrying 500 ten-pound bombs of, let us suppose, mustard gas, might cause 200,000 minor casualties and throw into panic 1,000,000 people within a few minutes of their arrival."[26] As a British historian later put it, "the apocalyptic conception of the bombing war of the future pervaded much of the culture of the interwar period."[27] Nor was that conception limited solely to the sensation-mongering popular media. Here is Stanley Baldwin addressing the House of Commons on November 10, 1932:

> What the world suffers from is a sense of fear . . . [and] it is my own view . . . that there is no one thing that is more responsible for that fear . . . than the fear of the air.
>
> Up to the time of the last war civilians were exempt from the worst perils of war. . . . In the next war you will find that any town within reach of an aerodrome can be bombed within the first minutes of war to an extent inconceivable in the last war. . . . I think it is well . . . for the man in the street to realize that there is no power on earth that can protect him from being bombed, whatever people may tell him. The bomber will always get through.[28]

All over the "civilized" world, newsreels showed footage of the wars in China and in Spain, complete with burning cities, demolished houses, and dead bodies lying about.[29] The climax of these developments was the attack on Guernica, an unremarkable town in the Basque country of northeastern Spain, which at that time had a population of about 5,000.[30] Its military importance, if any, consisted of the fact that it commanded some roads and a bridge. In April 1937 it was in the hands of the Republicans, though some doubts exist as to whether Republican troops were actually stationed inside it. On April 27, the bridge was attacked by five waves of aircraft belonging to the German Condor Legion and Italy's Regia Aeronautica. As the smoke dissipated, it became clear that the town had been hard hit. However, the bridge, which was the real object of the attack, still stood. Most modern estimates put the number of dead at between 250 and 300, which was about twice as many as had been killed in the deadliest single World War I raid. Yet by subsequent standards the operation was small indeed. No more than 40 tons of bombs were dropped. The most important thing about the entire episode was the amount of media attention it received. For example, the London *Times* ran stories about the bombing every day for a week. At that time Pablo Picasso had just received a commission to do a painting for an exhibition on twentieth-century technological progress to be held in Paris. He went to work, producing a canvas that caught the surprise, the horror, the helplessness, and, perhaps best of all, the blind confusion that war in general, and air warfare in particular, can inflict. Since then, the fame of *Guernica* has grown to the point where many now consider it the most important artwork of the entire twentieth century.

Attempting to justify his policy of appeasement at the Munich Conference to the members of his cabinet, Prime Minister Neville Chamberlain told them:

> He had flown up the river over London. He had imagined a German bomber flying the same course. He had asked himself what degree of protection they could afford for the thousands of homes which

> he had seen stretched out below him and he had felt that we were in no position to justify waging a war today.[31]

Once the conference was over and Czechoslovakia had surrendered the Sudetenland, he explained that he had wanted to avoid "people burrowing underground, trying to escape from poison gas, knowing that at any hour of the day or night death or mutilation was ready to come upon them."[32] In France, too, fear of air attacks played a large part in bringing about the policy of appeasement.[33] East of the Rhine it was inconceivable for people in responsible positions to utter such thoughts. Still, under the surface the situation was not very different.

Meanwhile, how did the organizations that were supposed to bring about apocalypse develop? Once World War I had ended, most of the world's armed forces, their air components specifically included, entered a period of retrenchment. By the provisions of the Treaty of Versailles, the major country most affected was Germany. It was prohibited from having an air force at all—a fact that could well be seen as a tribute to the extraordinary growth of a service that, less than a decade previously, had been seen by many as a mere toy. Nevertheless, the air forces and air industries of other countries fared almost as badly. Between 1918 and 1920, U.S. production of aircraft went down from 14,000 to 328. In Britain, which during the war had built up the largest air force of all, the number of personnel was cut by 90 percent, that of aircraft by an astonishing 99.

To make things worse still, neither the army nor, even less so, the navy wholeheartedly accepted the RAF's independent existence. As chief of staff, Trenchard had his hands full fending them off. One way of doing so was to persuade the cabinet to allow his service to assume "humdrum responsibility in peace time"[34]—specifically including that of policing Britain's newly acquired, very large, and often very sparsely populated, imperial possessions in the Middle East and in Africa. Yet the other services kept on hammering away on the issue; in 1937–38 the navy succeeded in restoring carrier-based aircraft, though not land-based maritime aviation, to its own control. To fend off the army, the RAF consistently pushed strategic bombing over CAS and interdiction. Even during the early years of the war, when the Germans tried to bring down Britain by means of the Blitz and air defense was understandably given top priority, these forms of war were still neglected. Consequently when the time came, there was neither an organization nor a doctrine nor personnel suitable for the purpose, so that everything had to be rebuilt from the beginning.

Elsewhere the first major country to build an independent air force was Italy, whose Regia Aeronautica was established soon after Mussolini assumed power in 1922. The French Armée de l'Air became independent in 1934. A year later the new Luftwaffe also became an independent force.[35] Yet in 1939 three major powers, the Soviet Union, the United States, and Japan, had still not moved in that direction. In any case the establishment of independent forces did not solve all problems even in the countries that adopted this solution. Take the case of Italy. To be sure, the Italian Air Force was in charge of all the country's military air assets. However, since most of the brass consisted of former army officers, they did not appreciate the role of naval aviation. As a result, all the navy got was a handful of obsolescent reconnaissance aircraft. To make things worse still, whenever the navy (and the army) required air support, it had to go through the Commando Supremo in Rome, a weak and ineffective organization. Italy never developed either torpedo planes—a grave shortcoming, since those planes soon turned out to be the most fearsome weapons of all—or squadrons of dive-bombers trained, equipped, and organized for air-to-sea missions. Thus the Aeronautica was reduced to attack enemy ships by means of high-level bombing, which did not prove effective.[36]

In Germany, the creation of the Luftwaffe as an independent service led to somewhat similar problems. Since Germany during the Weimar years had not been allowed to have any air force at all, inevitably many of the Luftwaffe's senior commanders were former army men—for example, its first chief of staff, General Walther Wever, and the future field marshal Albert Kesselring. Both were supremely able men, but they had no appreciation for the navy's special requirements. The Luftwaffe's founder and commander in chief, Hermann Goering, insisted that "everything that flies belongs to me." As a result, in 1939, the naval aviation arm consisted of just 200 operational aircraft. Almost all were based on land, and many were obsolete. Training courses in such specialized work as naval navigation and reconnaissance, anti-shipping attacks, and mining were only just being instituted, and a torpedo capable of being air-delivered became available only in 1941.[37] No wonder the memoirs of many senior German admirals consist of one long complaint about the failure of the Luftwaffe to support the submarine war in particular.[38] So bitter were the sailors that, when the West German Bundeswehr was created in the mid-1950s, they deliberately selected British aircraft so as to make sure they were incompatible with the American equipment their colleagues in the air force used.[39]

As previously noted, the Soviet Union, the United States, and Japan did not set up independent air forces. In the Soviet Union, this may have had something to do with the fact that a strategic bomber force never emerged. The responsibility rested with Joseph Stalin, whom some authors have accused of everything that went wrong with the Soviet military.[40] Unquestionably the Soviet dictator made mistakes, and this may have been one of them. Still, taking World War II as a whole, would the Soviets really have done better if, instead of focusing on the land army and the kind of airpower needed to support it, they had devoted greater resources to building up an independent air force? Should they have put greater emphasis on strategic bombing? Should the Soviet High Command have included a flying Field Marshal Zhukov, a flying Field Marshal Konev, or a flying Field Marshal Shaposhnikov in its ranks? The United States and Japan, too, might have followed the British example; what cannot be proved is that their conduct of air operations in 1941–45 would have been more efficient or more effective than it actually was.

Passing from interservice relations to the organization of each service separately, one comes across several very different models. With the RAF, the most important divisions were Fighter Command, Bomber Command, Coastal Command, and, after 1943, Transport Command. As the name implies, Coastal Command specialized in conducting land-based naval operations. Though it was clearly separate from Bomber Command, the two were interchangeable to some extent. On one hand, Coastal Command often asked Bomber Command to assist in anti-submarine warfare, as in targeting submarine pens, or else in laying mines. On the other, Bomber Command sometimes demanded that Coastal Command release some of its aircraft so that they could participate in the strategic bombing campaign. Whereas these divisions applied to the home islands, a sizable part of the RAF was always stationed overseas. The units in each theater came under an air commander in chief who served the theater commander. Each overseas command naturally consisted of an appropriate mixture of aircraft of various types.

In the United States, defending the homeland against naval attack, anti-submarine warfare included, was initially the responsibility of the U.S. Army Air Forces (USAAF), as they were known from March 1942 on. It is a telling comment on how much autonomy the air commanders already possessed that it took the army chief of staff, General George Marshall, months of pressure before he succeeded in making his subordinates surrender some bombers to the navy to assist it in this task.[41] As the war continued and expanded, most of the USAAF's operational units were deployed overseas where they were grouped in huge formations known as air forces. Thus there was the Eighth Air Force in Britain, the 12th and 15th Air Forces in the Mediterranean, the 20th Air Force in China, and the 21st Air Force in the Pacific. All these consisted primarily of bombers with various fighter, reconnaissance, and transport units thrown in. The exception was the Ninth (Tactical) Air Force, also stationed in Britain, which was made up entirely of fighters.

By contrast, neither the Soviet Union nor Germany built its air forces for large-scale strategic bombing. Accordingly they did not organize those forces by commands but by armies, corps, and regiments (the Soviet Union) or by fleets, corps, and divisions (Germany). Each formation was complete in itself, comprising several different types of aircraft, though of course the units of which they consisted could be changed like so many building blocks. They came with their own headquarters, signals, and ground services. Each fleet, army, corps, division, and regiment could be moved from one theater of war to another as circumstances dictated. In the case of Germany, internal lines, as well as an exceptionally homogenous system of organization and training, helped. A good example is the X Fliegerkorps. In 1941–42, it found itself moving from Norway to the Mediterranean to Russia and back to the Mediterranean again, along with all its equipment, a good example of the Luftwaffe's almost uncanny ability to change its bases rapidly and without undue friction.

As Allied bombing of Germany increased, a new command, responsible for fighters, was set up in 1943. In the Soviet Union, this never happened. Normally each Army Group or, to use Soviet terminology, Group of Fronts, had an air fleet or army assigned to it. The difference was that major Soviet air formations always remained part of the Red Army and were subordinated to the senior ground commanders whom they supported.[42] By contrast, the Luftwaffe kept operational command firmly in its own hands. As one of its senior commanders wrote after the war, it was neither a whore to follow where the army led nor a fire brigade on call to put out even the smallest conflagrations.[43] That said, it must be added that, whereas the navy was full of complaints about the Luftwaffe, cooperation between the latter and the ground forces was generally excellent.[44]

Another question in need of an answer was how to organize each country's anti-aircraft defenses, and here again Britain and Germany provided very different models. In the former, the defenses in question formed part of the army. In the latter they were part of the Luftwaffe. By facilitating cooperation among guns, balloons, and fighter aircraft this solution had much to recommend it, and many other countries also adopted it. In the Soviet Union anti-aircraft artillery was part of the Red Army just as the air force itself was. Yet it must be noted that these and more or less similar arrangements in other countries applied only to their respective homelands. Field formations invariably had organic anti-aircraft defenses consisting of light, mobile artillery batteries and heavy machine guns. The same applied to navies, which used both heavy and light artillery to defend their bases.

In September 1939, Germany was said to have 4,509 aircraft in its order of battle. Britain had 4,111, and France 3,392.[45] Even without Poland, the Allies outnumbered the Germans 1.6 to 1. When Italy entered the fray in June 1940 it had about 2,300 military aircraft.[46] Yet even without taking into account qualitative differences, on which more in a moment, these numbers mean little. For example since Germany prepared to fight short, sharp campaigns, it kept only 20 percent of the available machines in reserve. By contrast, Britain had more aircraft in reserve than in the front-line units and was thus better prepared for a long war. Readiness rates, which provide one of the best indications of the quality of an organization as opposed to that of the machines it uses, also varied. The Luftwaffe only had 2,893 serviceable aircraft out of 3,609 first-line ones; for the RAF, the corresponding figures were 1,600 and 1,911. France suffered from a shortage of qualified pilots, whereas Italy signally failed to build up sufficient stocks of munitions and spare parts. So badly maintained were Mussolini's aircraft that, in one of his periodic letters to Hitler, he half complained, half boasted, that he had to do the work himself.

While these and other air forces organized and reorganized, technical progress proceeded at a dizzying pace. In 1920 the winner of the Schneider Trophy contest for seaplanes was an Italian-built Savoia S.12bis. Powered by a 500-horsepower Ansaldo engine, it covered the 230.68-mile course at an average speed of 105.97 miles per hour. When the race was held for the last time in 1931 the winner, a British Supermarine S.6B equipped with a monstrous 2,350-horsepower Rolls-Royce engine, raised the record to 340 miles per hour;[47] later the same aircraft was clocked flying at 408 miles per hour. As important as speed was flight ceiling. In 1920 the world record, set by an American machine, stood at 33,000 feet. Ten years later it had been pushed to 43,000. The long-distance record went up from 1,967 miles in 1925 to 4,911 four years later.[48] These, of course, were exceptional performances, achieved by custom-built aircraft flown and serviced by handpicked personnel; even in 1931, few fighters had engines developing more than 600 horsepower or were capable of speeds far in excess of 200 miles per hour. Yet the figures, as well as the fact that the races were held at all, do create an impression of the dizzying rate at which technical progress was proceeding and of the enthusiasm it was generating.

Until 1931, too, most military aircraft were little but souped-up versions of those developed late in World War I. Made of wood, fabric, and wire, they were biplanes fitted with fixed undercarriages and open nacelles. Yet change was already under way; the most important one was the shift to metal construction. Among the earliest attempts was the Soviet Tupolev TB-1, the world's first all-metal bomber.[49] By that time performance had improved to the point where the aerodynamic advantages of a retractable undercarriage justified the added complexity and weight. Some light liaison and artillery spotting aircraft apart, eight years later only a few military aircraft still had fixed undercarriages. The most important factor driving improved performances was increasingly powerful engines. In 1937, the Klimov M-100 engine of the Soviet Polikarpov I-17 developed 860 horsepower. Just one year later the Merlin engine of the first model British Spitfire fighter was rated at 1,030, almost exactly the same as the Daimler-Benz 601 D mounted in its German opposite number, the Messerschmitt Me-109, developed. Both engines were 12-cylinder, V-shaped, and liquid-cooled; obviously the laws of engineering and aerodynamics that dictated the choice were the same in both countries.[50]

Apparently the first cannon-armed fighter of all was the above-mentioned Polikarpov I-17. It was quickly followed by the British Hurricane Mark II C, which carried no fewer than four 20-millimeter ones, as well as the Me-109. By 1941 the Spitfire had also been equipped with these weapons. When the first jet fighter, the German Me-262, became operational late in 1944, it came with an even more powerful armament consisting of four 30-millimeter cannon. At least two other German aircraft that made their appearance toward the end of the war, namely a late-model Stuka and the experimental Focke-Wulf Ta-152 fighter, were armed with 37-millimeter cannon. The former served as a tank buster; the latter was designed to blast its enemies out of the air as quickly and economically as possible. By contrast, the North American P-51 Mustang, an excellent all-round fighter that deserved its nickname, the Cadillac of the Sky, never received anything heavier than six 0.5-inch Browning machine guns.[51] But then this fighter, unlike most others, was intended to bring down not bombers but the fighters that escorted them.

The Spitfire Mark IX had a maximum speed of 408 miles per hour and could reach 44,000 feet. For the Me-109G the figures were 406 and 39,400 respectively. Most bombers fell far short of such performances. Even if they could climb that high, they were hampered by the loads they had to carry. Nor, owing to their multiple engines and considerably greater weight, could they compete with the fighters' maneuverability. Yet taking into account the very different requirements they had to meet, the technical progress bombers made was as impressive as that of their smaller rivals. The Tupolev TB-3 of 1931 had four engines rated at 715 horsepower each. Maximum speed was 179 miles per hour, the ceiling 12,500 feet, the bomb load a disappointing 4,800 pounds, and the range almost 2,000 miles. Among the bombers produced by other countries perhaps the best known was the American B-17. Built to meet the army air forces' demand for a daylight "precision" bomber, the Flying Fortress, as it was known, appeared on the scene for the first time in 1936–37. It had four Wright R-1820 Cyclone nine-cylinder radial air-cooled engines rated at 1,200 horsepower each. The machine could fly at a maximum speed of 267 miles per hour to a maximum distance of 3,400 miles and carry as much as 17,600 pounds of bombs. The flight ceiling stood at 35,600 feet; few other bombers could fly that high.

Needless to say, this short discussion is much simplified. There were single-engine fighters and two-engine fighters. There were also numerous ground-attack aircraft, though later during the war there was a growing tendency to replace them with high-performance fighter-bombers. Fighter-bombers came with one engine, light and medium bombers with two (here and there, as with the Italian Siai-Marchetti SM-79 of 1937, three), and heavy ones with four. The Germans developed a famous dive-bomber, the Ju-87 Stuka (*Sturzkampfflugzeug*, meaning, literally, "falling fighting" aircraft), for close support. Specialized night fighters, equipped with radar, made their debut in 1941. Other aircraft, such as the British Mosquito, were originally developed for reconnaissance purposes but later adapted to carry cannon and bombs too. In other cases things worked the other way around as fighters and light bombers were equipped with cameras. Even this list does not take into account entire families of light reconnaissance liaison and transport aircraft.

Nor was technological progress limited solely to new aircraft. For example drop tanks, which greatly extended the range of aircraft even though they somewhat reduced performance, were first used during the Spanish Civil War. By 1939–40 many aircraft also incorporated self-sealing fuel tanks. By 1941–42 the first fighters equipped with bubble canopies, which provided pilots with much-improved all-around vision, started making their appearance. Perhaps the most important, and certainly the most sophisticated, innovation of all was the Norden bombsight,[52] named after its inventor, the Dutch-American engineer Carl Norden. So secret was the mechanism that crews in training had to take an oath to defend it with their lives, if necessary. The army air forces need not have bothered. In 1937 one of Norden's employees went to Germany. There he reconstructed the device for the Luftwaffe, which produced a simplified version.[53] In practice the performance of the device fell short of its theoretical capability. Still it was a remarkable achievement, and later models were used in both Korea and Vietnam.

At the time the war broke out, some even more revolutionary innovations, such as jet engines and helicopters, were in the early stages of development. Of the two, the former made it into the last stages of the war itself; although some prototypes flew even before 1939, the latter never did. Though there were some differences in emphasis, technologically speaking the most advanced countries were the United States, Britain, and Germany. The heaviest bombers were built by the Americans, who had both the industrial resources and the longest distances to cover in the Pacific. Loaded, a B-29 weighed 141,000 pounds, a British Lancaster only half that. Though it could carry a similar weight of bombs, its range and ceiling were much lower. The Germans never developed a good heavy bomber. At a time when their enemies and even the U.S. Navy were arming their fighters with cannon, the U.S. Army Air Forces continued to rely on machine guns.

Other countries lagged behind the leaders. During World War I, France had developed a military air force second to none; however, it did not keep up, so that in 1939 it was no longer a serious competitor, a fact that played a major role in the "strange defeat" it suffered the next year. After 1930, Italy too fell behind. Until 1935 or so, the Soviet Union was able to compete with the West in the quality of its military aircraft. Later, though, it committed the classic error of switching from development to mass production too early. Consequently the Red Army entered the war mainly with masses of obsolescent aircraft.[54] The situation in respect to ancillary equipment such as radio sets, landing and navigational aids, and the like was even worse. Later the USSR caught up to some extent, developing some powerful and well-armored ground-attack aircraft in particular. Yet it was only able to match the Luftwaffe because the latter had withdrawn its best aircraft to the west.

For the Japanese, things worked the other way around. During the interwar years observers in the West tended to underestimate all things Japanese and did not count them as a fully civilized people. The setback they suffered at Khalkin Gol in 1939 did nothing to raise the esteem in which they were held. All the greater the surprise when they opened the war with some excellent machines, including, above all, the Zero fighter. Later, though, they fell behind. This was especially true in regard to radio and other kinds of electronic equipment; so feeble were Japanese attempts to produce radar that the Allies hardly even became aware of its existence in the enemy's hands. Closing the circle, the Germans resembled the Japanese in that they lost their initial advantage. At the end of the war all of their aircraft except for fighters were obsolescent. Nobody was more aware of this fact than the man in charge of the Luftwaffe technical department, General Ernst Udet. In November 1941, he shot himself.

Of the three great pioneers of aviation whose works we have analyzed, none was a navy man or took a particular interest in naval aviation. Understandably in view of the pressure coming from the other two services, Trenchard's main concern had been to make sure that anything that could take off and fly should belong to his own service. To a large extent, he achieved his aim, and it was only in 1937–38 that his successors had to make some concessions and acquiesce in the establishment of the Fleet Air Arm. Testifying before Congress in February 1925, Billy Mitchell asserted that the fleet could not "resist attack from even an insignificant flock of airplanes." In *Winged Defense* he wrote that coastal defense had "ceased to exist." In the future, all the sailors would be able to do was to "control . . . the waters outside of the cruising radius of aircraft, [but] these areas are constantly diminishing with the increasing flying powers of aircraft. It will be impossible for them to bombard or blockade a coast as they used to." As a result, "the surface ship as a means of making war . . . will gradually disappear." In the entire volume Mitchell does not make a single reference to carriers and only a single brief one to seaplanes.

Finally, Douhet was even less interested in naval questions. In the first version of *The Command of the Air* he did not have one word to say about the subject. Criticized by his fellow officers, he tried to correct this deficiency in the second edition. "If we are in a position to dominate our own sky," he now wrote, "we will automatically be in a position to dominate the Mediterranean. . . . Since aerial operations can be directed against both land and sea objectives, while the reverse is not true, it is logical to agree that aerial operations are the only ones which can be carried out independently of the others."[55] Flying from Italy, aircraft could dominate the entire Mediterranean; unlike some of his domestic critics in particular, though, Douhet understood that, outside the relatively limited space of that sea, the situation was very different. Since he did not believe that Italy had the means to fight Britain and break out of its "prison," as Mussolini would later put it, he did not see any need to discuss carriers even though he cannot but have been aware of the experiments other nations were conducting with them. Those nations, bordering on the open oceans and dependent on much longer maritime communications, saw things in a different light. Whatever Mitchell and others might say, the time when aircraft would be able to dominate the vast expanses of the oceans as they were already beginning to do shores and inland seas was some way off. Surface fleets would continue to exist and, if they were not to be blind, had to be capable of taking aircraft with them.

During World War I, navies had used two kinds of aircraft capable of operating from the water, seaplanes and flying boats. However well designed and successful they were, the laws of physics dictated that their performance should always lag far behind that of land-based machines that did not have to float. To improve performance, it was necessary to build an entire new class of ships capable of launching aircraft and recovering them. Of the seven major belligerents that had survived World War I, Italy, being confined to the Mediterranean owing to its geography, never developed such a vessel. Each for its own reasons, the Soviet Union and Germany did not do so either. France did convert a former battleship into a carrier, but once it had been completed it was judged unsuccessful.

This left the field exclusively to the three nations with the largest navies and the longest maritime lines of communication—Britain, the United States, and Japan. No sooner had the war come to an end than some pundits started claiming that the time of battleships had passed and that carriers should take their place. One letter to the London *Times*, written by a retired admiral who was a well-known gunnery expert, claimed:

> Criminal woeful, wicked, wanton, willful waste of the British taxpayers' money—this is my label for our government if they sanction the building of two battleships. . . . The Royal Navy is under the new conditions of warfare no longer our first line of defense or offense. The air is. . . .
>
> If we have a few aeroplane carriers out on the ocean with a speed of nearly double that of a battleship, the battleship will stay at home, as it did in the last war.[56]

Across the Atlantic, some American officers were equally outspoken. Yet this did not prevent the so-called battleship admirals from fighting hard to retain their floating castles. While they admitted that carriers were indispensable for providing the fleet with air defense, reconnaissance, and artillery spotting, they thought that the vessels should be ancillary to the battle fleet and should not seek to take its place.[57] Still they could only slow down, not stop, the process whereby battleships were finally consigned to oblivion. The very first ship equipped with a full-length flight deck, HMS *Argus*, was completed in September 1918 though it came too late to see action. In the same year, the Royal Navy laid down its first purpose-built carrier, the 10,850-ton HMS *Hermes*. They were followed by the *Courageous* and the *Glorious*, the former with 22,500 tons and the latter with 29,500.

The first American carrier, the USS *Langley*, was designated as an experimental vessel so that it would not count against the carrier tonnage America was permitted to have under the Washington Treaty of 1922, which limited the naval armaments of the great powers. She was followed by the *Lexington* and her sister ship, the *Saratoga*, which were rated at 36,000. True to the American tradition, these ships had monstrous engines rated at no fewer than 180,000 horsepower, twice as much as the *Glorious* had. Even this proved an underestimate; during their trials in 1930, the ships developed 210,000 horsepower and more. They reached the unheard-of speed of almost 35 knots, earning their nickname as fast carriers.[58] On the other side of the Pacific, the first Japanese carrier, IJN *Hosho*, joined the fleet in 1921. With only 8,000 tons, it was intended mainly for further trials and experimentation. Later in the decade the *Akagi* and the *Kaga* were added. Displacing 33,800 and 38,200 tons respectively, they stood somewhere between the British carriers and the American ones. By this time American pressure on Britain had persuaded the latter that its 1902 treaty with Japan should be allowed to expire. As the 1920s turned into the 1930s, all three powers were actively preparing for the clash in the Pacific that many contemporaries saw approaching.[59]

As important as the development of carriers was that of naval aircraft, but there was a catch. As we saw, the true believers, as they have been called,[60] in the future of airpower were primarily interested in strategic bombing. Owing to constraints of space and weight, carriers could not operate bombers. Essentially this reduced carrier aircraft to three main types:

light ones for liaison, reconnaissance, and artillery spotting; fighters for dealing with enemy aircraft; and torpedo bombers as perhaps the most effective anti-shipping weapon of all. Since bombers were excluded, a fourth type, the dive-bomber, made its appearance. Though the amounts of ordnance it could deliver were small, it was much more accurate; whereas horizontal bombing from 10,000 feet only scored one hit in ten, dive-bombers hit their targets four times as often.[61] Whatever the type, the outstanding characteristic of most carrier aircraft, as compared with their land-based counterparts, has always been their folding wings. First introduced in 1913, such wings imply greater weight, lesser strength, and added complexity. However, in most cases they are absolutely essential if the limited space aboard ship is to be fully utilized.

As the great British naval author Julian Corbett had written early in the century, naval power has three main tasks: to defend the motherland by preventing an invasion, to protect one's own trade and attack that of the enemy, and to "project force" across the sea.[62] Since the geographical constraints surrounding the three interwar carrier-owning powers were very different, and since they also had very different national aims, comparing them is hard. To start with Britain, it was a small offshore island entirely dependent on its foreign trade. Its imperial possessions and sources of supply were scattered all over the globe. These facts obliged the Royal Navy, its carriers and carrier aviation included, to operate in theaters as far apart as the Atlantic (the most important by far), the Mediterranean, and the Indian and Pacific oceans. Worse still, the long dispute between the RAF and the Royal Navy caused carrier aviation to be badly neglected.[63] In the end the Royal Navy entered World War II with seven carriers and six more under construction, though most of the aircraft these vessels operated were badly out-of-date.[64] Fortunately for Britain, at first neither of its enemies, Germany and Italy, had carriers. However, when Japan struck, there were no British carriers available to oppose it.

America's situation was entirely different. In relation to the rest of the world the United States is also an island. However, as its great enemy, Adolf Hitler, once said, the distance between it and other continents, as well as its sheer size, meant that the possibility of invasion could only occur to a disturbed military imagination.[65] America's foreign trade was nowhere as critical to its survival as Britain's. Its few overseas possessions were also relatively unimportant. To be sure, geography dictated that America's naval strength was divided between the Atlantic and the Pacific with only the Panama Canal to link them. Still there could be no doubt that, should war break out, its most urgent task would be to keep open the sea-lanes in the Pacific in order to defend forward bases such as Hawaii, Midway, and the Philippines. The second step would be to focus on Japan's lines of communication so as to cut the maritime communications on which that country was even more dependent than Britain was. The third and final step would be to occupy bases near the Japanese home islands so as to tighten the siege and, perhaps, prepare an invasion.

During the second half of the 1930s the technical quality of U.S. carrier aviation was probably somewhat inferior to that of its Japanese opposite number. As late as 1937 the admirals were still replacing one antiquated biplane with another that was almost as antiquated. In typical American fashion they believed that by simply equipping aircraft with increasingly powerful engines they could make up for structural defects. It was only in 1938 that the navy finally woke up to the fact that no biplane, however powerful, could compete with the new all-metal, low-wing monoplanes then starting to enter service in the world's main armies and air forces. From then on things gradually improved. Yet the machines delivered by the navy's favorite constructor, the Grumman Corporation, tended to be chunky. This earned the company its nickname, the Iron Works.[66] In December 1941 the gap, though smaller, persisted.

Finally Japan was at least as dependent on foreign trade as Britain was. To defend its own sea-lanes and attack those of the enemy, the Imperial Japanese Navy (IJN) had to operate over vast distances in the Pacific and the Indian Ocean. But at any rate it was free to concentrate most of its ships against the main enemy, the United States, and did not have to send them literally to the other side of the world, as Britain did. Thanks to years of concentrated effort, in 1941 Japanese carrier aircraft were far superior to anything the British possessed and probably somewhat superior to their U.S. counterparts too. They were more modern, lighter, faster, and more maneuverable. Another extremely important Japanese asset consisted of the Type 91 torpedo. With its long range, extraordinary speed, and large warhead, so superior was it to anything in the British and American inventories that there was simply no contest.

Still the IJN's greatest advantages consisted of the superb training of its aircrews and the experience gained during the war against China. The former consisted of something known as "combat skills," which included not merely the ability to fly their aircraft well but leadership, communications, and more; before being allowed to join their squadrons, Japanese pilots received four times as many flying hours as their opposite numbers in other forces did. Since death in training was considered acceptable, even necessary and heroic, some officers later complained that, compared with what they had endured during exercises, war was easy.[67] The latter meant that, at the time they entered World War II, some Japanese pilots already had the right to call themselves aces. Compared to their Japanese opposite numbers, British naval pilots only received a third as many training hours before joining their units; no wonder they could not compete.[68]

Since carriers could not operate bombers, their ability to "project force" from the sea to the land was limited. Conversely, as long as they stayed away from the land they themselves were safe because land-based fighters often did not have the range to reach them, whereas bombers were insufficiently accurate to seriously threaten them. Close to the shore, the situation was different. Carrier fighters were generally inferior to land-based ones; besides, the ships could be attacked by submarines and mines. Consequently carriers did their best to stay out of coastal waters. They were safest on the high seas, where their most dangerous opponents were similar groups. Yet operating on the high seas created other risks. From the early days of carriers on, those in charge were troubled by the question what to do if the vessels, large, expensive, but lightly armored and having no heavy guns, ran into the opposing battle fleet. Since the carriers had reconnaissance aircraft, in theory this should never happen. In practice the weather, the need for aircraft to pause between sorties in order to refuel and rearm, as well as human error, meant that it sometimes did. When it did happen, as for example during the Norwegian campaign of 1940, which saw the sinking of the *Glorious* by German heavy cruisers, the results could be catastrophic.

The conclusion from all this was that carriers should never operate without an escort. Depending on circumstances and availability, the latter might consist of battleships—in the early days, there was often some question as to who was escorting whom—destroyers, frigates, and submarines. When the group engaged on long-range missions, supply ships might also be needed. The need for extensive escort and support helped turn carrier warfare into an enormously expensive proposition, which of course is one more reason why it was limited to just three nations. It also made things extremely complicated; throughout the 1930s, one key issue that preoccupied navies was how to ensure that all those ships did not get in each other's way but supported each other as effectively as possible.

In 1939, Britain had 15 battleships and battle cruisers and seven operational carriers. For the United States, the late 1941 figures were 18 and eight, for Japan 13 and 11. Though the carriers were much smaller than those that the United States in particular built after the war, aircraft too were smaller and lighter. This meant that each of the former might be able to carry up to 90 of the latter; the U.S. Navy alone had a little over 1,000 carrier-capable aircraft though not all of those were up-to-date. Though the balance between the old and the new was shifting, every country still had naval officers who insisted that battleships were the core of the fleet and carriers, merely an adjunct to them. Aircraft, like various light vessels and submarines, were seen as essential, even indispensable, but not as the real strength of the fleet on which its striking power depended.

Douhet had argued that so-and-so many aircraft could be had for the price of a single battleship and that, in each sortie, they could drop an incomparably greater weight of bombs than any battleship could fire in a broadside.[69] Now, others turned his argument upside down. They calculated that a single surface ship could carry as many tons of ammunition, whether in the form of shells or as torpedoes, as so-and-so many aircraft could. An aircraft attacking a battleship, one officer claimed in 1936, stood a 94 percent chance of being shot down by the latter's anti-aircraft guns. By contrast, the aircraft's own chance of scoring a hit only stood at 1 percent of all the ordnance it expended.[70] As always, opinions reflected men's interests, and their interests, the positions that they occupied and the schooling they had received. Carrier officers for their part left no stone unturned in their efforts to persuade their superiors that the future belonged mainly if not exclusively to their own arm.

Facing one another across the Pacific as they did, the two navies that had invested most in carriers, those of the United States and Japan, thought in terms, outlined by the nineteenth-century American naval strategist Alfred Thayer Mahan, of a decisive battle. The goal would be to achieve command of the sea as a prelude to cutting lines of communication and projecting force. Consequently both of them concluded that, except when carriers acted in escort and anti-submarine duties, they should operate not individually but together so as to maximize striking power while at the same time reducing the number of escorts each one needed. By contrast Britain, thanks to its geographical position and the weakness of Hitler's navy, was much less interested in the prospect of fighting large fleet actions on the high seas. Consequently its carriers were more likely to be found operating individually while escorting convoys and hunting submarines.

To complete the cycle, recall that, of the three nations that operated carriers, Britain, owing to its geographical position, was the only one that stood in imminent danger of coming under air attack. Its priorities reflected this fact; those of the other two did not. It was this factor, rather than any inherent conservatism, that explains why, when war broke out, Britain lagged behind the other two in deploying modern carrier aviation.

CHAPTER 4

FROM WAR TO WAR

As I wrote in another book, one may divide the wars of the years 1919–39 into two kinds, "civilized" and "uncivilized." In fact, that was the way contemporaries themselves looked upon the matter.[1] The former were waged between, or else inside, more or less organized states with both sides making use of more or less well-organized, bureaucratically managed, uniformed, armed forces clearly separate from the population at large. The latter were fought by self-proclaimed "civilized" nations against all kinds of "uncivilized" people in Asia and Africa. This chapter will discuss the role of airpower in the former type of conflict. The part it played in the latter will be reserved for the last part of the book.

The first "civilized" war, growing directly out of the Revolution of 1917, was the Russian Civil War (1917–20). To put things in perspective, in 1918 alone Britain produced over 30,000 aircraft. However, over the three and a half years from the outbreak of the war in August 1914 to the time the Treaty of Brest-Litowsk was signed in March 1918, the Russian armed forces received only 7,400 aircraft (1,800 of them imported). Out of 5,500 engines, 4,000 were also brought from abroad.[2] To make thing worse still, many of Russia's aircraft manufacturing companies had been set up with the aid of foreign capital. No sooner did the Revolution break out than that capital started to be withdrawn, all but bringing production to a halt. By the beginning of 1919 the country was in near-total chaos as Reds and Whites, including Russians and foreign interventionists on both sides, fought each other on many fronts.

During this period, air operations were conducted by a small number of aircraft haphazardly assembled. None of the warring parties were exactly known for their highly developed aviation industries, so they seldom had enough spare parts and were often unable to maintain their aircraft properly. The forces on both sides were spread over vast spaces and huge distances; from Leningrad to Batum, which the Turks in 1918 tried to seize for themselves, it is 1,200 miles as the aircraft flies. Of the Tsar's aircraft, about two-thirds had fallen into the hands of the Whites, especially those operating on the southwestern front (Odessa) and in the Caucasus. To make things worse for the Reds, some of the foreign contingents and the Poles, with whom they were simultaneously engaged, had their own rudimentary air forces.

Operating on external lines and widely separated from each other, the various armies fighting the Reds could only use airpower in dribs and drabs. The fact that their aircrews were a motley assortment of ex-Tsarist, ex-German, ex-Austrian, Polish, British, French, and American pilots did not help. As it turned out, it was the Poles, in their war against the Soviets, who made the most effective use of what aircraft they possessed. In August 1920 they flew 190 sorties and dropped nine tons of bombs on the forces of Mikhail Tukhachevsky that were then approaching Warsaw. More important, a combination of cryptology and air reconnaissance enabled the Poles to track Tukhachevsky's moves, thus helping them to save their capital; yet all they had at this time were about 60 machines.

Initially the Reds had only 238 operational aircraft. During the wars themselves, the factories under their control, especially in Petrograd, Moscow, and Kiev, provided them with another 670. The Bolsheviks had the advantage of internal lines, but apart from that their situation was little better than that of their opponents. Now they sent 12 to combat the Allies at

Murmansk, now 30 to drop pamphlets over the Czech Legion, and now 30 more to Tsaritsyn, which was later renamed Stalingrad, on the Volga. Only once, during the above-mentioned advance on Warsaw, did they bring together as many as 200 aircraft for a single operation. They even bombed the headquarters of the Polish field marshal Józef Pilsudski, but neither this operation nor any of the rest could prevent the offensive from ending in failure. Aircraft are also said to have played a part in the recapture of the Crimea toward the end of 1920.[3] Losses, especially those that resulted from accidents, were very high.[4] Perhaps a better perspective on all of this is gained by the fact that the entire Red Army numbered between two and a half and three million men. While the vast majority moved on foot or on horseback, aircraft merely formed a drop in a bucket.

The next "civilized" war during the period was the Spanish Civil War. It opened on July 17, 1936, when some units of the Spanish Army joined right-wing paramilitary forces and attempted a coup. They did not, however, succeed; though some points were taken, loyalist forces defeated the principal uprisings in Madrid and Barcelona, thus setting the stage for a long and extremely bloody conflict. Enter Francisco Franco, the youngest and most highly decorated general in the Spanish Army. From the Canaries he flew to Spanish Morocco and assumed command over the troops there. No sooner had he done so than he sent representatives to Hitler and Mussolini, asking for aid. Both responded positively; of the former, we know that he was persuaded by Goering to use the opportunity both to assist in the spread of fascism and to test the nascent Luftwaffe.[5] The first ship, loaded with equipment, left Hamburg on July 31. Just a few days later, the airlift from Africa to Spain, the first of its kind in history, got under way. From that time to mid-October, when air transport became superfluous because the rebels had seized control of the sea, German and Italian aircraft flew some 20,000 troops across the Mediterranean. With them came 270 tons of weapons and ammunition. By the end of September the Luftwaffe contingent in Spain had grown to several thousand men. Working side by side with them were units of the Regia Aeronautica. However, the Germans and Italians did not have things all their own way. As early as October Soviet arms and equipment started arriving and reinforced the other side.

Early on, air superiority was in the hands of the Soviets, whose aircraft soon came to form 90 percent of the entire Republican air force. Hoping to put a quick end to the war, at first the Nationalists focused on the capital. The city came under air attack for the first time on October 27, when a Ju-52 dropped six bombs on it, killing 16 and injuring 60; at this time there were no anti-aircraft defenses to fire back. In response the Soviet commander, the 34-year-old Jewish-Lithuanian brigadier Yakov Vladimirovich Shmushkevich, who was known by his codename Douglas, deployed his forces around the capital. On November 15, they scored their first kill, shooting down an Italian reconnaissance aircraft. Taken by surprise by the strength of the Reds, the Germans built up their Condor Legion. It consisted of a bomber group with three squadrons, a fighter group, a reconnaissance group with two squadrons, and a seaplane group with two squadrons. The total authorized strength stood at 136 aircraft. A signals battalion, an anti-aircraft battalion, and two field maintenance battalions completed the picture. At peak, these forces numbered some 12,000 men. The Italian contingent was much larger, with as many as 70,000–80,000 men and a total of 759 aircraft.[6] As was also to happen during World War II, the Italian troops quickly became the subject of numerous jokes.

Except for landing troops by parachute or glider, two kinds of operation that were then in an experimental stage and were never attempted, the opposing forces undertook almost every conceivable mission airpower could accomplish. At the time, it was the strategic bombing—known to the Germans as carpet bombing—of important cities that attracted the most attention, although, by subsequent standards, the amount of ordnance dropped was less than impressive. Other frequently practiced missions included liaison, reconnaissance, close air support (CAS) by bombing and strafing, interdiction, casualty evacuation, and transport. Initially the Republicans, thanks to their Soviet-provided aircraft and pilots, had the upper hand. In the words of Werner Beumelberg, a Nazi writer who reported on the conflict, they involved their opponents in "bitter and bloody battles."[7]

However, late in 1937 the Germans sent in their most modern Me-109 fighters, He-111 bombers, and a small number of Ju-87 dive-bombers. German pilots developed new tactics, including the famous finger-four formation, which consisted of two pairs of fighters forming a loose, asymmetric, staggered group capable of providing mutual support in air-to-air combat. So heavy were the Red casualties that, come August 1938, Stalin chose to withdraw his Falcons altogether—which did not prevent him from organizing a victory parade in Red Square. Though the Soviet aircraft remained in the country and were subsequently flown by Republican pilots, from then on the skies were increasingly dominated by the Germans and the Italians.

This was anything but a small war; geographically it spread over much of Spain's 200,000 square miles. The number of dead ultimately reached 600,000. Moreover, it was fought not in some colonial country but in Europe itself. Transport in and out of the theater of war was easy and telecommunications for passing and receiving news were readily available. For these reasons, but also because of its markedly ideological character, it was closely observed both by military experts and assorted civilian reporters who flocked to it like flies to a dustbin. To the Soviet Union, it offered proof that strategic bombing was of no use and reinforced the decision to concentrate on army support instead. The Luftwaffe, the Regia Aeronautica, and the Armée de l'Air all reached similar conclusions; whatever Douhet and others might say, the bomber did not always get through and was not always effective. But whereas the first of these went on to develop the aircraft and the doctrine to implement it, the second and the third were unable to.

In the United States, one of the very few commanders to take any interest in the Spanish War was the assistant chief of staff of the U.S. Air Corps (USAC), Brigadier General Henry H. (Hap) Arnold. In an editorial for the *U.S. Air Services* issue of May 1938, he explained that the war, which he described as a mere civil conflict unfolding in a not very developed country, did not involve strategic bombing on any scale; therefore, he went on, it did not cast doubt on the USAC's doctrine in this respect.[8] The horse having spoken in this way, it is hardly surprising that other USAC officers echoed this assessment. They refused to allow their existing views to be questioned; in their favor, it must be said that they did recognize the importance of air transport. No more than the USAC was the RAF prepared to let its doctrines be influenced by events, least of all events unfolding in a supposedly third-rate, out-of-the-way country like Spain. In the most prestigious journal of all, *The Royal Air Force Quarterly*, the conflict was all but ignored. Yet at least some British officials agreed with the Germans that strategic bombing had yielded disappointing results and that unescorted bombers could hardly survive in the face of enemy fighters.[9] Much more important, those very same officials were just about to go ahead and force the RAF High Command to put fighters, rather than bombers, at the top of its list of priorities. By thus preparing it for the coming Battle of Britain, they quite possibly saved the country.[10]

Whereas most contemporaries seem to have paid more attention to the Spanish Civil War than to any other armed conflict of the time, that conflict was by no means the only one. In June 1937 the Imperial Japanese Armed Forces launched their invasion of China. Over the next few years it provided them with precious experience, thus in some ways doing for them what the Spanish Civil War did for the Luftwaffe. Ill-equipped and ill-trained as they were, the Chinese ground armies greatly outnumbered their Japanese enemies on the ground. Not so in the air, where the latter's much more highly developed industry always gave them a superiority of at least four to one. The Japanese also had superior organization and superior command arrangements. In spite of these advantages, so huge was the country, and so persistent the opposition, that they never got to the point where they enjoyed full command of the air. Time and again they thought they had achieved it and could focus on supporting ground operations as well as terror-bombing Chinese cities; time and again Chinese aircraft would emerge out of nowhere and inflict a sharp reverse. So highly motivated were some Chinese pilots that they tried to ram their enemies.

Early in the war, the U.S. colonel Claire Chennault described the Japanese pilots as able, experienced, well trained, and aggressive.[11] Later, things changed. Contrary to their reputation for discipline, the Japanese started operating in a disorderly, even sloppy, manner. So contemptuous did they grow of their enemies that they flew over their targets with open bomb bays, making three of four passes before releasing their loads. They were also slow to adopt lessons learned elsewhere; for several years after German pilots had revolutionized fighter tactics in Spain, Japanese pilots continued to fly into combat in tight Vs of three.[12] Like the Germans and Italians in Spain, the Japanese learned that the bomber would not always get through; if, in the face of enemy fighters, losses were to be kept to acceptable levels, a fighter escort was needed. Like the Germans and the Italians, too, the Japanese learned that pilots' reports concerning the results of their attacks both on troops in the field and on industrial targets were often exaggerated. Either the damage inflicted was relatively small or else it could be quickly repaired. Finally, also like their future Axis allies, they were forced to recognize that there were limits to what bombing cities could achieve. Burning houses, screaming women, and dead children abounded. For example, in the summer of 1940 Chunkin, which was then serving as China's capital, received 2,000 tons of bombs and was reduced to rubble. Yet such Japanese "victories" did not translate into political action; at no time was there any question of breaking the Chinese people by such means. As in Spain, there were signs that the attacks reinforced the will to resist.

Japanese policy during these years can only be called idiotic since they managed to clash with all four of their principal neighbors, China, the Soviet Union, Britain, and the United States, almost at the same time. Airpower played an important role in each of these conflicts, and it is to the second of them that we must now turn. The Khalkin Gol War, as it is known, had its origin in a dispute between the Soviet Union and the newly installed Japanese masters of Manchuria over the location of the border between them. In the spring of 1939, the clashes grew into full-scale war between the two countries. The Japanese Kwantung Army had some 500 aircraft in Manchuria. The Soviet Far East Army probably had more. On both sides, the aircraft suffered from the usual problems when it came to trying to accurately deliver their bombs onto relatively small targets. They were also plagued by other defects, such as lack of oxygen equipment to enable pilots to function at high altitudes and a shortage of radios.[13] On both sides the air contingents formed but a small part of the order of battle. The latter consisted of ground forces numbering in the hundreds of thousands, again with the balance strongly tilting toward the Soviet side.

During the first weeks of the hostilities, both sides discovered that the vast distances, the flat open terrain, the difficulties of navigation, and the vagaries of the weather greatly hampered air operations. Such conditions did not prevent them from using their aircraft for air-to-air combat as well as ground attack missions. Since neither Siberia nor Manchuria contained any large cities, those attacks were limited very largely to military targets. As the fighting escalated, its character changed. Instead of operating in dribs and drabs, the Soviets in particular started using their aircraft in large, concentrated formations. When General Georgi Zhukov, the future savior of Moscow, launched his final offensive in August, he had three rifle divisions, two tank divisions, and two independent tank brigades with a total of almost 500 tanks—the largest number used in any campaign since 1918. He also had 200 bombers and 300 fighters.[14] The bombers launched their attacks in massive waves from an altitude of 6,000–8,000 feet; at that height, they were often able to make their escape before the Japanese defenders could reach them. If they did reach them they would encounter the Soviet fighter escort, leading to heavy air-to-air battles. As so often was the case, there are conflicting accounts as to losses. Yet there is no doubt that, following a few weeks' heavy fighting, the Japanese were soundly defeated.

The war between Russia and Japan seems to have excited but little interest among contemporaries. The same cannot be said of the one between the Soviet Union and Finland. Considering how vast the difference in size between the belligerents was, inevitably the balance of forces was one-sided. This was as true in the air as on the ground; to oppose an estimated 900 Soviet aircraft available in the theater, the Finns had only about 200. The most modern machines in the Finnish inventory were Dutch-built Fokker D.XXXI fighters and British-produced medium Blenheim bombers. Both were quite respectable for their time, but unfortunately they only numbered 41 and 18 respectively. As the war went on, additional aircraft were ordered from various countries. The most important ones were 30

French-built Morane-Saulnier fighters, sleek machines with a maximum speed of 302 miles per hour, superb handling characteristics, and armament consisting of one 20-millimeter cannon and two 7.5-millimeter machine guns. Serving both as interceptors and in the ground attack role, they were superior to any other aircraft in the theater and did excellent work in spite of their vulnerability to anti-aircraft fire.

At 0920 hours on November 30, 1939, the Soviets opened hostilities by means of a surprise air attack. The targets selected were Helsinki and some other cities, and the objective was to break enemy morale with a single blow. First leaflets were dropped, then bombs. However, as was so often the case, the Soviet planners had overestimated the damage bombs could do. In these and other raids that followed, the only heavy damage done was in Viipuri, a small town at the head of the Bay of Vyborg. Another favorite target was the port at Turku the Finns used to import foreign war materials. In all, during the next three and a half months, the Red Air Force is said to have attacked 2,075 civilian targets in 516 different localities. Some 650 Finnish civilians died—an average of six a day—and 2,000 were injured. Two thousand buildings were destroyed and 5,000 damaged. In the words of former U.S. president Herbert Hoover, the Russians had reverted to "the morals and butchery of Genghis Khan."[15]

Finnish pilots formed a corps d'elite. Unable to match the Soviet numbers deployed against them, they sought to solve the problem by developing extremely aggressive tactics. Unlike their enemies, they had very close ties with the Luftwaffe (Finnish aircraft were also painted with the swastika, except that the arms pointed in the opposite direction). Following the lessons of the war in Spain, they adopted the finger-four formation, used it to considerable effect, and allegedly shot down ten times more Soviet aircraft than they lost.[16] As always, the defenders enjoyed the advantage of being able to recover more downed aircraft and pilots. Powerful anti-aircraft defenses, in the form of excellent German 88-millimeter guns, as well as superb civil defense discipline, helped.

The ground war proper has been described as "frozen hell" and with very good reason. Amidst bitter cold, often made worse by snowstorms and frozen mist that shrouded the endless, equally frozen, forests, the Soviet columns plodded toward their objectives. With visibility often reduced to zero, airpower could do relatively little either to assist ground operations or to prevent them from going forward. Only during the last weeks of the war did visibility improve somewhat, permitting airpower to play a larger role. Even so, in the end, the Finnish Mannerheim Line, which had hitherto remained unbroken, had to be breached by means of methods more like those of World War I than like those of the Blitzkrieg to come. General Semyon Timoshenko, who assumed command in January 1940, was one of those broad-shouldered, no-nonsense, occasionally brutal commanders of low-class origins whom the Red Army seemed to breed. Given a four-to-one superiority over the Finns—he had no fewer than 600,000 men and 2,000 tanks—he used masses of heavy artillery to fire hundreds of thousands of rounds at the opposing trenches.[17] Close behind the creeping barrage came the usual mass of infantrymen whose task was to turn the break-in into a breakthrough. Here as at Verdun, which might have served as a model, once the battle had begun the role of aircraft was necessarily marginal. Though the most detailed available account says that the Soviets had "total air superiority," it hardly has a word to say on what they did with it; elsewhere, the same account says that communications between ground and air forces were so bad as to prevent the former from having any effect at all.[18]

When we reflect on these wars, probably the one thing almost everybody could agree on was that the importance of airpower kept growing. Yet this widespread realization did not automatically tell people just how important it actually was for any one country, at any one moment, and for any one purpose. As we saw, the Spanish experience in particular helped the Germans and Italians to develop their respective air doctrines without, however, pushing them in a fundamentally new direction. Thanks to their much greater technical and industrial capacities, the former profited more than the latter did. During the same time frame, 1936–39, several air forces, with the USAC and the RAF at their head, simply refused to open their eyes to the lessons of the Spanish Civil War. Instead, postulating all kinds of excuses of the Not Invented Here (NIH) variety, they went on preparing themselves for what, perhaps guided more by instinct than by reason, they preferred to do.

When we turn the argument around, it would seem that, of all the major countries, the only one that allowed the experience gained in any one of the various wars to have a really decisive impact on the doctrine and equipment of its own air force was the Soviet Union. In view of its essential character as a land power above all, the 1937–38 decision to abandon large-scale strategic bombing in favor of ground attack and interdiction was probably correct. However, this could not make up either for Stalin's consistent refusal to set up an independent air force capable of doing more than acting as flying artillery in support of large formations or, even less so, for the failure of his commanders to study and adopt the most advanced air combat tactics. Only toward the end of 1943 did the Red Army finally begin to learn how ground and air forces could be integrated into a team. If all this proves anything, surely it is how difficult, how fundamentally unscientific, the military decision-making process at the top levels really is. So it was then, and so, in spite of all the numerous newfangled methodologies that have been invented to serve the purpose since, it remains today.

PART II

THE GREATEST WAR OF ALL

1939–1945

The day before Nazi Germany started World War II on September 1, 1939, Hermann Goering, as Hitler's deputy and the commander of the Luftwaffe, ordered his pilots to observe the laws of war and make sure they only attacked military targets, broadly defined as anything that is important for the enemy's conduct of war. Less than six years later, an American aircraft dropped the most powerful bomb in history until then on Hiroshima, a city devoid of major military significance, killing an estimated 75,000 civilians and bringing the greatest war of all time to an abrupt end. What had happened to airpower in the meantime, and how did it make the transition from the one to the other?

CHAPTER 5

FROM TRIUMPH TO STALEMATE

Historically, the speed with which a war could be launched was inevitably limited to that at which men's legs, or those of the animals they rode, could move them. Since railways are not suitable for tactical movement, with very few exceptions this remained the case even as late as World War I.[1] Though the motorized and armored forces that saw their debut during that year can do much better, before and after 1939 rare were the occasions when large formations of this kind advanced more than a few dozen miles a day; even in 2003, while enjoying absolute domination of the air and faced with very little opposition on the ground, the Americans took three weeks to cover the 300 miles from Kuwait to Baghdad. By comparison airpower, even the relatively primitive airpower available at the beginning of World War II, was able to carry war into the enemy's deep rear within a matter of hours or less. Scant wonder it became the favorite instrument in the hands of commanders intent on delivering the most powerful blow possible as quickly as possible.

The story of the first two years of the war in the air is largely that of the Luftwaffe's offensives and the Allied attempts to respond to them. Among those Allies, the first to feel the full weight of modern airpower were the

Poles. Outnumbered six to one at the beginning of the war, attacked simultaneously from three sides, the Polish Air Force, like the rest of the country's armed forces, stood no chance; in fact, having dispersed its most modern machines in time, the best it was able to do was to escape destruction on the ground. But supporting facilities such as hangars, repair shops, and ammunition dumps could not be so easily removed. All these were hit and, if not completely eliminated, had their capacity greatly reduced. Two days after September 1, the Polish Air Force had been broken up into small units with hardly any central direction. Still it did what it could to continue the fight, sending up as many as its 463 mostly obsolete aircraft as possible only to see them shot down in great numbers by the far superior Luftwaffe machines. It was heroic, magnificent even, but it can hardly be called war.

Each one of the two German army groups invading Poland was supported by a Luftflotte consisting of a suitable mixture of aircraft of all types and cooperating with the ground forces by means of specially trained liaison officers. Each Luftflotte also had organic motorized supply columns and airfield construction companies directly under its own command.[2] As the armored spearheads advanced, the Luftwaffe, partly supported from the air by its trusty Ju-52s, moved its bases with them. Once command of the air had been ensured, the Luftwaffe devoted most of its efforts to interdiction. During the first five days alone, it flew almost 5,000 sorties of this kind.[3] The main targets were the Polish rail network as well as marching columns. Military installations such as bases, depots, and the like also came under attack. On several occasions the Stukas provided close support, helping break up some of the fortified perimeters that threatened to hold up the tanks.

Amidst all this there were certainly cases when civilian refugees came under attack, sometimes deliberately, sometimes not; still, by and large the Germans, following Goering's order, which was issued August 31, seem to have adhered to the laws of war as they then stood. Certainly they did not do so out of what they called humanitarian tomfoolery, which God forbade. Rather it was because their "operational" doctrine called for the destruction of the enemy's armed forces as the condition for everything else.[4] Only late in the campaign, when the Poles refused to surrender, did the Luftwaffe systematically bomb Warsaw with masses of small incendiaries. Absent more advanced means of delivery, the latter had to be dumped out of the cabin doors of Ju-52s by shovel-wielding men.

Seven months later, in April 1940, the Luftwaffe turned its attention to Denmark and Norway. To forestall the British, who had been making their own plans for a landing at Narvik, the operation had to be prepared in great secrecy. As a result, intelligence was minimal and the Germans found themselves using Baedeker tourist maps. Occupying nearby Denmark presented no special problem either to the Luftwaffe or the other German forces and will not be discussed here. However, Norway lay across the sea where the Royal Navy enjoyed a much greater superiority than had been the case during World War I. In fact some of the points the Germans selected for the initial landings were closer to the British Isles than to their own home ports. All this made the undertaking risky, almost foolhardy; but for the Luftwaffe, its execution could not even have been considered.

Comprising the air component of the invading force, X. Fliegerkorps had 360 bombers, 50 dive-bombers, 50 single-engine fighters, 70 two-engine fighters, 60 reconnaissance aircraft, 120 coastal aircraft, and as many as 500 Ju-52 transports.[5] The campaign opened with seaborne landings at Oslo, Arendal, Kristiansand, Egersund, Stavanger, Bergen, and Trondheim. Of these, Oslo, Stavanger, and Trondheim were also attacked from the air. First the Luftwaffe's bombers and twin-engine fighters focused on the Norwegian Air Force, most of which was destroyed on the ground, and on the enemy's anti-aircraft defenses. Next troops were landed either by parachute or by means of transport aircraft. The defenders of Oslo succeeded in sinking one of Germany's most powerful warships, the *Bluecher;* yet in the end all it took to occupy the city was a military band that was landed on the nearby airfield and marched in without meeting resistance. By contrast, the airfield at Trondheim did not fall to the initial German attack; hence they quickly improvised an airstrip on the snow and landed their Ju-52s on it.

With the airfields in German hands, it was mainly a question of using every available transport to fly in more supplies so that the Luftwaffe's own aircraft could make use of them. This was accomplished within days, enabling the Germans to reconnoiter the theater of operations, gain intelligence on enemy movements, attack British shipping on its way to Norway, and prevent British attempts to establish improvised airfields of their own. The Luftwaffe was also able to provide effective support to the ground forces in their fight against the retreating Norwegians, particularly in the valleys between Oslo and Trondheim and Oslo and Bergen. The one thing it was unable to do was to prevent the British forces from being withdrawn; this was due above all to the near absence of specialized naval aviation as well as the fact that the Luftwaffe itself did not operate at night.[6]

On paper, the forces facing each other in the west appeared much more balanced than had been the case in Norway. The Germans had 3,578 aircraft—1,563 bombers, 376 dive-bombers, 1,279 single-engine fighters, 311 twin-engine ones, and 49 Schlachtflieger, or close support aircraft, in the form of Henschel 123 biplanes. Of those aircraft, 2,589 were operational. The Allies had 4,469, of which, however, only 1,453 were immediately ready for action.[7] The mystery as to why only 32 percent of the Allied aircraft in France, but a full 72 percent of the German ones about to attack them, could be thrown into the struggle is soon solved. Recalling the events of 1914–18, the French High Command believed that it was facing a long war in which the side with the last reserves would win. Hence they stationed almost three-quarters of their aircraft so far to the rear as to be out of the Luftwaffe's reach. Unfortunately this meant that they were also unable to help in repelling the German invasion. Indeed not the least remarkable feature of the "strange defeat," as it has been called, was the fact that the Armée de l'Air ended the campaign with more operational aircraft than it had at the beginning.[8] Qualitatively speaking, the Luftwaffe was about equal to the RAF but superior to the French, Belgian, and Dutch air forces. The French in particular did possess some modern aircraft, such as the Dewoitine D.520 fighter, which were a match for the Messerschmitts.[9] However, owing to the above-mentioned considerations, few of them were used where and when it mattered.

Truth to say, the real advantage of the Germans was in neither the number nor the quality of their aircraft. Instead it consisted of their unified command, imaginative planning, and the unparalleled élan with which they threw themselves into the battle, which Hitler told them would decide the fate of the Reich for a thousand years to come. Again there were two Luftflotten, one for each of the two principal Army Groups, B and A, which were involved in the campaign. Each Luftflotte came with a mixture of aircraft of all kinds, and each was provided with its own organic ground organization as well as anti-aircraft defenses. As in Norway, the first attacks were directed against Dutch airfields. The objective was to knock out the opposing air force, neutralize the anti-aircraft defenses, and seize the airfields themselves so that the Luftwaffe could use them for its own purposes—namely, to take the Grebbe Line, which defended the country to the east, from the rear. At the same time, paratroopers were dropped over Rotterdam to seize the vital north-to-south railway bridges over the River Maas.

But things did not work out quite as planned. The Dutch Air Force and anti-aircraft artillery did their best but were quickly neutralized. However, Dutch ground forces near The Hague prevented the Germans from taking over the airfields; as they did so, their colleagues in Rotterdam successfully fought off the paratroopers.[10] As Hitler himself recognized in his Directive No. 11 of May 13, Dutch resistance to the Wehrmacht's ground forces trying to breach the Grebbe Line was skillful and determined.[11] It was only after the Germans bombed Rotterdam, killed 980 people, and destroyed a large part of the city—by accident, they later claimed—that the Dutch gave up.[12]

Further south, in Belgium and northeastern France, the Luftwaffe also focused on airfields and anti-aircraft defenses. Wehrmacht communiqués claimed that, during the 12 days of the campaign, almost 2,000 Allied aircraft were destroyed either on the ground or in the air, as they rose to meet the attackers; while the figure was probably exaggerated, it is certainly true that, after the first week, the Luftwaffe had the sky almost entirely to itself. On the ground, blocking the way into Belgium, were the Albert Canal and the Eben Emael fortress that protected it. Aware of their importance, the Germans had been studying them for months. In the end, using gliders, they landed troops on the fortress's roof, where the defenders could not fire at them. Coming like a bolt from the blue, the operation succeeded in opening the road to the ground forces. Subsequent attempts by Allied aircraft, carried out at great cost, to destroy the bridges over the canal failed.

Further south still, the Luftwaffe covered the main German *Stoss*, or thrust, which proceeded by way of the Ardennes forest. The roads in the area were narrow and winding, barely able to carry the huge German forces committed—from the foremost spearheads to the rear echelon, they stretched over 60 miles and more. The outcome was monumental traffic jams, which the Allied air forces, partly because the Luftwaffe operated overhead and partly because they were holding back, failed to exploit. Once the German spearheads reached the River Meuse with its steep banks and strong fortifications they called on the dive-bombers to help them cross it. Some 300 aircraft participated in the operation, flying in relays; as in Poland, post-action inquiries revealed that the physical destruction the Stukas wrought was not as extensive as thought at first. As in Poland, their psychological impact on the French troops on the receiving end, French now, was very great.[13]

Once they had broken into the open plains of northern France, the tanks, still covered and supported from above, rolled westward very quickly. Twice, on May 19 and 22, did French forces try to mount a counterattack against the long and vulnerable German flanks.[14] Twice, their efforts were detected and defeated by Luftwaffe aircraft flying in the interdiction mode and *not* in close cooperation with the ground forces. There was a lesson here, which the future was to confirm time and again. Assuming reasonable freedom of action in the air, the best way in which an air force can assist in a war against a "trinitarian" army, by which I mean one that is state-owned, bureaucratically organized, uniformed, and clearly separate from both government and population, is almost certainly neither CAS nor strategic bombing, but interdiction.[15] On the other hand, interdiction itself is best carried out over wide-open terrain where enemy troops cannot hide or find cover.

It was at Dunkirk that the Luftwaffe, unable to prevent the evacuation of over 300,000 British and French troops, suffered its first real setback in the war. Much of this is attributable to the fact that the 850 aircraft, mostly fighters, the British had held back from the battle of France were now available to fight the Germans over the English Channel. The RAF itself had changed greatly. We have left the service in 1937–38 when, partly because of Trenchard's legacy and partly because the governments of the day hoped to deter Germany from going to war, it was still strongly committed to strategic bombing operations directed against enemy urban centers. At that point, a deus ex machina appeared. Having started in 1935, experiments with radar were already well under way. Almost from the beginning they were successful. By permitting incoming bombers to be detected in time for fighters to scramble and meet them, they promised to change the entire nature of war in the air as it had been understood from the time of Douhet on.[16]

Thereupon the Air Ministry, through its control over the purse strings and the factories, forced the RAF into a near-complete change of direction.[17] Fighter Command, long the RAF's neglected stepchild, suddenly received priority over everything else. Hurricanes and Spitfires, both of them among the most advanced fighters of the age, started rolling off the assembly lines in ever growing numbers. Spitfires in particular, having a very simple structure, were easy to build. This was one reason why, as early as 1940, the British were able to manufacture more aircraft than Germany, with its considerably larger industrial base, did. British production of fighters exceeded that of Germany by better than two to one.[18] Meanwhile, a chain of radar stations was speedily erected along England's east and south coasts. A command-and-control system, based on the one used to defend London in 1915–18, linked them to headquarters. It was Britain's good luck that, when the Luftwaffe started its assault, the system was just about ready for action.

The air assault on Britain began on August 13, 1940. The objective, in Hitler's own words, was to "overpower the English Air Force . . . in the shortest possible time" so as "to create the necessary conditions for the final conquest of England." As in Poland, Norway, the Low Countries, and France, the first objectives were "flying units, their ground installations, and their supply organization."[19] Easier said than done; as is often the case, the defender enjoyed some important advantages. The RAF could keep many of its fighter squadrons in north and west England and Wales, where they were out of range of most of the Luftwaffe's aircraft; compared with the German need to coordinate bombers and fighter escorts with their very different characteristics, sending up fighters to counter them was simple. German pilots shot down over England were invariably lost. By contrast, British ones, provided they managed to crash-land or parachute to earth, were often able to fight another day. Occasional help came from Ultra, the organization responsible for monitoring, intercepting, and deciphering German military wireless traffic in general and that of the Luftwaffe in particular. Yet perhaps the most important single factor was the failure of the Germans, whose aircraft were equipped for offense rather than defense, to recognize the critical role that the Chain Home radar stations were playing in the battle. Had they attacked those stations first of all and sustained the offensive, preventing them from being repaired, the outcome might well have been different.[20]

The turning point in the battle came early in September. The RAF inflicted such heavy losses on the Luftwaffe, its bombers in particular, that it had to switch from day to night bombing. Yet in the Second World War, as in the First, bombers operating by night could not hit their targets nearly as accurately as those operating by day. Any attempt to focus on militarily and economically valuable ones became a question of sheer luck. The signal was given by a German squadron that had lost its way and struck London. In response Churchill, who had become prime minister in May 1940, sent the RAF to bomb Berlin. Whether he had been waiting for such an opportunity in the hope of making the Germans change targets and taking the pressure off his hard-pressed few remains in dispute; certainly Hitler was the last man to take an attack on his capital lying down. To the "hysterical applause" of an audience consisting mainly of "raving maidens," he promised thousandfold retaliation.[21]

These events may also be interpreted in a different way. By early September, Hitler and Goering were confused as to the state of the RAF. On one hand they greatly underestimated its strength and believed it had become a spent force. On the other, the British fighters kept coming.[22] Meanwhile autumn and its storms were fast approaching, which meant that a seaborne invasion would soon no longer be practicable. They therefore switched to bombing urban targets, a decision for which Churchill had given them the perfect excuse. The Blitz, as it was called, lasted until May 10, 1941. It killed 43,000 civilians, half of them in London, and destroyed or damaged a million houses in London alone. Yet in truth the Germans, having built up an operational air force consisting mainly of light and medium bombers, did not really have the heavier, four-engine machines they needed for the job. In the end, the impact of the Blitz on Britain's economy was limited. Only 1.7 percent of the entire stock of machine tools was destroyed. Production of critical items such as electricity, aluminum, iron ore, aircraft, artillery barrels, and bombs was higher in 1940 than in 1939 and was to go higher still in 1941.[23]

Above all, the will to resist was not broken. Civil defense measures, which started to be implemented on a large scale in 1938, proved quite effective and reduced casualties to a small fraction of what had been expected.[24] The mere spectacle of British fighters and anti-aircraft defenses engaging the enemy, coupled with considerably exaggerated daily reports concerning German losses, was heartening. To be sure, there were many complaints, especially in London's hard-hit East End. However, never was there any question of the bombing forcing a change in the nation's determination to pursue the struggle. It was a story that was to be repeated many times both in World War II and later on. While some people died or were injured, sometimes in large numbers, only very few lost their mental balance as the pessimists had predicted. Far more suffered and grumbled; however, since they generally stood up and went about their business as best they could, governments rarely listened until there was almost literally nothing left to defend.[25]

During World War I, except for the operations of some German submarines, the Mediterranean had been an Allied lake. Italy's entry into the war on June 10, 1940, changed this situation. Except for convoys coming from either Suez or Gibraltar and heading for Malta, Allied maritime transport had to be suspended and could only be resumed in 1943. As it turned out, Mussolini's vaunted air force suffered from poor preparation and low serviceability rates.[26] As his son-in-law, the minister of foreign affairs, Galeano Ciano maliciously wrote in his diary, it sometimes looked as if the Regia Aeronautica and the Regia Marina hated each other more than they did the British. The former told Il Duce that it had eliminated "50 percent of the British naval potential" in the Mediterranean, whereas in reality the damage it had done mounted to exactly zero. The latter complained that its sister service bombed its ships for six hours.[27] In September 1940 the Italians invaded Egypt, but three months later they found themselves reeling back into Libya. In October of the same year they invaded Greece, but soon found themselves in headlong retreat into Albania. In both theaters the hapless Regia Aeronautica did what it could. It provided close support to the ground forces—in the Balkans, this meant operating in the teeth of absolutely atrocious weather conditions—and flew in some men and supplies. To no avail; by the beginning of 1941, out of 700 Italian aircraft stationed in Libya, only one-tenth were still operational.[28]

At sea, things went no better for the Italians. Repeatedly, their attempts to use their bombers in high-level attacks on British warships proved ineffective. What *did* prove effective was a well-planned, well-executed attack by British carrier-borne torpedo bombers on the port of Taranto; on the night of November 11–12, 1940, about half of the Italian battle fleet was put out of action for a long time to come. Only when the Germans, in the form of X. Fliegerkorps and the soon-to-be-famous Africa Corps, began arriving in force in December 1940–February 1941 did the balance of forces change. Some of the troops, incidentally, were flown across the Mediterranean in transport aircraft. As we saw, the Luftwaffe had not really been built with maritime operations in mind. Nevertheless its dive-bombing attacks on British ships proved incomparably more accurate than the Italian ones had been. German bombers flying from bases in Sicily also blockaded Britain's "unsinkable aircraft carrier" in the Mediterranean, Malta. Launching countless determined attacks on it, at times they came close to forcing it to surrender.

In the spring the Wehrmacht, strongly supported by the Luftwaffe, went on the offensive in southeast Europe. As Hitler had explained in his Directive No. 19, one of the objectives was to deny the RAF the use of Greek bases from which it could threaten the Romanian oilfields at Ploesti.[29] As it turned out, the first country to feel the effect was Yugoslavia, where a pro-British revolution had broken out on March 27, threatening the German plans. Its capital, Belgrade, was heavily bombed with little attempt to distinguish between military and civilian targets. As the campaign unfolded, the Luftwaffe, enjoying absolute command of the sky in the face of the hapless enemy, used its aircraft very effectively to disrupt the mobilization and deployment of the 800,000-strong Yugoslav Army.

In Greece, too, the Germans enjoyed complete command of the air. They used their aircraft as flying artillery, bombing and strafing first the Metaxas Line and then the Greek- and British-occupied positions that blocked or attempted to block the valleys further south. Distances in this theater of war were rather large—from the Bulgarian-Greek frontier to the southern tip of the Peloponnesus it is over 300 miles. As on previous occasions, the Germans' most impressive quality was their amazing ability to seize enemy airfields and move their logistic organization forward so as to use them almost immediately. For example, when the chief of the Army General Staff, General Franz Halder, flew to Larissa, in Thessaly, on April 22, he found the airfield there in full operation.[30]

It was precisely this ability that permitted the most spectacular German air campaign of all, the capture of Crete, to begin on May 20, barely three weeks after operations in Greece had ended.[31] First, several waves of parachutists were dropped at different spots over the island in order to capture its principal airfields. While the operation was ultimately successful, it proved very difficult to carry out and led to heavy casualties among the paratroopers. Next, the usual squadrons of Ju-52s brought in General Kurt Student's airborne troops. Some of these transports had to come down on the beach because the airfields on which they were supposed to land had not yet been secured. In the process many of them were wrecked either by accident or by enemy fire. Once the German troops had reached the ground they fought like devils. Nevertheless, since they had hardly any heavy weapons and no mechanized transport except some motorcycles, they found themselves at a grave disadvantage and the number of casualties kept growing. If the undertaking nevertheless ended in victory this was due largely to the fact that the Luftwaffe, in a spectacular display of anti-shipping operations on May 22, was able to prevent British reinforcements from reaching the island. This in turn enabled German mountain troops, embarked on Italian barges, to land on it, and the rest is history.

Once the campaign was over, Hitler told the Reichstag that, "to the German soldier, nothing is impossible." Behind the scenes, things were very different. Thirty-two years earlier that extraordinarily prescient writer, H. G. Wells, had correctly pointed out that airpower, while capable of inflicting "immense . . . destruction," was unable to "occupy or police or guard" assets on land.[32] Hitler evidently agreed with him; so heavy were casualties among the paratroopers that he told Student that their day was over. From then until the end of the war, they were only used as crack infantry. Still, much of the Mediterranean coast and islands, including Libya, Sicily, the Peloponnesus, and of course Crete itself, was now in Axis hands. This enabled Luftwaffe units stationed in those areas to all but close the sea to British shipping. While the Regia Aeronautica was still present, it hardly counted. Until the Battle of El Alamein in October 1942 finally turned the tide, German fortunes in the Mediterranean theater waxed and waned almost exactly in proportion to the strength of Luftwaffe units Hitler thought he could spare for that theater of war.

Thanks to its operational doctrine, its forward observation officers, and its now considerable experience in conducting air-to-ground operations, the Luftwaffe proved extremely adept at supporting the Africa Corps. Not so the RAF, which, though it now had many aircraft suitable for the purpose, had to learn everything from scratch. As late as June 1941, during the British attempt to relieve the German siege of Tobruk, the RAF and the U.S. Eighth Army Headquarters were set up eighty miles apart, making cooperation all but impossible. It was only in mid-1942 that things started changing. The two headquarters were moved closer to one another. Proper communications were established, and forward air observers equipped with radio were appointed. These measures reduced the average time it took the RAF to answer a request for air support from three hours to as little as 35 minutes.[33] Consequently carpet bombing played a critical role in defeating Erwin Rommel's last attempt to reach the Suez Canal. From this point on, the German commander, having experienced at first hand what airpower could really do, made it into a crucial factor in his entire strategy.[34] Needless to say, the fact that the RAF greatly outnumbered the Luftwaffe helped.

Compared to the momentous events then going on in the Soviet Union, the Mediterranean was a sideshow. The number of divisions Hitler committed in order to defeat Stalin exceeded those under Rommel's command by about 36 to one. Serious preparations for the campaign, the largest of all time, got under way in December 1940. As so often in the past, the task of the Luftwaffe was to cooperate with the ground forces in the common task of "crushing" the Soviet Union without, however, being subordinated to them. When Operation Barbarossa started on June 22, 1941, Goering had concentrated 2,713 combat (bombers, fighters, close support, and transport), of which 2,080 were operational. These figures do not include 639 liaison and reconnaissance aircraft (551 operational).[35] The Luftwaffe's order of battle as a whole was no larger than it had been in the previous year, nor had its composition changed to any considerable extent.[36] Given how vast was the country to be overrun, and how gigantic the Red Air Force, this is surprising.

The Luftwaffe's Intelligence Service was inclined to look down on everything Soviet. It estimated that the Red Army had about 10,500 machines, of which 7,500, or two-thirds, were stationed in Europe. Supposedly there were 1,360 reconnaissance aircraft and bombers as well as 2,200 fighters.

The Germans believed that most of these aircraft were inferior to their own, and this belief turned out to be correct. They also thought that Soviet ancillary equipment such as radios and navigation aids was on the primitive side, and in this, too, they turned out to be correct. Soviet organization was judged as being heavy-handed, overcentralized, and inflexible, Soviet training as below par. Where they were wrong was in their belief that, once the industrial centers in the USSR's western provinces had been overrun, Soviet production, including the production of aircraft, would all but collapse. As it turned out, they could not have made a greater mistake.

As in Poland, Norway, and the west, the Luftwaffe started the war with a devastating strike directed against Soviet airfields—by the end of the first week, the number of those attacked reached 130. Then and later the German aircraft, the Stukas in particular, flew as many as four, five, six, or even seven missions per day—astonishing figures made possible by the relatively simple construction of the machines, the excellent training of the ground crews, and a special apparatus that allowed no fewer than nine aircraft to be refueled at the same time. The Armed Forces High Command proudly claimed the elimination of 4,017 Soviet aircraft against the loss of just 150 of their own; by July 9, the Soviets, in a highly unusual statement, admitted that 3,985 had been destroyed.[37] Most of the losses were incurred on the ground; however, entire Red bomber squadrons, flying without escort in a desperate attempt to stop the Wehrmacht, were shot down. Whatever the precise figures, clearly command of the air was won easily and at a low cost. As early as June 25, the Luftwaffe began allocating part of its sorties to support the army's ground operations by attacking the Soviet transportation system in particular.

Since the Luftwaffe's central archives were destroyed at the end of the war, all we have is the scattered records of individual units. Take the case of a Kampfgeschwader (bomber group) made up of Ju-88 light bombers and stationed at the central part of the front, where it formed part of II. Fliegerkorps. From June 22 to September 9, it claimed to have destroyed 356 trains and 14 bridges, interrupted railway traffic 322 times, and flown 200 sorties against troop concentrations, barracks, and supply depots in what the Germans called "indirect" support for the ground troops. In addition, acting in the CAS mode, the group claimed to have destroyed 30 tanks and 488 motor vehicles. It also flew 90 sorties against artillery positions. Another Kampfgeschwader, made up of Me-110 twin-engine fighters, claimed to have destroyed 50 trains and four bridges over a slightly longer period. This came on top of 148 tanks, 266 guns, and 3,280 vehicles of various kinds.[38]

There was a price to be paid for this—between August 10 and 21, VIII Fliegerkorps, trying to help the ground forces by cutting the main railroad from Moscow to Leningrad, lost 10.4 percent of its aircraft. Another 54.5 percent were damaged but could be repaired.[39] As in World War I, the flat, often featureless terrain made navigation difficult, but it also meant that cover was hard to find, thus facilitating reconnaissance. Yet in some other ways things had changed considerably. Many of the Red Army's most powerful formations, instead of marching along on their and their horses' stomachs, were motorized and thus much more dependent on their logistic tails than their predecessors. In the entire European USSR there were only 52,000 miles of rail, many of them single-tracked. Consequently, disrupting the network was easier than in the more developed countries of the west, and the impact on the ground forces was greater. On the other hand, the same flat terrain, plus the fact that few Soviet roads were paved, meant that they were hardly ideal targets for air attack. Whereas in the west one could often hamper ground movement by reducing villages to rubble, in the Soviet Union such methods were of no avail.

Yet the most serious problem facing the Germans was the sheer size of the theater of operations. As the Wehrmacht marched east, the length of the front increased, funnel-like, from 1,000 to 1,500 miles. There simply were not enough aircraft, let alone ground troops, to thoroughly reconnoiter, conquer, occupy, and master such gigantic tracts of land. Here and there extensive forests covered the terrain, providing cover against air reconnaissance and enabling entire armies to disappear as if by magic. By this time the Luftwaffe's operational style of warfare, as the counterpart to the army's preference for combined arms maneuver warfare, had been fully developed.

Though some air attacks were mounted on major industrial cities such as Leningrad, Moscow, Bryansk, Orel, Tula, Kharkov, Rostov, and Odessa, they were met with unexpectedly ferocious resistance by the anti-aircraft defenses in those cities. This was one more reason why, on the whole, the Germans, or at any rate the Army High Command, much preferred to focus on the Red Army in the field. Invariably the goal was not simply to hold and wear down. Instead it was to use superior organization, superior intelligence, superior mobility, and a superior command-and-control system to drive deep wedges between the opposing enemy formations, separate them from each other, and if possible force them to surrender.

The Luftwaffe's assigned mission in all this was to gain air superiority (accomplished, as we saw, early in the campaign), reconnoiter, and interdict. From time to time it also concentrated as many aircraft as possible to deliver massive blows on targets immediately ahead of the attacking ground forces. It was by such means that it helped capture Novgorod and Tallinn (Reval) on the northern front; in the summer of 1942, in one of its last large-scale offensive moves, it was to play a similar role at Sebastopol in the Crimea. So accurate were its dive-bombers, and/or so great the commanders' determination to win even if it meant taking some casualties by friendly fire, that bombs were sometimes dropped within 600 feet of the German troops. One Stuka pilot, Hans-Ulrich Rudel, was ultimately credited with busting no fewer than 519 Soviet tanks; such were his exploits that a whole series of medals had to be designed especially for him.[40]

Up until the end of September the system yielded very good, indeed unprecedented, results. Entire Soviet armies were surrounded, cut to pieces, and smashed. Millions of Red soldiers were killed or injured or taken prisoner, booty sufficient to equip dozens of divisions was taken, and hundreds of thousands of square miles were occupied so that their populations and much of their economic resources were lost to the Soviets. At that point, however, diminishing returns set in. One reason was that the German lines of communication had become too long. The outcome was constant logistic problems from which the Luftwaffe, desperately trying to move its bases forward as fast as it could, was not exempt.[41] In October the rains arrived, followed by frost. The former turned practically all roads into bottomless quagmires, bringing most ground movements to a complete halt; the latter hampered all operations and badly reduced serviceability rates.

Behind the front, large numbers of Soviet soldiers whose units had ceased to exist refused to give themselves up. Instead, seeking and finding shelter in the woods, they joined a growing force of partisans. As the Germans found to their cost, in this kind of operation neither aircraft nor most other heavy weapons were of much use. All along the front, these factors caused operational moves to be stymied. Hitler himself had begun to question their value, telling Halder that Stalin's hordes of subhuman Slavs were too primitive to understand when they were beaten and that, in the future, it would be necessary to proceed more slowly and systematically.[42] The greater the problems of the Luftwaffe, the less it was able to support whatever bold and deep-thrusting, operational movements the army was planning. The less bold and deep-thrusting the army's movements, the more the Luftwaffe was reduced to a mobile fire brigade. This was especially true in the northern sector of the front. There the Wehrmacht, having laid siege to the great city of Leningrad, was doomed to remain practically stationary for almost three years on end.

Relatively little information is available on the operations of the Red Air Force during this period.[43] We know that Stalin, alerted by the bad performance of his forces during the war against Finland, was aware of the shortcomings of his Falcons and doing what he could to correct them. As far as may be determined, the purpose of his preparations was to anticipate a German attack. But given enough time—a matter, I think, of a year or two rather than of days or weeks as has been claimed[44]—he might very well have used them, along with the rest of the 200-division-strong Red Army, to stab Hitler in the back. As it was, the invasion caught the Soviets in the midst of a major expansion of their airfields and communications infrastructure, which, however, could not be completed. The result was that warning orders arrived too late and hundreds upon hundreds of aircraft were left standing wingtip to wingtip on the aprons. Losses were immense and the confusion perhaps even greater; never in history has any air force met a worse disaster.

For several weeks, even months, what operations the Red Army was still able to mount tended to be scattered, uncoordinated, frequently ineffective, and, at times, truly desperate. For example, large numbers of obsolete bombers were sent to attack the German spearheads and entire squadrons of them shot down like turkeys. As German intelligence had correctly perceived, a large part of the problem lay with the centralization of the command system. Another was rooted in the fact that, before the war, the Red Army's doctrine, whether the one centering on strategic bombing or the one that advocated deep operations, had been almost purely offensive. Taken by surprise by the outbreak of hostilities, the Stavka, the General Staff, in Moscow did not know how to use aircraft for defensive purposes. Stalin's interference, which was always backed up by the not too remote possibility of drastic punishment for failure, did not help.

By the time the battle of Smolensk was fought in mid-July the Red Air Force had fewer than 2,000 serviceable aircraft left. Still, as had also been the case in China and for many of the same reasons, Soviet air operations never came to a complete halt. Not every airfield could be located and subjected to attack. Not every attack inflicted irreversible damage. So many aircraft having been destroyed on the ground, for a time the Soviets even had a surplus of trained pilots. Often operating under the most primitive conditions, they took off whenever they could, only to find that their machines, such as the I-16, Yak-1, and MiG-3 fighters and the LaG-3 ground support aircraft, were no match for the Messerschmitts. In a wordplay on the manufacturer's initials, the LaG-3 even acquired the nickname of "varnished guaranteed coffin." Outflown, outmaneuvered, and outgunned, the pilots sometimes resorted to desperate measures, as in trying to ram their enemies. This was done often enough for a technical term, *taran*, to be invented for it. While many died, some survived; a few were recognized as heroes of the Soviet Union.

Eventually, like their comrades on the ground, Soviet air commanders learned. But at what cost! By the end of the year the German High Command claimed to have destroyed no fewer than 20,392 enemy aircraft. As opposing narratives go, this is remarkably close to the 21,200 mentioned in Soviet sources. The cost to the Luftwaffe was 2,505 aircraft lost. Another 1,895 were damaged, but since the Germans were on the offensive and constantly overrunning more and more territory they must have been able to recover and repair more of them than the Soviets did.[45] Thus the overall balance was almost five-to-one in favor of the Luftwaffe. Yet it was already beginning to feel the weight of the British air offensive in the west that was eventually to force it almost entirely on the defensive.

Much worse for the Germans, in 1941 their output of aircraft was lower than that of the Soviet Union—11,776 versus 15,735—and only slightly higher than it had been in 1940.[46] It is true that, across the board, Soviet aircraft remained inferior. Many of them suffered from various technical defects. Paint peeled off, cables snapped, engine blocks cracked, machine guns were improperly mounted, and so on. Once the initial surplus of Soviet pilots had been used up, the prevailing conditions made it very difficult to train successors, with the result that quality suffered. Against this stood the fact that Stalin, thanks to his master spy in Tokyo, Richard Sorge, knew Japan was not about to attack him. As a result, whereas the Germans were compelled to disperse their forces, air forces included, among several different theaters, the Soviets were able to concentrate almost all of theirs against a single enemy. By the end of the year, atrocious weather, primitive airfields, and other ground installations, and impossibly long lines of communications over even more impossible roads had reduced the Luftwaffe to a shadow of its former self.

CHAPTER 6

WAR OF FACTORIES, WAR OF WITS

After the opening moves, during which some of the belligerents engaged in large-scale maneuver warfare, World War I developed into a struggle of attrition. After the opening moves, during which some of the belligerents also engaged in large-scale maneuver warfare, World War II also developed into a struggle of attrition. This was not because there was prolonged stalemate at the front—there was not—but because the opposing sides were so large, or else ruled such vast stretches of land and sea, that even the largest operational movements, such as the Battle of Stalingrad and its successors, did not suffice to bring about a decision. Time after time, the front stabilized and the attacker, who was usually one of the Allies, had to start all over again. Inevitably, attrition meant a long war, and inevitably, a long war meant that the factories were called upon to play a critical role.

In 1939 the power with the greatest industrial potential was the United States. If we put that potential at 3, then that of the runner-up, Germany, stood at 1.2. That of the British Empire stood at 1; and those of the Soviet Union, Japan, France, and Italy at 0.8, 0.5, 0.3, and 0.24, respectively.[1] The gap between the United States, Britain, and the Soviet Union, on one hand, and Germany, Japan, and Italy, on the other, was 2.4:1. Of course, industrial potential did not translate directly into airpower. Depending on geography, national objectives, the characteristics of enemies and allies, doctrine, and so on, some belligerents put much greater emphasis on their air forces as opposed to the older two services. Some belligerents focused on relatively small and cheap single- and twin-engine machines; others, again for various reasons, produced a greater number of large, heavy, and expensive four-engine ones. The precise mixture was not necessarily fixed but might change sharply over the years. Briefly, a detailed comparison of the number of aircraft produced by the various countries is both impossible and meaningless. On the other hand, since God so often supports the large battalions, there is no alternative to trying our hand at it in spite of all the difficulties.

Not much needs to be said here about the two smallest powers, France and Italy. From 1937 until 1939 inclusive, France produced 4,288 aircraft against Germany's 19,136 and Britain's 12,920.[2] In the next year, the country was knocked out of the war. French aviation firms such as Amiot, Morane-Saulnier, and Potez continued to work and certainly made some contribution to the Luftwaffe's order of battle. However, for various reasons, productivity was abysmally low; it took four times as many man-hours to assemble the same aircraft in France as it did in Germany. Consequently the number of French-built aircraft that the Germans were able to put their hands on was rather small, never exceeding 100 per month. Much more important were French deliveries of bauxite and aluminum. Were it not for those critically important raw materials, the German aircraft industry could never have expanded as much as it did or maintained output for nearly as long as it did.

Whereas the French economy assisted the German aviation industry to some extent, Italy and the Regia Aeronautica were a burden on the German one. As in France, production was carried out in rather small factories. Machine tools were scarce, and attempts to increase output by using masses of semiskilled labor did not get far. Production peaked in the second half of 1940 when it reached just over 300 machines per month. Even so, the refusal of the aero-engine manufacturers to allow large constructors of automobile engines to enter the field meant that only barely enough engines could be delivered to match the supply of airframes, forcing the Germans to step in. From early 1941 on, the situation was reversed. The production of engines, many of them license-built Mercedes-Benz ones, almost doubled from 600 to 1,100 a month. Yet that of airframes started declining, at first slowly and then much more rapidly. In 1943 the country became a battlefield. The south was occupied by the Allies, but the north remained in German hands. Thereupon production, and with it the Regia Aeronautica, collapsed.[3]

During all the six years from 1939 to 1945, Japan only produced 79,123 aircraft.[4] Output peaked in 1944, when it stood at 28,180. Even at the end of the war, only 15 percent of all Japanese machine tools were of the general-purpose, as opposed to specialized, type.[5] This both accounts for, and was a result of, the fact that much of the empire's industry, the aviation industry specifically included, was scattered among thousands of small firms, even family workshops, acting as subcontractors to large corporations. Consequently productivity was low—between 1941 and 1945 it went down from 44 percent of the U.S. level to a mere 18 percent. As in other countries, competition by the armed forces drained the labor force and made it hard to use the remaining workers in a rational way. Given that the United States produced almost 100,000 planes in 1944 alone, and that at the time of the attack on Pearl Harbor it was not yet at war with Germany, it is a little hard to understand how Japan's leaders could have hoped to win the unequal struggle.

The way the German war economy functioned, whether or not it was deliberately geared to provide what was needed for Blitzkrieg campaigns and no more, and why it produced as much or as little as it did during the years that it was so geared have been the subject of a huge literature. Here all that needs to be said is that, notwithstanding Goering, who once said that Germany "armed until it bristled,"[6] at first there was no attempt to bring about a major expansion of the aircraft industry. Production, which as we saw had stood at 11,776 in 1941, only went up to 15,409 during the next year. This was much less than that of the United States, the Soviet Union, and Britain, which stood at 64,706. The great leaps came in 1943, when 24,807 were built, and in 1944, when the number increased to 39,087.[7] Even so, of course, there could be no question of Germany even coming close to matching its enemies.

Supposedly the Third Reich was governed by the *Fuehrerprinzip*, the leader principle, according to which decisions at all levels were made by a single man, and Hitler himself, standing at the top of the hierarchy, made the most important ones of all. In practice, owing not least to Hitler's somewhat lackadaisical leadership style, it tended to be surprisingly decentralized. Both before and during the war, this left plenty of room for the top figures to fight fierce turf battles among themselves. In the field of aircraft production, Goering, as minister of aviation and commander in chief of the Luftwaffe (among his numerous other titles), fought the air inspector general, Erhard Milch, whom he once described as "a fart in my ass." Milch tried to impose some kind of order on leading manufacturers such as Heinkel, Messerschmitt, and Junkers. He was foiled by the fact that, making use of Hitler's tendency to put his understanding of technology on display,[8] the heads of those and other firms had fairly easy access to him. In theory, they ought to have been coordinated by Udet as chief of the Luftwaffe's technical office; in practice, as he himself complained not long before his death,[9] nobody listened to him. The outcome was that, long before 1939, each went his own way, fighting all the rest for resources such as labor, energy, raw materials, and factory space.[10]

This competition went on throughout the war. It led to an extremely inefficient use of the chief raw material, aluminum, as well as endless duplication and a very large number of prototypes, the great majority of which never entered production. Another result was constant modifications that disrupted production plans. Perhaps worst of all, after 1941–42 a great many types were obsolescent. By 1943–45 the British and the Americans had a clear technological lead. Against this background, the feat of doubling of output between 1942 and 1944 was almost a miracle—one that is hardly diminished by the fact that it was done partly by switching from twin-engine to industrially less demanding single-engine machines. The Germans had always known that, quantitatively, they could not cope with their enemies.

Both in general and in the air, their operational doctrine was meant to overcome that difficulty by focusing on the enemy's armed forces and defeating them before their enemies' superior resources could be fully mobilized and brought to bear.

The "lightning campaigns" of 1939–41 having failed to bring a decision, the Germans sought to redress the balance by producing an entire generation of revolutionary weapons. The most important one was the Me-262, the world's first operational jet fighter. In the words of one pilot, it gave the term "flying" an entirely new meaning[11]; had it been available somewhat earlier in sufficient numbers, it might well have brought the Allied bombing offensive to a halt. Less successful were the V-1 and the V-2. Developed by the army, the latter was a magnificent technical achievement but owing to its inaccuracy and the relatively small warhead it carried, it never justified the vast resources invested in it.[12] Developed by the Luftwaffe specifically to compete with the army, the former did not do much more for the *Endsieg* (final victory), but at any rate it was much cheaper.

This brings us to the real heavyweights, Britain, the Soviet Union, and the United States. Throughout the years 1940–43 the British outbuilt the Germans, let alone the Japanese, by a considerable margin. The same happened once again in 1945, when the German and Japanese war economies were approaching collapse. Furthermore, once the Battle of Britain had been won, the British again started producing large numbers of heavy bombers. To this extent, they replaced quantity by quality. In each of the years 1940, 1941, and 1942 Britain built more aircraft with fewer laborers than Germany did. As early as March 1942 it had a surplus of fighters that could be delivered to its newly found Soviet ally.[13] Yet nothing could be more mistaken than to think that cooperation was smooth and efficiency maximized. As in Germany, the RAF and the navy were not able to agree who would get how many aircraft first, and the establishment in 1938 of an Air Council in which both were represented did little to resolve their differences. Some of the worst errors were committed early on. Grossly overestimating the output of Germany's aircraft factories, the Air Ministry sought to close the gap as quickly as possible. To do so it compelled the

RAF to accept several types of bombers that turned out to be obsolescent; early on they were shot out of the sky and had to be withdrawn. Retooling the assembly lines to build their successors took time, which meant that production was slowed down or had to be halted.[14] This was one reason why, once the British were able to turn back from defending themselves against the Luftwaffe toward strategic bombing, it was found that the available forces were totally insufficient for the purpose.

This brings us to the largest belligerents of all, the Soviet Union and the United States. Over the first six months of the war the Soviet Union lost a huge part of its territory, population, raw materials, energy sources, and industrial potential. Either they were destroyed or they were overrun by the advancing German armies. In the face of such problems, the country's ability to maintain and even expand production can only be called a miracle. Much of the miracle was due to the evacuation of an entire plant from the western USSR to locations east of the Urals. However, compared to the rest, the Red Air Force also enjoyed some advantages. Owing to the circumstances of geography and the limited role that the sea played in the conflict, it never had to build up a really strong naval arm with all the complications it creates.[15] Owing to a deliberate decision, it only ever produced a single heavy bomber. Even this machine could only carry half as many bombs as the American B-17.[16] Only a few were built, and a few nuisance raids on Berlin apart, even these were used mainly for tactical and operational purposes, as during the Battle of Kursk in 1943. The Soviets did produce some two-engine machines—the Ilyushin Il-4, the Peltyakov Pe-2, and the Tupolev Tu-2—that could be classified as either light or medium bombers. However, from the beginning of the war to its end, the emphasis was clearly on single-engine fighters and ground support aircraft; indeed it is said that the number of Ilyushin Il-2 Shturmoviks built exceeded that of any other military aircraft in history.[17]

From 15,735 in 1941 the number of aircraft built jumped to 25,346 in 1942, 34,900 in 1943, and 40,300 in 1944, only to drop back to 20,900 in 1945. The longer the war, the greater the emphasis on fighters and ground-attack machines as opposed to bombers. In each of these years, the Soviets outproduced the Germans by a smaller or larger margin. Though both countries resembled one another in that they focused on land-based aircraft and produced very few heavy bombers, in other ways they were opposites. The Germans developed a very large number of prototypes of which only a comparatively small number were ever produced; the Soviets went the other way. They discontinued the production of some models so as to free machine tools and factory space, limited the number of different engines, and rationalized production so that building an Il-4 only required 12,500 man-hours in 1943 as against 20,000 two years earlier.[18] They also skimped on ancillary equipment and on finish; then as later, compared to their western opposite numbers, Soviet weapons, aircraft included, always had something crude about them. This, however, does not mean that they were always ineffective. For example, the Shturmovik, whose armor made it particularly hard to shoot down, was the only World War II plane constructed in such a way that the armor actually contributed to its strength, leading to a weight saving of approximately 15 percent. Even if some Soviet aircraft were relatively ineffective, at any rate they were expendable and, therefore, usable.

Standing like a colossus, the most successful World War II producer of aircraft—as of practically everything else—was the United States. In 1940, a total of 12,804 machines left the assembly lines, 26,277 in 1941, 47,836 in 1942, 85,898 in 1943, 96,318 in 1944, and 49,761 in 1945. At peak, therefore, one aircraft did so every five minutes, 24 seconds. Furthermore, this output was perhaps more varied than that of any other country: it consisted of small aircraft, large aircraft, single-engine aircraft, multi-engine aircraft, combat aircraft, noncombat aircraft, land-based aircraft, and carrier-based aircraft. Nothing like it had ever been seen before; nothing like it has been seen since, and almost certainly nothing even remotely resembling it will ever be seen in any kind of future.

As with every other country, this is not to say that perfect coordination of all production factors was achieved. The mere title of one book, *The Mess in Washington*, ought to rule out any such belief.[19] A look at the index shows that the aviation industry suffered from labor shortages, disastrous turnover rates (often caused by employers trying to steal skilled workers from each other), and even a production crisis that occurred in the summer of 1943 and led to serious problems in the manufacture of B-17s. It appears that, when President Franklin Roosevelt in May 1940 put forward his "50,000 aircraft" program for 1942 he had taken the figure out of thin air.[20] After Pearl Harbor he raised it to 125,000 aircraft per year, again with no solid basis of facts to back it up. As in other countries, delays in starting the production of some aircraft, notably the B-24 Liberator bomber, meant that, by the time they could finally be deployed, they were approaching obsolescence. That was one reason why many of them were used in the antisubmarine role over the Atlantic whereas others were converted into transports. Nevertheless, these problems ended up being overshadowed by a number of advantages no other country had.

Throughout World War II, the United States was the only major belligerent whose territory was neither invaded nor bombed. Following the Great Depression the country had a huge unused manufacturing capability and an equally large pool of surplus labor. Thus, from 1940 to 1942 alone, the size of the workforce went up by nine million.[21] Compared to the population, the United States called up fewer men than any other major belligerent did, which translated into a larger workforce. In 1944, the U.S. aircraft industry employed more people than that of any other country. American industrial plants in general, and aircraft-manufacturing factories in particular, were much larger than their British, German, and Japanese opposite numbers, though in comparison with the Soviet Union the difference was probably not as great. U.S. productivity in the field was also much higher than in Germany and Japan.[22]

There is another way of looking at the figures. Of the five main belligerents, two entered the war in 1939. One did so in mid-1941, and two at the end of the same year. Taking the period 1940–45 as the best available compromise, we find that, in those six years, the United States produced 309,761 aircraft. Germany built 109,586, the British Empire 143,234, the Soviet Union 147,836, and Japan 74,646. Earlier in this chapter it was estimated that, if America's industrial potential in 1939 stood at 3, then the figures for Germany, the British Empire, the Soviet Union, and Japan were 1.2, 1, 0.8, and 0.5 respectively. Combining the two sets we find that Germany produced somewhat less than its fair share of aircraft. The British Empire produced considerably more, and the USSR many more. Japan, too, produced more than its share. This calculation ignores many factors, including the extent to which the various countries mobilized their resources and the types of aircraft each produced. Still we conclude that, relative to their overall industrial potential, *all* the main belligerents except Germany built more aircraft than the United States did.

Surprisingly enough, the country that put the greatest emphasis on the air arm turns out to have been the Soviet Union. This even held true at the time U.S. production peaked, in 1944. Still following the same calculations, during the same year the Soviet Union should have produced 25,648 aircraft; instead, it came up with no fewer than 40,300. These figures represent a useful corrective to the oft-heard claim that the Soviet Union was basically a land power that neither put sufficient resources into airpower nor, perhaps, fully grasped its significance. The truth seems to be that, relative to the resources at their disposal, the Soviets devoted a greater effort to creating and maintaining its air force than did anyone else. Where they differed was the purpose for which they planned airpower and used it—that is, at the front and comparatively close behind it. Still, given that three out of every four German soldiers killed in World War II met their fate at the hands of the Red Army, perhaps Stalin's choice was not so bad after all.

As much as the war in the air was a battle of factories, it was also a battle of wits. Throughout the years that it lasted, all the belligerents assiduously collected intelligence on the opposing air forces. Doing so, they made use of every possible method, including, to name but a few, perusing the media, agents' reports, pilots' reports, and captured enemy pilots' reports. To this were added technical intelligence (finding out whatever they could about the characteristics of enemy machines), photo intelligence, signals intelligence (SIGINT, reading enemy radio messages), electronic intelligence (ELINT, learning about the enemy from the frequency of his radio transmissions, the direction from which they come, and so on), and much more.

Few, if any, of these methods had not been tried during the First World War. Few, if any, were not practiced on a much larger scale during the Second. As specialized equipment was added, they also became more sophisticated. An excellent example is Ultra, the later-to-be-famous British project that intercepted, deciphered, and exploited German radio traffic. Of course it was not the Luftwaffe's fault that, with its "teeth" consisting of flying units, it was more dependent on wireless than the army. It *was* its fault that, compared to the navy, its communications discipline was lax.

Not surprisingly, the various air intelligence services got some things right, others wrong. Perhaps the most important thing almost everybody (except for the Soviets and the Japanese, who never went for it in the first place) got wrong was the effort strategic bombing would require if it were to have any real impact. Simply deciding which elements were critical to the German economy in particular proved much harder than anyone had anticipated. The result was repeated disappointments and frequent shifts from one kind of target to another, not to mention unnecessary losses. Beyond that, the situation varied. Starting around 1935, the British greatly overestimated the speed at which the Germans were building up the Luftwaffe, an error that contributed first to appeasement and then to every sort of dire prediction and to accelerated rearmament on their part.[23] On the German side things worked the other way around. During the Battle of Britain, the Luftwaffe not only missed the role of radar but underestimated the number of the RAF's remaining fighters, a truly critical error. Worse, the basic idea, for which there was as yet no evidence whatsoever, that a large and powerful country could be forced to its knees simply by means of terror bombing directed against its civilian population, proved to be false.

Born out of arrogance, this tendency toward underestimating the enemy reappeared in 1941, when it was a question of confronting the Soviet Union, and again in 1941–42 in relation to the United States. In both cases the Luftwaffe's appreciation of its enemies' weaknesses in regard to doctrine, training, and technology proved approximately correct—for example, it never followed the U.S. Army Air Force in its belief that bombers, however well armed and however good their flying discipline, were invulnerable to the activities of fighters. What the German Air Staff did not understand, and consequently take into account, were the dramatic changes that time and mobilization would bring. Nor did the list of intelligence failures end at this point. Early in 1944, confronted with evidence that Mustang fighter-bombers were escorting formations of B-17 bombers deep into German and German-controlled airspace, Goering at first thought that his intelligence officers had gone stark raving mad and berated them. Something similar happened in the Pacific; though Japanese planners did receive an occasional warning concerning their enemy's ability to outbuild them in the air, they chose to look the other way.

As the war changed course, various kinds of intelligence either gained or lost in importance. For example, Soviet codes were notoriously difficult to crack. Moreover, the Red Army placed a greater reliance on landlines than any other armed force did; thus there were limits to what SIGINT and ELINT could do to gain information about it. Preparing for Operation Barbarossa, the Luftwaffe placed much reliance on photoreconnaissance. Its chosen instrument in this task was the Ju-86, a magnificent diesel-powered, exhaust-driven, turbocharged, twin-engine machine that was first tested in 1939. It had a service ceiling of 42,640 feet; some later models could rise as high as 52,500 feet, but they were only produced in very limited numbers. By comparison, the famous British de Havilland Mosquito Mark XVI only made it to 39,400 feet.

Later, as their own offensives ran out of steam and they were confronted by the Allies' growing superiority in the air, the Germans found that their ability to conduct this form of reconnaissance declined almost to the vanishing point. The consequences of this situation can only be called momentous; for example, it enabled the Allies to keep the location of the Normandy landings secret and thus contributed to their success. Allied command of the air also induced Rommel, who had experienced its results in North Africa and was in charge of the German defenses, to try to meet the landings on the beach instead of concentrating his reserves in the rear and counterattacking at a later point.[24] Both in Europe and the Far East, for the Allies things worked the other way around. The longer the war went on, the better able their pilots were to fly over enemy territory and photograph every inch of it. Entire teams of specialists developed the photos and interpreted them. They turned their craft into a highly specialized, if sometimes arcane, art.

As important as the battle for intelligence was the effort to achieve and maintain technological superiority. Improved aircraft, as well as the even more numerous improvements *in* aircraft, followed each other at a pace never equaled before or after. Still, except for the atom bomb, about which more later, probably the most important single contribution science made to the field was the above-mentioned introduction of radar. To this day it remains an indispensable tool of air warfare. It was from there that it spread to sea warfare, space warfare, and, much more slowly but surely, land warfare. The leaders in the field were the British and the Americans. The Germans were only slightly behind, the Soviets considerably so, whereas the Italians and the Japanese hardly counted.

The first operational radar sets were installed in large ground stations and used to serve as early warning against approaching enemy aircraft and to track friendly ones. Somewhat later they also started to be used to direct anti-aircraft artillery fire, a function that gave rise to the first computers. The Allies even mounted a sort of miniature radar set inside anti-aircraft shells, allowing the latter to explode when they passed near the target and not just when they hit it head-on.[25] At about the same time, smaller radar sets capable of being mounted aboard aircraft made their appearance. In this form, shortwave radar, used by Coastal Command, played a critical role in the defeat of German submarine warfare during the spring of 1943.[26] Conversely, an increasingly sophisticated combination of ground radar, anti-aircraft artillery radar, and radar mounted inside twin-engine night fighters allowed the Luftwaffe to wage a years-long fight against the Allied strategic bombing campaign.[27] Late in the war, radar was also mounted aboard bombers and used to penetrate through cloud cover, but its effectiveness in this role remained somewhat dubious. Since water reflects radio waves in an entirely different way than land does, radar was most useful for finding targets located near the coast. However, only in December 1944 did it reach the point where it could reliably identify a large urban target such as Berlin.

The real battle of wits consisted not just of introducing new devices but also of inventing others to counter them. Right from the beginning it was clear that radar, while vital to intercept enemy aircraft at night in particular, also gave warning about its own presence. Instruments could be and were built to warn pilots that they were being targeted. One way to counter radar was by using paint that absorbed at least some of the radio waves; another was to drop masses of tinfoil specially cut to such dimensions that they would appear on the screens in the form of vast clouds, thus blinding the operators. Nor was radar the only form of electronic wizardry aircraft used or had used against them. As important were navigation aids used to guide bombers to their targets. Methods of interfering with the operation of each of these devices were conceived almost as soon as the devices themselves were introduced. From idea to operational deployment, of course, it took longer.[28]

As successive devices were introduced, each radio beam by its very existence became a treasure trove of information not only on the type and apparatus that generated it but also, often enough, concerning enemy capabilities and intentions. Vice versa, the same applied to aircraft shot down over enemy territory and which carried either radar or some device for countering it. No sooner had it touched down or crashed than teams of technicians swarmed over it, trying to learn its secrets, examining the surviving crew members if any, and immediately setting to work in an attempt either to counter them or to copy them. The difference was that, from the second half of 1942 on, increasingly it was the Western Allies who penetrated Axis airspace. The opposite happened less and less frequently; thus, paradoxically, an advantage was turned into a disadvantage. That this was by no means a theoretical problem only is demonstrated by the fate of the proximity fuse. Having invented it in 1942, the Allies delayed its operational use until late 1944 because they feared it might assist the enemy more than it benefited them.

Though not every problem required a scientific breakthrough, many demanded a great deal of technical ingenuity. An excellent example comes from the field of anti-submarine warfare. German submarines in the Atlantic usually stayed submerged during the day, but at night they rose to the surface to stalk their prey. Once the presence of a submarine had been determined by airborne surface vessel (ASV) radar, it had to be illuminated so the Coastal Command aircraft could drop depth changes on it. The problem was made more difficult by the fact that, at first, it was confused with the one of illuminating German cities so that bombers could attack them. Once this hurdle had been cleared—in other words, once it had been determined that submarine hunting required a searchlight and not some kind of flare—an aircraft had to be found with enough room to permit the searchlight and the dynamo it needed to be installed. Next, a method had to be found for clearing away the fumes generated by its carbon lamp. All this explains why it took about a year and a half to bring the idea from the drawing board to full operational use.[29]

Intelligence and technical excellence are one thing, the ability to use them effectively and translate them into military results, another. Because air warfare, which takes place in a relatively simple environment, is easier to analyze than what takes place at sea or on land, as early as World War I attempts were made to apply mathematics to it. The objective was to substitute scientific calculation for trial-and-error-based guesswork, to improve performance, and to reduce casualties. A pioneer is this field was the British specialist Frederick W. Lanchester. In 1939–45 his scientific work developed into operations research (OR), and the best-known practitioners of the craft were the American mathematician and game theorist John von Neumann and two Britons, Patrick M. S. Blackett, a physicist who later went on to win the Nobel Prize in his field, and Solly Zuckerman, a zoologist specializing in the study of primates.

OR could answer, or at least provide better instruments with which to answer, such questions as whether the best way to protect aircraft was by adding extra cannon or armor, how many of the available aircraft to commit and how many to keep in reserve, what formations to adopt under what kind of circumstances in order to minimize casualties, how many aircraft to use against what kinds of targets, what routes of approach they were to follow on their way, and what types of ammunition they should fire or drop. OR was equally useful in planning and deploying anti-aircraft defenses, logistic systems, training schedules, and, above all, communication systems.

The following is a summary of a document that spelled out the results of applying OR to air attacks on submarines:

1. [Since a submarine only took 25 seconds to submerge] the attacking approach was to be made by the shortest path and at maximum speed.
2. The actual attack could be made from any direction relative to the U-boat.
3. The depth of setting of all depth-charges was to be 50 feet, the spacing of depth-charges in a stick was to be 60 feet and all depth charges carried were to be released in one stick.
4. The ideal was to attack while the U-boat or some part of it was still visible. Data was given, however, to enable pilots to estimate quickly how far ahead of the point of final disappearance their stick should be placed if the U-boat got under just before release was possible.
5. In cases where the U-boat had disappeared for more than 30 seconds it was pointed out that success was unlikely owing to the progressive uncertainty of the U-boat's position either in plan or depth.
6. The height of the release must not be greater than 100 feet.[30]

Though air warfare was better suited to OR than almost any other form of war, the extent of the role it played on the latter's conduct remains difficult to assess. Much depended on access to enemy information—in other words, knowledge of the results. Such knowledge might or might not be available. Throughout the war, pilots on all sides greatly exaggerated the number of enemy machines they had shot down. In air-to-ground warfare, too, attempts to find out how much damage this or that strike had really inflicted often yielded results very different from pilots' reports.[31] Nor could the question always be resolved by means of photoreconnaissance; furthermore, a ground survey could only be contemplated by the side in possession of the battlefield, and even then it was often hard to carry out. To this is added the fact that generals are extremely status conscious and tend to have huge egos. As Harris's correspondence in particular demonstrates, they were not necessarily prepared to accept "a panacea plan devised by a civilian professor whose peacetime forte is the study of the sexual aberrations of the higher apes."[32]

In this respect, as in so many others, there may have been some differences among the belligerents, and, *pace* Harris, of the five principal armed forces the ones most open to seek the advice of OR experts were those of Britain and the United States. Not accidentally, the societies they served were the least militarized and the ones that, in peacetime at any rate, held uniforms in relatively low esteem. Roosevelt and Churchill appointed scientific advisers, and some of their subordinates followed their example until having a scientist at one's beck and call became something of a status symbol. On the other side of the hill, things were entirely different. Hitler never had a scientific adviser—with the result, as he himself commented, that he had to learn about the possibility of setting off a nuclear explosion from his postmaster general.[33] Many German and Japanese generals had too good an opinion of their profession, and of themselves, to allow civilians to tell them what to do. Little is known about the Soviet Union in this respect, but it may well have stood somewhere in between. It always had excellent mathematicians and chess players. On the other hand, owing to its size and the relatively low educational level of its people, most of whom were only one step removed from the peasantry, it was inclined to solve military problems in a somewhat heavy-handed manner. In such a climate the finesse of OR may have played a lesser role in the conduct of the war.

As it turned out, the Allies won the struggle in the air as they did those that were waged on the ground and at sea. Certainly the intelligence men, the scientists, the technicians, and the operational researchers contributed to the final victory. Still there can be little doubt that the ultimate factor was quantitative superiority. Some evidence for this comes from the father of OR himself. Again referring to the industrial potential of the five main belligerents, the difference between the two sides was (3+1+0.8) to (1.2+0.5)=2.8:1. Again referring to the number of aircraft produced, the difference between them was 599,964 to 130,902, or almost 4.6 to 1. Even if we factor in the hapless Italians, these figures remain almost as they are. In one of his best-known equations Lanchester argues that, in modern warfare, to offset a numerical handicap of two to one, an armed force needs to be not twice as good as its enemy, as common sense would suggest, but four times. If, as in this case, one side outnumbers the other 4.6 to 1, then a qualitative advantage of no less than 4.6 times 4.6=21.16 is needed. If we assume that this is even approximately correct, the real miracle is not why the Allies eventually won the air war but how the Axis powers were able to hold out for as long as they did.

CHAPTER 7

CLOSING THE RING

While the Second World War resembled the First in that the largest operations of all were waged on one continent, Europe, it also resembled its predecessor in that much of the struggle took place at sea. Until the spring of 1943, submarine warfare probably represented the one method by which Germany could have beaten Britain and forced it to surrender. Conversely, first Britain's survival and later its ability and that of its larger and more powerful American ally to bring forces to bear against Germany (and Italy) depended on their command of the sea-lanes. Though the Mediterranean was never more than a side theater, here, too, ultimately it was command of the sea that decided the issue. The difference between the two world wars was that, from 1918 to 1939, military aviation developed far more rapidly than warships and merchantmen did. By the time World War II broke out, there was still much argument about how much air support navies required, how it should be organized, and what tasks it should carry out, but the principle that they could not operate without such support had been firmly established.

Having already said something about the Mediterranean, and leaving the Pacific until later, here we shall focus on the Atlantic. In 1939–45, as in 1914–18, without the sea-lanes across the Atlantic, Britain could not exist and would have to surrender sooner rather than later. As in 1914–18, what decided the issue was not so much a Mahan-like encounter between opposing fleets as a long struggle of attrition. That struggle was waged mainly by light naval units and the aircraft that worked with them. As in 1914–18, one of the first things the British did was to revert to the convoy system and to blockade Germany. The Germans on their part used their submarine fleet to impose a counter-blockade.

Seen from the viewpoint of airpower, the struggle was not symmetrical. Wherever they went, the British could and did use aircraft, whether land-launched or carrier-borne, to hunt for German submarines as well as the few other blockade runners, armed and unarmed, that got through. Whatever may be said about relations between the navy and the RAF, cooperation between it and Coastal Command was always exemplary. Meanwhile the German Navy, the Kriegsmarine, owing partly to geography—Britain still stood between it and the open ocean—and partly to its peculiar relationship with the Luftwaffe, did not have nearly as much support from the air. Lacking it, the Naval War Command, the Seekriegsleitung, in Kiel had to rely mainly on RDF (radio direction finding), ELINT, and SIGINT to receive warning that Allied convoys were setting sail, on what course, with what destination, and so on. The ability of submarine captains to locate their prey was greatly, perhaps fatally, reduced. They were forced to spend more time on the surface, where they were vulnerable both to surface ships and to aircraft; coming under attack by the latter, all they could do was either submerge or fire a few shots from the guns some of them started carrying from 1943 on.

From the Allied point of view, the worst moments in the anti-submarine struggle were the first half of 1942 and the first half of 1943. The worst month of all was June 1942, when 700,000 tons of merchant shipping were lost.[1] During both periods, airpower played a critical role in defeating the menace. Based in Scotland, Ulster, Iceland, Greenland, and along the North American coast from Newfoundland to the south, aircraft protected convoys and searched for submarines. Either they attacked those submarines on their own, dropping depth charges on them, or else they acted as the eyes of hunter-killer groups made up of destroyers and other light naval vessels. The more time passed, the more technological progress and the introduction of more long-range aircraft limited the ocean spaces where submarines could operate in relative safety. Some historians claim that this factor was the most important reason why the Allies eventually came out on top.[2] As one German U-boat captain told his commander in chief, successful attacks on convoys were only possible as long as there were no Allied aircraft around.[3]

Another means for closing the gap were escort carriers—meaning small and relatively cheap ones—and so-called merchant aircraft carriers (MACs). The latter were simply merchantmen, often grain ships or tankers. They were converted for the purpose by being made to carry a catapult, a few antiquated Swordfish biplanes, and a crane or two for lifting them out of the water once they had accomplished their mission. As often happens, their very simplicity and low cost caused them to be disliked by "real" navy commanders; no sooner had the war ended than the latter did what they could to make people forget they had existed at all. Nevertheless they were very effective. The record shows that no MAC-escorted convoy ever lost a ship to a submarine, nor was any MAC lost.[4]

Still other Coastal Command aircraft, operating from airfields in the eastern part of Britain, visited the submarine bases in an attempt to learn more about the submarines' arrivals and departures. Often encountering intense anti-aircraft fire, these aircraft suffered the heaviest losses. While many factors played a role in the submarines' ultimate defeat, probably the most important one was a shortwave (decimetric) radar set known as SCR-517 introduced in the spring of 1943. Though its range in anti-submarine work was limited to six miles, for the first time it enabled the aircraft carrying it to reliably and accurately locate submarines operating on the surface even at night, their favorite time in which to recharge their batteries and stalk their prey. Since a different version of this set, known as the H2S, was carried by Bomber Command in its raids over Germany it was feared that the Germans would be able to quickly capture it and counter it. As it turned out, a set *was* captured almost immediately, but a countermeasure was only built after eight months, because, as Goering himself was forced to admit,[5] their scientific research in the field of shortwave radar was falling further and further behind.

After June 1943 the submarine menace ceased to play a major role in the war. This enabled the Allies to start closing the ring on Nazi-dominated Europe and begin sending massive troop-carrying convoys across the Atlantic. If no troop-carrying ship ever went to the bottom, then one reason for this was the air escort that the RAF and the USAAF provided for them. Even earlier, in November 1942, the Allies had landed in North Africa. After conquering Algeria and Tunisia, in July 1943 they went on to organize invasions of Sicily and Italy. Each of these undertakings relied on massive air support, and none would have been possible without it. Each time it was aircraft that provided intelligence on the landing sites as well as on the enemy forces defending it; covered the convoys on their way across the sea; provided firepower during the landings themselves, demolishing coastal fortifications and interdicting German reinforcements further inland; and brought in supplies where conditions were suitable and other means unavailable. In Sicily they also dropped parachutists to assist the seaborne troops, with very mixed results.

Even as their aircraft helped fight and win the war at sea, the Allies mounted their strategic bombing campaign against Germany. The two were often in conflict. Throughout the war, RAF Coastal Command was always calling for more aircraft to support its operations, only to have Bomber Command retort that releasing them meant weakening the strategic bombing campaign as the most effective way to bring Germany to its knees. Arthur Harris, the chief of Bomber Command, also strongly objected—with good reason as it turned out—to using his bombers against submarine pens. During the first two years of the war, British attempts to bomb Germany had been almost entirely ineffective. Mediocre aircraft such as the Blenheim and the Wellington, highly inaccurate navigation and bombing aids, and unexpectedly strong, increasingly radar-assisted, German defenses both in the air and on the ground all contributed to this. Only in the spring of 1942, after new aircraft such as the Avro Lancaster entered service, did things change.

The shortage of resources apart—what general in history has not called for more men and materiel?—the principal obstacle facing Bomber Command during this period was that no long-range fighters were available to escort the bombers. Unable to defend themselves effectively against the Luftwaffe, they were compelled to operate mainly, indeed almost exclusively, at night. Operating at night, they at first had great difficulty finding their targets in the darkened countryside below. Often they missed it not by yards but by miles. Even after that problem had been solved, accuracy remained, to put it mildly, doubtful. To make up for this, their normal aiming point was the central railway station. Over time special mixtures of incendiaries and high-explosive bombs were developed, resulting in firestorms and widespread destruction of everything around.

At the time the U.S. Eighth Air Force, commanded first by General Carl Spaatz and then by General Ira Eaker, joined the campaign in 1943, they at first tended to look on their British allies with some contempt, which the British heartily reciprocated. As we have seen, during the interwar period the chief fount of U.S. Army Air Corps doctrine had been the Tactical School in Alabama. Few instructors posted to this backwater allowed foreign writers, let alone an Italian one, to influence them. Some mimeographed extracts of Douhet's works were indeed circulated in translation. But they were by no means universally welcomed; there were even claims that applying his ideas would turn the United States into a nation of baby killers.[6] Good, bad, or merely indifferent, U.S. doctrine concerning so-called precision daylight bombing was largely homegrown. USAAF commanders insisted that, in the B-17 with its 13 machine guns, they had an aircraft capable of penetrating the defenses in daylight and hitting targets much more accurately than could be done at night.

It took several defeats to convince the Americans that they were barking up the wrong tree. The most serious one was the raid on Schweinfurt on October 14, 1943, when 60 (20.7 percent) out of 289 bombers were destroyed. Seventeen were irreparably damaged, and another 121 damaged but judged reparable. On this day alone, about 600 highly trained crew members were either killed or taken prisoner.[7] German production of ball bearings, to paralyze which had been the object of the exercise, suffered badly, but, since on this and numerous other occasions there was no follow-up on the attack, it quickly recovered. So heavy were the losses that General "Hap" Arnold, who was commanding the USAAF, was forced to suspend deep raids into Germany until the Mustang fighters began arriving in February of the next year; thanks to their thin "laminar flow" wings, these aircraft had a longer range than any previous fighters. Even then it took some time before the U.S. Eighth Air Force changed its tactics, freed pilots from their close ties to the bombers, and allowed them to engage the German fighters wherever they were found.[8]

In the summer of 1943, acting on Hitler's direct instructions, the Luftwaffe shifted the emphasis from interdiction and CAS toward defending the Reich. Eventually 70 percent of all fighter squadrons were so employed. The outcome was to leave much of the Wehrmacht's field formations without cover to match the growing airpower that the western Allies, and in their own way the Soviets too, were using against them; the few units that remained often consisted of inferior aircraft. Worse still, many of the anti-aircraft guns, especially the excellent 88-millimeter one, were dual-purpose. Consequently the front was starved of anti-tank weapons as well. As in other countries, the defenses consisted of fighter aircraft, anti-aircraft artillery units, and a civil defense. As in the Soviet Union, but unlike the situation in Britain both during the Battle of Britain and later, the first and the second of these were both under Luftwaffe command, facilitating coordination. Most of the night fighters were Do-17, Ju-88, and Me-110 aircraft. None of them had been designed for the purpose, and by the end of the war all were obsolete; yet all had the advantage that, being twin engined, they were large enough to carry radar sets. The pilots were directed to their targets by a series of control centers. Approaching, first they would spot the enemy on their own radar screens and then, closing to within gunshot, visually. The control centers in turn relied on data provided by a chain of layered, overlapping, interlocking radar sets first established in 1940 and reaching from Denmark to central France. Down almost to the last days of the war, the bombers and their nemesis continued to face each other, with each side introducing successive improvements to its methods.[9]

Until the beginning of 1943, daytime defenses hardly existed. From this point on they were systematically built up with single-engine fighters such as the Me-109 and the FW-190, and twin-engine Me-410 fighters predominating; the last named was heavy enough to carry a 50-millimeter cannon originally developed for use on tanks. As with the night defenses, radar sets detected the bomber swarms when they were still as much as 60 miles away (the fact that they were coming was noted much earlier, given that the radio traffic they generated was easily intercepted). Once approximate numbers, altitude, course, and the prospective target had been determined, the controllers would alert the nearby fighter squadrons and guide the pilots toward the approaching enemy. As with the night defenses, too, both sides, but the Allies in particular, did what they could to study one another and mislead one another by mounting diversions, changing direction, and broadcasting false messages.

On both sides, casualties were extremely high—the British Bomber Command alone lost 55,000 aircrew killed. This figure represented one-quarter of all military dead and fully 44 percent of the 125,000 aircrew who served under Harris at one time or another. But Allied crews in any case knew that, if they survived their tour, they would be withdrawn and used on less demanding duties. By contrast, German ones flew until they could no longer—which is one reason why they racked up much larger numbers of kills. As more than one record, both contemporary and postwar, by German pilots shows, hunting bombers could be great fun.[10] Reading British participants' memoirs of the Battle of Britain, one sometimes gets a similar impression.[11] The situation of the bomber crews was quite different. As one U.S. aviator, the navigator Lieutenant James Goff, wrote:

> I can remember few specific details of those terrifying twenty-five minutes over Muenster [in October 1943] when all hell broke loose. My mouth felt as though it was full of cotton, and in spite of the numbing subzero temperature, I was perspiring freely. I can recall slipping and sliding on the growing mound of shell casings as I moved hastily and clumsily from the left nose gun to the right nose gun and back again. I found later that I'd fired some 1,600 rounds. If

> I did any damage to the German fighters, I never knew, because they were coming in so fast and furiously. It all seemed like a lurid nightmare . . . wave after wave of enemy fighters . . . pieces of aircraft littering the clear blue sky . . . ugly black smoke of flak bursts . . . men in drifting parachutes . . . burning bombers and fighters all around us. . . . Twenty-five minutes that lasted an eternity.[12]

As time went on, the bombing increased in intensity. In 1941 the RAF dropped 35,509 tons on Europe; in 1942, the RAF and USAAF together dropped 57,550. In 1943, the figure was 226,513; in 1944, it was 1,188,577; and in 1945, it was 477,051—bringing the total to just under two million.[13] The attacks were not always continuous. Now the weather, now German opposition, could cause them to be interrupted for days and even weeks on end.

Though the difference might not always be apparent to those on the receiving end, the Americans proceeded in a somewhat more systematic way than the British did. Instead of deliberately setting out to wreck cities and de-house workers, they concentrated on specific industrial targets. The ones that, in retrospect, proved the most rewarding were Germany's aircraft factories, its transport system, and its installations for producing synthetic oil. The first type did not succeed in causing production to break down—in fact, German production of aircraft peaked in 1944—but it did cause untold difficulties and forced the entire industry to disperse with all the inefficiencies that such a program entails. By the end of the war, the second had produced a situation where such raw materials as could still be extracted and such materiel as could still be produced often could not be assembled or put to use. The third hit both the ground forces and the Luftwaffe very hard, forcing the former to place growing reliance on horses and helping create a situation where German flight cadets could not get sufficient training. Sent into the air nevertheless, many were shot down before they could properly learn to handle themselves.

In the entire history of World War II, probably no campaign has given rise to more controversy than this one. Which method, the British or the

U.S., was preferable? Was strategic bombing the best way to use airpower, or was it merely a diversion from other forms of employing it, such as CAS and interdiction? Were the targets correctly selected, or would a different approach have led to better and faster results? What was the effect on the German conduct of the war, and how much did it contribute to victory? Could strategic bombing be morally justified? Proceeding in reverse order, if the raids on Cologne, Hamburg, Dresden, and so many other cities constituted war crimes, then so, without doubt, did the ones on Warsaw, Rotterdam, London, Coventry, and Birmingham. Given how inaccurate the means of delivery of the time were, it was completely unrealistic to expect that targets hit would be exclusively, and in many cases even mainly, of a military nature. Bombing did not prove decisive in the sense of forcing Hitler and his government to surrender.[14] What it did do was to kill about 350,000 people and injure 800,000 more, render 10 percent of the population homeless, and paralyze many industries and transportation arteries. To counter the strategic bombing campaign, the Germans in 1944 used 55,000 guns and 2,100,000 men (900,000 in the defenses proper, 1.2 million in damage repair).[15] These were no mean figures, but whether they were greater or lower than the cost of the campaign itself is impossible to say.

In spite of everything Joseph Goebbels's propaganda machine could and did do, in spite of the terror measures liberally applied to those who "undermined morale," bombing certainly did not improve the morale of those on the receiving side. In soon-to-be-occupied Berlin, German women told each other that "a Russian on one's belly" was better than "an American [in a bomber] overhead."[16] Yet it did not bring the German people to the point where they ceased to resist, let alone made them rise against their government. Even in the face of infernos such as Hamburg, social cohesion proved much stronger than anybody had expected. Streets were quickly cleared of rubble, essential services restored. Moreover, bombing gave German fighter pilots something to fight and, if necessary, die for. One of them, 22-year-old Heinz Knoke, flew his Messerschmitt over Hamburg not long after the city's destruction. Having observed the "monster cloud of smoke" and the "horror of the scene," he wrote in his diary: "I resolve with grim determination to return to operations in spite of my wounded hand."[17] By the end of the war the anti-aircraft defenses were staffed not merely by men but by women and youngsters; in Berlin, a 16-year-old Hitler Jugend member noted in his diary how proud he and his comrades were to be called up and serve so that nobody could call them cowards.[18] To this extent, bombing actually helped the Nazis stiffen their people's resistance.

The Luftwaffe also built up formidable anti-aircraft defenses. By the end of 1942 there were over 200 heavy flak batteries and 300 light ones. The number of troops was over 100,000; as had previously happened in Britain, a growing number of them were women.[19] In July–December 1942, whereas fighters shot down 169 British bombers, flak accounted for 193.[20] Yet this was just the beginning. During 1943, the number deployed within Germany went up to 1,300 heavy and 728 light batteries. They were supported by 395 searchlight batteries. In time, the quality of the defenses improved. Much heavier guns—up to 128-millimeter caliber—were introduced; flak towers, providing unobstructed vision and fields of fire, were built; increasingly sophisticated radar sets were added; and the problem of coordinating with the fighter units and thus preventing friendly casualties was tackled if never completely solved. The first three months of 1943 showed that, whereas fighters and flak each finished off about equal numbers of bombers, taking into account damaged machines the balance in favor of the latter was nine to one.[21] Late in the war, after the Luftwaffe's fighters had been all but eliminated, flak remained almost the only means by which the Germans could fight back at all.

Would the Allies have used their airpower to better effect if, in 1944–45, instead of building thousands of bombers and sending them over the skies of Germany, they had focused on ground support as the Luftwaffe had done during the early years? Some authors think so, but proof is hard if not impossible to get. This particular problem may also be turned around; some authors argue that the greatest benefit of the strategic air campaign consisted less in any damage it inflicted on the German people and economy than in that it compelled the Luftwaffe to abandon its doctrine and focus on defending the Reich. This was taken to the point where, from mid-1943 on, many of its ground forces were left almost unprotected from the air, greatly facilitating the Allied advances on many fronts. Finally, was the U.S. method preferable to the British one, or vice versa? Again a definitive answer is very hard to get. One reason for this is that, in reality, precision bombing was not nearly as precise as its advocates claimed. Even according to the U.S. *Official History of the Army Air Forces in World War II*, the longer the campaign went on, the more the U.S. bombers found themselves engaged in RAF-style area attacks.[22]

Historical truth is no doubt a very important thing to have. Nevertheless, looking back, it would seem that the true significance of these and similar questions does not consist of the answers that were provided for them either at the time or later. Instead, what matters is the fact that, for years and even decades after World War II had ended, they continued to form the framework for thinking about air warfare.[23] Later in this book we shall have occasion to see the "lessons" of the war being applied in subsequent ones: what part in the overall war effort that airpower should play, in what manner it should be waged, what kinds of targets it should focus on, what it could reasonably be expected to achieve, whether it could be morally justified, and so on.[24] Meanwhile, though, there was still the Wehrmacht to beat.

We left the Allied struggle to close the ring on the Axis in Europe at the time they invaded Italy, landing first at Salerno and then at Anzio. Taking the Italian campaign as a whole, the performance of the Allied air forces proved disappointing. To be sure, one German general writing not long after the war expressed the view that Allied air support at the beachhead, and later at the battle of Monte Cassino, was "magnificent." He personally had witnessed the density of the bomb patterns, the accuracy with which they were delivered, and the destruction they wrought. However, he also noted that "on entering a position immediately after the bombardment one would find that, aside from a few exceptions, the guns, machine guns, and observation instruments were intact, and that even the effect on the men's morale, which initially had reached critical proportions, wore off after the initial experience." An "exact" check of the casualties inflicted by a "heavy" air attack near Monte Cassino showed that they were far lower than those caused by artillery. "Apparently," the general concluded, "an air attack accomplishes its objective only to some extent if its effect on morale is immediately exploited by a ground attack."[25]

The remarkable thing about this campaign is that, from its inception in July 1943 to its end in April 1945, the Allies always enjoyed a very clear edge in the air. The few remaining Italian Air Force units in the area could do very little; the Luftwaffe, whose aircraft were increasingly diverted to protect the Reich, was not in a much better position. Another reason for this was that Allied radar worked so well that their fighter-bombers were always able to elude the Axis fighters trying to intercept them. Nevertheless, if ever there was a campaign that unfolded slowly and with great difficulty it was this one. It was really and truly a tug-of-war. In what was known as Operation Strangle, on countless occasions the Allied air forces bombed and strafed German communication lines, both rail and road, all over the country. Almost completely defenseless from the air, all the Wehrmacht's ground troops could do was to deploy anti-aircraft artillery and set up dummy motor columns, depots, loading sites, and the like. Still, Allied airpower never really succeeded in depriving them of so many supplies as to paralyze their ability to resist.[26] In particular, the vital Brenner tunnel, without which the Germans in Italy could not have existed, was never closed for long. The difficult topography, as well as the inability of Allied pilots to attack by night, both contributed to this.

When the time came to invade northwestern Europe, airpower once again played a critically important role. The officer in charge of drawing up the preliminary plans, the British general Frederick Morgan, later explained how he went about it.[27] Dividers in hand, he ruled out any coasts that could not be effectively covered by fighters operating from air bases in the British Isles. Nor was it a question of using fighters and fighter-bombers alone. Anxious to prevent the Germans from rushing in forces to oppose the landings, the commander in chief, General Dwight Eisenhower, decided to use his heavy bombers to destroy road and railroad communications in northwestern France. Anxious to conceal the exact point where the landings were to take place for as long as possible, he also decided that, for every sortie against the Normandy area, two would be flown against other targets.

Both bomber generals, the American Spaatz and the Briton Harris, objected to the plan. Seeing it as yet another attempt to divert their crews and aircraft from their proper task of launching strategic attacks on German cities and industries, they claimed that it would result in heavy casualties—also among France's civilian population—and have little impact. But they were overruled. From March to June, 76,000 tons of ordnance rained down on the French transportation system. In the end, the effort was a considerable, though not an absolute, success. On D-Day itself no fewer than 12,000 sorties were flown by aircraft of all kinds, surely an all-time historical record. By that time every bridge over the Somme from Paris to the west had been demolished and rail traffic in the area had been reduced by almost two-thirds. To the end of his life, Eisenhower remained convinced that insisting that the bombers be put under his control and directed against the French transportation system represented his own greatest contribution to the success of the landings;[28] in fact, however, much of the damage had actually been the work of the smaller, more agile fighter-bombers.[29]

After the invasion, with Allied fighter-bombers constantly roaming overhead in search of targets, the German reinforcements were slowed down and condemned to make their way almost exclusively by night. In July, with the Allies preparing to break out of their bridgehead, U.S. and British bombers also launched massive attacks on the Wehrmacht's ground troops that were trying to hold the ring. In this too they were ultimately successful, though their accuracy left something to be desired. The outcome was numerous friendly casualties; among them was the U.S. Army Ground Forces commander, General Leslie McNair, who had come over and was watching from his foxhole.

Once the war of movement got under way on July 31, the bombers were switched back to their strategic task, leaving the skies to the fighter-bombers. France, it quickly transpired, was not Italy. Not only was Allied strength in the theater much greater, but the open, flat terrain helped pilots to find targets and attack them. This, moreover, was not 1940–41. The campaigns in North Africa and Italy had taught the Americans and the British how to run their systems of air-to-ground, ground-to-air cooperation. Both had copied the German system whereby forward observers, riding special vehicles and equipped with radio-telephones, accompanied the forward troops and talked directly to the pilots. To quote one German Panzer commander referring to the failure of his division's attempted counterattack at Avranches on August 7, "they [the Spitfires, Typhoons, and Mustangs] came in hundreds, firing their rockets at the concentrated tanks and vehicles. We could do nothing against them and we could make no further progress."[30]

As was often to happen following the wars that came after 1945, too, a fierce debate soon developed as to who had done what, how effective the attacks had really been, and what the overall contribution of airpower to the unfolding of operations was. This was all the more so because all parties had some interest in presenting events in the most favorable light for themselves. As the statement just quoted implies, German commanders, especially those writing in the 1950s against the background of their country's efforts to join NATO, wanted to justify their defeat by showing that, in the face of overwhelming Allied superiority in the air, there was nothing they could have done. Allied air commanders wanted to show how indispensable their own contribution to victory had been; approaching the problem from the opposite side, Allied ground commanders sometimes tried to minimize that contribution, insisting that aviators made exaggerated claims. Disputes between the bomber pilots and the fighter "jocks" complicated the issue even further to say nothing of the "objective" interventions by military historians.

The first factor governing the effectiveness of tactical airpower (Tac/Air, as it was called), whether it is employed immediately behind the front or used to interdict enemy movements and supplies at some distance behind the front, is the weather. Where the weather did not cooperate, as happened during the first days of the German Ardennes offensive in December 1944, fighter-bombers, in this case Allied ones, were all but impotent. Next in line come timeliness and accuracy. Timeliness itself is a function of several factors, including the number of available aircraft, organization, communications, and, last but not least, the distance between the air bases and the front.[31] During the early years of the war, the Luftwaffe had often performed miracles in rapidly pushing its bases forward behind the armored spearheads. Now the British and Americans, whose forces had far more motor vehicles and construction equipment per soldier than the Germans ever did, showed that they could do the same. Operating on a much larger scale, they took over abandoned German airfields in France, restored them to working condition, and provided them with everything they needed by way of facilities, supplies, communications, and so on.

Even so, ground troops who asked for air support could hardly expect to receive it within less than an hour of the request being made. One hour might entail extraordinary efficiency on the part of a host of forward observers, communicators, air traffic directors, and commanders at many levels. Yet to men who sought to defend themselves against a counterattack or met unexpected resistance when they themselves took the offensive, it seemed like an eternity; after all, in that period a tank might easily cover 15 miles. To be sure, much shorter response times might be achieved by diverting fighter-bombers already in the air. However, doing so was not always technically possible and inevitably entailed abandoning other missions. Furthermore, it carried the danger that airpower would be turned into the handmaiden of the ground forces and thus lose its greatest advantages, namely, its flexibility and its ability to concentrate.

There never was any doubt that, thanks to their agility and their ability to operate at low altitudes, fighter-bombers could deliver ordnance much more accurately than bombers could. Before the invasion, certain experts—perhaps with an axe to grind since they were employed by RAF Bomber Command to show how wasteful the policy of diverting the heavy planes away from the strategic bombing of Germany was—estimated that it would take 1,200 tons of bombs to knock out a single bridge. Next the commander of the U.S. Fighter Command, Major General Elwood Quesada, showed that eight P-47 Thunderbolts, carrying just 0.4 percent of that amount between them, could accomplish the mission just as well.[32] Yet this episode, too, was misleading. Fighter-bombers had a field day destroying stationary and moving targets in the open field. Locomotives, which could not engage in evasive maneuvering and which when hit gave off a spectacular cloud of steam, were a special favorite. However, they could hardly do the same inside cities with their often tall structures and narrow, sometimes canyon-like, streets.

Operating over open country, fighter-bombers were more effective against large, stationary targets, bridges included, than against smaller, moving ones. They were also more effective against infantry in the open, especially if it stood or moved in dense concentrations, than against entrenched troops; once again, whether the enemy would be caught in the open was very much a question of precise coordination and timing. When fighter-bombers were used in close support the small caliber of their ballistic weapons, such as machine guns and cannon, and the inaccuracy of the non-ballistic ones, such as rockets, made them much more effective at suppressing enemy fire than at destroying its sources,[33] and more so against soft vehicles than against armored ones. To this extent those who favored interdiction over close support were doubtless correct, the more so because second-echelon troops were usually less well provided with anti-aircraft artillery than front-line units. Again, the question is not merely who was right and who was wrong; rather the debate helped shape the post-1945 world. In the end, all that can be said is that the role of Anglo-American Tac/Air in defeating the Wehrmacht was considerable. However, it must also be said that we shall never know just how considerable it was, or whether the industrial and manpower resources it consumed might have been more effectively used if they had been assigned to the ground troops on one hand or to the strategic air forces on the other.

In all this it is useful to recall that three-quarters of all Wehrmacht soldiers who were killed in World War II lost their lives on the Eastern Front. Compared to that, the Western one was almost a picnic. Until the autumn of 1942 the German Army and the Luftwaffe units supporting it, though weakened to the point where they were no longer able to attack all along it as they had done during the previous year, still enjoyed superiority over the Soviets. The outcome was a series of spectacular victories that brought it to Stalingrad and to the gates of the Caucasus. While the quality of Soviet aircraft was improving, German pilots and organization, including above all the critically important field of communications, remained superior. Concentrating its forces, the Luftwaffe was still able to obtain clear air superiority at the time and at the place it wanted. The problem was that, given the relatively low number of machines and the huge spaces to be overrun, there were never enough forces to do a really thorough job. This was reflected in the tremendous effort of the Luftwaffe transport command; during this period it flew 21,500 sorties, covered over ten million miles, and delivered 42,000–43,000 tons of supplies.[34]

Determined to dislodge the last remaining Soviet forces still clinging to the right bank of the Volga at Stalingrad, in October the Luftwaffe concentrated 80 percent of all its combat power against that city. During that month the bombers and dive-bombers of Luftflotte 4 flew approximately 20,000 bomber and dive-bomber sorties to assist General Friedrich von Paulus's Sixth Army. Targets consisted of remaining pockets of resistance as well as Soviet traffic across the river. However, the Germans did not have a free hand. As enemy resistance stiffened, the number of serviceable machines dropped by almost half. By the time the Soviet counteroffensive got under way on November 20, the Red Air Force, constantly growing in numbers and operating from bases east of the Volga, was in control of the sky. Particularly important was the German pilots' inability, made worse by the closeness of the fighting on the ground, to identify their targets at night. For just that reason, it was at night that the Soviets sent most of their reinforcements into the beleaguered city.

The Soviet counteroffensive quickly led to the encirclement of the German Sixth Army. Some months earlier, in February–May 1942, about 90,000 German troops had been cut off by the Red Army, forming two pockets south of Leningrad. During that period the Luftwaffe was able to keep the encircled forces alive by flying in supplies and replacement troops and taking out the wounded. In the end the encircled formations were able to break the siege, although doing so cost them much of their heavy equipment. Now Goering told Hitler that the Luftwaffe might repeat the performance. Yet conditions were entirely different. Whereas the battle for Demyansk took place toward the beginning of spring so that the weather could be expected to improve, that for Stalingrad got under way just when winter was setting in. Whereas the troops at Demyansk needed a minimum of 265 tons a day to survive, the 220,000 at Stalingrad needed at least twice as much. Flying in and out of the city, the distances the aircraft had to cover were also much longer.

Mobilizing every aircraft and every crew, braving nights that were becoming increasingly longer, atrocious weather conditions, and growing Soviet resistance in the air and from the ground, the Luftwaffe, still flying mostly obsolescent Ju-52s, did what it could. However, during the entire period when the air-bridge was in operation only once did it succeed in delivering as much as 280 tons, whereas the daily average stood at a mere 90 tons. Toward the end, as more and more airfields were lost to the advancing Soviet columns, the Germans were reduced to dropping supplies by parachute, with the result that many were lost or fell into enemy hands. None of this could save the doomed Sixth Army; by the time it surrendered, the Luftwaffe's transport command, having lost almost 500 aircraft and many experienced crews, had received a blow from which it would never recover.[35]

The last occasion when the Luftwaffe on the Eastern Front was able to intervene effectively in the ground battle was at Kursk in July 1943, when it saved the German Ninth Army from encirclement and possibly annihilation. From this point on, in the air as on the ground, the boot was clearly on the other foot. Already during 1942 the quality of Soviet airpower had begun to improve; aircraft received wireless—from early 1943 on, every new machine was equipped with a set—and modern navigation aids. Soviet ground radar had now developed to the point where it was able to provide 15 minutes' advance warning against approaching German aircraft, greatly facilitating interception and enabling commanders to do away with the wasteful practice of mounting air patrols around the clock. Stalin's Falcons finally got around to adopting the staggered four-finger formation, the outcome being a notable improvement in the scores of air-to-air combat.[36]

By this time the Soviet aviation industry, much of which had been hastily evacuated to the territory east of the Ural Mountains in 1941, was back in full operation. Partly for that reason, partly because of the Luftwaffe's decision to focus on the defense of the Reich, the Red Air Force also enjoyed a very great quantitative advantage. One result was that the number of air-to-air encounters actually declined, as was later to happen in the west too; there simply were no German planes or pilots left to carry on the fight.

This in turn meant that the Soviets, assured of air superiority at most times and places, were able to focus on air-to-ground attack. Like their enemies and their allies, they developed a system of forward air observers. They were fully motorized and used radio telephony to work with ground commanders down to the regimental level. Tactics, too, improved. At Stalingrad, deficient arrangements for air-to-ground cooperation made Soviet air support almost totally ineffective. Now, with the battle moving to and fro (but mostly to) over the enormous, almost featureless expanses, things became a lot easier. Smaller, more flexible formations numbering three or four aircraft were adopted. Pilots learned to launch their attacks from the west, especially during the late afternoon when the sun would blind the German defenders. While tactical bombers—the only ones the Soviets had—fighter-bombers, and ground attack aircraft flew both battlefield support and interdiction sorties, the Soviets continued to differ from the western Allies in that they always preferred the former to any other kind. By one calculation they devoted as many as 40–50 percent of all sorties to that task. This was almost as many as those devoted to air superiority (35–45 percent), interdiction (4–12 percent), and reconnaissance (2–13 percent) combined.

The number of Soviet combat aircraft grew from 1,327 at Stalingrad to no fewer than 7,496 during the climactic Battle of Berlin. The daily number of sorties went up from 500 at Stalingrad to 2,600 at Kursk to 4,157 at Berlin.[37] Whereas at Stalingrad each aircraft flew 0.37 sorties per day on the average, two years later the figure stood at 0.55. Losses were heavy in proportion. Out of 33,700 ground-attack aircraft built, no fewer than 23,600, or 70 percent, were destroyed—12,400 by enemy action and 11,200 by accidents of every kind. All this fits in well with a report that, soon after the war, Stalin was shocked to learn that fully 47 percent of all losses had been due to accidents. As so often was the case, the discovery immediately led to an investigation into the nefarious activities of assorted so-called wreckers and enemies, though its results are not recorded.[38] Yet in one respect the Soviets were fortunate. Given that almost all their aircraft were single- or twin-seaters, personnel losses were proportionally much smaller than those suffered by the western Allies in particular; in the long run, smaller losses translated into greater accumulated experience.

As so often was the case, just how much Soviet airpower affected ground operations is impossible to say. To be sure, we are told that "air cover and support from the tank armies that carried the burden of the major Soviet offensives after 1944 were critical to the overall success" and that "the [Frontal Air Force] was the most mobile, flexible, and powerful means for supporting tank armies during deep operations."[39] However, the question remains as to how critical "critical" really was. Whereas German records and memoirs pertaining to the West often stress the role of Allied airpower, when it comes to the Red Air Force they are of little help. To the very end, the German generals tended to look down on their Soviet enemies, attributing the latter's victories, and their own defeats, to hammer-like blows delivered by overwhelming numbers rather than to any tactical and operational finesse. Always it was the supply system that broke down, or some neighboring unit that gave way, rather than they themselves who were defeated. For most of these generals, admitting that Soviet successes in the war in general, and in the air war in particular, might be due to qualitative superiority was little but heresy; during the Cold War, such an admission would cast doubt on Germany's usefulness to its newly found NATO allies.

As we saw, early in the war the Luftwaffe had enjoyed some notable successes in its conduct of airborne operations—successes, however, that were made possible partly by the enemy's weakness, as in Norway, and partly by the fact that sea and land forces were close at hand and came to the rescue.

The latter factor in particular was critically important; where no supporting forces were available, as happened around The Hague in particular, the German airborne troops barely survived. At Crete, so appalling were the losses among the paratroopers that from this time on they were used only as ground troops. On the whole, the Allied experience was not dissimilar. Airborne forces assisted the landings in Sicily in July 1943. However, bad weather caused the U.S. paratroopers to be scattered over 50 miles. Out of 134 British gliders, 47 landed in the sea with heavy loss of life. Their activities made little impression either on the Italians, who surrendered with hardly a shot, or on the Germans, who fought with their usual tenacity. On the Eastern Front, too, the largest Soviet airborne operation, mounted at Burkina in the Ukraine in September 1943 and lasting into November, was not a great success either.

Perhaps the most successful airborne operation took place in Normandy in June 1944, when British paratroopers and glider-borne troops, sent to capture bridges, road crossings, and key terrain features, achieved all their objectives and held most of them against German counterattacks until help arrived. Their American colleagues were not as fortunate. So scattered and confused did they become that their divisional commanders were only ever able to gather 2,500 men out of 13,000; consequently their operations only amounted to pinpricks. For all sorts of airborne operations, the turning point came at Arnhem three months later. Operation Market Garden, as it was called, involved no fewer than 34,600 U.S., British, Canadian, and Polish troops.[40] It was much the largest of its kind ever attempted. Yet intelligence failures caused it to run into fierce resistance by armored SS troops. It never achieved its objectives of securing the bridges over the Dutch rivers and cost the Allies at least 15,000 casualties. To make things worse, these were enormously expensive operations. Not only is air transport the most costly form of transport—to say nothing of losses—but organizing it entailed selecting the cream of the available manpower, providing them with special training, and keeping them in reserve—and thus out of combat—for months on end until a suitable opportunity for their employment arose.

With that, our account of the role of airpower in Europe during World War II must close. As had also been the case in World War I, the struggle consisted of attrition. There were no clear decisive battles or turning points. Attrition occurred primarily because the number of aircraft involved on both sides was huge, much larger than in Asia and the Pacific. There the United States deployed only part of its forces, the British and the Soviets deployed a comparatively small number, and Japan as the common enemy produced fewer machines than any other major belligerent except Italy. Yet it was precisely the huge number of aircraft employed in both theaters—even heavy four-engine aircraft carrying ten crew members and more each—that made them expendable. It was precisely because they were expendable that they were able to take a part, however great or small, in the conduct of hostilities. Conversely, weapons and weapon systems regarded as too expensive and too few in number to be lost cannot be used in war either. It was a lesson that, during the decades after 1945, came to be increasingly neglected.

CHAPTER 8

FROM CARRIER WAR TO GRANDE FINALE

The war in the Far East was separated from the one in Europe by thousands of miles and was very different from it. Ground operations, even famous ones such as the advance through Malaya and the capture of Singapore, were relatively small in scope; until the Soviet Union entered the war during its very last days, the most important theater where such operations took place was China. Here airpower, some of it Russian, some Chinese, and some American, had played a considerable role in resisting the Japanese invasion from 1937 on.

Something has already been said about Japan's own use of airpower in China and the inability of Hirohito's pilots to finish off their enemies there. Chinese persistence and determination, as well as the sheer size of the country and the undeveloped nature of its infrastructure, which meant that there were few targets to attack, played a large role in this. So, however, did U.S. intervention. The first American-built aircraft, Curtiss P-40 fighters, arrived in 1940. By and by so did some 300 pilots who posed as tourists. In the summer of 1941 they started training, and after Pearl Harbor they officially joined the Chinese in fighting the Japanese.[1] In the summer of 1942 they were incorporated into the USAAF. Later the Flying Tigers, as they were known, were incorporated into the 14th Air Force. Until late in the war their missions fell into two main categories. One was to defend against further Japanese advances, including any directed against their own bases, in southeastern China. In this they were largely successful. The second was to assist in the reconquest of Japanese-occupied Burma so as to open a road from India through the latter country to China. In the end, though the Burma Road was built and was in operation, so difficult was the topography that its performance did not meet expectations. The opposite applied to the airlift over the Himalaya range, the Hump, as it was known, which did much better than expected. During the war it delivered to China no fewer than 650,000 tons of supplies, which made it into one of the greatest triumphs of air transport of all time.

Burma also witnessed the first large-scale attempt to free a ground force of its dependence on lines of communications by supplying it entirely from the air—a feat pundits and generals had been contemplating ever since the end of World War I. The scheme actually put into operation was the brainchild of an eccentric British officer, Brigadier Orde Wingate. He hoped that, leading a brigade-sized force into the country and conducting a kind of guerrilla warfare behind the lines, he might loosen the Japanese hold on it. In February 1943, some 3,000 men, divided into seven columns, set out. The operation was not a success; Japanese intelligence had been aware of it from the beginning. Their forces progressively hemmed in the Chindits, as they were called. After more than two months only 2,200 men returned. Of those, 600 were too debilitated by hunger and disease to take a further part in the war—losses largely occasioned by the fact that, despite the aircrews' best efforts, they often failed to locate the troops on the ground or deliver supplies accurately to them. Nothing daunted, in February 1944 Wingate returned to the attack with considerably larger forces. This time they were delivered to their targets by gliders, thus avoiding the arduous jungle marches of their predecessors. Wingate himself died in an air crash in March—according to Field Marshal Bernard Montgomery, getting himself killed was the best thing he ever did.[2] Yet the operation, which lasted until July, did not prove more successful than that of 1943. At one point so desperate did the situation become that the Chindits were forced to shoot their own wounded.[3]

Events in the Pacific were much more important than those in either China or Burma. On December 7, 1941, Japan opened hostilities against the United States by delivering a powerful blow from the air at Pearl Harbor. Acting on the belief, which was quite possibly mistaken, that the United States would take military action against any attempt on their part to expand into the Dutch and British colonies of Southeast Asia, the Japanese planned to knock out the U.S. Pacific Fleet. By so doing, they would make such interference impossible or at least postpone it until after the Americans had recovered and they themselves established a defensive perimeter in the Pacific. Relying mainly on six carriers with 405 aircraft among them, the attack was brilliantly planned and executed. First, observing radio silence, the Imperial Combined Fleet approached Hawaii from the north, avoiding detection and, in effect, escaping the order of battle as traced by U.S. intelligence. Next cruisers, covering the carriers, sent up their reconnaissance aircraft to report on the precise positions at which ships were anchored at Pearl Harbor as well as on any possible U.S. preventive attacks. Putting everything on a single card, the Japanese commander on the spot, Admiral Chuichi Nagumo, left just 48 aircraft in reserve to defend the fleet.

American (and British) military commentators of the period tended to underestimate the Japanese. It was claimed that their aircraft were inferior and the people myopic and suffering from heritable "defects of the tubes of the inner ear" that prevented them from ever becoming really good pilots.[4] Now, as two waves, each numbering some 180 machines, roared low over Pearl Harbor they received a rude awakening. The first wave consisted of torpedo bombers, which the Japanese, having carefully studied the 1940 British attack on the Italian fleet at Taranto, had selected as their main weapon. A special aerial torpedo capable of making its way in the shallow waters of Pearl Harbor was even developed. The principal objective of this wave was to destroy as many capital ships as possible. This accomplished, a second wave consisting of light bombers, dive-bombers, and fighters was dispatched to attack harbor installations, aircraft, and, above all, fuel depots.

The operation was much the largest of its kind in history until then—a fact that helps explain why U.S. radar operators mistook the approaching Japanese aircraft for American B-17 bombers that were due to arrive as reinforcements.[5] As a result, surprise was total and resistance initially very slight. Most of the troops were caught in their barracks, fast asleep. Rushing to their battle stations, they found the guns covered and the ammunition boxes locked. This explains why the first wave of attackers only took light losses, but also why the second one suffered considerably more. These losses in turn led Nagumo to abandon his plan for launching a third attack wave consisting of aircraft that had returned from the first. As it turned out, the attackers failed to sink the carriers of the U.S. Pacific Fleet. Unknown to the Japanese, they happened to be absent on exercises. Still the sinking of several battleships and the damage inflicted on others left the Western Pacific essentially a Japanese lake, where, over the next few months, the Imperial Navy did much as it pleased.

Following their prewar plans, Japanese strategists divided their war effort between two prongs. One pushed southward by way of the Philippines (and Indochina, which was already under Japanese control) into British Malaya, the Dutch East Indies, and a number of smaller islands near them; here the objective was to seize raw materials, primarily rubber, nonferrous metals, timber, and oil. The other was directed eastward into the Pacific. Here the intention was to capture as many islands as possible as far away from home as possible and fortify them—which, of course, also meant preparing them for use as air bases—against an American counteroffensive. All this came on top of the four-year-old war in China. Thousands of miles separated the three theaters from each other. The Japanese resembled their German allies on the other side of the world in that, operationally speaking, initially their strikes were highly successful. Strategically, though, seldom in history can any nation have overestimated its own capabilities to such an extent; perhaps this explains why, faced with his country's plans to go to war with the United States, Isoroku Yamamoto, naval marshal general and commander in chief of the Combined Fleet, at one point wrote that all he could rely on were "the Emperor's virtue and God's help."[6]

Wherever the Japanese went, their aviation, especially their naval aviation, not only went with them but helped open the way. Only three days after Pearl Harbor, 86 aircraft of the Imperial Navy operating from airfields around Saigon sank the British battleships *Repulse* and *Prince of Wales.* Churchill personally had sent the two vessels to Singapore in the hope of deterring Japan from attacking. Originally they were supposed to be accompanied by an aircraft carrier, the *Indomitable*. However, at the time the war in the Far East broke out, that ship was undergoing repairs and thus not available for action. Consequently when the two battleships and the four destroyers that escorted them left Singapore to hunt for the Japanese, they did so without air support of any kind. Except for radar, which as it happened did not function very well, they were blind. Unsurprisingly, instead of locating the Japanese they themselves were discovered by a Japanese submarine. The latter radioed their location, speed, and course to headquarters, and the rest followed.

Of the two ships, the *Repulse* was relatively old, having been launched in the midst of World War I. Since then, however, she had been refitted several times, specifically in order to strengthen her defenses against air attack. By contrast, the *Prince of Wales* was among the most powerful gun-carrying naval platforms anywhere. She incorporated the latest in anti-aircraft and anti-torpedo defenses, including both guns and specially designed underwater armor. Yet this did not prevent her from becoming one of the two first capital ships ever sunk solely by airpower in the open sea; as a result, in the vast naval battles that followed, battleships, to the extent that they were present at all, were overshadowed by the carriers. On the Japanese side, this even applied to the largest battleships ever built, the *Yamato* and *Musashi,* both of which had their short, but exciting, careers terminated by U.S. Navy aircraft. On the American one, it meant that the big gunships' principal remaining use was not in the fleet actions for which they had been designed but in providing cover to amphibious landings by bombarding coastal defenses.

The two naval engagements later recognized as turning points, those of the Coral Sea and Midway, took place in May and June 1942, respectively. They illustrate the above developments almost to perfection. The former grew out of a Japanese attempt to seize the British-held island of Tulagi as well as Port Moresby on New Guinea. The ultimate objective was to extend the protective ring around the newly won empire in Southeast Asia, gain a base from which Japanese aircraft could bomb northern Australia, and threaten communications between Australia and the United States. The Japanese Task Force MO consisted of three carriers as well as assorted cruisers, destroyers, minesweepers, submarines, a seaplane tender, and various supply and transport vessels. The American Task Force 17 had two carriers and a similar, if smaller, array of warships, but no transports.

This was the first naval battle in which the naval forces of both sides never even sighted one another. Operating over vast distances and maneuvering at high speed, they searched for one another by means of wireless interception and code breaking, radar (the Americans), and land- and sea-based air reconnaissance. Once the enemy had been located, and assuming his position was not misreported and that he was not lost again or concealed by bad weather, they sent out their land- and sea-based aircraft. The trick, an intricate one depending on elaborate calculations of distance, speed, and time, was always to catch the other side's aircraft while they were being refueled and re-equipped and thus unable to respond; insofar as doing so required high-quality, real-time intelligence that might not always be available, a good measure of luck was also needed. As it turned out, since Admiral Shigeyoshi Inoue's experienced aircrews sank more American ships than the other way around, he was able to claim a victory. However, losses among those crews were heavy, and unlike their enemies the Japanese were unable to replace them; above all, though Tulagi was in fact occupied, Port Moresby, as the operation's more important objective, remained in British hands.

By contrast, the Battle of Midway took place in the Pacific, where it formed part of the second Japanese effort. This time the intention was to strengthen the Japanese perimeter facing east as well as prepare for further landings on Fiji and Samoa. Acting on the assumption that his forces had won the Battle of Coral Sea, Admiral Yamamato also hoped that another crippling blow at the U.S. Navy would paralyze America's will to continue the war. Again the two forces, centered on their respective aircraft carriers but also including three Japanese battleships, maneuvered against one another over vast stretches of ocean. Once again, they did their best to track each other by means of radio direction finding, code breaking, radar (in the last two fields the Americans now had a considerable, and growing, advantage), and sea- and air-reconnaissance. The enemy's strength, location, course, and speed having been determined, quite often not without any number of errors, again it was a question of striking without being struck. In doing so the Americans were greatly assisted by the fact that, though they only had three carriers against the Japanese four, they used Midway itself as an unsinkable aircraft carrier. Thanks to this fact the Americans could deploy 362 aircraft versus the Japanese 254;[7] as it turned out, it was U.S. land-based machines that drew first blood even though their operations were not terribly effective.

In the end, surprise determined the outcome at Midway just as, seven months earlier, it had at Pearl Harbor. Just as the Americans in December 1941 had been unaware of the Japanese approaching them, so, but with far less excuse, the Japanese in June 1942 were unaware of the presence of three American carriers. In fact Nagumo only learned of that presence after his planes returned from their first mission against the island and reported. Next, though an entire squadron of U.S. torpedo bombers was shot down, it was American dive-bombers that were able to catch the Japanese with their pants down. Having lost four out of four aircraft carriers present (the Americans lost only one), the Imperial Navy was crippled. Never again was it in a position to mount an operation nearly as large as the one at Midway. Now it was the American forces' turn to engage in a two-pronged advance, one leading northwest from Australia and one west from Hawaii. Their common destination was the Philippines, from which the invasion of Japan would have to be launched. As the Americans fought to conquer one island after another so as to get within striking distance of Japan proper, inevitably the outcome was a long struggle of attrition. In this struggle American industrial superiority, which Yamamato personally had always feared would end up by grinding his country down, could not but make itself felt.

Within two weeks from the end of the battle, the House Naval Affairs Committee drew the conclusions from this fact by unanimously scrapping the plans for five 58,000-ton *Montana* class battleships with their twelve 16-inch guns each. At the same time it approved the construction of no fewer than 500,000 tons of new carriers. It was clearly the end of an era; from now on, it would be the principal mission of the remaining battleships either to escort the carriers or to bombard coastal targets in preparation for amphibious landings. The carriers themselves gradually grew in size from 20,000 to 30,000 tons at the beginning of the war to as much as 45,000 tons at its end. Doing so, they took on larger and heavier aircraft, which in turn led to larger carriers, and so on in an endless cycle that, involving phenomenal cost increases, continues to the present day. They ruled the seas—or, in the view of those who did not have what it took to own them, tyrannized them.

Outside the range of land-based aircraft, and leaving aside submarines, which form a separate story, carriers were invulnerable. The only enemies capable of taking them on were others similar to themselves. Provided only it had been located and identified, as far as the carriers' aircraft could range no other vessel could sail without their captains' permission. In most of the long series of operations that followed Midway, carriers formed the backbone of the fleet. All other kinds of ships found themselves operating in such a manner as to protect them and support them. Light and escort carriers used their aircraft to cover the hundreds of convoys that crossed the Pacific carrying troops and equipment. In the huge naval battles for the Philippine Sea (June 1944) and Leyte Gulf (October of the same year), it was mainly carrier aviation that fired at the enemy by bombing, launching torpedoes, and strafing. At the latter in particular, U.S. carrier aviation first sank four Japanese carriers and then prevented the Japanese force of four battleships and eight cruisers in the San Bernardino Strait from mauling the American invasion fleet. Lieutenant Donald Lewis, who piloted a

Douglas Dauntless dive-bomber in the first of these battles, recalled what it was like:[8]

> Everywhere I looked there seemed to be ships with every gun blazing. The sky was just a mass of black and white puffs and in the midst of it planes already hit, burning and crashing into the water below. It's strange how a person can be fascinated even in the midst of horror. . . . I was employing the wildest evasive tactics possible. I would be down low on the water and then pull up quick and hard rudder one way, hold it for a moment, then kick rudder the opposite way. I had decided it didn't make any difference which way I went. . . . Any direction I went, I would still have to run the gauntlet.

Whenever there was an amphibious invasion to be carried out, aircraft, launched from light and fleet carriers, protected the naval task forces. They fought off counterattacks at sea and in the air, and struck at ground targets beyond artillery range just before the landings proper began. In principle, once an island had been occupied, carriers could also be used to transfer aircraft to it; even though, since many land aircraft could not take off or land on them, doing so usually required fairly extensive port facilities at both ends of the journey.

Qualitatively, too, the advances of these years were impressive, and here again the Japanese were less and less able to match their enemies. During the early months of the war, U.S. carrier commanders had experienced difficulty in coordinating their various types of aircraft as well as their anti-aircraft defenses. These problems are said to have played a role at Coral Sea in particular.[9] Later, things changed. The new *Essex* class carriers began joining the fleet during the second half of 1943. Capable of carrying almost a hundred aircraft each, they bristled with anti-aircraft guns. Above all, they made good use of radar—both to direct their anti-aircraft fire, which was becoming increasingly automated as new direction finders and ballistic calculators were introduced, and to fight at night. Since the Japanese did not have anything as sophisticated, within a short time they found themselves at a decisive disadvantage when darkness fell. In particular, this factor played an important role in the Battle of Leyte Gulf. During the four days it lasted American radar detected several key Japanese movements that were made at night.[10] By this time almost the only remaining qualitative advantage Japanese naval aviation still enjoyed consisted of the longer range of their (land-based) Nakajima C-6 reconnaissance aircraft; yet even this was obviated by the fact that the quality of the pilots was no longer what it had been.

War, least of all modern naval war, rarely consists of large battles alone. Going on day in, day out, was submarine warfare. In it, too, naval aviation played a decisive role. As we saw, the German Navy in the Atlantic was badly handicapped by the almost total absence of naval aircraft to work with. By contrast, both sides in the Pacific used aircraft not just in anti-submarine warfare but in their efforts to combat the enemy's merchant shipping as well. Again, the U.S. Navy enjoyed the inestimable and growing advantage of radar as well as code breaking. Gradually its commanders learned how to weave surface ships, submarines, and aircraft into a near-seamless web. In that web, as authors of the *Strategic Bombing Survey* put it, "carrier-borne air attacks, when directed against large concentrations of merchant shipping, were by far the most devastating attacks of all." Between them, the aircraft and submarines they often directed to their targets sent 81 percent of Japan's merchant fleet to the bottom. As imports of raw materials and energy declined, between 1941 and 1945, Japanese industrial production fell by 80 percent.[11]

By this time the cream of the Imperial Navy's aviators had been lost. As the Americans kept introducing more modern aircraft such as the F-6 Hellcat and the F-4 Corsair, the Japanese also found themselves technologically outclassed. The solution, which had some precedents in Japanese history, was to call for volunteers ready to serve their country by crashing their aircraft into American warships. Most were earnest young men of good families. Some of the aircraft they flew were standard fighters and dive-bombers modified for the purpose and packed with explosives; others had been specially designed for the purpose, being made of wood and provided with obsolete engines. Training began in August 1944, and the first attack clearly identified as such took place at Leyte Gulf in October of that year. From then on the number of kamikaze missions flown increased, peaking in April–May 1945. At this point it went down—not because of any difficulties in recruiting volunteers, of which there were plenty, but because the Japanese General Staff had begun to husband aircraft in anticipation of an American invasion.

Having received only rudimentary training, many volunteers made the mistake of going after all kinds of ships rather than focusing on the vital carriers. To defend against the attacks, the carrier commanders themselves started flying constant air patrols. That was an expensive tactic, but thanks to Allied technical superiority it was able to keep many Japanese pilots away from their intended targets. Needless to say, as each Japanese aircraft appeared, it was also met by fire from every available anti-aircraft gun. The total number of attacks was probably around 2,800; they appear to have sunk anywhere between 35 and 60 ships, damaged 368 more, and killed or injured some 10,000 sailors.[12] On the whole, the campaign was not a success. By the time it was started, and even more so when it ended, the imbalance of forces between the two sides was simply too great.[13]

One thing that the relatively small naval aircraft, including carrier aircraft, were never able to do was to engage in strategic bombing. The Japanese tried it in China, but never to very great effect except, perhaps, in terrorizing the populations of cities such as Nanking. Even so, airborne terror on its own achieved little, and it was left for Imperial Army units to enter the city and commit the famous "rape." The islands of Southeast Asia and the Pacific contained few, if any, strategic targets worthy of the name. As the string of Japanese victories early in the war showed, the navy's aircraft sufficed to help combat and occupy them. Japanese land- and sea-based aircraft even attacked Darwin, at the northern tip of Australia. Though the damage they inflicted, especially during the first raid on February 19, 1942, was considerable, they did not really manage to disrupt the functioning of the town as a center for mining operations as well as a major basis for Allied troops. Lacking heavy, long-range bombers, the Japanese could not attack the western coast of the United States either. During three and a half years of war, their attempts in this direction were limited to launching paper balloons loaded with incendiaries so as to set California's forests alight—with precious little success, as it turned out.[14]

Japan was a densely populated, heavily urbanized, industrialized country. It contained plenty of targets suitable for strategic bombing of the kind Trenchard, Douhet, and their U.S. successors had advocated. As early as 1943, the Joint Targeting Group (JTG) in Washington, D.C. (some of whose members would be counted among the most prominent postwar defense officials and intellectuals), referred to these facts and recommended the use of incendiaries against Japan's cities.[15] This was premature; though the United States had begun to build large numbers of four-engine bombers, such were distances in the Pacific that those bombers were unable to reach the targets in question. True, in April 1942, sixteen B-25 light bombers took off from the carrier *Hornet*. Since they would not be able to land on it, though, it was planned that they should fly over Japan, drop their bombs, and proceed to China. The total distance to be covered was 2,400 miles, at the bombers' extreme range; had it not been for a fortuitous tailwind, they would not have made it at all. Even so, every single aircraft was lost, some after their crews had abandoned them and parachuted to safety, some after crash-landing at their destinations, and one after landing on neutral Soviet territory (the Soviet Union was not at war with Japan). Eleven crew members were killed or captured. The Doolittle Raid, as it was called after its commander, Colonel Jimmy Doolittle, created headlines in the United States, and indeed doing so seems to have been the real reason why it was mounted at all. Being unexpected, it lifted American morale—it showed that the United States could actually *do* something—and temporarily rattled that of the Japanese; yet materially its results were close to zero.[16]

After overcoming many teething problems, the new B-29 bombers reached operational status during the first half of 1944.[17] These aircraft could reach Japan from airfields in east China, and they started being used in that way in June–July of that year. Yet getting them to China was difficult and time-consuming. The normal route was from the West Coast, where the Boeing Corporation built them, to Hawaii. From there they went to Australia and on to India, and from there, over the Himalayas to Chinese bases that were not always well prepared to receive them. It was only after the Americans had finished clearing the Marianas in October 1944 that an alternative presented itself. Even so, there was plenty to be done before the bombers could land and take off again. Runways had to be built—the heavy machines needed no less than one and a half miles, considerably more than any aircraft in history until then. With runways came a demand for parking spaces, command-and-control installations, repair-and-maintenance facilities, depots, and quarters for the personnel. All of these went up with amazing speed; indeed throughout the Pacific War a major advantage the Americans enjoyed was their extensive use of earthmoving machinery to construct bases on newly conquered islands. By contrast, the Japanese relied on gangs consisting of thousands of half-naked men laboring in the sun—with the result that they took weeks to accomplish what the Americans did in days.

The first B-29s left the islands on their way to attack Japan in November. However, their efforts, based on the same theories as had governed the use of B-17s in Europe and aiming at the destruction of large industrial installations, were not a success. Thanks to their pressurized cabins, a technological first, they could cruise comfortably at 30,000 feet and more. But at this altitude they ran straight into what was later known as the jet stream. Severe buffeting and problems in navigation also made aiming very difficult. Most of the time, the aviators had no idea where their bombs had gone. As one story has it, so many bombs missed their intended targets and fell into Tokyo Bay that the city's residents told one another that the Allies had decided to reduce them to starvation by killing all the fish.[18] Owing to the weather, many missions had to be canceled or aborted. Even so, weak though the opposition was, losses were not negligible but ran at a steady 4.5 percent per mission. Thus things continued until January 1945, when the Army Air Forces kicked out the commander and brought in a new one, Major General Curtis E. LeMay. Not yet 38 years old, LeMay had gained his spurs by commanding first B-17s in Europe and then B-29s in China. He was regarded as an expert navigator and a hands-on, no-nonsense commander. Others, less polite, described him as a "hard-headed bastard."[19]

Having studied the situation, LeMay took the revolutionary step of switching from day to night operations—thus jettisoning the doctrine preached and practiced by the Army Air Forces from the early 1930s on. Yet there was logic behind the madness. Since Japanese radar was rudimentary, night flying meant that its fighter defenses would find it very difficult to engage the incoming bombers; so much so, in fact, that LeMay ordered his crews to remove their defensive armament, thus increasing the aircrafts' range and enabling them to carry a greater weight of ordnance if so desired. The other change—one that also ran straight in the face of every tenet of strategic bombing ever since it had first been practiced by the German Zeppelins in 1915—was the decision to fly low. Instead of trying to cope with what contemporaries called "hellacious" winds howling along at as much as 180 miles an hour, the bombers, roaring in at no more than 5,000–9,000 feet, would move at such high angular speed as to leave gunners on the ground with no time to respond.[20]

Thus reorganized, 346 heavy bombers took off on March 9 and headed for Tokyo, which, at the time, was defended by just eight fighters. In the whole of Japan, only 300 were available. On this and subsequent occasions Japanese pilots did what they could but were overwhelmed. Though LeMay may not have been familiar with the conclusions of the JTG in Washington,[21] he had loaded his aircraft with incendiaries. Almost 2,000 tons were released. So intensive was the resulting heat wave that it buffeted some aircraft—which, empty, turned the scales at 34 tons each—to a height of 1,500 feet above their predetermined course. The city, which until then had only suffered some 1,300 dead, became a blazing inferno in which at least 83,000 people perished. That was about equal to the figure that resulted from the destruction of Hamburg and Dresden combined.

By the end of March, Nagoya, Japan's third largest city, as well as Osaka and Kobe, had shared Tokyo's fate. Detailed calculations determined how many bombs were needed to set what area afire; as one observer wrote, it was "like throwing many matches on a floor covered with sawdust."[22] Not only was the loss of life very heavy, but the raids disrupted or stopped the work of numerous small enterprises that Japan's great arms-manufacturing firms were using as subcontractors to produce parts. In April there was a pause. Partly this was because LeMay had run out of ammunition; partly because, like Harris before him, he was made by his superiors to divert some of his bombers to other missions. This time it was to mine Japan's straits and harbors. For heavy four-engined machines to operate on such a mission was somewhat of an innovation but one that, using their now standard low-flying tactics, they carried out with great success. By May, mines of various types were sinking three Japanese ships per day.

In May, the city raids were resumed. As Japanese resistance diminished, LeMay felt confident enough to mount some of them in daylight so as to improve accuracy. Even before atomic bombs were dropped on Hiroshima and Nagasaki, the total number of Japanese his men killed exceeded 300,000. Adding the injured, probably over 1 percent of the entire population was physically hit. The list of targets included Tokyo again—after 56 square miles of urban land had been razed, the city was no longer considered worth attacking—as well as Yokohama. Losses went down to an acceptable 2 percent. As had happened in Germany, and as was also to happen in Vietnam 20-something years later, in time the heavy bombers, joined by medium ones and fighter-bombers operating from Okinawa, turned their attention to smaller and smaller objectives. By July, cities numbering just 100,000–200,000 inhabitants were being hit. The last ones to be attacked during the early days of August had fewer than 50,000. Two months earlier, in June, LeMay had already warned the Army Air Forces commander, General Hap Arnold, that he was about to run out of targets. In the whole of Japan, there were no cities of any size worth bombing left.[23]

Perhaps the most remarkable aspect of the entire campaign was the vast scale on which it was conducted. Each of the dozens of city-burning missions had to be prepared by many thousands of technicians and other personnel. Each involved hundreds of heavy bombers and several thousand aircrew. Each had to be flown over distances of well over a thousand miles in each direction. Each consumed millions of gallons of fuel. The amount of ordnance dropped increased from 13,000 tons in March to 42,000 in July; had hostilities not come to an end, by September it would have risen to 100,000. All this had to be done on or from island bases that could provide practically nothing by way of food, supplies, or even simple accommodations. Everything had to be transported from the American homeland, which was thousands of miles away. Losses, too, were anything but light, amounting to no fewer than 309 machines between January and August. It is indicative of how weak Japan's anti-aircraft defenses had become that two-thirds of these resulted from accidents. Yet since each B-29 carried a price tag of $600,000—the 2009 equivalent of $11,000,000—that was scant consolation; indeed developing the aircraft cost as much as building the first atom bomb did. No other country in history has ever carried through anything nearly as large. Since 1945, however, the U.S. ability to do so has, on the whole, undergone nothing but a prolonged and very sharp decline.

Meanwhile, proceeding in such secrecy that even Vice President Harry Truman was only informed after he became president, something much greater still was going on. Late in May, aircraft and personnel of the 509th Composite Group started arriving on one of the islands, Tinian. It was exceptional in the sense that it consisted of just one bomber squadron, plus a transport squadron, plus supporting units. In charge of the outfit was a 29-year-old lieutenant colonel, Paul W. Tibbets Jr. Having flown combat missions over Europe and the Mediterranean, he was reputed to be the best pilot in the Army Air Forces.[24] Preparations were long and elaborate; the last rehearsal was held on July 31. Three out of Tibbets's 15 B-29s took off with replicas of Little Boy, the gun-fired, uranium-powered bomb of which the scientists in Los Alamos felt so sure that they never even had it tested. Their destination was the island of Iwo Jima, where they rendezvoused. From there they returned to base, dropped their dummies into the sea, and practiced the maneuver, known as toss-bombing, needed to prevent the aircraft from being destroyed by the bomb's blast. The second bomb, a rather larger and heavier plutonium-powered device known as Fat Man, which had been test-fired in New Mexico on July 16, arrived on August 2; the one factor that still delayed the go-ahead was the weather.

Though they did not know it, the inhabitants of the two doomed cities, Hiroshima and Nagasaki, were also being prepared for the ordeal. Both cities were of some importance as manufacturing centers, depots, and embarkation ports. Hitherto they had been spared specifically so that the first atom bombs could be tested on them and the precise results studied in detail. On the evening of August 5, the American crews were briefed amid heavy security. Tibbets's plane, which he had dubbed *Enola Gay* after his mother, took off at 0245 on August 6. Six hours later, at 0840 in the morning, it was flying at 32,000 feet over Hiroshima. Earlier the city had been reconnoitered by a weather plane, which made sure everything was clear. The unintended result was to convince many people on the ground that the second American aircraft was nothing very dangerous, a fact that may well have prevented them from taking shelter and thus helped increase the number of casualties. Now everything worked just as planned; the bomb doors opened and Little Boy dropped out. Fifty-seven seconds later, having reached approximately 2,000 feet, it exploded. By that time *Enola Gay* was already 11.5 miles away and escaping as fast as it could. Even so, it was badly buffeted by the shock wave and the crew, afraid of being blinded, had to use goggles to observe their handiwork.

As the doomed city disappeared under a mushroom cloud that rose to 60,000 feet, 75,000 people lay dead or dying. Later on, another estimated 75,000 died of their injuries or else as a result of the radiation they had received. Within a radius of one mile from point zero, only a few steel-framed buildings, built to resist earthquakes, remained standing. Yet even that was not the end of the horror. Three days later the second bomb was dropped on Nagasaki. Though it was considerably more powerful than the first, thanks to the hilly topography the number of immediate casualties was considerably smaller. So terrible were the death and the destruction that the U.S. Army decided to keep the 100,000 feet of color film its photographers had shot in both cities under lock and key so as not to ruin the public taste for dropping more bombs if necessary.[25] Regardless of whether the bomb should or should not have been dropped, was or was not responsible for the Japanese surrender that followed almost immediately,[26] clearly never before had airpower been used to such awesome effect. Mercifully, as it turned out, never again would it be so used.

PART III

THE WAR THAT NEVER WAS

1945–1991

So far we have described the way air warfare, having started from very humble origins indeed, developed. Until World War II, no large-scale military operation, whether on land or at sea, that did not at least take it into account—and sought to deal with it—stood the slightest chance of success. As the fate of Germany and Japan shows, by 1944–45, it had reached the point where it was quite capable of wrecking entire countries. Hundreds of thousands of dead, industries that all but ceased to function, and cities so thoroughly demolished that they were deserted even by the birds testified to this fact. To speak with the Bible, though, power does not forever last.[1] Though the process did not unfold in the same way at all places, and though it has certainly had its ups and downs, seen in retrospect airpower has now been in decline for six decades and more.

CHAPTER 9

THE DOMINANT FACTOR

In the introduction to their 1983 book *Air Power in the Nuclear Age*, Air Marshal Sir Michael Armitage, KCB, CBE, and Air Commodore R. A. Mason, CBE, MA, wrote that airpower represented the "dominant factor" in post-1945 war.[1] For support they quoted Churchill, who in a 1949 speech said that "air mastery is today the supreme expression of military power" side by side with which "fleets and armies . . . must accept subordinate rank." In fact, World War II had proved that, both on land and at sea, no large-scale military operation could have any hope of success unless it was properly covered and supported from the air. But these statements, and a thousand others like them, were wrong. In reality, the dominant factor that distinguishes post-1945 warfare from all its predecessors is not airpower but nuclear weapons. And efforts at disarmament notwithstanding, almost certainly nuclear weapons will dominate warfare as long as the latter itself exists.

On the face of things, "nucleonic" weapons, as one group of scientists called them during the late 1940s, should have turned the armed forces, and specifically the U.S. Army Air Forces, which was the first to deploy and use them, into the undisputed master of the world—the destroyer of cities and the agents of death that would return future opponents to the Stone Age if necessary. Some air force officers, determined to make their own service *primus inter pares*, saw it exactly that way. Take Major General Orville Arson Anderson, a former altitude-record-setting balloonist and deputy director of operations for the Eighth Air Force in Europe. After the war he served as a key member of the United States *Strategic Bombing Survey* along with such luminaries as Paul Nitze, George Ball, and John Kenneth Galbraith. In March 1946 he wrote that "since airpower is the only force capable of being launched directly against the enemy economy, it has become the primary weapon and must dictate the overall strategy of another war." American airpower had to be emancipated from army control and made into an independent service such as most other countries already had; unless this was done, the future was "fraught with grave warning."[2]

Faced with this challenge on the part of the air force, which became independent in September 1947, the other U.S. services were also determined to get nuclear weapons and their delivery vehicles. The most celebrated episode in the struggle that followed was the so-called Revolt of the Admirals of 1949.[3] At issue was the question whether the navy would get a number of new carriers sufficiently large to carry nuclear-capable aircraft. After much controversy during which the secretary of the navy, Francis Matthews, fired the chief of naval operations, Admiral Louis E. Denfeld, the navy got its way and was allowed to build the carriers it wanted.

Meanwhile the army, equally determined to get its hand on nuclear weapons and their delivery vehicles, achieved the same goal in a different way. At the end of World War II, it had captured the SS-run underground factory where V-2 missiles were produced. Not only did it put its hands on some of them, but it found and brought to the United States the team of experts, led by Wernher von Braun, who had been responsible for developing them.[4] From that point on it concentrated on the accelerated development of nuclear-capable surface-to-surface missiles with ranges in the hundreds of miles. By the mid-1950s it was working on the Jupiter, which had a range of 1,500 miles, only to have it taken away and entrusted to the air force. Technically there was no reason why the army could not have designed, built, and deployed its own intercontinental ballistic missiles

(ICBMs). Some of the missiles von Braun did develop in the United States in 1948–55 could have carried a satellite into space if only the Eisenhower administration, which backed the air force, had given him the go-ahead.[5] Thus the net effect of introducing nuclear weapons was to make the navy even more concerned with air operations than it already was. At the same time, it caused the army to enter space operations for the first time. To this extent, the two services formed part of airpower and thus of the subject of the present volume.

While the air force chiefs were arguing for a monopoly over nuclear weapons and their delivery vehicles, and while the navy and army chiefs outdid one another in painting the dire results that would follow if they did not get them too, the realization gradually dawned that the weapons in question were not just more powerful versions of older ones. Instead, they were of an entirely new kind. Nuclear weapons were about to alter, perhaps had already altered, not merely the way wars were fought but the purpose for which they were fought and, perhaps, whether they could be fought at all. In retrospect, the most important early bearer of this message was Bernard Brodie. In 1946, while on the faculty of Yale University, he edited a volume called *The Absolute Weapon*. In the first chapter, which he wrote and which carried the same title, he wrote:

> I. *The power of the present bomb is such that any city in the world can be effectively destroyed by one to ten bombs. . . .*
>
> II. *No adequate defense against the bomb exists, and the possibilities of its existence in the future are exceedingly remote. . . .*
>
> V. *Superiority in number of bombs is not in itself a guarantee of strategic superiority in atomic bomb warfare. . . .*
>
> VII. *In relation to the destructive powers of the bomb, world resources in raw materials for its production must be considered abundant. . . .*
>
> VIII. *Regardless of America's decisions concerning retention of its present secrets, other countries . . . will possess the ability to produce the bombs in quantity within a period of five to ten years.* [all emphases are in the original][6]

Truisms they were then, and truisms they remain now. Given the presence of practically unlimited destructive power, and given the absence of any meaningful possibility of preventing that power from doing its work, the conduct of war, here understood as the *mutual* use of organized violence in pursuit of one's interests,[7] simply no longer made sense.

Intellectually speaking, it took time for Brodie's theses to be widely accepted, and even today there are those who hotly dispute them.[8] There were two reasons why this was so. First there was the revolutionary nature of the argument and that of the weapons on which it centered; not in tens of thousands of years of human history had there been anything like them. As the greatest nuclear strategist of all, Thomas Schelling, was later to explain, what nuclear weapons had really done was to cut the link between victory and survival so that a belligerent might "win" a war and *still* have a large part of his population killed and his country reduced to a radioactive desert.[9] The other reason was institutional interest; if war had become too dangerous to wage, then the long-term consequences for the armed forces, first of the United States and then of other countries that Brodie foresaw would soon join the nuclear club, were obvious. Short of serving as instruments for national suicide, at best they might still engage in preparation, not for waging war but to deter potential enemies. At worst, lack of funding would cause them to gradually wither away.

Early on, Harold Urey, who had won a Nobel Prize in 1934 and played a key role in the Manhattan Project, said that the one thing worse than one nation having the bomb was two nations having it.[10] That was wrong; in reality the balance of terror, as it was known, prevailed. Throughout the 45 years of the Cold War the nuclear arsenals of the two superpowers, the United States and the Soviet Union, easily overshadowed all the rest, a situation that was later known as bipolarity. Yet contrary to all historical experience—Athens versus Sparta, the Roman Empire versus the Parthian one, the Ottoman Empire against the Habsburgs, and so on right down to World Wars I and II—and contrary also to what many people believed during the first decade or so after 1945, World War III did not break out. By some eyewitnesses' accounts, even during the most dangerous crisis of all, the October 1962 Cuban one, it did not come close to breaking out.[11]

In time it became evident that, understood as an intellectual construct, the balance of terror, or Mutual Assured Destruction (MAD) as it was called from the 1960s on, suffered from many weaknesses, though certainly not more so than any other strategic theory ever devised. Not only were its fundamental tenets open to question, but hardly a year passed without them being questioned.[12] Many of these polemics grossly exaggerated Soviet power and the willingness of the men in the Kremlin to risk the destruction of the world. Others were designed to serve special interests. Nevertheless, considered as an "actually existing" state of affairs (to borrow a phrase from the former East German leader, Erich Honecker), MAD turned out to be not only sturdy but practically inescapable; indeed any comparison of 1950s-vintage strategic writings with those that followed will quickly show that belief in it has become much stronger than it used to be.[13] Exercises held in the Pentagon have demonstrated that it is hard to find officials willing to cross the nuclear threshold even during wargames, let alone in reality.[14]

Much less is known about the doctrines of other nuclear countries. Still, looking back, there is no question that, broadly speaking, the same processes were at work. Under Lenin and Stalin the Soviet official position had been that a frightful clash with the capitalist West was certain to take place one day and would lead to the final victory of socialism over its enemies. During the early decades of the Cold War some Soviet leaders, including onetime minister of defense Field Marshal Andrei Grechko, kept emphasizing that their country did "not absolutize nuclear weapons."[15] In other words, a nuclear war was possible, and should the United States provoke it, then the Soviet Union fully intended to fight it and win it. In practice, this stance did not prevent the emphasis from shifting toward deterrence from 1956 on.[16] Deterrence in turn led first to Nikita Khrushchev's policy of peaceful coexistence and then to détente. To be sure, much of the latter was little more than rhetoric. One could even argue that it was a delusion that Western leaders used to conceal their countries' weakness from their peoples and from themselves.[17] Nevertheless, when the rhetoric died down after 1976, the balance of terror *still* held.

Not only in the Soviet Union, but in Britain, France, China, Israel, India, Pakistan, and—presumably—North Korea too, doctrines were written for using the weapons if necessary.[18] As with the superpowers, from time to time there was talk about the "dangerous dilution of nuclear deterrence."[19] As with the superpowers, too, what evidence is available suggests that, in time, those countries' rulers were forced to the conclusion that there is no escape from MAD.[20] Among these countries, too, there were moments when the balance of nuclear forces was completely lopsided in favor of one side or the other. Such was the case during the Soviet-Chinese confrontation of 1969–70 and probably also during the one between India and Pakistan in 1989–90.[21] Since a lopsided balance turned out to be just as effective in preventing war as a more symmetric one, once again it did not matter; whatever some people might say, no major war has taken place among South Asia's three nuclear powers, China, India, and Pakistan, over the last 40 years.

Early on, the service primarily affected by the various nuclear doctrines was the air force with its aircraft and missiles. Later, as the navy deployed its own nuclear-capable aircraft and submarine-launched strategic missiles, it felt the impact to an almost equal extent. Of the three services, the poor relation was the army. It focused its efforts in the nuclear field on short-range "atomic bazookas," artillery, and missiles. It is, however, important to repeat that this situation was an entirely artificial one. In Germany it had been the army, not the air force, that developed the V-2. If the U.S. Army did not engage in space operations and develop the hardware for doing so, then this was due to neither lack of will nor capability, much less to some fundamental principle. Instead, it was due solely and exclusively to the restrictions that Congress had placed on it.

To deliver *its* nuclear weapons, the Soviet Union had set up a special command, known as Long-Range Aviation, which received its orders directly from the Ministry of Defense.[22] No sooner had the first ICBMs become available than the Soviets started placing much greater reliance on them than on manned aircraft. The Strategic Rocket Forces having been created in 1959, a few years later it absorbed Long-Range Aviation. Not counting the navy's air arm, this decision left the Soviet Union with two separate air forces.[23] Depending on strategic requirements as well as other factors, other countries developed their own organizations. The conclusion from all this is clear: to deliver nuclear warheads, even the largest nuclear warheads meant to strike strategic objectives thousands of miles away; an independent air force with power over everything that flies through the air or reaches its targets through space is not necessarily the only possible organization.

As the first and by far the greatest nuclear power, right from 1945 the United States has always done whatever it could to prevent other countries from obtaining weapons similar to those it already owned (and has used). Indeed the man who built the bomb, Manhattan Project chief General Leslie Groves, wrote that, "if we were ruthlessly realistic," Washington should destroy the capacity of any other country "in which we do not have absolute confidence" to build the bomb "before it had progressed far enough to threaten us."[24] Since America's nuclear primacy was seen as a "wasting asset," there were at least some who openly called for it to be used while the going was good; fortunately for the world, nothing came of it. For decades on end, making full use of what Joseph Nye, President Clinton's assistant secretary defense for international security affairs, calls its "soft power," the United States flooded the world with a vast literature on the need to prevent proliferation.

Each time another country looked ready to acquire nuclear weapons Washington came up with detailed explanations why doing so posed a grave danger to the world. Also, why a few nuclear countries were preferable to many; why a multipolar nuclear world would be less stable than a bipolar one; and why the new candidates were less rational, less responsible, and less deserving to enter the club than their predecessors. The arguments varied—now it was communists who were particularly nefarious, now Muslims, and now terrorists. In the process, it often happened that onetime "irresponsible" actors such as the Soviet Union were metamorphosed into "calculable ones." Thus China, whose leaders were at one time seen as stark raving mad, gradually had its image changed into that of a responsible strategic partner; if it were not so serious, it would have been comic. Ignored was the fact that *none* of the thousands of warnings ever came true—the United States stuck to its guns and, which is more surprising, made many other countries follow.

Moreover, the factors that governed relations between the lions quickly started affecting the mice as well. Within a fairly short time it became clear that deterrence worked from the top downward; for fear of escalation, increasingly it prevented not only nuclear war but large-scale conventional war too from breaking out. The outcome has been that, in all the years since 1945, not once did two countries armed with nuclear weapons, or even believed to be so armed, engage in more than border skirmishes against one another. Here and there they also supported terrorists, as between Pakistan and India. Large-scale armed force, with land- or sea-based airpower serving as its cutting edge, was turned into something to be employed solely against countries that did not have nuclear weapons or else in wars between such countries. This was a far cry from 1939–45 when the great powers of the day relied on such force in their efforts to tear each other to pieces, and, as the ruins of cities such as Warsaw, Rotterdam, London, Coventry, Cologne, Hamburg, Dresden, Hiroshima, and Nagasaki showed, did so with considerable success.

While nuclear deterrence was gradually undercutting the uses to which air- and space power, along with all other forms of military power, could be put, that power also came under attack from another, somewhat unexpected, direction. As even a cursory look at history shows, most of the time political power and military command have been concentrated in the same hands. In practice, indeed, very often it was military command, legitimately or illegitimately obtained, that formed the key to political power; as late as the beginning of the twentieth century, all European monarchs habitually wore uniforms. It was only during the eighteenth century, and then only in very few democratizing countries, that the two began to be separated and elected civilians were put in firm control of the military. Even so, it took another two centuries of often very bloody struggles before the majority of states on earth finally concluded that, in theory at any rate, this was indeed the best system.

Now, to paraphrase the French World War I prime minister Georges Clemenceau, nuclear war had become too important to be left to the generals, those in charge of airpower as well as all the rest. One of the first generals to feel the effect of this truth was Eisenhower. In November 1945 Eisenhower, who after George Washington was probably the most popular commander in the whole of American history, took over as chief of staff of the army, which, at that time, still included the Army Air Forces. Even before he did so, his superior, President Truman, personally made sure that he would have no say in setting a policy in respect to the atomic bomb.[25] This turned out to be just the first move in a long series. The details differed over time and also from one country to another. Yet the intent was always the same: namely, to deprive the generals, and the airpower generals in particular, of much of their power by taking the most powerful weapons away from them and making sure they would be able to use them only on the politicians' direct order.

In the United States as the first nuclear power, a fierce debate soon developed as to how this objective might be accomplished. Even before the first nuclear test took place in June 1945, President Roosevelt's secretary of war, Henry Stimson, had set up a committee charged with considering postwar control over the weapon. Its recommendations later served as a basis for the May-Johnson bill being debated in the House of Representatives.[26] However, since the bill left atomic research in the hands of the military, it was opposed by a coalition of scientists, who wanted free research, and politicians and went down to defeat. A contributing factor in that defeat was news concerning General Douglas MacArthur's order to destroy some captured Japanese nuclear equipment, a decision many in Washington saw as both high-handed and stupid.[27] By January 1946 a different piece of legislation, known as the Atomic Energy Act, or the McMahon Act after its sponsor, Democratic senator Brien McMahon from Connecticut, was being debated and was passed in July. On August 1, 1946, less than a year after Hiroshima, Truman signed it. It established the United States Atomic Energy Commission (AEC) and put it in charge of developing nuclear weapons.

To the generals, with the now independent air force generals at their head, the act came as a rude surprise. Probably never before in history had the armed forces of any nation been told that they would not be allowed to control their own weapons in peacetime, storing them, deploying them, and exercising with them as they saw fit. According to David Lilienthal, as head of the AEC, they "*assume[d]*" [emphasis in the original] that, in the future as in the past, they would be the ones to decide when to use the new weapons, under what circumstances, and against what targets.[28] Early on, some of the strongest opposition came from Stuart Symington, a Missouri businessman whom Truman had appointed as the first secretary of the air force. But Truman would have none of it. "You have got to understand," he told Symington, "that this is not a military weapon. It is used to wipe out women and children and unarmed people, and not for military uses. So we have got to treat this differently from rifles and cannon and ordinary things like that."[29] Truman's logic might be faulted—after all, in 1942–45, the United States, along with several other belligerents, had used conventional bombs "to wipe out women and children and unarmed people" by the hundreds of thousands. That night Lilienthal noted in his diary: "if what worried the President . . . was whether he could trust these terrible forces in the hands of the military establishment, the performance these men gave certainly could not have been reassuring."[30] Truman himself seemed to agree; somewhat later he drafted a note to "Dear Stu," calling the latter's proposals "drivel" and "bunk."[31]

By issuing Executive Order No. 9816, Truman ensured that the agency and not the military controlled them. Two years later, on August 29, 1949, came the first Soviet nuclear test. Since no defense was available or even on the horizon, the result was to make those responsible for doctrine emphasize the importance of getting in the first blow.[32] But how could this need be reconciled with the fact that the military did not have physical custody over the bomb? As Lilienthal's diary shows, hardly a month passed without some general taking up the subject with him. Among those who did so was Omar Bradley in his capacity as the first chief of the Joint Chiefs of Staff.[33] Just weeks before the Korean War broke out, Curtis LeMay, now commanding the newly established Strategic Air Command (SAC), referred to the dilemma in a talk he gave to Air War College students. He told them that, *"given proper intelligence and authority,"* his bombers were able to meet an enemy offensive before it could "get rolling." He kept returning to the issue; within days of the war's start, he told the air force chief of staff, General Hoyt Vandenberg that "a major weakness in our planning" was "the process by which the execution of an air offensive might be ordered and the necessary atomic weapons made available to me."[34] It must have rankled—decades later, a long since retired LeMay was still referring to this period. He told interviewers that neither he nor any of his fellow generals had been allowed to have "a single [atomic bomb]" to quickly drop if necessary; evidently the weapons were considered "too horrible and too dangerous" to be entrusted to the likes of himself.[35]

Yet not even Truman, while determined to ensure that the nation's nuclear weapons remained under his exclusive control, could ignore the realities of modern air warfare. By denying the military custody of nuclear weapons, a situation might be created in which those weapons would not be available to repel aggression in time. On July 12, 1950, three weeks after the Korean War began, a compromise was worked out. At that time it was thought North Korea was acting directly on Stalin's orders and that the war might merely be a maneuver designed to distract attention from Western Europe. Fearing a possible Soviet assault on that continent, and in the belief that the West could not stop such an assault by conventional means alone, Truman ordered that the nonnuclear components of nuclear bombs be transferred to the air force for storage on its British bases. A few weeks later, with Kim Il Sung's army apparently threatening to push U.S. forces off the Korean peninsula, similar components were sent to the Pacific. This meant that the bombs could be assembled and used much more quickly than would otherwise have been the case.[36] According to the diary of Lilienthal's successor at the AEC, Gordon Dean, on April 6, 1951, the president, faced with a renewed Chinese offensive in Korea, went a step further. At a one-on-one meeting with Dean, he agreed to transfer custody of nine bombs out of some 200 that were available at that time. As he did so, however, he said that "in no event would the bomb be used" over the North.[37]

Whether Eisenhower did or did not resort to nuclear blackmail in order to end the Korean War is moot; in the end, what mattered is that the threat, if one there was, was not put into effect and the weapons remained unused. During the eight years of Eisenhower's presidency, America's nuclear arsenal grew from 800 to over 18,000 bombs; at that time, indeed, the United States was producing more bombs *each year* than the total arsenal had been under Truman.[38] Not counting the navy's aircraft carriers floating around the oceans, these devices, large and small, were now spread over bases as far apart as South Dakota and Texas, Britain and Okinawa, West Germany, Turkey, and Libya. Plans were also being formed to carry them aboard Polaris and Poseidon missile-launching submarines, which made the problem of communication all the more difficult. Eisenhower himself was very different from Truman. Personally he may have been less assertive and more inclined toward delegation of power. More important, as the originator of the strategic doctrine known as the New Look, he was determined to turn nuclear weapons and their delivery vehicles, primarily the air force's heavy bombers, into the mainstay of America's defense.[39]

Against this background, no sooner did the new president enter office than the newly established Joint Chiefs of Staff (JCS) started asking him to hand over custody of nuclear weapons to them. In May 1953, the pressure appears to have borne some fruit. Enough nuclear components were transferred into the hands of the military, the air force above all, to match the number of nonnuclear components already in their possession. Next, on December 1, 1954, Eisenhower decided that "custody of weapons shall be transferred to the Department of Defense in accordance with mutually acceptable arrangements between the AEC and the Department of Defense." Apparently the order only referred to overseas bases; weapons stored in the continental United States (CONUS) still remained under centralized AEC control. Even so, Eisenhower must have remained doubtful of his own policies. In August 1955, perhaps after having gone through the scary experience of the Taiwan crisis of the previous year, he directed that all weapons above 600-kiloton yield be restricted to bases under complete U.S. control and subjected to AEC custody.[40]

All this merely served to highlight the extreme difficulty of reconciling dispersion and readiness, needed to frustrate a possible Soviet first strike, with the very tight controls necessary to rule out accidental or unauthorized use. Technically Eisenhower's order was carried out by separating the nuclear capsule needed to activate the weapon from the weapon itself and putting it under separate lock and key. Thus the only person with access to it was the AEC representative on each base or carrier. But since those representatives were dependent on the base or carrier commanders for everything, in practice the arrangement meant that civilian control was weak, perhaps merely symbolic.

Still the tug-of-war, constantly refueled by the generals' and admirals' claims that the above arrangements compromised national security, went on. In 1956 Eisenhower seems to have reversed himself. Not only did he agree that the distinction between small and large weapons should be abolished, but control over them was entrusted to the base or ship commanders who wore a double hat as the AEC representatives. Whereas in 1954 only one in ten of the available nuclear weapons were held by the Department of Defense, five years later the figure was two out of three.[41] Yet Eisenhower, who is known to have been appalled by the possible results of a nuclear war and whom his recent biographers have portrayed as a strong president in full control,[42] must have retained some kind of ace up his sleeve. According to his aide Colonel (later General) Andrew Goodpaster, he never doubted that, as commander in chief, he alone had both the right and the ability to decide exactly when and how the country's nuclear arsenal would be put to use.[43]

Highly esoteric though it was, the debate did not always remain behind closed doors. By the early 1960s, first any number of successful novels and later the famous movie *Dr. Strangelove or: How I Learned to Stop Worrying and Love the Bomb* (1964) had firmly imprinted the consequences of a nuclear war on the public mind. Such a war might well spell "the end of civilization as we know it," as the phrase went. Those who argued that nuclear weapons were like any others and should be deployed and, if necessary, used could not expect a favorable reaction. One such was LeMay himself. Keeping in the public eye by means of newspaper articles and interviews, and having joined George Wallace as the latter's vice presidential candidate in 1968, he became known as the "caveman with the cigar." Four years earlier, the 1964 Republican candidate Barry Goldwater, himself a retired air force general, suggested, or seemed to suggest, that certain American commanders in overseas theaters should be given authority to use some of the nation's nuclear weapons on their own initiative.[44] By so doing, he made it easy for the supporters of President Johnson to portray him as a wild character who might just lead the country into Armageddon. This in turn helped bring about a landslide Democratic victory; since then other leading politicians seem to have learned the lesson.

The shift from manned aircraft to ballistic missiles, which got under way in the late 1950s and early 1960s, reduced the time available for deliberation and response from hours to minutes. It thus made the problem much more serious still. At this point, as so often was the case, new technologies came to the rescue. Work on these technologies, which eventually came to be known as Permissive Action Links (PALs), started at various nuclear research centers around the country as early as the mid-1950s. Whether the initiative was taken by the scientists involved, or by the AEC, or by the Congressional Joint Commission on Atomic Energy (JCAE), is moot. What does seem clear is that the issue was taken up by the Eisenhower administration, which ordered research to go ahead. Many officers, understanding its significance, were originally anything but supportive and kept raising objections. While claiming that PALs would interfere with command and control, they also saw them as a slur on their own loyalty and professional competence—which, in one way, they were.[45]

Installation of PALs on the nation's nuclear weapons started in 1962 when President John F. Kennedy signed National Security Action Memorandum No. 160. Kennedy's secretary of defense, Robert McNamara, is known to have been contemptuous of the military, which he saw as both reckless and reactionary. That fact may well have played a role, if not in the decision to go ahead, at any rate in accelerating its implementation and making sure, as far as possible, that no commander would be in a position to make an independent decision. All this was very much in line with the development of the new World Wide Military Command and Control System (WWMCS, pronounced wimex) from 1962 on.

The first warheads to receive PALs were those held by the SAC forces in CONUS and the army's short-range nuclear ones. As far as the latter were concerned, this meant that they could be deployed much closer to the front, and hence presumably brought into action at an earlier stage, without fear that they might be captured. Later those with SAC squadrons based in other parts of the world, as well as naval task forces, were added.[46] Last in line were submarine-carried weapons, which, according to some sources, received their PALs only in 1997. Top-level command over all nuclear forces is exercised by the president with the aid of the famous "football," the briefcase-like device that follows the president much as the wanderer is followed by his shadow; conversely, the role of the forces themselves, including that of the air force, has been reduced to storage and portage.

These things have always been shrouded in secrecy and are bound to remain so in the future. Even so, much more is known about the way they are done in the United States than in any other country—a fact, of course, that speaks volumes about American democracy and also about its relative sense of invulnerability. For this reason, but also because the United States was the first nuclear power and probably still maintains a technological lead, inevitably it served the rest as a model. As best we know, when Stalin first got his nuclear weapons he was careful not to give exclusive control of them to the Red Army, some of whose heads he regarded as his potential rivals. Instead commanders had to share responsibility with the KGB, which maintained its own separate system for communicating with the Defense Council as the supreme decision-making body.[47] It appears that, until the mid-1960s, the weapons were stored separately from their delivery vehicles. Only with the introduction of second-generation ballistic missiles were they mated with the latter. Even so, Soviet nuclear forces always remained under unusually tight operational restrictions well short of the preparations necessary for engaging in combat.[48]

Finally, information that came to light after the Cold War indicated that the Soviets had developed their own PALs. As in the United States, the ultimate decision whether to use nuclear weapons rested with the head of state and the minister of defense, each of whom was in possession of one-half of a binary code. These facts help explain why, following the disintegration of the Soviet Union, the newly independent republics of Ukraine, Belarus, and Kazakhstan all agreed to surrender the nuclear warheads stationed on their territory. Without the codes, those warheads would have represented nothing more than rather heavy, unwieldy metal containers. Once they were gone the missiles on which they were mounted became worthless; ultimately they too were handed back to Moscow.[49]

Other sophisticated nuclear nations such as Britain and France have probably developed their own PALs. In doing so, the British may have received some technical assistance from, or worked closely with, the United States.[50] Almost nothing has been published about the way China, India, and Pakistan handle these matters. This is even truer of the latest member of the nuclear club, North Korea. Concerning the first three, all that may safely be said is that, in all of them without exception, authority over the bomb's use has been taken out of the hands of those responsible for delivering them. Instead it is reserved solely for the head of state, perhaps in consultation with one or two other persons. To ensure that it should remain firmly in his or her hands, various organizational, procedural, and technical safeguards have been devised and installed.[51] Both India and Pakistan seem to store the warheads separately from their delivery vehicles.[52] Yet these countries' nuclear arsenals are much smaller and not nearly as widely dispersed over much of the earth as American warheads and delivery vehicles are. Hence the problem of command and control, while similar in principle, may be somewhat easier to solve. For example, a country that does not have submarine-launched ballistic missiles (SLBMs) does not have to worry how to communicate with its submarines either.[53]

All these countries have long lived under the nuclear gun, meaning that their enemies, real or presumed, also have nuclear weapons in their arsenals. So far, the only exception to this rule is Israel. Under such circumstances time is less critical and is probably measured not in minutes but in hours or more; hence, early on at least, Jerusalem may well have kept its weapons in a dismantled state. This would have the added advantage of lending support to its long-standing, if hardly credible, promise not to be the first to introduce nuclear weapons to the Middle East. Another method would be to store the bombs or the warheads separate from their delivery vehicles. However, why bother? Foreign sources claim that, quantitatively and qualitatively, Israel's nuclear arsenal is on par with those of Britain and France.[54] This small country has excellent scientific institutions and a world-class computer industry. It should be able to construct its own PALs; given the allegedly growing threat from Iran, which requires much faster reaction times than were needed in the past, very probably it has gone ahead and done just that.

As so often is the case, the technical details are less important than the political and military implications. The nuclear weapons first introduced in 1945 seemed to have given the military, and the air commanders responsible for delivering them to their targets in particular, absolute power over the life and death of tens of millions. In reality, it quickly became clear that the opposite was the case. Whatever commanders and strategists from Paul Nitze to Henry Kissinger and beyond might say, deterrence, or the balance of terror, or MAD, has worked very well indeed. This has been true regardless of whether the nuclear system was bipolar or multipolar, whether the nuclear powers involved were geographically close or far apart, whether the weapons and their delivery vehicles were primitive or sophisticated, whether the balance of forces was about even or lopsided, and whether they were democratic or totalitarian or Christian or Jewish or Hindu or Muslim. It even applied when the leaders were mad, as Stalin during the last years of his life may well have been, or drunk, as Nixon in the last year of his presidency was.

Furthermore, no sooner had the weapons been introduced than the politicians started making sure that they, rather than the top brass, would control them. In the United States, nuclear weapons research was taken from the army and entrusted first to the AEC and later to the National Nuclear Security Administration (NNSA) as part of the Department of Energy. In the Soviet Union, it was the province of a somewhat shadowy organization known as the Ministry for Medium Machine Building.[55] In the United States, owing to the conflicting demands of control and readiness, the process of centralizing command and control in the president's hands seems not to have unfolded in a straight line but undergone some ups and downs. Whether the same applies to other countries is impossible to say, but it is known that, in the Soviet Union, the KGB was responsible for guarding the weapons.[56] Whatever the exact arrangements, essentially they have reduced the generals and admirals, those in charge of airpower more than anybody else, to jacks in gold-braided uniforms. Though they must always be ready to jump out of their boxes, they are always securely locked into them. Definitely in the United States, and perhaps in other countries as well, the installation of PALs has allowed the generals to regain physical custody over their countries' most powerful weapons. However, that is only because that custody has become illusory since they no longer have what it takes to put the weapons to use.

Perhaps the most remarkable fact about all this is that, over 60 years after the first introduction of nuclear weapons, most people take these arrangements for granted. Even in democratic countries, any commander who tries to question them in public can expect to be instantly dismissed. One supposes that, in nondemocratic ones where such an attempt may be considered equivalent to a military coup, the consequences are much worse. Few even remember the days when many senior commanders, air force commanders in particular, saw them as a threat to national security, objected to them, and did what they could to prevent them from being implemented. About this one might truly say, *Sic transit gloria belli.*

CHAPTER 10

THE JET AND THE HELICOPTER

While nuclear weapons revolutionized airpower, they also it put into shackles from which it has yet to emerge and from which, one hopes, it will never emerge. These were momentous developments; compared with them the introduction of jets and helicopters, which started at about the same time, was a trivial event. It is true that jet engines made for more powerful, larger, and faster aircraft. Helicopters gave air forces, navies, and armies some entirely new capabilities, including that of taking off and landing almost anywhere and attacking some kinds of targets much more accurately than fixed-wing aircraft can. Nevertheless, neither faster flying machines—jets—nor more agile ones—helicopters—affected the basics of air warfare or even the main forms in which it was waged. As we shall soon see, no new missions were added whereas some old ones have almost entirely disappeared. Only at the time of the Gulf War of 1991 could it be said that new technologies, consisting mainly of precision-guided weapons (PGMs) and the sensors and data links and computers on which they rely, had really revolutionized airpower. By that, time, though, so different had conditions become that, in many ways, it hardly mattered.

As early as 1910 a French-Romanian inventor, Henri Coanda, built and flew the first "thermo-jet"–powered aircraft. In this machine a four-cylinder piston engine, instead of driving a propeller, was coupled to a compressor. The latter fed air into a combustion chamber, where it was ignited; leaving the device through a nozzle, it pushed the aircraft forward. Though several inventors continued to develop the idea during the 1920s, it was only in the late 1930s that they began to receive serious support from their countries' ministries of defense. At that time it was becoming clear that propeller-driven aircraft had inherent problems that limited their speed. Efforts to overcome those problems went on simultaneously in Italy, Britain, and Germany. It turned out that the key to a practical jet engine was to install a turbine in the way of the exiting gases and use it to drive the compressor; essentially, then, this was a gas turbine working in reverse. By 1939–40 British and German engineers were hard at work building the first jet aircraft. They came up with two quite similar machines, the Gloster Meteor and the Messerschmitt M-262. Both were straight-wing, two-engine designs, and both carried the engines under their wings.

The first squadron of Meteors became operational in 1944 and played some role in the fight against the German V-1s. Later, as that threat receded, the jets were moved to Belgium, where they participated in the final battles without, however, ever meeting their German opposite numbers. The story of the M-262 was more complicated. According to Albert Speer, Hitler's minister of armaments, its introduction into service was delayed by the fact that Hitler at first ordered it to be produced as a bomber whose speed would make it immune to Allied fighters. Unlike the British, who had full access to the world markets, the Germans had difficulty in securing the kinds of special metals needed to make the engines resistant to high temperatures. This handicap slowed down the process of development and led to numerous accidents. The first jet-equipped squadrons only became operational in January 1945. They might just have put an end to the Allied strategic bombing campaign against Germany—but by then it was a question of too little, too late.

Though the first operational jet aircraft were fighters, perhaps it is best to open this account of their subsequent development with bombers. As we saw, heavy bombers had played a very important role in air warfare as waged by the British and the Americans in World War II. Yet no sooner had the first jet fighters appeared than it became clear that existing piston-engined bombers were too large, too heavy, too slow, and too cumbersome to cope. These aircraft also had another limitation; even the largest of them, the B-29 Superfortress, did not have the range to reach many targets in the Soviet Union from bases outside that huge country, let alone the continental United States. It was to overcome these limitations that the U.S. Air Force built its next bomber, the B-36. The original aircraft, work on which started as early as 1940, was propelled by six piston engines. Later versions added two jet engines, one under each gigantic wing. The idea was to fly across the Atlantic, drop a bomb load on Germany, and return. Given the difficulties of the journey, the cost of the aircraft—they came at $4.1 million each—and the fact that it could only carry some 30 tons of TNT, one can only describe the scheme as ridiculous. It was like trying to use a long-handed hammer with a pea-sized head to batter a pot standing a mile away. Luckily for the air force and the company that built it, the aircraft was saved by the appearance of nuclear weapons. In the end, no fewer than 385 were produced.[1]

Even with the jets turned on, at 420 miles an hour the B-36 was not much faster than the B-29 it was supposed to replace. Certainly that speed was not enough to escape the MiG-15, which was not only fast but small and agile—and had not World War II shown that, without a fighter escort, daylight bombers did not stand a chance against well-organized air defenses? In the early 1950s, so acute did the problem become that SAC saw itself as forced to abandon its doctrine of daylight precision bombing. Some attempts were made to look for a remedy by making the B-36 carry "parasite" aircraft, but these led nowhere.[2] Worse still, at this time it was already becoming clear that the future of anti-aircraft defenses did not belong to artillery but to surface-to-air missiles (SAMs) such as the Soviet SA-1 and its American counterpart, the Nike Ajax. Against those missiles, intercontinental-range fighters, even if they had been available or could be developed, were of no use.

Both the SA-1 and the Nike were radar-guided, and both were designed to shoot down aircraft flying at up to 60,000 feet and more. As so often was the case in the history of arms races, it would be hard to say where the egg ended and the chicken began. Did the development of the bombers lead to that of SAMs, or the other way around? Well aware of the B-36's shortcomings, the U.S. Air Force started work on two other jet bombers, the B-47 and the B-52. Over 2,000 of the former were built; yet the B-47, which entered operational service in 1953, was insufficiently large to lift the first cumbersome hydrogen bombs. While that problem was soon solved, the aircraft did not have intercontinental range. This meant that the wings and squadrons equipped with it had to be based in countries as far apart as Britain, Morocco, Spain, Greenland, Guam, and the remote state of Alaska. To realize its dream of a truly intercontinental bomber, the air force had to wait for the B-52.

The Stratofortress, as it was called, was said to have been "the most formidable expression of airpower in history"[3]—though this statement must be qualified by the fact that it was never used on the mission for which it had been intended. Powered by eight jet engines, four under each wing, it had a maximum speed of 650 miles per hour and a combat radius of a little less than 5,000 miles. It could operate at 50,000 feet and was capable of carrying about 30 tons of bombs. These figures refer to the B-52H, the last model that entered service in 1961. By that time the place of the original turbojet engines had been taken by turbofans, which yielded considerably greater range for less fuel. Though even these mighty aircraft could not reach some Soviet targets from CONUS, that problem was solved by the development of air-to-air refueling. A complicated and very costly procedure, it had been experimentally demonstrated as early as the 1920s when two American brothers, Fred and Al Key, kept a Curtiss Robin monoplane in the air for no fewer than 27 days. However, it only came into widespread use 30 years later.

The total number of B-52s built was 744, the peak number of those in operational service at any one time around 650. For about a decade and a half they formed the backbone of SAC. Either they stood on the runways in a state of full alert or, until 1968 when accidents brought to light the dangers involved, flew round-the-clock air patrols. Had SAC unleashed the full power of these and other assets, the outcome would have been an estimated three to four hundred million Soviet, Chinese, and satellite fatalities.[4] In the 1970s, by which time the B-52s would have fallen easy victim to the fighters and anti-aircraft missiles of the period, their operational life was extended by adding electronic countermeasures as well as cruise missiles, so-called standoff weapons capable of reaching their targets from as much as 1,500 miles away. For years and years, the massive machines came to stand as the symbol of strategic deterrence and, in this way, the ability of the West to defend itself if necessary. As of 2008, there were 94 still in service.[5]

No other strategic bomber of the period was nearly as successful as the B-52 had been. At one point the United States developed a supersonic bomber, the B-58 Hustler. With its sharp nose, sleek silhouette, and delta wings it was specifically designed to penetrate Soviet defenses in ways that its older, slower, and more cumbersome predecessor could not match. However, it had neither the B-52's range nor its bomb-carrying capacity, and only 116 were built;[6] unlike the B-52s, too, it was never once used for dropping conventional ordnance. Next the air force came up with an even more ambitious project, the even faster supersonic B-70. It was resisted by Eisenhower, who was always asking his air force generals how many times they thought they could kill the same man, and finally canceled by Kennedy's secretary of defense, Robert McNamara. Their reasoning, which can hardly be faulted, was that the Mach 3 aircraft had no chance of escaping the SAMs that would be aimed at it. Besides, the solid-fuel Minuteman ICBMs then entering service stood a much better chance of surviving a Soviet first strike. Since there was no defense they were also much more likely to reach their targets, to say nothing of their lower cost.[7]

Yet the air force, always worried about its independence, refused to give up. At one point it even tried to convince Eisenhower of the urgent need for a nuclear-powered aircraft as well as a nuclear-powered missile for colonizing the moon. Fortunately for the national debt, these bright ideas were rejected. However, the air force did succeed in developing and producing what will almost certainly be the last two American strategic bombers, the B-1 Lancer and the B-2 Spirit. The first made its debut under President Ronald Reagan at the very end of the Cold War, the second some years after it had ended. Of the first, 104 were built, of the second a mere 21. Each one, but the B-2 with its stealth configuration in particular, was a miracle of technical progress. However, by the time they entered service the mission of strategic deterrence had long been taken over by ICBMs, SLBMs, and to a lesser extent, cruise missiles. Thus neither aircraft was ever used on the mission for which it had been designed. Given how expensive they were to procure and operate, using either to carry conventional ordnance almost amounted to a bad joke; indeed it has been claimed that the B-2 in particular became a pariah to many pilots.[8]

No other country put nearly as great an emphasis on heavy bombers or built as many of them. In late 1944 a few B-29s, having flown over Manchuria, landed in the Soviet Far East. While the crews were quietly repatriated, the aircraft were not, and the design bureau headed by Andrei Tupolev was charged with reverse-engineering it. The aircraft, which was given the designation Tu-4, remained in service during most of the 1950s. Later the Soviets came up with the Tu-95 Bear/Bison, a larger and in some ways very successful aircraft. It was powered by four enormous turboprops, a variant of a jet engine in which the hot exhaust gases, instead of pushing the aircraft forward by reaction, drive a turbine, which is coupled to a propeller. They gave the aircraft a speed of 575 miles per hour, a flight ceiling of 45,000 feet, and an intercontinental range of over 9,000 miles.[9] Only in terms of payload, which was around 15 tons, did the Tu-95 lag far behind the B-52. In 1958, U.S. intelligence estimated that the Soviets had some 135 operational machines of this kind. From its introduction to the present, about 500 were produced. The decisive fact about the T-95 is that, like the B-52, it was never used on the mission for which it had been built, that is, carrying thermonuclear weapons over intercontinental distances in war.

Like the B-52, too, it is still in service in limited numbers—either because of its versatility or because a successor would be too expensive.

After 1960 the Soviet Union only built one more strategic bomber, the Tu-160 Blackjack.[10] In many ways it was the equivalent of the American B-1. Both aircraft had variable geometry wings, an arrangement that, at the cost of additional weight and complexity, allowed them to operate at both low and high speeds. Like the B-1, too, its range was too short to qualify it as a truly intercontinental bomber, a fact that caused some complications during disarmament talks when the U.S. negotiators wanted to include it and the Soviets refused. Apparently 35 of the machines were built, not many, considering that, at peak in the early 1980s, the Soviet Union had no fewer than 1,398 ICBMs and 912 SLBMs.[11] No other country has followed the superpowers' example or is at all likely to do so in the future. Indeed during all the years since 1945 only two countries, the Soviet Union and Britain, even went ahead and built any medium bombers at all.

The Soviet machine of this kind was the Tu-16, a subsonic aircraft capable of carrying nine tons of bombs over 4,500 miles. The British came up with no fewer than three different aircraft, the Victor, the Valiant, and the Vulcan. Collectively known as the V bombers, their performance was quite similar to that of the Tu-16. The objective was to deter the Soviet Union from attacking Britain by threatening to strike demographic and industrial targets in European Russia. A total of 431 machines were built, representing an extraordinary effort for a relatively small country. The French on their part never developed medium bombers, but they did try their hand at building a supersonic one. It took the form of the Dassault Mirage IV, an elegant, delta-winged, and comparatively light machine. Like all the rest, it never carried out its stated mission to carry thermonuclear weapons in war and "tear off a [Soviet] arm" as strategist André Beaufre put it.[12] Before long they were replaced by intermediate-range ballistic missiles (IRBMs) and SLBMs.

In this way, strategic bombers slowly went the way of all flesh. The culminating point came in 1991 when, in a long-overdue step, Strategic Bombing Command, the USAF's once-dominant SAC, was abolished. This author well remembers meeting pilots who, understandably, were in tears when it happened. Whereas America's ICBMs were grouped in a new space command, the remaining bombers joined other "shooters" in a newly established combat command. By that time medium and light bombers had all but disappeared. This is hardly the place to list them all; the Soviet Il-28, the British Canberra, the French Vautour came and went. All three machines are perhaps best understood as replacements for World War II–vintage light bombers such as the American Mitchell and the British Mosquito. All were powered by two wing-mounted engines, could operate at high subsonic speeds, had a comparatively long range, and were able to carry a bomb load of between three and four and a half tons. Designed primarily for deep interdiction behind the front, by the time effective, mobile, ground-to-air missiles started making their appearance in the late 1960s and early 1970s, all three were obsolete; perhaps the most significant point about them is that they have had no successors.

This brings us to some of the smallest jets, the fighters and fighter-bombers. Like their larger brothers they were the product of a tight oligopoly; essentially they were built by only five countries, the United States, the Soviet Union, Britain, France, and Sweden. Others, such as Italy, Germany, Israel, South Africa, and even poor underdeveloped Egypt, tried their hand at this game at one time or another; yet without exception they ended by dropping out of the race, which proved to be exceedingly expensive. Others still built their fighters by license, tried to modify their foreign-bought ones by putting in new avionics, or else entered joint ventures with other countries so as to share the development costs. By the early 1950s, first-generation machines, such as the above-mentioned Meteor and the Me-262 as well as the American F-80 Shooting Star and the French Ouragan, were giving way to second-generation ones capable of flying at just over the speed of sound for short periods. Some had to roll on their back and enter a shallow dive in order to do so.[13] The best known were the American F-86 Sabre, F-84F Thunderjet, and F-101 Super-Sabre; the Soviet MiG-15, 17, and 19; the British Hawker Hunter; and the French Mystère IV.

All these were single-seat, single-engine, swept-wing designs. Several of them owed something to German engineers who, willingly or not, were now working for new masters. To gain an impression of the progress made, compare the F-86 Sabre with the World War II P-51 Mustang. It had a top speed of 687 miles per hour (versus 437) and a ceiling of 50,000 feet (versus 42,000). The greatest advance was in climb rate, which reached 8,100 feet per minute instead of a mere 3,300; such machines could compel slower opponents to accept combat while they themselves were able to avoid it if the pilot so desired. Higher performance also made necessary, or was accompanied by, many new features such as improved gunsights, pressure suits, and ejection seats. Yet all these aircraft still had an armament consisting of rapid-firing cannon—except for some very light trainers adapted for ground support, machine guns had finally gone by the board. They could also carry air-to-ground rockets and a load of unguided iron bombs. At about two tons, the bomb load of an F-86 Sabre was about twice as large as that of a P-51 Mustang. Reliance on cannon meant that, in air-to-air combat, dogfights remained the norm as they had been since World War I. Iron bombs meant limited accuracy, the more so because of the increase in speed.

A third generation of jet fighters started entering service around 1960. Most, such as the U.S. F-102 Dagger and F-106 Dart, the Soviet MiG-21, the French Mirage, and the Swedish J-35 Draken, had delta wings. The principal exception was the American F-104 Starfighter, an extraordinary machine that looked almost like a rocket with stub wings and a cockpit added. Some of its versions, notably the G variant, a thousand of which were bought by the renascent German Air Force, proved so dangerous to fly that they were known as widowmakers. All these aircraft were capable of reaching Mach 2 and more, albeit only by using their afterburners and at the cost of a greatly increased fuel consumption that limited endurance and range. To enable more fuel to be carried, bubble canopies, offering much improved visibility, that had been characteristic of fighters from about 1944 to 1954 were done away with. Since speed and climbing rate were considered the most important qualities—the F-104 could shoot up at no less than 48,000 feet per minute—maneuverability had to be sacrificed and turning radii greatly increased. These characteristics made many third-generation aircraft less suitable for dogfighting than their predecessors had been.

What made the sacrifice possible, or at any rate was supposed to make it possible, was the introduction of early-generation air-to-air missiles such as the U.S. Sidewinder and others. As the gospel of air tactics now had it, the age in which pilots made visual contact with their enemy was over. Instead they were to rely on the radar sets all these aircraft carried and which, incidentally, did away with the traditional distinction between day and night fighters. Next the missiles, which were guided to their targets by infrared homing apparatus, were to shoot down the enemy at much longer ranges and without the pilots having to maneuver in such a way as to aim their own aircraft straight at the target.

In practice many early-generation air-to-air missiles did not work too well—in Vietnam between 1965 and 1968, only one out of nine hit its target.[14] One problem was that, by relying on their radar, aircraft revealed their presence long before they could be visually detected; to solve this difficulty pilots often switched off their radar sets, thus returning to square one. Another was that whereas cannon could hit an opponent from any angle, missiles had to be launched from behind so as to home in on his exhaust. This meant that much of their supposed advantage was canceled out. Sometimes they missed their targets or else could be shaken off by pilots alerted to their presence. These difficulties caused designers to retrace their steps and equip the next, or fourth, generation of fighters with both missiles and cannon. The new cannon were of the rotary type also known as Gatlings. This allowed a rate of fire as high as 6,000 rounds per minute to be achieved, but it also meant that the aircraft in question could only carry a few seconds' worth of ammunition. To improve maneuverability some machines such as the American F-111 Aardvark received variable-geometry wings similar to those of some of the bombers. Others, notably the American F-16 Falcon, had so-called thin wings. Much lighter and simpler, they dramatically improved the maneuverability needed for air-to-air combat.

At some time in the mid-1980s, this author had the good fortune of having the essentials of the system explained to him by its originator, the late Colonel John Boyd, during a lunch at the Pentagon cafeteria. The way he saw it, the performance of any given fighter aircraft reflected its "energy maneuverability." Energy maneuverability was obtained by means of a series of mathematical formulae that he—using stolen computer time, it was claimed—had developed and tested. They took account of engine thrust, drag, weight, wing area, and similar factors in order to predict how they would relate to each other at different altitudes and under various flight conditions. In this way, a scientific basis for comparing the overall performance of different aircraft was created.[15]

Previous generations of fighters had been designed for stability, meaning that, when buffeted by atmospheric conditions, they tended to right themselves. Not so those entering service during the 1970s. To maximize energy maneuverability, they deliberately had instability built into them. Such aircraft are always on the verge of going out of control, especially at subsonic speeds (fighters still spent most of their time flying, maneuvering, and fighting at subsonic speeds, using their afterburners only in an emergency). To stay aloft, they rely on their built-in sensors and computers. Under this system, known as "fly by wire," the computers automatically adjust the state of the aircraft's control surfaces to the prevailing flight conditions. They thus relieve the pilot of a large part of his workload and enable him or, rarely, her to concentrate on his proper mission; indeed pilots sometimes claim that the aircraft controls them as much as they control it. To ensure reliability, triple and even quadruple computer systems are provided. Yet all this ultrasophisticated electronic gear has to be crammed into the extremely limited space available onboard. But this was not all: to allow the aircraft to withstand the very high G-forces its maneuvers created, both fuselage and wings had to incorporate advanced, nonmetallic, composite materials such as very few countries were capable of manufacturing.

By the 1990s, with the exception of the United States with its dwindling number of ancient B-52s still in service, just about the *only* kind of combat aircraft left in the inventories were fighter-bombers. Fighter-bombers, which have a history going back to 1944–45, started becoming more common in the 1950s. In large part this was the result of escalating cost, which led designers to try to combine the capabilities of what had been two very different types in one. An excellent early example of the species was the U.S. Navy's F-4 Phantom. Developed in the 1950s and much used in Vietnam, in its role as a fighter the F-4 relied mainly on air-to-air missiles though it also had a 20-millimeter M-61 Vulcan rotary cannon. What made it unique was its ability to carry as much as eight tons of ordnance, which was more than most World War II bombers. Convergence operated in both directions; whereas some aircraft, such as the American F-15 Eagle, started life as air-superiority fighters and were later modified to serve as ground-attack aircraft too, others, such as the American F-16 Falcon, developed in the opposite direction.

Yet even fighter-bombers were present only in ever-declining numbers. To justify the decline, some experts explained that modern aircraft of this kind were qualitatively different from their predecessors. Equipped with much more accurate air-to-air missiles and sophisticated long-range radars that allowed them to engage numerous opponents at once, they would gain command of the air by virtue of their technological superiority, making large numbers superfluous. The argument appears attractive, especially to the bean counters. However, on closer examination it turns out to be specious. The reason why it is specious is that when one fighter is made to confront another, the new machines remain as evenly balanced as their predecessors have ever been. For example, an American F-15 confronting a Russian MiG-29 was no more capable than a British Spitfire or American Mustang when fighting a German Messerschmitt or a Japanese Zero. In other words, the technological advances on both sides canceled each other out; as a result, the real difference between, say, 1991 and 1945 was that, in case a serious war led to serious losses, building new machines, training new pilots for them, and providing them with the infrastructure they needed took years and years. Thus all the declining numbers really meant was that, in case of a war, the belligerents operating these machines would have to win very quickly indeed. Failing to do that, they would be forced to revert to older, more primitive weapons and methods—something that actually happened in some cases.

The second and even more important reason why the argument is wrong is that it ignores the nature of war as a two-sided, interactive activity. It looks at the enemy as a mere gathering of targets, some more important, others less so, that have to be identified and, once identified, hit as accurately and as economically as possible.[16] It does not consider him as a living, thinking being who can and will find ways to resist. The more powerful and the more sophisticated the means at one's disposal, the greater the temptation to think in terms of one's own capabilities alone; this phenomenon, which is typical of air force personnel though by no means limited only to them, is sufficiently well-known to have acquired a name, "coning."[17] Reality, of course, is very different. Targets will shoot back; after all, an electronics package very similar to the one that is used to guide an air-to-surface missile to its target can do the same for a surface-to-air one. Even if the answering fire is ineffective, it will usually force the attacker to take some precautions that will reduce his effectiveness. Targets will also be dispersed or camouflaged, or else decoys will be used in order to draw attention away from them. Like the mythological shape-shifters who could turn from men into animals and back again, the enemy will modify his tactics, his modus operandi, even his very nature, in order to counter the threat. At best, anyone who ignores these facts will find his own performance lagging far behind what is theoretically possible. At worst, the outcome will be ignominious defeat.

The earliest designs for so-called fifth-generation aircraft were conceived in the 1980s, and the first experimental machines made their appearance about 20 years later. By that time the research and development costs associated with each new machine had risen from the billions into the tens of billions of dollars. Consequently fewer countries considered participating in the race worthwhile, and fewer prototypes reached maturity and became operational. Compared with their predecessors, these aircraft were to be characterized by greater maneuverability—an improved "flight envelope," as it is known—greatly reduced visibility to radar and, above all, improved electronics. Increasingly, pilots have the information they needed presented to them by means of their head-up displays (HUDs) and even inside their flight helmets; computers allow all these data to be exchanged with other aircraft, permitting them to operate as a coordinated team. An interesting, if seldom noticed, aspect of all this was the fact that, from the pilot's point of view, it mattered little whether the electronic blips he saw did or did not represent anything in the real world. Thus air warfare became almost indistinguishable from a video game, and, conversely, video games edged closer to faithfully representing air warfare.[18]

Even so, the truth is that most fifth-generation aircraft being developed during the first decade of the twenty-first century were not really fifth-generation at all. Instead they are best described as fourth-and-a-half generation, meaning that they represent more or less straightforward developments of fourth-generation machines. Examples are the British-German-Italian-Spanish Eurofighter or Typhoon, the French Rafale, the Swedish Gripen, and the Russian MiG-35. What all have in common is that they come in a very large number of variants. Each one incorporates different engines and different avionics and can carry different kinds of weapons tailored for different kinds of missions against different kinds of targets. The outcome is that, instead of being mass-produced as they used to be, these machines have to be handcrafted, which, of course, contributes mightily to cost and makes it impossible to replace them should losses occur.

The American F-35 Joint Strike Fighter does meet the criteria of a true fifth-generation aircraft in that it has a new airframe with stealth characteristics and new avionics. Nevertheless, insofar as it was conceived as a kind of single-engine substitute for the unaffordable F-22 and also because it has a lower thrust-to-weight ratio than the F-16, which it is meant to replace, it still does not stretch technology to the limit. This leaves just one aircraft, the F-22 Raptor, to boldly take air forces where none have gone before. The F-22 is the first aircraft in history capable of flying at well over the speed of sound without the benefit of a fuel-thirsty afterburner. Thanks to thrust vectoring, it also has a shorter takeoff distance than earlier fighters as well as extremely high maneuverability—to the point where it is somewhat questionable whether the pilot will be able to withstand the full G-forces that result.[19] Specialized for air-to-air combat (although, judging by experience, other versions providing an improved all-round capability will almost certainly appear later on), it presents a threat no other aircraft can live with. Fighter jocks, a unique breed who are said to be taken into the air force at 19 and leave it 20 or so years later at the same age, are literally prepared to get themselves killed if necessary in order to be allowed to fly it. Faithfully supporting the pilots are legions of public relations men and women who, by way of the official website, have covered it with superlatives. It is the "First and Only 24/7/365 All-Weather Stealth Fighter," "provides 'first-look, first-shot, first-kill' transformational air dominance capability for the twenty-first Century" (which means, in plain words, that "it can see the enemy first while avoiding detection itself"), and is "a key asset in our Expeditionary Aerospace Force."[20]

Assuming the hype reflects reality—and there are some who have serious doubts about this[21]—these and many other capabilities are well worth having. Nevertheless, in the summer of 2009 U.S. Secretary of Defense Robert Gates, supported by Congress, which for once put aside objections concerning the impact on employment and so on, decided to kill the program by capping the number to be produced at 187, less than one-quarter of the original figure.[22] Considering that, depending on the way one calculates, each machine produced so far has cost the taxpayer anything between $137.5 and $340 million,[23] the decision is understandable. Yet the F-35, which is being touted as a substitute for the F-22, is itself expected to cost $125 million per unit, trend rising.[24]

The need to spend such sums helps explain why, whereas at one time each leading country had several major manufacturers of military aircraft, nowadays they tend to have just one or, at most, two. Outside the United States, where Lockheed and Boeing have swallowed up all the rest, even most of those are often forced to enter joint projects with foreign competitors. Many companies do not produce entire aircraft but focus on subsystems such as engines and avionics. Either they work as subcontractors for the few manufacturers left or else directly for air forces that want to upgrade existing machines. Exploiting their advantage, consumers very often insist that their own firms manufacture parts of the aircraft they purchase. On the other hand, the manufacturers sometimes refuse to equip the machines they build to export with certain kinds of sensitive equipment, mainly electronics. At times, this unheard-of industrial concentration leads to truly strange results. For example, Russia's president Vladimir Putin on one occasion proposed developing a new fighter that would incorporate a Russian airframe, American engines, and Israeli avionics; apparently no attempt was made to find out who might want to use such an aircraft against whom. Clearly, the entire process can only end in a cul-de-sac.

Decades earlier, during the mid-1950s, the size and weight of tactical nuclear weapons had been reduced to the point where the fighter-bombers of the period, such as the U.S. Air Force's F-84 Thunderchief and the navy's F-8 Crusader, could carry them. Later this was to become true of any aircraft adapted for the purpose, including, to mention but a few, the F-4, the F-15, and the F-16. Anxious to keep as free a hand as possible, many senior commanders tried to draw a sharp line between these weapons and their larger cousins, insisting that the former were like any others, only more powerful and more destructive.[25] However, escalation has its own logic; though some tried to present it as a controllable, step-by-step process, no one could guarantee that, if even a single small nuclear weapon were used, all the more powerful ones would not end up by being used as well.

Under such circumstances, scant wonder that *no* two combat aircraft produced and owned by nuclear countries ever fought one another while forming part of the air forces of those countries. To be sure, American F-86s did fight Soviet MiG-15s in the skies of Korea, but only because both sides pretended that the latter were flown by Chinese and North Korean pilots rather than by Soviet ones as was actually the case. Captured Soviet pilots were ordered to say they were Chinese of Russian extraction; President Eisenhower personally was informed and participated in the coverup.[26] American-built F-4s met Soviet-built MiG-17s over Vietnam, but only when the latter were piloted by North Vietnamese. British-built Harriers engaged U.S.-built Skyhawks over the Falklands, but only because the latter were piloted by Argentineans. The list could be continued indefinitely. As several of these examples show, the process affected naval aviation just as much as it did its land-based counterpart; after all, had any war gone nuclear, carriers would have led an exciting, but very short, life. Originally only countries capable of *producing* the most advanced combat aircraft had what it took to manufacture nuclear weapons. As the examples of China, Israel, India, Pakistan, and North Korea showed, however, after 1960 this was no longer true. Increasingly, any country capable of *operating* a modern—or even not so modern—air force was able to join the nuclear club if it decided to do so. To date, this rule applies to several dozen countries—with the result that, like an inkstain, the restrictions on the use of airpower continue to spread.

Jet engines have also revolutionized other military aircraft such as reconnaissance and transport. Though there were some exceptions, notably the famous American U-2 and the above-mentioned SR-71, since 1960 or so specialized reconnaissance aircraft have all but disappeared. Their place is being taken by satellites and unmanned airborne vehicles (UAVs). Using either jets or turboprop engines—only some small aircraft still rely on piston-driven ones—military transport has increased enormously in terms of power, speed, range, and load-carrying capacity. One aircraft, the American C-17 Globemaster, can lift 77 tons, a load equal to that of almost 30 World War II C-47s and almost three 1960s-vintage C-141s. The C-17's high wings and low-slung body enable it to load and unload cargo with the aid of its doors, which serve as ramps, without any special equipment. The same qualities also enable it to turn around even on a fairly narrow runway.

All these are impressive capabilities that greatly enhance their owners' ability to deliver men and supplies when and where they are needed. Nevertheless, in other ways the picture so eagerly presented by the airpower enthusiasts is misleading. Large and capable as modern transport aircraft are, when it comes to intercontinental transport, they still cannot compete with ships—or why else do thousands of the latter, heavily loaded with containers, continue to sail the seas? Furthermore, in some ways the larger the machines, the more serious the problems are. With the usual exception of the United States, most countries that bought the C-17 only own a handful of machines. Since the loss of each one would represent a major national disaster, they can only be used with extreme caution. In turn, the need for caution is hard to reconcile with the fact that the greatest problem facing military air transport has always been the aircrafts' inability to defend themselves.

If the big lumbering machines are to be of any use at all, then it is first necessary to secure near-complete command both of the airspace through which they fly and of an area around the bases that may be measured in dozens of square miles, probably more. For example, the bases used by the U.S. Air Force to fly in troops and supplies during the 1991 Gulf War were located several hundreds of miles behind the front. Over there cheaper, more readily available, civilian airliners and transports could have served, indeed did serve, quite as well; similarly, the French contingent that was sent to put an end to genocide in Rwanda in 1994 arrived in civilian aircraft leased from Russia.[27] In other words, large-scale air transport cannot operate anywhere near the front. Conversely, the closer the front and the more powerful the opposition, the lighter the aircraft have to be, and therefore the smaller the loads they can deliver to the forces on the ground.

One prominent victim of these considerations has been airborne operations. Dreams concerning "vertical envelopment" that would cut off sizable enemy forces and attack them from the rear are now some eight decades old. Such operations did play some role in World War II, but rarely if ever did they lead to the grand results that their advocates had hoped for. Since then, H. G. Wells's prophetic dictum that the greatest problem of airpower is its inability to hold ground has proven itself. Given how vulnerable transports are, airborne forces just cannot be reinforced as fast as ground forces can. As a result, the dreams have remained just that, dreams. Rarely if ever since 1956 has any single airborne operation involved more than a battalion of troops; essentially, it has become a question of inserting a handful of commandoes for carrying out special missions, then withdrawing them before the enemy can concentrate his forces and counterattack.

Perhaps this explains why, in one recent survey of "air and space power in the new millennium," neither airborne operations nor vertical envelopment are mentioned at all.[28]

At the lower end of the scale, military air transport has been supplemented by helicopters. The idea of the helicopter, meaning a device that uses an airscrew or screws to propel itself upward as well as forward, goes back at least as far as Leonardo da Vinci at the end of the fifteenth century. In Aldous Huxley's futuristic novel *Brave New World,* which was published in 1932, ordinary people fly helicopters—in reality, vertical takeoff and landing (VTOL) aircraft that use their rotors until they gain sufficient speed to rely on their wings—as a matter of course. As so often was the case, Huxley knew what he was talking about. The first autogiro, a machine that uses a free-spinning rotor to increase lift as it is pulled or pushed forward by a propeller, had flown in 1923; in 1938 Hanna Reitsch, a German female test pilot, flew the world's first fully controllable helicopter. Built by Focke-Wulf and given the designation FW-61, it was a twin-rotor machine equipped with a forward propeller. To increase the effect, a demonstration was held inside a large hall crowded with spectators.[29] During World War II both the Germans and the Americans used helicopters, but the numbers were so small that most soldiers probably never set eyes on them.

From 1951 on, helicopters were equipped with turboshafts, that is, gas turbines specifically engineered to produce the greatest possible rotary power. The first war in which helicopters were used on any scale was the one in Korea, when they served for the tactical transport of troops and material, casualty evacuation, observation, and liaison. It quickly reached the point where having a helicopter at one's beck and call became the number-one status symbol of many commanders. Compared with aircraft, even light ones, the helicopter's greatest advantages were their ability to take off and land almost anywhere and their extreme maneuverability. These qualities should have encouraged their use as convenient flying gun platforms, but in reality this only happened on a fairly small scale. The main reason why it did not happen was that the machines' extreme vulnerability—unlike aircraft, which will stay airborne for a time even after their engines have been shut down, a helicopter with a badly damaged engine or rotor will drop out of the sky like a stone. First rapid-fire light artillery and heavy machine guns, and later shoulder-held anti-aircraft missiles, all proved easily capable of shooting down a helicopter.

Some helicopters carry armor, but given that weight limitations are even more important than in fixed-wing aircraft, clearly there are limits to what can be done. The solution was to equip helicopters with their own standoff weapons, guided air-to-surface missiles. Specially designed machines of this kind, such as the American Huey Cobra and the Soviet Mi-24 Hind, debuted in the 1970s. By the end of the decade several other countries were producing them as well. Originally their armaments consisted of television- and laser-guided missiles that required the weapons operator—most of these machines have two seats—to follow them to their targets. Later, so-called fire-and-forget missiles such as the Hellfire were introduced. Thanks to infrared sensors and other electronic wizardry, the pilot and his weapon operator can launch them even at night. Each of these machines comes with a price tag of several tens of millions of dollars; scant wonder that most countries have bought them only in very limited numbers.

Originally developed in the late 1960s, attack helicopters, as they are known, were meant to be used as tank-busters. Accordingly, throughout the 1970s and 1980s, elaborate calculations were made to see how to best organize them for that purpose and how many tanks each helicopter would be able to take on.[30] At least one well-received book argued that, by making possible an altogether new degree of mobility, the "rotary wing revolution" was about to do for land warfare what tanks had done for it during the Blitzkrieg era.[31] Yet in this case as in so many others, reality refused to follow theory. It turned out that, the term "attack" notwithstanding, helicopters could not survive in the face of enemy fighters. Even when air superiority was ensured, they were best used on the defense. Taking up concealed positions well behind the front, where enemy fire was sparse or absent, they would rise suddenly, fire their missiles, and disappear, perhaps to repeat the performance somewhere else. If helicopters were to be used on the attack, it was vital to ensure there were no dense concentrations of enemy troops in the area. In wars with no fronts, except when the opposition did not have anti-aircraft defenses and was too weak to respond, they could only be used at the cost of extreme precautions. If the precautions were taken, then performance would be reduced; if not, then high losses could be expected.[32]

Helicopters' ability to take off and land almost anywhere makes them ideal for liaison, the rapid insertion and extraction of troops, and medical evacuation; indeed one reason for the steady decline in the ratio of wounded who die of their injuries is the speed with which they can be flown out of the combat zone and gotten into the hospital. Yet these qualities have to be balanced against the helicopters' enormous demand for maintenance and spare parts. Starting with the two- or three-man machines of the early 1950s, helicopters became bigger and faster. The largest one, the Soviet Mi-26 Halo, can lift 80 troops or 20 tons of cargo. Yet for all the improvements in performance, helicopters never even came close to matching fixed-wing aircraft in terms of load-carrying capability, speed, or range. The same applies to reliability. Attempts to combine their advantages with those of fixed-wing aircraft proved much more difficult than was thought at first and have only recently begun to bear fruit in the form of the U.S. Marine Corps V-22 Osprey tilt-wing aircraft.

Not only are modern aircraft themselves much more expensive than their predecessors, but most of them also require ground facilities incomparably larger and more complex than those that served their World War II predecessors. Few people remember that, as late as 1945, the B-17 bombers that helped bring Germany to its knees were still able to operate from grass runways. The B-29 could no longer do so, however, and the results of trying to make today's heavier, faster aircraft follow suit will hardly bear thinking about. A Spitfire or Me-109 could operate off any desert strip or stubble field. Their direct successors, the Meteor and the Me-262, could not. Since then, though some aircraft are more demanding than others, things have scarcely changed for the better.

As a rule, the more advanced the aircraft, the more maintenance it requires. True, with each new generation, the manufacturers, well aware of the problem, always promise that their future products take this problem into account and will be designed in such a way as to require less maintenance. That may indeed be true in some cases, but it ignores the fact that the most recent combat aircraft are so sophisticated that they require tons of computerized equipment to carry out the necessary corrections, calibrations, and tests. Either the equipment is driven about in container-sized trailers or it is built into the walls of the hangars where the aircraft spent the time between sorties; indeed the entire hangar itself may well have to be air-conditioned. To make things worse still, once the aircraft reach operational status many assurances tend to go up in smoke. For example, the F-15 needs fewer hours of maintenance work per hour of flight than its predecessor, the F-4, did. However, this advantage is canceled out by the fact that the spare parts needed to keep it flying during its operational lifetime cost three times as much.[33] The B-2 is said to require 119 hours of maintenance per hour of flight vis-à-vis 60 and 53 for the older B-1B and the B-52H, respectively; operating costs are in proportion.[34] One reason for this is that, to protect the skin that endows it with its stealth properties, the B-2 must be stored and taken care of in air-conditioned hangars large enough to take its 172-foot wingspan.[35] In most cases this means that the aircraft can only be operated from bases in the United States, thousands of miles from the targets.

Before it was canceled, the F-22 provided another example of the way things work. Originally it was meant to replace America's aging fleet of F-15s. As the numbers on order were reduced and the decision was made to extend the latter's life, the F-22 turned out to be the only U.S. warplane that did not have the capability of exchanging data with other types of warplanes, greatly degrading its combat performance. After all, it had been designed to replace older warplanes, not to operate with them! That problem alone was estimated to require $8 billion—$43 million per aircraft—to fix. Another problem was the canopy. Originally touted as providing the pilot with the best optics in aviation history, it turned out to lose its transparency so that it must be replaced almost three times as often as the manufacturer had hoped.[36] Depending on how one calculates, flying the F-22 costs close to $50,000 an hour. On a per mission basis the cost is almost five times as high as that of an F-15, and 16 times that of an F-16.[37] But why go into this kind of detail? As a look at international digests will show, so expensive has airpower become that few countries can afford any amount of it and only one is still desperately trying to run it in all its forms.

Along with the constraints that nuclear proliferation has imposed, the declining order of battle has created a situation where many elements of airpower are very far from constituting the "dominant factor" in war. Instead, they seem to be in the last stages of turning themselves into white elephants if indeed that has not happened already. This is all the more so because of the appearance of competitors, such as ballistic missiles and earth-circling satellites on one hand and drones on the other.

CHAPTER 11

MISSILES, SATELLITES, AND DRONES

Since the Soviet Union never built nearly enough intercontinental bombers to match the capabilities of SAC, and since the latter's importance started declining from the mid-1960s on, it might well be said that, of all the arms races that took place between the superpowers during the Cold War, the missile race was the only one that mattered.[1] It is true that, especially during the early years, not every feat carried out with the aid of missiles was essential for military purposes. Some, notably the American quest to put a man on the moon, were almost entirely irrelevant to them. Still the missiles came to stand as the very symbol of that conflict. Comparisons between the orders of battle of both sides regularly carried pictures of little bullet-like devices, which, on paper, looked harmless enough.

The basic principles of ballistic missiles have been known ever since the Chinese invented firecrackers not long after 1200 B.C. In 1792 primitive rockets were employed by Tipu Sultan, of the kingdom of Mysore in India, against the troops of the British East India Company. During the early nineteenth century, some small ones, known as Congreves after their British inventor, William Congreve, were actually used on a few occasions. The line in America's national anthem, "the rockets' red glare," refers to these devices. Rockets, however, were insufficiently accurate to take the place of artillery. Serious work on larger ones, capable of reaching greater altitudes and of carrying payloads over longer ranges, only got under way during the 1920s. The work took place mainly in Britain, Germany, and the United States, where the physicist Robert Goddard launched several of these contraptions between 1926 and 1940. Not by accident these were the same countries where jets were developed; after all, except insofar as rocket-powered craft carry their own supply of oxygen whereas jets obtain theirs from the atmosphere, the underlying principles are similar. Experimental rockets were also launched in the Soviet Union, but the arrest in 1938 of the chief engineer terminated the project for the time being.

By the early 1930s, the Germans were pulling ahead. Their principal researcher was Wernher von Braun, whom we have already met. Von Braun was an aristocrat whose original goal was to make possible space travel, or so he always claimed. However, since the necessary funds, raw materials, and research facilities could only come from the German Army, he threw himself into working for it heart and soul. The army in turn was looking for a way to circumvent the limits imposed on it by the Treaty of Versailles, which prohibited long-range artillery. Later, after Hitler had abolished those limits, it became a question of competing with Goering and the Luftwaffe. The ultimate product was the A-4, a rocket that could carry a 2,200-pound warhead to a distance of 190 miles. To do so it had to reach an altitude of over 50 miles, far higher than any aircraft had ever flown. This fact made it into the first weapon that passed through space on its way to target.

Starting in September 1944, about 3,000 of the missiles were launched at targets in Western Europe and Britain. Since they traveled at several times the speed of sound—the noise of their arrival actually came *after* they had hit their targets—there was no advance warning whatsoever. The one way to defend against them was by bombing the launching sites, which, however, were soon redesigned so as to make them mobile and easy to camouflage. In the end they could be launched from almost anywhere. The preferred locations were forest clearings or even the parks of country houses. Preparations for the flight were made under the cover of trees. Next, as soon as the launch was over, that cover would be resumed. Fortunately for the Allies, the missiles were none too reliable so that quite a few of them never even came close to performing as planned. Gyroscopically guided, they were also extremely inaccurate. On the average, each launch only led to less than one person being killed. Indeed it is estimated that the number of slave laborers who died building them was far greater than the number of people actually killed by the missiles. The impact on Allied morale was considerable, but one can only concur with the historian who argues that, considered in terms of cost/benefit, they represented an extremely wasteful effort.[2]

For all its shortcomings, nobody doubted that the V-2 pointed the way to the future. The relevant technologies having been studied and mastered, development went on throughout the 1950s. Power, reliability, and range all increased. By the last years of the decade the first ICBMs, missiles with an intercontinental range, were tested in the United States and the Soviet Union. As we saw, different countries had different ideas as to which organizations should be in charge of the R & D process on the one hand and of operations on the other. Though the missiles ultimately acquired a range as long as, or longer than, that of any combat aircraft, there was no reason why the air force should necessarily be in charge.

To be sure, accuracy, measured in terms of CEP (circular error probability, that is, the probability that 50 percent of the missiles would land within so-and-so many feet from their target), also improved during the 1950s and continued to do so thereafter. On the one hand, launching a missile from one side of the planet to the other merely in order to deliver a few tons' worth of explosive still did not make sense. On the other, it took but little foresight to understand that missiles would end up by being married to the smaller, lighter nuclear warheads then being developed. It might also be possible to make them much more accurate; in that case, wrote our old acquaintance Hugh Trenchard as early as 1946, "the Air Force as we know it today [would become] as obsolete as battleships . . . are today."[3]

Shortly after Trenchard's death in 1956, his vision started turning into reality. Up until this time bombers still enjoyed some advantages over missiles. Among them were a much larger payload needed to carry the early, large, and heavy atom- and hydrogen bombs; greater reliability; and, most important of all, the much shorter time needed from alert to launch. A squadron of B-47s or B-52s on full alert could take off within 15 minutes of being ordered to do so. With radar providing warning, that was fast enough to escape any ICBMs coming from the other side of the world (though not fast enough to avoid missiles launched from enemy submarines near the coast); those on airborne patrol did not even need that much. The case of first-generation ICBMs was very different. Like the V-2, on which they were ultimately based, they were liquid fueled and could not be kept in a state of permanent readiness. The fuel, which was highly corrosive, would eat through the tanks, and its weight would warp the missile's thin fuselage and render it unusable.

By the late 1950s the problem was well on its way to being solved; as so often was the case, the first to solve it were the Americans. Solid fuel, which is combusted gradually by means of a process known as deflagration, enabled designers to do away with most of the complexities associated with liquid fuel engines such as pumps, tubes, and controls. Essentially it provided very powerful thrust at relatively low cost. The resulting Minuteman missiles could be kept in a permanent state of readiness, and indeed the manufacturer was said to guarantee their performance for a period of ten years. Once the order to do so had been received, they could be launched almost immediately. Requiring as it did very little pre-launch handling also allowed the Minuteman to be mounted in hardened, widely dispersed, underground silos, a method that made it invulnerable to anything short of a direct nuclear hit. Given the much less developed state of their civilian industry, especially that which dealt with plastic products, the Soviets found it hard to match these achievements. Although, from about 1970 on, they too began mounting their missiles in silos, most of them still used liquid fuel. Apparently they were also less accurate, thus forcing the Soviets to focus on larger boosters capable of carrying larger warheads.[4]

To be sure, the achievement of nuclear parity, which seems to have taken place around 1969–70, did not mark the end of the missile race. Much of it was driven not by strategy—that is, by what was required—but by advancing technology—that is, by what was actually or potentially possible. As always, special interests played their part. Had it been up to the air force, the number of America's ICBMs would have stabilized not at 1,054, as eventually happened, but at over three times that figure—if, indeed, it would have been capped at all.[5] As new onboard computers were developed, missiles kept becoming more accurate. Late in the 1960s, the same computers also enabled each missile to carry first several warheads (MRVs, for multiple reentry vehicles) and then several independent ones (MIRVs, for multiple independently targetable reentry vehicles). By the 1980s one Soviet missile, the dreaded SS-18, could carry no fewer than ten MIRVs, each with an estimated yield of just under a megaton. Its American equivalent, the MX Peacemaker, could deliver a similar number of smaller warheads but do so more accurately.[6] Thus a single missile, launched from thousands of miles away, could annihilate practically any country on earth. Coming on top of their ICBMs, both sides also had their SLBMs. The most powerful of the breed was the Trident, carried aboard submarines of the same class, and was as powerful as its land-based opposite numbers.

Though medium- and intermediate-range missiles have been deployed by several nations, as long as they were only armed with conventional warheads, their bang stood in no relation to their buck. The lucky hit apart, they could be of little more than nuisance value. To really make a difference these missiles had to be available in very large numbers, an enormously expensive proposition. Alternatively they had to be armed either with nuclear warheads or with chemical and biological ones. Even so, since missiles cannot loiter over a target but must drop straight on it, as platforms for delivering the latter two types they are far from ideal. One way or another, manned aircraft still retained some important advantages. Among them were the ability to carry considerably greater payloads, flexibility, and reusability. This explains why, even as ICBMs were slowly replacing manned bombers, fighter-bombers continued to be produced and deployed, albeit in steadily declining numbers. Yet the more time passed, the less inclined were countries such as India and Pakistan to rely on manned aircraft to carry their nuclear weapons, and the more they focused on developing ballistic missiles instead. More recently the same has applied to North Korea and Iran, both of which have been able to build and deploy medium-range missiles even though neither is exactly famous for its well-developed aviation industry.

Almost from the beginning, plans, some of them grounded solely in the overheated imaginations of generals and journalists, were made to counter ballistic missiles by developing antiballistic missile (ABM) systems.[7] However, the high hypersonic speed of ICBMs made the task a formidable one indeed. Nor are countermeasures hard to think of. The simplest tactic would be to swamp the defense with more missiles than it can cope with. Others are decoys, multiple warheads, and electronic warfare aimed at disrupting the defenders' tracking and targeting system. As a result, few of these schemes ever produced more than a handful of prototypes. Of those that were produced and tested, some were so inaccurate that they depended on megaton-sized warheads to do their deadly work, thus posing almost as great a hazard to their owners as to the attackers. Interest in the subject was revived by the Reagan administration in the 1980s. The outcome was much research and development as well as some limited deployment of defensive missiles by the United States, Russia, and Israel. Other countries such as India and Japan have expressed interest in such missiles, purchased them, and performed some tests.[8] Yet so complex and so expensive are the systems in question that it is uncertain whether any of them has been, or even can be, tested under realistic conditions—for example, against multiple incoming warheads instead of just one. Not to mention the fact that the most recent Russian ICBM, the RT-2UTTKh Topol, is said to carry a maneuverable reentry vehicle (MARV) specifically designed to evade an ABM and sufficiently hardened to withstand the electromagnetic pulse (EMP) generated by a nuclear explosion taking place near it.[9]

Judging by publicly available sources, as of 2010 no country possessed a system capable of providing its cities with 1,000 percent protection against a determined attack. Indeed those responsible for developing the Israeli system fully admit that fact.[10] Given what we know about the operation of Murphy's Law, the chance of its being made available appears slim indeed; early in the year yet another American test ended in failure owing to problems with radar.[11] Nevertheless, in a world where a single missile or bomb can do almost inconceivable damage as well as lead to escalation, such protection would be the only kind worth having. Some analysts argue that, by creating the illusion of security and thus perhaps encouraging leaders to take unwarranted risks, a deployed system is worse than a nonexistent one. Instead of generating stability, the proclaimed goal, it would lead to the opposite.[12]

Whereas ballistic missiles of all types had to pass *through* space on their way from launching site to target, they did not make use *of* space. The first to work out the detailed mathematics of artificial satellites was a Russian scientist, Konstantin Tsiolkovsky, in 1903. He was something of a mystic, and his goal was to make possible space travel, the colonization of other planets, and prepare the ground for a more perfect race of men who would live forever. In the 1940s, the possibility of using satellites for communication purposes by relaying and amplifying radio waves began to be discussed. A landmark of sorts was presented by a 1946 RAND study, *Preliminary Design of an Experimental World-Circling Spaceship*. A decade later, given how closed the Soviet Union was to ordinary espionage, the possibility of launching a satellite for reconnaissance purposes was on the mind of the Eisenhower administration. Such a device might take the place of reconnaissance aircraft, which were becoming increasingly vulnerable; in the end, though, it was the Soviets who put the first one into orbit in October 1957.

The Soviet achievement stunned and amazed the world. Supposedly it revealed a "missile gap" that politicians, including our friend Stuart Symington, now a senator, did what they could to exploit in order to get to the White House; in the end, it was Kennedy who won the race. Yet it was not long before the Americans recovered their nerve. The first reconnaissance satellites went into orbit in 1961. They made it possible to dispense with

U-2 overflights of the Soviet Union even though that and similar aircraft continued to violate the airspace of many other countries, friends and enemies alike, almost as a matter of course. During the next decades satellites took on a vast number of military uses. Chief among them are surveillance (optical, infrared, magnetic, gravity-centered, radar-based, and electronic), communication, mapping, and weather prediction. The development during the 1990s of the global positioning system (GPS) made it possible to add navigation to the list. In each of these critically important fields, the more sophisticated, the more capable, and the more reliable the satellites grew, the stronger the temptation to allow older methods and skills to go by the board. If only for that reason, over time dependence on them steadily increased.

As of the second decade of the twenty-first century, about the one military use of space that has *not* yet been tried is to station weapons in it. Such weapons might be used either against other nations' space and air assets or against targets on the surface of the earth. Whether or not the former would be worth having is subject to a hot debate that may still lead to the "weaponization" of space; indeed the launching in April 2010 by the USAF of the robotic X-37 B may well present a giant step in that direction.[13] Something known as a fractional orbit bombardment system (FOBS) was developed by the Soviet Union during the 1960s. It was, however, never tested while carrying a live hydrogen bomb. Such a bomb, orbiting in space, would have had the advantage that the time from warning to impact would be considerably shortened. Too, an attack, instead of being limited to the established paths between two nations, might be launched from any direction of the compass. Nevertheless, deploying FOBS was prohibited by the second Strategic Arms Limitation Treaty (SALT), of 1979. Since ballistic missiles already have the ability to destroy practically any point on earth from any other, perhaps its loss was not too keenly felt.

Looking back, one can observe the impact of space on the military extending from the top down. First to be affected was strategic nuclear warfare or, rather, since no such warfare has taken place so far, preparations for it. Often satellites provided the only means of mapping a country with sufficient accuracy or else for providing early warning that an enemy missile had been launched and was on its way. As time went on lesser operations were drawn inside the orbit, so to speak. Whereas, in 1977, Israel's prime minister Yitzhak Rabin claimed that his country did not need satellites,[14] since then the country has launched several of them and is becoming more dependent on them with each passing day. Ultimately every soldier and every bomb received his or its own satellite-based GPS, the former for orientation and navigation and the latter for accurate delivery to target.

To put the argument the other way around, the more modern any armed force, and the larger the geographic area over which it operates, the more dependent it is on satellites. As a result, the greatest single user of all is said to be the U.S. Navy. Deprived of their space assets, the armed forces of modern nations would be rendered blind, deaf, and mute. Communications, logistics, and even day-to-day administration would all be disrupted. At best, the outcome would be a somewhat chaotic period of adjustment during which many kinds of capabilities would be badly degraded. At worst a country could be exposed to what some analysts called a "space Pearl Harbor," an all-out attack delivered without warning.[15] The term was used in a 2001 report on space warfare said to have been personally drafted by Donald Rumsfeld, President George W. Bush's secretary of defense.[16]

Worldwide, the value of space-based equipment of every kind is estimated at close to a trillion dollars. Hardly a week passes without some new satellites being launched, whether to replace existing ones or to carry out new functions. Ten countries—Russia, the United States, France, Japan, China, Britain, India, Israel, Ukraine, and Iran—have sent them into space aboard their own missiles. Dozens of others have done the same by borrowing other people's launch vehicles. An extensive breakdown of the equipment in question would make its effects felt rapidly and across a huge spectrum of day-to-day activities. Satellite phones would no longer work; TV and radio broadcasts would cease to reach viewers. Parts of the Internet would cease to function and credit cards would turn into worthless pieces of plastic. Transportation networks would break down, ships and aircraft would find themselves forced to rely on older methods for accurate navigation, and so much more as to boggle the mind. In civilian as in military life, a piecemeal attack carried out over a relatively long period would create serious problems as now this asset, now another, dropped out of use. A comprehensive one, carefully planned to target the most critical satellites and simultaneously executed to knock out or neutralize as many of them as possible, might result in something very close to social and economic collapse.

What kind of weapons might serve to attack another nation's space-based assets?[17] If the objective were to deliver a single knockout blow, then the best method would be to explode one or more hydrogen bombs high over the earth. The resulting EMP would incapacitate any satellite that has not been especially hardened to resist it. However, such an attack would be indiscriminate. Not only would it be impossible to target the assets of any specific adversary, but friendly satellites, unless carefully hardened and protected in advance, would suffer just as well. Another possibility would be to physically shoot down or destroy individual satellites. That might be done either from the ground or from some orbiting space vehicle. Two countries, the United States and China, are known to have developed the technologies needed to do so. The United States has tested an anti-satellite missile that can be launched from an F-15. Later the program was canceled, but one never knows if some missiles are not being kept in storage somewhere. In 2008 China generated much publicity by successfully testing a ground-to-space missile.[18] The Soviet Union long ago tried to develop a hunter-killer satellite capable of blowing others to pieces, but in 1983 these efforts were suspended.[19] Whether some kind of alternative has been developed since is not known.

A third possibility would be to use some sort of electromagnetic attack. Powerful radio waves might disrupt a satellite's electronics; a laser or particle beam might blind it or destroy it. In principle such an attack might be launched either from space—that is, from a "non-kinetic" killer satellite—or from the ground. The former has the advantage that no power would be wasted trying to penetrate the earth's atmosphere, the latter that the facilities for generating the pulse would not be limited in bulk and weight. Indeed one of the more interesting questions surrounding space-based weapons of every kind has always been where the necessary energy is to come from; aiming space-based lasers and similar weapons from one unstable spacecraft at another would also represent a major technical problem.

Whatever the technology, so far the same fear of escalation that prevented U.S. and Soviet warships from shooting at each other during the Cold War has prevented it from being used in real-life interstate armed conflict. Considering their past behavior, there is good reason to expect that the same will be true of other powers, such as China and India, whose presence in space is growing. But it is too early to heave a sigh of relief. ASAT (anti-satellite) missiles and killer satellites are probably too complex and expensive to be secretly built and operated by non-state actors. However, the same may not be true of some of the above-listed electromagnetic weapons. As present-day international law goes, such actors' use of such weapons would be akin to terrorism or piracy. This is certainly a scenario worth thinking about and, perhaps, taking some precautions against. On the other hand, clearly there are limits to what can be done. Given the large number of satellites orbiting the earth, any attack by a non-state actor will almost certainly be a piecemeal one. The outcome would not be a sudden and complete collapse, but merely a more or less serious, more or less temporary, degradation of existing capabilities.

As already mentioned, it is possible to imagine counter-countermeasures. Physical and electronic hardening apart, satellites can be made stealthy just as aircraft can, making them much harder to track. A country concerned about the survivability of its space assets might design those assets in such a way as to enable them to take over from each other if necessary. Miniaturization, which makes satellites cheaper, would be a step in that direction, enabling them to be put into orbit and operate in clusters. The same country could also develop the means to replace its satellites quickly. Doing so might involve simple things such as having a supply of satellites and missiles ready at hand. It might, however, also mean building some kind of reliable, instantly usable, reusable craft for putting new satellites into orbit as well as accessing old ones that are defective, retrieving them, and perhaps repairing them. Three decades ago, the space shuttle was supposed to provide precisely such a capability. However, it has notoriously failed to serve its purpose; promoters of space warfare would argue that a replacement is long overdue.

How does all this affect the subject in which we are interested, airpower? In many ways, space power is the natural continuation of airpower, and it is scarcely an accident that the same people and organizations are often put in charge of both. Here and there attempts to entrust the development of ballistic missiles to other organizations, such as the artillery arm, had disastrous consequences because those organizations were not accustomed to working with the light materials and very fine tolerances required. Yet this coin also has an obverse side. Already now, high in outer space, a number of critically important missions that used to be carried out by aircraft—if, indeed, they were capable of being carried out at all—are being performed by satellites instead. With each passing year, the number of countries that put them into orbit and use them for this purpose or that is growing. One interesting outcome of this is the change in career tracks. Down to the mid-1990s only pilots could expect to rise to the top of the air force hierarchy. Since then, slowly but steadily, they are being joined by officers who made their mark on the space side. Things seem to work as the old adage says: If you can't lick 'em, join 'em.

Closer to the surface of the earth, a somewhat similar process is underway. The first attempts to build robotic, pilotless aircraft were made during World War I. British inventors hoped to use them to fight Zeppelins; not having human pilots, they should have been able to climb faster and rise higher than manned aircraft could. They could also serve as targets for pilots to practice on. American inventors, the most important one of whom was Charles Kettering, later head of General Motors, built a primitive cruise missile designed to strike ground targets. Powered by a 40-horsepower engine, it was a forerunner of the World War II German V-1. In 1925, the ubiquitous Trenchard had a gyroscopically operated autopilot mounted into a small monoplane of the period. The ensuing contraption, code-named Larynx, could be flown both from shipboard and from the ground.

It was intended for use against shipping, and experiments were also made toward employing it to bomb rebellious villages in Iraq. However, the technical means of the day did not permit reasonable accuracy to be achieved. In 1936, after many ups and downs, the project was abandoned.[20]

The next ones to try were the Germans, this time with some success. Just as the army had developed the V-2 in order to compete with the Luftwaffe, so the Luftwaffe, starting much later, developed the V-1 specifically to compete with the army. It was powered by a pulse jet, a kind of engine in which the fuel, instead of being continuously fed into the combustion chamber, enters it in sequential pulses. The engine gave the V-1 a speed of about 400 miles per hour and a range of 150 miles. The warhead had a weight of a little under a ton. Like some of its predecessors, the V-1 was kept on course by an autopilot. Range was determined simply by counting the number of revolutions of a small propeller fixed to the nose, after which the fuel supply was cut off and the missile dived toward the ground.

The missile was so inaccurate that it was hardly capable of hitting a target smaller than a large city. To remedy that problem it was proposed to develop a manned version intended for suicide missions, but Hitler did not like the idea, and by the time he finally gave his approval it was too late.[21] Since the buzz bomb, as the Allies called it after the characteristic sound it produced, was relatively slow, it could be engaged by ground-based antiaircraft defenses and fighters just as ordinary aircraft could. Some missiles were shot down, others made to change course when a fighter, gingerly flying on a parallel course, used its wing to tilt them on their side. The V-1's greatest advantages were its simple construction and low cost—just 3,500 Reichsmarks ($900) per machine. Instead of an expensive-to-produce and dangerous-to-handle mixture of ethanol and oxygen, the fuel it consumed consisted of simple kerosene. From June 1944 until the end of the war in May 1945, some 8,000 were launched, killing 1.34 people on the average.[22] Though less spectacular than the V-2, compared with the latter it was a bargain.

During the 1950s both the United States and the Soviet Union developed cruise missiles, and some of them reached operational status. On the

U.S. side, work on them ceased after they were overtaken by the much faster, hence harder-to-shoot-down, ICBMs. On the Soviet one, it led to various models intended to be launched from the air or the sea so as to take care of U.S. carrier task forces. Thus the P-5 Pyatyorka (Fiver) was estimated to be capable of a speed of about 0.9 Mach and a range of up to 600 miles. To make up for their relative inaccuracy (CEP was probably around two miles), these missiles carried 200- and 350-kiloton nuclear warheads.[23] The real turning point came in the 1970s with the introduction of TERCOM, for terrain contour matching, a navigation system that made use of an on-board radar and computer to achieve much greater accuracy. As it happened, lighter, composite materials and much smaller, more economical jet engines became available at about the same time; this "confluence of technologies" made possible an entire new generation of cruise missiles.[24] Some were slung underneath heavy bombers, thus extending their range and their operational life. Others were designed to be launched from ground vehicles, or from ships, or submarines, in which case they required different guidance systems because TERCOM will not work over water.

Compared with manned aircraft, cruise missiles have both disadvantages and advantages. Their main disadvantage is their lack of reusability, which increases cost. Another was inflexibility, which made it impossible to switch them from one target to another, though the substitution of GPS for TERCOM during the 1990s seems to have solved that problem.[25] While cruise missiles are accurate enough to be used against ships at sea, it is not clear whether they can hit moving targets on land. Their main advantage is their small size, which makes them easy to disperse and camouflage. A second-strike force made up of mobile devices of this kind would be hard to detect and destroy. To this must be added their ability to fly very low, which makes them difficult to intercept. Should one of the robotic aircraft crash or be shot down, it is unnecessary to worry about the pilot. Rescue operations, which are often among the most demanding of all, can be dispensed with. Above all, cruise missiles were and are comparatively simple and cheap, so that many countries are able to produce them. It has been claimed that, given the necessary know-how, a fairly effective device could be built in a garage at the cost of $10,000 or so.[26]

Like many types of aircraft and ballistic missiles, originally cruise missiles were designed to deliver nuclear weapons to target. Like those types of aircraft and ballistic missiles, not once have they been used on that mission. Carrying conventional warheads, cruise missiles *have* been used against targets that posed high risks, such as anti-aircraft defenses, and against those hard to hit, such as bunkers located at the heart of cities. Another use has been against real or suspected terrorist sites in countries such as Afghanistan and Sudan. Apparently one reason why they were preferred was the belief that a robotic strike maintained a lower profile, and would give rise to fewer diplomatic complications, than one carried out by manned aircraft. Whatever the mission, it is clear that cruise missiles are already taking the place of their older rivals. Given how fantastically expensive the latter have become, one can only expect that process to continue.

Whereas cruise missiles carry their own navigation equipment, drones are controlled by radio from the ground (or from shipboard, or from another aircraft) as model aircraft are. The U.S. Army alone is said to have purchased 15,000 of them during World War II, using them as targets to help train pilots and anti-aircraft gunners; a few are still around and command high prices. On both sides of the iron curtain, the 1950s saw the development of a large number of drones of this kind. Some were intended as targets, others as decoys to mislead enemy radar. Later their successful performance in those missions led to their development as platforms for carrying all kinds of reconnaissance equipment. Drones were used in Vietnam, without great success as we shall see later on.

It was in 1982, during the Israeli invasion of Lebanon, that drones really came into their own. Originally the Israelis had hoped to use their drones in order to locate their enemies on the ground. Yet what left much of the military world gaping was their use against the Syrian SAM batteries in the Beqa Valley. First, the drones flew over the area for months to pinpoint the missile batteries and learn as much as possible about them. Next, before the actual attack, other remotely piloted vehicles (RPVs) were sent out as decoys. They made the Syrians switch on their radar sets, thus revealing the frequencies on which they operated. Once this had been done, other drones, or perhaps they were the same ones, were sent to home in on those sets and destroy them. Missile-carrying aircraft, helicopters equipped for electronic warfare, and long-range artillery may also have taken part in the operation. The total number of sorties is said to have been just 125, with 56 more in support. Sixty more sorties had been planned but were canceled because things went better than expected. Though both the Israeli Air Force commander, General David Ivri, and the Syrian minister of defense, Mustafa Tlas, have written accounts of the battle, details are scarce.[27] On the Israeli side some of those available in the public domain are probably part of a disinformation campaign.

Since then the use of RPVs, as well as that of the larger unmanned airborne vehicles (UAVs), has exploded. Hundreds of different types have been produced by various countries, including some, such as Iran, which are incapable of producing a modern manned combat aircraft and will almost certainly never do so. Both RPVs and UAVs are designated by incomprehensible combinations of letters and numbers followed by some short, easy-to-remember name, usually of some animal or bird. Some are tiny, intended to be carried on a jeep or even on the back of an individual infantryman so as to help him find out what is happening on the other side of the nearby hill. Most are the size of large-model aircraft with a wingspan of, say, 15 or 25 feet. A few are the size of small-passenger aircraft and, as the name Global Hawk, for example, implies, intended for very long-range missions.[28]

Three decades after Lebanon, probably the most important mission of all remains intelligence (photo, video, infrared, radar, electronic, and signals) gathering, a purpose for which UAVs have some advantages over both manned aircraft and satellites. Compared to the former, their radar signature is much smaller; some are even said to have achieved true stealth capabilities at much lower cost. Compared to the latter, they are able to fly closer to the earth's surface and can remain over the same area for a considerable time. Other frequently mentioned missions are communication, over-the-horizon identification, tracking and targeting, and electronic warfare such as anti-radar work. Some UAVs are used as targets; others, notably the American Predator, can carry and fire air-to-surface missiles, which effectively turns them into unmanned killing machines.

UAVs, especially the larger and more complex among them, are not cheap. One reason for this is that they pack some of the most sophisticated electronics in existence into a very small space, including computers, communications gear and the associated encryption equipment, every imaginable kind of sensor, and, more and more often, the systems needed to activate weapons too. The unit price of a Global Hawk is said to be $35 million, a figure that is more than trebled if development costs are included.[29] But not everything is painted in red ink. The infrastructure that UAVs need is much smaller and simpler, which is one reason why operating costs are said to be only about 5 percent of those of manned aircraft.[30] Some models are sufficiently small and cheap to be purchased and operated by nonstate organizations such as the Lebanese Hezbollah. Others are operated by industrial firms on behalf of governments that do not have what it takes.[31] Relatively low cost also means that, as technology advances and existing models become obsolete, UAVs are more easily replaceable than manned aircraft are. Finally, low cost means that the number of corporations that can build them is much larger.

As is the case with sophisticated video games, "flying" the largest and most sophisticated UAVs requires a very high level of training and skill. Some UAVs are so complex that more than one operator is needed to handle the workload, which of course makes things more complicated still. Yet in the end doing so is not nearly as demanding as piloting many kinds of conventional aircraft. Whereas concentration and good coordination are essential, qualities such as physical fitness and excellent eyesight are much less important. Training is carried out in a matter of months rather than of years.[32] The task itself may well be performed in air-conditioned rooms located hundreds if not thousands of miles away from the battlefield. For example, some U.S. Air Force UAVs operating in Iraq and Afghanistan are "flown" from a headquarters in the Nevada desert.

Since the factor most characteristic of war—that is, risk to life and limb—is absent, in many ways the job is the exact opposite of what pilots used to face and more like an ordinary nine-to-five one. Gone is the freedom, the sense of adventure and of being different from other people, that used to be among the main attractions of flying. Gone, too, is the physical stress. One drives to work, is admitted to the secure room, sits down, and relieves one's predecessor at the computerized controls. Those controls themselves are becoming so sophisticated that they carry out many tasks on their own, leaving the operators with little more than a supervisory function. Having completed one's shift, one drives home while picking up one's offspring from school or stopping at the supermarket on the way. Later that evening one sips a cocktail and complains to one's spouse about how hard it is to look—by television, of course—into the faces of people who, in a second or two, are going to be dead as a result of one's actions. Some UAVs are used not against the enemy but to guard bases at home, thus raising the question whether their operators deserve to be considered warriors at all or should be seen as some kind of policemen.

Some operators would much prefer to take off in "real aircraft," but others rather like the ongoing shift to unmanned ones. Most have never flown any other kind. The exception to this rule occurs in the U.S. Air Force, which for reasons of its own insists on only employing pilots, that is, officers. As a result, many are vastly overqualified for the job. One side effect of all this is that, whereas the percentage of females among military pilots of every sort has always been extremely low, among UAV "pilots" it is higher and growing. In Israel, a country that produces and operates some of the most sophisticated UAVs anywhere, the accident rate of female operators is said to be lower than that of their male colleagues.[33]

Some UAVs are launched by aircraft or else cooperate closely with them, as apparently was the case in Lebanon in 1982. The British are said to be developing software that will enable pilots to control two or more UAVs even as they fly their own machines.[34] Quite a number of others are used independently on missions that would previously have taken aircraft to execute, be they reconnaissance or shooting up terrorists. Overall, the best indicator of the direction in which things are moving is money. During the first decade of the twenty-first century, U.S. investment in UAVs is expected to be over three times as large as it was in the 1990s; in 2007–2013 alone $22 billion will be spent.[35] Whereas combat aircraft have been disappearing, UAVs are multiplying like the proverbial rabbits. Their operators are gaining recognition and being grouped into a separate career track; in the United States, they have even succeeded in getting flight pay.[36] On the border between India and Pakistan, both sides are even now using UAVs in the skirmishes between them. Whereas the loss of a manned aircraft could conceivably lead to nuclear escalation, by tacit agreement shooting down an unmanned one is considered acceptable.[37]

A standing joke among pilots is that no other guidance system can be produced so cheaply by unskilled labor; hence, they say, there will always be a demand for manned aircraft. In reality, things are different. In outer space as well as close to the surface of the earth, over both land and sea, on missions that do not consist of directly engaging the enemy as well as on a growing number of those that do so, the drones are coming.

CHAPTER 12

PAPER WARS

Whereas, until 1945, works on armed conflict had been one of the principal factors driving war in general and air war in particular, after that date they tended to become a substitute for it. The principal reason for this was the presence of the "dominant factor," discussed above. Another factor working in the same direction was the vast proliferation of institutions, both military and civilian, that devoted themselves to researching war, studying war, and teaching war.[1] Where the demand for texts exists, supply will surely follow.

Vast as it is, the literature in question is hard to categorize. For our purposes, it may be divided into three kinds. The first, and the one supposedly most relevant to actual war, is doctrine. In air forces as in armed forces in general, normally those responsible for producing doctrine are colonels and their immediate assistants, military or civilian, working for their superiors, the generals. As one air force intellectual with experience in the matter once put it to me, the generals arrive at certain "conclusions." Next, it is up to the colonels to justify those conclusions and flesh them out. Though the generals themselves hardly ever write doctrine, invariably it is over their signatures that it is issued. In theory, the readership consists of officers of all ranks. The objective is to help them develop a common vision concerning the way their country's armed services understand their mission and go about carrying it out. In practice, doctrine, with its frequent elaboration of the obvious, its tendency to split hairs (as in trying to define the difference between air superiority and air supremacy),[2] and dry, often very convoluted, language aimed at covering all possibilities, is hardly ever read by anybody at all. Yet this is not to say that it is not influential. Though few may actually be familiar with all the details, the basic concepts, propagated by a thousand means, are likely to be widely, if somewhat vaguely, understood.

Two other types of military writing must be mentioned here. The first is the kind one meets in specialized books and periodicals, military or academic. This kind is produced by serving and retired soldiers, defense officials, academics, and journalists. Except insofar as journalistic pieces tend to be more readable, the four are often almost interchangeable. Often their purpose, real or declared, is serious, namely to call attention to the fact that such and such a problem exists and/or to propose a solution for that problem. The second type is military fiction, including, in our case, fiction whose subject is air- and space power. It tends to be produced by members of the same groups with the occasional unlikely outsider thrown in. Its purpose, too, may be serious, namely to warn against possible future developments; most often, however, it is simply to sell and to entertain. Some of this material is made into movies or TV series, or else things work the other way around. Needless to say, a considerable degree of overlap among the three types exists. Partly this is because all three share the same objective, namely to provide a game plan for the future, partly because the same people are often involved. Needless to say, too, they do not exhaust all the different categories into which military literature may be divided.

In air warfare as in other kinds, doctrine, defined by NATO as "fundamental principles by which the military forces guide their actions in support of objectives,"[3] is a comparatively recent phenomenon. Even as late as the first decades of the twentieth century, armed forces had theories and regulations, but not doctrines. Theories dealt with fundamental principles. However, they were not tailored to the needs of specific countries, did not prescribe anything, and were not binding on anyone. Regulations, or instructions as they were sometimes called, did prescribe how things should be done and *were* binding up to a point. However, they only dealt with the lower, i.e., technical and tactical, aspects of war. For example, a discussion of "Posts of Officers and Non-commissioned Officers of a Company Acting Singly" or of "Formation of a Regiment of Five Squadrons in Column"[4] hardly counts as doctrine as NATO defines it. Not accidentally, neither of the two "prophets" of airpower discussed earlier in this volume, Douhet and Mitchell, produced doctrine; had they done so, then presumably they would have remained almost totally unknown. The former wrote theory, which differs from doctrine in that it attempts to go down to basic principles, and also tried to write fiction. The latter was mainly a polemicist, but of the more flamboyant and nonacademic kind. Focusing on airpower, it was only in 1922 that the RAF, as perhaps the most advanced air force of the time, issued its first doctrine manual, entitled CD-22 *Operations*.

This chapter will focus on what was eventually to become the most important air force of all, the American one. As already noted, the Army Air Forces first started looking for a doctrine in the late 1920s, and by the end of the following decade it was firmly committed to the one it had developed. The doctrine was written and taught by instructors at Maxwell whose names have long been forgotten; yet it was sufficiently detailed and sufficiently coherent to receive the ultimate accolade in the form of an acronym, HAPDB (for high-altitude precision daylight bombing), of its own. Some omitted the words "high altitude," putting in "strategic" instead.[5] Whatever the exact term, as early as 1940 the doctrine was behind the decision to develop the B-36, as yet without the jet engines, as America's first true intercontinental bomber. In 1943–45 it was applied on a huge scale. Whatever else the Army Air Forces did had to be seen in relation to it.

Since the so-called bomber mafia continued to dominate the newly established air force after 1945, it is not surprising that the fundamentals of doctrine remained largely unchanged. After all, America still remained a global island. Carriers and bases in foreign countries apart, the best way to reach the main enemy, the Soviet Union, was still the heavy long-range bomber. The bombers' main targets were still the "enemy's" (since there was no shooting war) principal concentrations of population and industry.

In the words of one historian, strategic bombing had become to the air force what the gospel was to Christianity.[6] It was not just doctrine, it was the organization's life and raison d'être. Nor did the appearance on the stage of nuclear weapons do much to alter the equation. To quote the conclusions of the Spaatz Board, appointed in September 1945 specifically in order to examine the question: "The atomic bomb does not at this time warrant a material change in our present conception of the employment, size, organization, and composition of the postwar Air Force. . . . The atomic bomb has not altered our basic concept of the strategic air offensive but has [merely] given us an additional weapon."[7]

Over time the details of the doctrine were modified to suit changing circumstances. Much greater emphasis was put on the need to prevent accidental or unauthorized war, a problem that became the subject of so vast a body of extremely detailed regulations that, at times, it came close to threatening the mission of warfighting itself. To minimize the possibility of a Soviet surprise attack, standing airborne patrols were introduced and went on until 1968, when they came to be seen as superfluous and were abolished. Daylight attacks were replaced by nighttime ones, high-altitude ones by low-level ones that, in the era of modern radar and surface-to-air missiles, supposedly had a better chance at "penetrating" enemy airspace and reaching their targets.[8] SAC's arsenal was expanded by the addition of standoff weapons and electronic warfare, leading to further changes in doctrine. No longer was it necessary for the bombers to fly directly over their targets in order to drop their loads; nor, with a force consisting of many hundreds of B-47s and B-52s, each carrying one or more thermonuclear weapons rated at between four and a half and nine megatons,[9] was there a need to lose sleep about possible inaccuracy or much room for claptrap concerning the desire to minimize civilian casualties.

Above all, President Eisenhower during his last months in office saw to it that the plans for operating the bombers should be coordinated with those being hatched by the army and navy in a unified scheme known as the SIOP, for Single Integrated Operations Plan.[10] From then on the SIOP has been continuously updated and a new one has been developed every few years. In theory the process was activated by the president and worked from the top down, passing through various layers in the air force hierarchy until it reached the actual planners. In reality few presidents knew or cared what it was all about.[11] Instead the planners, taking the existing SIOP as their starting point and poring over satellite images and other intelligence reports, were always trying to make their mark by identifying more targets and getting them into the list. This is one very important reason why, by the mid-1980s, the number of those targets had grown to a mind-boggling 16,000.[12]

Yet in view of the vast uncertainties involved and the horrific consequences that would follow if things did not go exactly as planned, the entire huge body of master directives, derivative directives and plans, and more detailed plans and operational plans (OPLANS) always contained a strong element of make-believe. This was recognized even by some of those in charge. The most important one was General George Butler. Before his appointment as commander of SAC in 1991 he had directed the planning process and thus probably knew more about it than anyone else. Later he said that "it was all Alice in Wonderland stuff . . . an almost unfathomable million lines of computer software code . . . typically reduced by military briefers to between 60 and 100 slides . . . presented in an hour or so to the handful of senior US officials . . . cleared to hear it."[13] So much for the hardware and procedures that could destroy the world in a few hours![14]

By the late 1960s, with thousands of missile-mounted warheads aimed at the Soviet Union from the land and from the sea, 24 hours a day, the role played by SAC's manned bombers in the national defense was clearly on the wane. Another factor behind the change in emphasis was the Vietnam War. Vietnam saw B-52s being used in action for the first time, albeit mainly in the interdiction role against lines of communication and not "strategically" against the kind of opponent for which they had been intended. The very fact that they could be diverted away from their original mission, that is, deterring the Soviet Union, to what was, in the final account, little but a side theater, speaks for itself. More important, the war, the domestic crisis that accompanied it, and its rather uncertain outcome left deep marks on the U.S. armed forces in general and the air force in particular. Paradoxically, though, it did not cause the forces to start thinking about how to win future conflicts of the same kind; instead, ostrich-like, they refocused their attention away from guerrilla warfare and toward large-scale conventional campaigning.

Another factor that helped the forces to put their heads in the sand was the October 1973 Arab-Israeli War. Coming just at the opportune moment, it seemed to show that large-scale conventional war was still possible even in the nuclear age. Tactical Air Command (TAC), which for decades had eked out a meager existence in the shadow of the strategic giant, began to re-emerge and spread its wings. A look at commanders' career patterns, always a good indicator of the way the wind is blowing, confirms this interpretation. After General John Ryan, who commanded SAC from 1964 to 1967, just one other SAC commander, General Larry Welch, made it to the position of air force chief of staff—and even he was originally a fighter jock who only spent less than one year at the head of SAC before being transferred to greener pastures. From this point on, not one chief of staff has started out as a bomber pilot.[15] Most other countries, of course, had hardly any bomber pilots left at all.

The outcome, a new doctrine known as AirLand Battle, was formally adopted in the early 1980s. It was the brainchild of the Air Land Force Application Agency, a joint outfit set up for the purpose by the air force's Tactical Air Command and the army's newly established TRADOC (Training and Doctrine Command). The result was *Field Manual 105*, or *FM 100-5* for short, a hefty tome whose purpose was to replace the earlier version of 1976. The best way to use tactical airpower, the new manual argued, was not at the front where the enemy is at his strongest and where he has concentrated most of his anti-aircraft defenses. Instead it should be employed further to the rear against Soviet communications and follow-up forces being rushed forward to reinforce the initial advance into West Germany. Rather than focusing on the enemy's front, a division commander was now supposed to look to a line 50 miles behind it. In the case of a corps commander the corresponding figure was 100 miles. The zone stretching back from that line to the front itself was the one in which tactical air, using the most up-to-date command, control, and communications technology to achieve full integration and synchronization with the ground forces, would show what it could do.

The term that described all this, AirLand Battle, was invented by TRADOC's second commander, General Donn Starry. Seen from the fliers' point of view, AirLand Battle had the advantage that it did not require them to provide direct battlefield support, a mission that many of them had regarded as anathema from World War I on. In fact, so much did the air force hate this particular task that even the aircraft designated for it, the slow but survivable A-10, was painted differently from the others. Under the new arrangement, not only would losses be less severe but the airmen's ever-present anxiety that the air force might again lose some of its independence to the organization of which it had originally been a part was assuaged.[16] Seen from the army's point of view, AirLand Battle was the next best thing to having a tactical air force of its own. Each service having received its pound of flesh, *FM 100-5* was presented with great fanfare as if it embraced some new and revolutionary concept. In fact, of course, it was merely a return to what the German general Walther Wever and his associates had advocated in the 1930s and what America's own tactical air forces had practiced, with growing success, in Italy and France in 1943–45.

Given that World War III never took place, whether the doctrine would have stood the rest of reality was never determined. The next important step in the evolution of U.S. airpower doctrine was taken six years later. Its initiator was an exceptional officer, John Warden. In 1985–86 Colonel Warden, with a fair but not stellar career behind him, studied at the National War College in Washington, D.C. His book, *The Air Campaign*, was published by the latter's press in 1988. Like Douhet, but with greater finality, the author ended up by suffering the consequences often reserved for those who rock the boat—after a spell at the Pentagon he was sent to Maxwell to command the Staff College and never made it to brigadier general. Nevertheless, he has been called "perhaps the single most influential individual in the development of concepts regarding the employment of air power in modern times."[17] As pundit-in-chief Edward Luttwak has put it, quite correctly, Warden "revived the art of strategically intelligent targeting," which, in an era when SAC prepared to destroy half the world with its megaton-sized weapons, had been put aside.[18] His work was arguably the most original done on the subject since Douhet's in the 1920s; this fact alone makes it worth discussing in some detail.

Ever since Douhet, the advocates of airpower had looked for a way in which their chosen instrument of power could win wars on their own or with minimum help from the army and the navy. The first mission of airpower had always been to achieve command of the air, that is, a situation in which friendly forces were able to fly whereas enemy ones were not; that accomplished, and leaving aside such fields as reconnaissance, transport, and so on, it could make its impact felt in one of three ways. It could shoot up enemy troops in what, in 1914–18, was known as "trench flying." It could focus on communications, reserve forces included, or it could go "strategic" by means of direct attacks on the enemy's supposedly "soft" civilian rear. All three methods were already in use during the last years of World War I. Since then, though aircraft had grown much more powerful, in principle at any rate they had remained just what they had been at that time.

Now, Warden wrote, developing technology had wrought some radical changes.[19] On the one hand, various kinds of sensors and satellite imagery made it possible to reconnoiter targets with a hitherto unimaginable degree of detail. On the other, the precision-guided munitions (PGMs) that began to be introduced during the second half of the 1970s made it possible to attack those targets without at the same time demolishing everything for miles around. In other words, and it is this point that represents the true core of Warden's argument, PGMs, being much more accurate than any previous air-to-ground weapons, had abolished, or at any rate could abolish, the distinction between strategic targets and tactical ones. To force an opponent to his knees it was no longer necessary to inflict large-scale devastation on his factories and cities, as Douhet, Trenchard, and the other "bomber generals" had argued and as the Germans, the British, and the Americans had tried to do or actually done during World War II. Instead, "strategic paralysis" could be achieved by means of precision attacks directed against his nerve centers.

Later, following up on this idea, Warden developed his model of the five rings. The first, or innermost, ring was the enemy commander and the apparatus through which he received reports and issued orders. The second was the logistic flow that provided the opposing armed forces with whatever they needed to exist and to fight—a flow that, under conditions of high-intensity modern warfare, might amount to as much as 1,500 tons per division per day. The third consisted of the vast network of roads, railways, pipelines, and similar installations over or through which the flow had to pass; in previous models, attacks on these two had been bundled together under the label "interdiction." The fourth ring consisted of the personnel who manned the enemy's zone of communications; the fifth, of his armed forces in the form of tanks, guns, vehicles, and troops.

Throughout history, armed forces could only tackle the enemy by moving from the outside in—to get at the soft fruit, it was necessary to break the hard outer shell first. By contrast modern air forces, relying on sensors and PGMs and the data links between them, could proceed the other way around. Starting from the inner ring, always thinking in terms not of individual targets but of the effect that destroying them might have on the enemy as a whole, they would proceed outward if doing so were necessary. However, with some luck doing so might *not* be necessary; the enemy, having been rendered deaf and blind by the loss of his command-and-control system, might collapse without further ado.

Both AirLand Battle and *The Air Campaign* were devised during the Cold War and very much as part of it. Both were directed primarily against the Soviet Union in Europe and meant to counter a possible Blitzkrieg-style offensive directed from East into West Germany.[20] Thus they ran straight into the fact that the Soviet Union was, after all, the second most powerful nuclear state on earth. Day and night, thousands of nuclear warheads of all sizes were ready to be dumped on that theater by every kind of artillery barrel; combat aircraft; short-, medium-, and intermediate-range ballistic missile; and cruise missile. Moreover, as if to save NATO from any illusions it might have, the Soviets had long doubted that war was as controllable, and escalation as preventable, as many Western analyses seemed to suggest.[21] In the United States itself there were those who shared this opinion.[22] Nevertheless both AirLand Battle and Warden resolutely closed their eyes to this issue. The former did so implicitly, by assuming that armed forces fielded by the two mightiest alliances in history, each one numbering hundreds of thousands of men, would be able to engage in World War II–like maneuvers deep into each other's rear, outflank each other, surround each other, and crush each other, without bringing the most powerful weapons of all into play. The latter did so explicitly.[23] In fact, by calling for attacks to be launched on the very heart of the enemy's battle array, which would normally be located in or near his capital city, he boxed himself into a corner where he was left with no other choice.

Yet both AirLand Battle and *The Air Campaign* formed only the tip of the iceberg. Hundreds, if not thousands, of books and articles sought to explain what war in general, and air war in particular, in the "Central Theater" might be like or raise suggestions as to how it might be won. Take *Race to the Swift*, one of the more thoughtful volumes of this kind. Written by a British general, Richard Simpkin, it carries a foreword by Donn Starry, the originator of AirLand Battle, himself. Starry in his foreword, and Simpkin in the text, explicitly say that their objective is to exclude nuclear weapons from the picture they are about to present. To the former, doing so is necessary because, given how powerful the Soviets' own nuclear forces had grown, a NATO threat to use such weapons in order to stop an attack on Western Europe was "no longer credible" (as if, since the early 1950s when the Soviet Union started building up its own nuclear arsenal, it had ever been). To the latter, it is possible because "many effects which 20 years ago would have called for a nuclear weapon can now be achieved with high explosive . . . conventional fire can now offer the same certainty of destruction as a nuclear strike."[24]

Having framed the picture he was about to paint in this manner, Simpkin proceeded to write as if Hiroshima and Nagasaki had never taken place. The way he saw it, modern military history, pushed along by technology,

German Zeppelins on maneuver, 1905.

Imperial War Museum, HU 68469.

A London street damaged by a German air raid, October 1915.

Imperial War Museum, H0 16

Most pilots died young: the funeral of Manfred von Richthofen.

Imperial War Museum, Q 10918

The V/1500 bomber came too late to be used against its intended target, Berlin.

Imperial War Museum, Q 66331

The new masters of the sea: HMS *Glorious*, 1935.

Imperial War Museum, FL 22991

Effective but expensive: German paratroopers floating over Crete, 1941.

Imperial War Museum, A 4154

Used for tank "plinking," the German Stuka could get down to 30 feet over the ground.

Author's collection

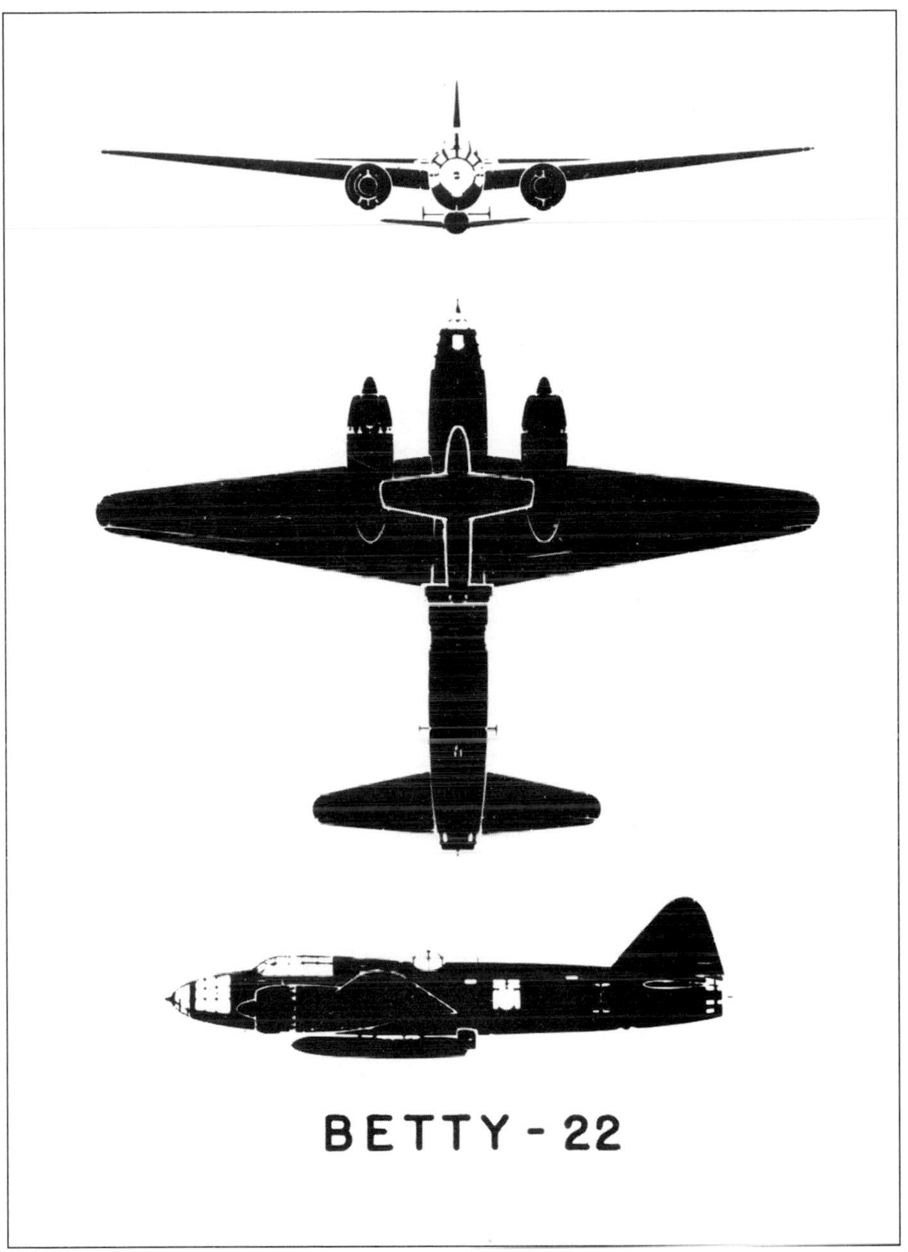

Recognition poster of a Japanese bomber with a Baka-type kamikaze aircraft slung underneath.

Imperial War Museum, HU 3515

B-29s, the first true strategic bombers, at Okinawa.

Photo courtesy of the defenseimagery.mil. Use of military images does not imply or constitute Department of Defense endorsement

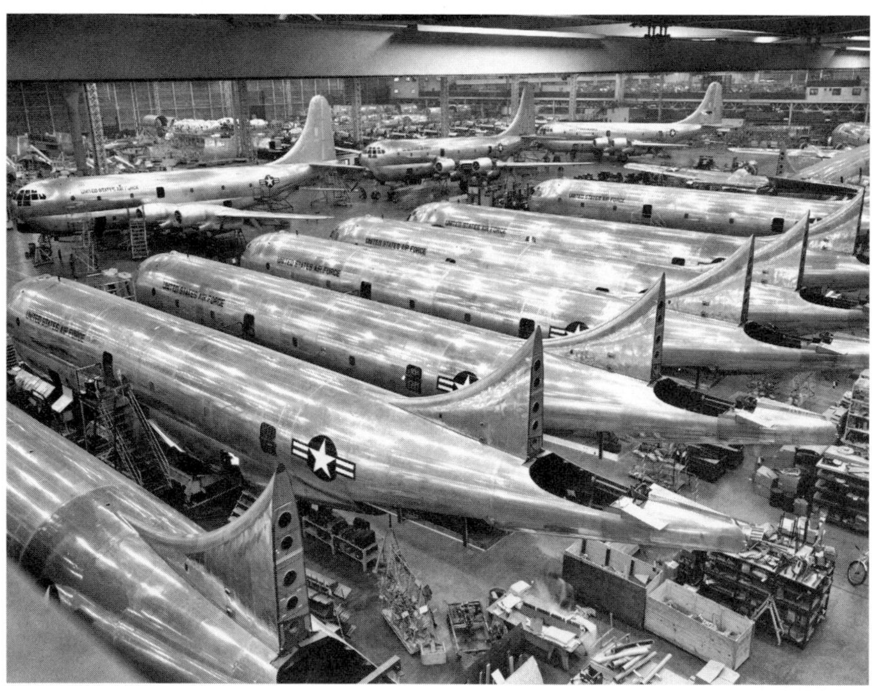

At peak in 1944, a military aircraft left U.S. assembly lines every four minutes.

Getty Images, RM 85903464

The *real* dominant factor: the explosion that demolished Nagasaki.

Photo courtesy of the defenseimagery.mil. Use of military images does not imply or constitute Department of Defense endorsement

It could have destroyed the world but did not; Soviet SS-15 ballistic missile on parade.

Photo courtesy of the defenseimagery.mil. Use of military images does not imply or constitute Department of Defense endorsement

Never used on the mission for which it was intended: a B-52 heavy bomber dropping its load.

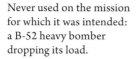

Photo courtesy of the defenseimagery.mil. Use of military images does not imply or constitute Department of Defense endorsement

The bomber nobody wanted: a B-70.

Photo courtesy of the defenseimagery.mil. Use of military images does not imply or constitute Department of Defense endorsement

The old anti-ballistic missile defenses failed; will the new ones work? Nike Zeus missiles on their launchers.

Getty Images, RM 85903750

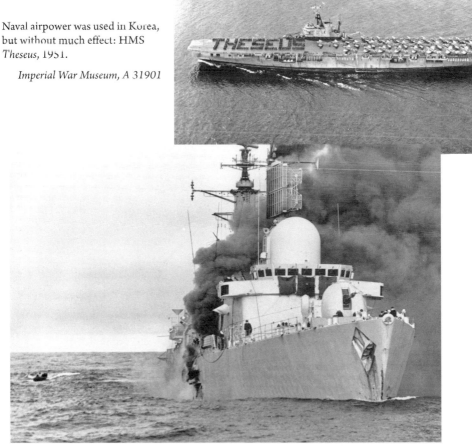

Naval airpower was used in Korea, but without much effect: HMS *Theseus*, 1951.

Imperial War Museum, A 31901

MS *Sheffield* on fire after being hit by an Exocet air-to-surface missile, 1982.

Imperial War Museum, FK D66

Versatile but vulnerable and expensive to run; U.S. Army Chinook helicopters.

Photo courtesy of the defenseimagery.mil. Use of military images does not imply or constitute Department of Defense endorsement

Celebrating the greatest victory of all: an Israeli Air Force fly-past, May 1968.

National Photo Collection, Israel, NPC

Use with caution: only when there is no enemy around.

Photo courtesy of the defenseimagery.mil. Use of military images does not imply or constitute Department of Defense endorsement

Air policing: a British Westland Wapiti over Mosul, 1932.

Imperial War Museum, HU 63062

Air mobility in Vietnam: over 5,000 helicopters were lost.

Getty Images, RM 70000563

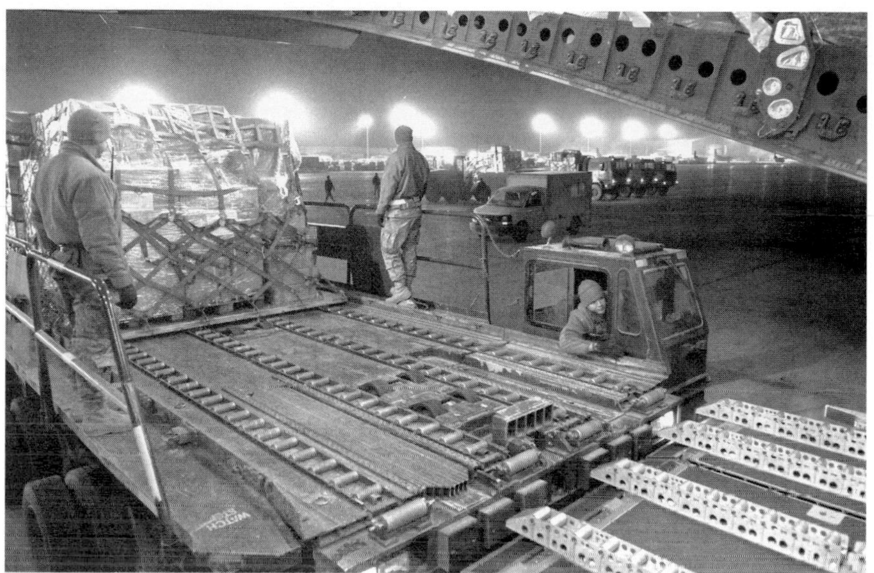

War amongst the people: A C-17 being unloaded in Afghanistan.

Photo courtesy of the defenseimagery.mil. Use of military images does not imply or constitute Department of Defense endorsement

Banned: no more F-16 strikes in Afghanistan.

Photo courtesy of the defenseimagery.mil. Use of military images does not imply or constitute Department of Defense endorsement

Capped: no more F-22 fighters.

Photo courtesy of the defenseimagery.mil. Use of military images does not imply or constitute Department of Defense endorsement

Taking over: a meteorological satellite.

Getty Images, RF 85784366

Taking over: an Israeli drone over Tel Aviv.

Courtesy of the Israeli Air Force

Taking over: a cruise missile being launched.

Getty Images, RF 57578009

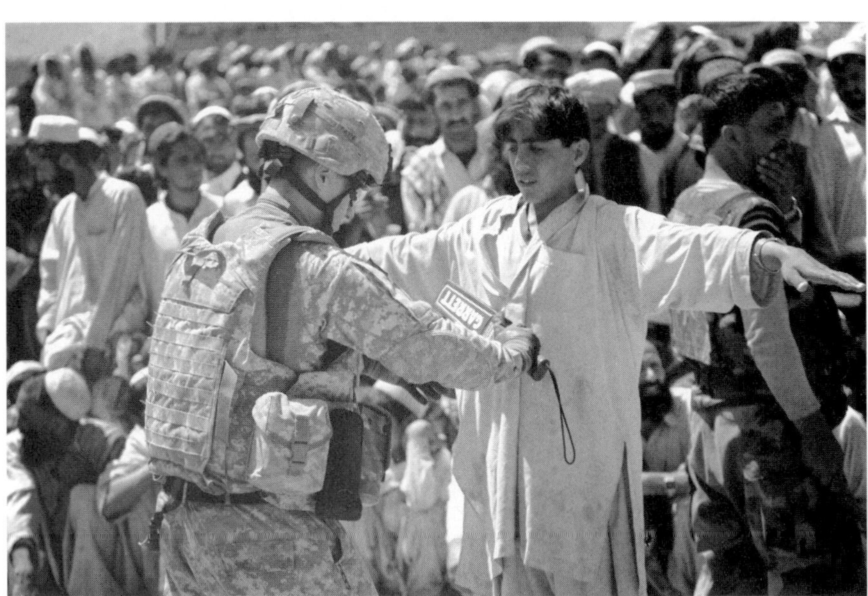

When it comes to deciding what is and is not a threat, airpower is often of no use at all.

Photo courtesy of the defenseimagery.mil. Use of military images does not imply or constitute Department of Defense endorsement

was advancing in leaps some 50 years apart. The next leap, which was just about to begin, would be brought about by the helicopter and the quantum jump in mobility that it made possible. Should war break out, following a Soviet attack needless to say, then first there would be mass attacks by the Red Air Force fighter-bombers and tactical missiles on targets not only at the front but also—this was presented as if it were some great and revolutionary innovation—deep into NATO's "soft" rear. Next, the Soviets might use their transport aircraft to fly entire brigades into that rear. The objective would be to seize key points such as bridges, ammunition dumps, fuel depots, and headquarters. Most important of all, they would occupy airfields on which more troops and more supplies could be landed later on. At that point Simpkin, with the "disaster" of Arnhem very much in mind,[25] seems to have felt some doubts as to whether all this was really feasible. Putting the brakes on his imagination, he wondered whether helicopters, which do not need airfields, would not be preferable.

Trying to cope with the Soviet offensive, NATO fighter-bombers would implement something known as "deep strike," a doctrine so similar to AirLand Battle that Simpkin found it difficult to keep the two apart.[26] Deep strike was promoted by the Supreme Allied Commander, Europe (SACEUR), the American general Bernard Rogers. It too was specifically designed to rely on conventional weapons while excluding the use of nuclear ones. If war did break out, and assuming that NATO's airfields would not immediately become the targets of tactical nuclear missiles that would render them unusable, then hundreds of NATO aircraft would take off. Flying very low to evade radar, they would fly out to strike targets deep in the Soviet rear. The objective was to slow down the Red Army's advance if not to bring it to a halt. Doing so, they would be supported by remotely piloted vehicles (RPVs), which were then at the beginning of their development; tactical ballistic missiles; long-range artillery; and intensive electronic warfare.[27]

None of this is to imply that Starry, Warden, Simpkin, Rogers, and legions of lesser Cold War warriors in the armed forces, defense departments, and academia of many countries, large and small, were not among the most knowledgeable experts of the time. It is, however, to suggest that what they were trying to do, namely find ways to use airpower to stop a large-scale Soviet invasion of Western Europe without necessarily blowing up the world, represented mission impossible. As we saw, some of them came very close to admitting as much. Rogers, as the most prominent of all, himself several times went on record as saying that operations in the "Central Theater" would develop on such a scale, and so fast, that the decision whether NATO should resort to nuclear weapons would have to be taken within days from the beginning of the conflict. If it were not done in order to stop the Soviets, then it would have to be done to prevent NATO's own nuclear weapons from being captured.[28] Use them or lose them; once the decision to use was made, presumably airpower, and indeed almost any other kind of power, would cease to matter.

The professionals' obvious inability to square the circle in "serious" literature, both that which was formally adopted as doctrine and that which was not, did not deter others from trying to do so in their own way. A favorite vehicle for the attempt was military fiction. Such works have a long history that goes back to the opening years of the nineteenth century. After the nuclear demolition of Hiroshima and Nagasaki, turning them out, reading them, and discussing them became something akin to a national obsession.[29] Most of those who wrote the books and magazine pieces were civilians, some of them very well-known. A few, such as Louis Ridenour, author of a play on the subject that was published in *Fortune*, were actually nuclear scientists who had lost confidence in their enterprise and were desperately trying to put the genie back into its bottle.

As one would expect, these people cared comparatively little about the precise way a nuclear war would develop in the air or anywhere else and had little to say about it. Instead novels such as Aldous Huxley's *Ape and Essence* (1948), Nevil Shute's *On the Beach* (1957), and Walter Miller's *A Canticle for Leibowitz* (1959) take us directly to the postwar world in an attempt to describe the collapse of organized society that a nuclear exchange would bring. The details differ—whereas the former two assume that some vestiges of civilization will be able to survive in the Southern Hemisphere, the last-named opens by describing a North American continent that has been bombed back into the early Middle Ages. All three assume that, to the extent that men would still be able to fight each other at all, they would do so armed with sticks and stones. One story, Ray Bradbury's "The Million-Year Picnic" (1946), approaches the topic from the point of view of a group of survivors who have escaped all the way to Mars; like several of the rest, it remains in print.

The men—not many women have ever bothered to write military fiction—who took up this subject from the late 1970s to the mid-1980s steered in a different direction. These were the years when calls for nuclear disarmament swept across the United States and Western Europe. In the latter they even succeeded in making their mark on national politics. What better way to silence them than by presenting war between the superpowers as a winnable, certainly interesting if not necessarily pleasant, enterprise? Besides, the years since 1945 had seen rapid military technological progress, some of which has been outlined in these pages. It was, however, a period of frustration; so many of the resulting weapons and weapon systems, into which so much effort had gone and on which so much money had been spent, had never been used against the opponents, and on the missions, for which they had been intended. Accordingly the authors' objective was to attract readers by showing what the newly developed weapons and weapon systems could do.

One of the better-known volumes of this kind was written by General John Hackett (1910–97), a onetime deputy chief of Britain's general staff, with the title *The Third World War,* and published in 1985. Some of the very first pages have a detailed description of American F-15 and German Tornado fighters flying missions over East Germany and attacking airfields there. Eight aircraft had "gone at high supersonic speed hugging the ground at 60 meters over the Harz Mountains." Following the "coordinated release of fire suppression and denial weapon," the navigator "had caught a glimpse of the airfield through the mist and was bubbling with confidence about the accuracy of the attack." "On the way home they had seen plenty of MiGs above them as they skimmed the trees but none of the Soviet fighters had been able to bring their guns or missiles to bear on the fast flying Tornados skimming the ground below. On this first evidence it certainly looked as if the ultra-low-level mode of operations was going to pay off in the penetration of heavy air defenses. No doubt things would get tougher as the enemy got the measure of theirs—but so far very good."[30]

The rest of the story proceeds in a similar vein. In the chapter called "The Battle of the Atlantic," the Soviet "C-in-C, Northern Fleet," sends 40 Tu-22 Backfires to attack American convoys carrying war material to Europe. "The approach of the Backfires was not detected in time for a fully effective air defense disposition to be taken by the . . . convoy escorts. . . . The Aegis-fitted support group was racing to position itself with the main body of the convoys. . . . Seven transports were hit, four of which sank quickly. The loss of life was appalling. Of the eighty AS-6 missiles launched by the Backfires, from ranges of 220 down to 160 kilometers, no less than thirty reached a target."[31] Separate chapters describe "the war in inner space," "air defense of UK and Eastern Atlantic," and "the air war over the central region." In the latter, Warsaw Pact aircraft, though they did manage "to achieve air super superiority on a number of occasions in the first week of the war," are nevertheless unable to provide "full air support" to their advancing ground forces owing to the "determined opposition from F-16s."[32] By now the reader will have got the idea.

Fifteen days after the start of the offensive, the Soviet advance, which at peak reached all the way to the city of Krefeld not far from the German-Dutch border, has been brought to a halt and begun to recoil back east. Thereupon the men in the Kremlin, following a long series of deliberations that we do not need to follow here, decide to escalate the war by going nuclear. At "twenty four minutes past ten [on 20 August] the digital display abruptly upgraded the threat as the [British] tracking radar picked up the [Soviet] missile soaring out of the atmosphere into space. The computer instantly calculated that it was on a sub orbital trajectory with 353 seconds to impact." "The SS-17 missile detonated its nuclear warhead 3,500 meters above Winson Green prison at 1030 hours. Within a fraction of a second the resulting fireball, with temperatures approaching those of the sun, was over 2,000 meters in diameter." A few minutes later, an "enormous mushroom cloud" rose 15 kilometers over the "totally devastated city of Birmingham."[33] In response the West drops a nuclear weapon that annihilates Minsk—this time we are spared the details—the Soviet Union falls apart, and the war comes to a rapid end.

Other military fiction works dating to approximately the same period follow a roughly similar plot and end in a similar way. Take the books of Tom Clancy (1947–), a man whose background is as unlike that of General Hackett as anything could be. Almost 40 years younger than the latter, Clancy originally hoped to serve in the U.S. military but was rejected owing to poor eyesight. Until 1984, when he brought out his best seller *The Hunt for Red October*, he made his living as an insurance salesman and businessman. Here I shall focus on his second volume, *Red Storm Rising* (1986). Like *The Third World War*, *Red Storm Rising* opens with a Soviet decision to attack the Persian Gulf in order to overcome an acute shortage of oil. As the war escalates, the Kremlin turns its attention to NATO in the West. This time the opening moves take place simultaneously on German soil and in Iceland. Using long-range airpower and a regiment of parachutists, the Soviets invade the island, occupy it, and turn it into an air base, a very serious loss to NATO indeed. Next, the inevitable Tu-22 Backfires make their appearance. They attack a NATO carrier group in the mid-Atlantic, sink the French carrier *Foch* and the U.S. amphibious carrier *Saipan*, and inflict such damage on two more American carriers as to render them hors de combat.

Meanwhile, in Germany things go somewhat better for NATO. "Colonel Douglas Ellington's fingertips caressed the control stick of his F-19A Ghostrider attack fighter, while his other hand rested on the side-by-side throttle controls on the left-side cockpit wall." American stealth fighters, assisted by other NATO aircraft, strike at Soviet air bases as well as the bridging equipment and crews so vital to any offensive in a river-crossed country as Germany is. Inter alia, "over two hundred Soviet all-weather fighters" are destroyed in just 27 minutes.[34] The battle turns into one of attrition, which the Soviets, thanks to their greater resources, are likely to win. However, at this point, NATO, using submarine-launched cruise missiles, cripples the enemy's naval air force. Near Iceland four American Phantoms fire eight Sparrow missiles at some MiG-29s, which turn tail and run. These air battles enable the convoys that carry reinforcements from the United States to Europe to resume. Meanwhile, a Soviet prisoner informs NATO commanders that the Reds are suffering from a shortage of fuel, whereupon those commanders focus their air attack against the enemy's fuel depots so as to stop the tanks. In one attack alone, 250,000 gallons of diesel, enough to power two Soviet divisions, go up in flames. The Politburo, in a desperate attempt to regain the initiative, considers the use of tactical nuclear weapons. At that point the good Communists on that body mount a coup against the bad ones, and the war is brought to an end even though we are not told exactly how.

Like *The Third World War, Red Storm Rising* both reflects and exploits the fascination of countless people in and out of uniform with the details of modern weapons—their names, their construction, and their capabilities. Prominent among those weapons are every type of aircraft, missiles, and cruise missiles, some of them so new that they have never been tested in battle and a few that exist only in the author's imagination. Though Clancy is a military buff and not a professional, and though his text is said to contain some technical errors, on the whole he shows a very good acquaintance with the way modern war is supposed to unfold. During his later years Clancy became a frequent guest of the American military whom he did so much to publicize. With some changes, his book could have served as the basis for a staff exercise aimed at gaming the best way to defend various parts of the world against a Soviet invasion. Indeed I vividly recall how, on a 1987 flight that took me from Washington, D.C., to Los Angeles and that happened to be filled with defense contractors, everybody seemed to be reading Clancy's book. Like *The Third World War, Red Storm Rising* is essentially a repetition of World War II waged against a different, but equally wicked and even more powerful, adversary and compressed into a much shorter time frame. Finally and, in the present context, most important, Clancy resembles Hackett in that the yarn he spins comes to an end almost as soon as nuclear weapons are introduced—though this time, fortunately for the world, the professional soldiers recognize the madness of using them before any cities are destroyed.

Whereas both *The Third World War* and *Red Storm Rising* were runaway best sellers, the third volume, I want to discuss here neither reached that status nor deserves to do so. I am referring to *Space Wars: The First Six Hours of World War III*, published in 2007, by William Scott with Michael Coumatos and William Birnes, with a foreword by George Noory, who all seem to have backgrounds in the military and in journalism. This time the year is 2010 and the United States is governed by a weak, naïve, and, though this is nowhere explicitly said, Democratic president who has taken over from that great statesman George W. Bush. Working for him is a disgusting bunch of double-dealing National Security Council "eunuchs" looking and behaving like "pompous little toad[s]." The action starts when some of the communications satellites America depends upon for its day-to-day existence suddenly cease to function. The military organizes a war game—in this volume, as in Clancy's, all U.S. military personnel are patriotic, straightforward, hardworking, and brave—and reveals that the source of the trouble is in Tajikistan. Further air reconnaissance focuses on an innocent-looking greenhouse from which a rogue Russian scientist and his daughter, who are controlled by a "fat" Latin American drug dealer, operate a maser weapon.[35] They neutralize the electronics of a spaceship, killing the five astronauts aboard.

A team of heroic American commandos goes out in a CV-22 Osprey tiltwing rotorcraft. They succeed in capturing the trio plus the scientist's wife, but that does not solve the problem. Behind the Russian scientist and the Latin American drug dealer are the unspeakably wicked Iranians. They treacherously execute a female Canadian negotiator with "ample breasts" who is sent to talk to them. A U.S. brigadier general, visiting northern Israel, is captured by Hezbollah terrorists (this part of the yarn reveals just how unfamiliar the authors are with the Israeli Army). The U.S. Air Force discloses the existence, previously kept secret even from the secretary of defense, of a single-seat space shuttle capable of being launched from one of the few remaining B-70s. It is used to put some new satellites in orbit, replacing the old ones and getting communications to work again. American hackers fire a worm into the computer system that directs Iran's antiaircraft defense, but it is detected and fails to perform its mission. The Iranians launch a nuclear-armed Shihab missile toward the U.S. air base at Aviano in southern Italy. It "leap[s] into the night air with a thunderous roar, trailing a multicolored palette of fire blasted from powerful rocket engines."[36] Luckily it misses its target and explodes in the Adriatic Sea; the fact that it causes hardly any damage is one of the major puzzles of the book. In response, an American superweapon that cannot be tracked back to its owners (having done its work, it leaves behind no traces whatsoever) is used to demolish the Iranian nuclear reactor at Busher. Since the Iranians' missile-guidance technology originates in France, two American F-15Cs are sent up and launch their anti-satellite missiles and destroy two European Galileo satellites. The world is safe, at least for the moment.

Like *The Third World War* and *Red Storm Rising, Space Wars* is full of pilot lingo: "Gaspipe, Control. Be advised: The Eagles just scored."[37] Even more than its two predecessors, it has at its epicenter descriptions of weapons and weapon systems, some real, some imaginary, and their supposedly marvelous capabilities. Not only do the authors pile one acronym upon another—we meet STRATCOM, POTUS, SIVTRIX, DEADSAT, AFFTC, ASAT, BOYD, ASM-135A, ASM-135C, MKV, CTF, and any number of others—but they even go so far as to invent some new ones of their own. An alphabetical list of them, such as is an essential part of most "serious" works in the field, would not have been out of place and might have helped the innocent reader find his arms and bearings in this mishmash. Like the works by Hackett and Clancy, *Space Wars* can be read, indeed is meant to be read, as a warning as to what could happen to the "West" in general, and to the United States in particular, if its nations and its mealy-mouthed, weak-kneed politicians do not wake up and confront the terrible dangers that are lurking just around the corner.

Last but not least, though it has the words *World War III* in the title, in fact *Space Wars* describes a series of comparatively minor incidents masterminded by a comparatively minor country, Iran. The fact that, in reality,

America's per capita GDP exceeds that of Iran by over eight to one ($47,000 versus $5,787) speaks for itself.[38] As things are now, the United States could wipe Iran off the map within minutes of the order being given. In response, all Iran would be able to do is stir up things in the Persian Gulf and have Hezbollah's guerrillas harass Israel. No wonder that country's rulers, wicked as they undoubtedly are—a key figure, Hassan Rafjani, is described as "clearly psychotic and dangerously unstable"[39]—hardly manage to do more than hire some foreign scientists, pay some foreign terrorists, kidnap a general, kill an envoy, and launch a single nuclear-armed ballistic missile that misses its target. There is no question here of massive armies and navies fighting one another, millions or at least hundreds of thousands of dead, and entire countries reduced to rubble. Instead, "World War III" is presented as consisting of a series of pinpricks. As the authors themselves point out, most of America's population is only dimly aware that it is taking place at all. Instead, what does get their attention is a suicide bombing in a Denver mall.[40] The reason is the same as in the two earlier volumes: namely, the overriding fear of nuclear weapons, which, if they were used in earnest, would very quickly bring about the end of the world. Worse still from the authors' point of view, there is no real defense and therefore no real interaction between the belligerents; thus introducing those weapons would make it impossible to devise any sensible plot at all.

Space forbids a detailed discussion of the countless other works of fiction, movies, TV series, and wargames that have sought to portray warfare in general, and air warfare in particular, over the last few decades. Clancy's books have been especially successful in this regard, giving rise to so many spin-offs as to make one's head spin and turn the author into a multimillionaire. Since his are works for adults, not children, one can only wonder what this success signifies concerning the mindset of those who purchase the products in question. From Kubrick's *Doctor Strangelove* (1964) to John Badham's *WarGames* (1983), films that deal with major war between the superpowers are overshadowed by the awesome destruction that nuclear weapons can and very likely will wreak. The former comes to an end at the moment when a B-52 drops the first hydrogen bomb; the latter ends with an explicit warning that the only way to win this game is not to play it in the first place. Incidentally one consultant for this movie was Peter Schwarz, an economist who also helped draw up threat scenarios for the office of the secretary of defense at the Pentagon. Some movies, such as Nicholas Meyer's *The Day After* (1983), which premiered on American television, represent a return to the attempts in the 1950s to portray a world that has gone through a nuclear war. Other movies whose topic is airpower, such as Tony Scott's *Top Gun* (1986), evade the question by having heroic American pilots fight some anonymous, but presumably nonnuclear, enemy.

In the air as on land and at sea, in fiction as well as in fact, such is the fear of, and the constraints imposed by, nuclear weapons that the days of large-scale military operations conducted by powerful nations against each other appear to be more or less over. However, the process of proliferation that got under way in 1945 was by no means even. In some places it did its work very quickly; in others it acted much more slowly or not at all, leaving states and their conventional forces with considerable room to fight each other to their hearts' content. And so it is to the "little wars" of this planet that we must now turn.

PART IV

LITTLE WARS
1945–2010

Whereas, at the time of writing in 2010, there are nine countries that possess nuclear weapons, the number of those that do *not* have them is around 180. Of those, 30 or 40, mainly in North America, Europe, East Asia, and Australasia, have a fully developed nuclear infrastructure and could have built the weapons in question relatively quickly if they wanted to. Some others, mainly in Latin America, the Middle East, and Southeast Asia, would probably require a sustained effort measured in years; others still, lacking even a rudimentary infrastructure, skilled personnel, and financial means, are unlikely to reach the nuclear threshold for several decades yet, if indeed they ever do so. To be sure, this highly uneven state of development hardly means that every one of the numerous nonnuclear states is automatically at the mercy of the few nuclear ones. On the other hand, it does present one very important reason why numerous interstate wars, some of them quite large and some of them very bloody, have continued to take place during the decades since Hiroshima. In these wars, all of which have been fought either between or against nonnuclear countries, airpower has often played an important role.

CHAPTER 13

THE TWILIGHT OF NAVAL AVIATION

Years ago, the kind of shop that specializes in jokes that people play on one another used to carry a volume entitled *Sex over Forty*. Opening it, the reader would be "surprised" to find nothing but blank pages. Since 1945, the situation in respect to air warfare at sea has been quite similar. Though it has not altogether disappeared, it has certainly gone into a steep decline in terms of the size and importance of operations. Above all, in over six decades, not on a single occasion did carrier-borne aircraft engage others of their own kind in combat. As more countries acquire nuclear weapons and as the costs of naval airpower continue to rise into the stratosphere, that decline seems very likely to continue.

Certainly the process has not been due to any lack of planning, spending, preparation, and training. Throughout World War II, naval aviation had played a key role in the war at sea. This was as true of the Pacific and the Indian Oceans as it was of the Atlantic and the Mediterranean. Navies that did not have a well-developed air arm, such as those of Germany and Italy, were at a grave disadvantage; looking back, one sometimes wonders how they dared enter the war in the first place. But for air cover, provided either by carriers or by land-based aviation, no major naval surface operations were possible at all. Nations that did not have aviation to support their submarines found themselves with a grave handicap. As Japan surrendered, the carriers' importance was underlined by the American prohibition on Japan ever to build them again. Since then the U.S. Navy, largely thanks to its carriers, has dominated the world's oceans and seas. It alone was in a position to go wherever it pleased and deny others the ability to do so if necessary.

One very important reason behind American dominance in the field was the question of cost. A first-class carrier represents one of the largest, and by far the most complex of, machines ever built by man. Those of the *Nimitz* class displace 78,000 tons when empty and just over 100,000 when fully loaded. Each of these Leviathans costs $4.5 billion to build and $160 million per year to run. These figures do not include their complement of 85 aircraft and the numerous vessels needed to escort, protect, and supply them. Representing the first of a new generation, the *Gerald R. Ford* is of similar size and will cost $9 billion to build. The designers claim that automation will reduce manpower requirements and, with them, operating cost, but whether this will really happen remains to be seen.

As also happened on land, there have been some attempts to bring down the cost of bases by introducing STOL (short takeoff and landing) and VTOL aircraft. However, the results have not been very satisfactory because the price, in terms of added complexity and reduced performance, is too great. True enough, the British Harrier, as the best known of these machines, which is also in use by the U.S. Marine Corps, is capable of doing some interesting things no other aircraft can do. Stopping in midair, turning on its own axis, or even flying backward, it will make spectators gape; assuming advanced electronics on both sides, though, it cannot take on an F-16 or one of its foreign equivalents.

By and large the limitations of modern carriers are similar to those of 1939–45. Though those with nuclear engines can remain at sea for practically unlimited periods, the amount of ordnance and fuel they can carry is limited so that frequent replenishment is required. Owing to the fact that the aircraft themselves have grown much bigger and heavier, the number carried by the largest vessels has remained static or may even have declined slightly. Owing to the need for short takeoff and landing capabilities as well as saving space, carrier aircraft continued to be somewhat more complex than their land-based opposite numbers. This was not without effect on performance; the first carrier aircraft only crossed the speed of sound in 1955, several years after land-based ones had done the same.

Furthermore, even the largest carriers, such as only the United States possessed, still could not take anything much heavier than twin-engine fighter-bombers and support aircraft. As long as wars remained conventional, which all of them did, this fact limited the amount of firepower they could deliver, restricting them to close support and interdiction missions. Another limiting factor was the need for interceptors to fend off enemy bombers and helicopters for conducting anti-submarine warfare. As a result, attack aircraft of every sort only formed approximately one-third of all the machines aboard each carrier. A fully manned carrier of the 1990s required a crew of 5,000 men and women, not counting several thousand more on the various escort and supply ships. The number of flying personnel aboard was about 300, the number of men and women who actually delivered fire to the enemy at any one moment a few dozen. All this turned carrier-based airpower into an even more expensive proposition than that which is based on land.

Within these constraints, the development of carrier aviation roughly paralleled that of land-based aircraft. First and most important was the switch from piston engines to jets. With the latter came turboprops, which were used to power some light transports and, later, AWACS (airborne warning and control) aircraft. Next, straight-wing subsonic machines such as the Grumman F-9 Panther were replaced by swept-wing transsonic ones such as the F-9 Cougar and F-8 Crusader. Then came delta-winged ones such as the A-4 Skyhawk light bomber and the supersonic F-4 Phantom fighter-bomber. The latter, a two-engine, two-seat, long-range machine capable of carrying an exceptionally heavy load of ordnance, acquired such a reputation that it was adopted by the U.S. Air Force as well as many foreign air forces.[1] In the 1970s third-generation delta-wing aircraft gave way to swing-wing F-14s and thin-wing F-18s, the U.S. Navy's equivalents of the air force's F-15s and F-16s respectively. As happened on land, each successive generation of aircraft was equipped with more advanced radar and other electronics. As also happened on land, though air-to-air missiles started replacing guns during the 1960s, later on the guns made a limited comeback and today's naval aircraft carry them.

Whatever else other countries may have done at sea during the decades after 1945, when it came to carrier aviation none came even close to matching the United States. During the 1950s and 1960s, Soviet naval commanders apparently believed that, in case a nuclear war broke out, the carriers' only role would be to be rapidly sunk by the air- and submarine-launched missiles of the period.[2] In this, incidentally, they were supported by the father of America's H-bomb, Edward Teller, who noted that the carriers would make "interesting targets."[3] Accordingly the Soviets limited their efforts to building a limited number of smaller vessels capable of carrying helicopters and VTOL/STOL aircraft and intended for covering the projection of force overseas, as was done opposite the coast of Angola in 1975–76. Only during the 1970s did the Soviet Union's top naval commanders start showing an interest in carriers capable of carrying conventional aircraft. To do so, it was first of all necessary to revise existing doctrine and assume that a nuclear war would not necessarily be short.

The leader of the Soviet effort was Admiral Sergey Gorshkov. In 1967 he had written that carriers were undergoing "a process of irreversible decline," a statement probably intended as much to explain away Soviet inferiority in this field as to reflect any "objective" truth. Five years later, in a 50,000-word treatise entitled "Navies in War and Peace," that statement was not repeated. During the 1970s other Soviet naval commentators were unanimous in holding that carriers should form a critical part of any naval buildup, a view that was only strengthened by the 1982 Falklands War. Yet Soviet carriers laid down from about 1975 to 1985 were much smaller than their American opposite numbers. They only carried about half as many aircraft and helicopters. Even so, the effort in this direction did not prove lasting. When Mikhail Gorbachev came to power in 1985, he apparently decided that Gorshkov's program to contest command of the sea with the Americans had been too ambitious and started cutting it back. Funding was cut, projects were canceled. Naval aviation declined from 1,354 aircraft and 312 helicopters in 1991 to 396 aircraft and 250 helicopters in 1996.[4] As of 2010, of the eight or so vessels that were laid down at one time or another, only one, the *Admiral Kuznetsov*, remained in service.[5]

Several other countries either constructed their own carriers or tried to build up their naval aviation by purchasing used ones and modernizing them. Britain and France both opted for the former course, but again their carriers never matched the American ones in point of numbers, size, and the quantity and quality of the aircraft they could operate.[6] As of 2010 these countries have two and one of these ships in service, respectively. If we limit ourselves to the post-1945 period, other countries that at one time or another bought foreign carriers or else are currently building their own include Argentina, Australia, Brazil, Canada, China, Germany, India, Italy, Japan, the Netherlands, Spain, and Thailand. For example, in 2004 the Indian Navy bought the former Soviet vessel *Gorshkov* and has since spent $2.5 billion trying to refurbish it. Hopefully it will be ready in 2012.[7] The Brazilian Navy operates the former French *Foch*. Its complement of aircraft consists of some upgraded Skyhawks bought thirdhand from Kuwait. Though on one occasion the ship raised steam and set sail in support of some fishing rights the Brazilians were claiming in the Atlantic, so far those aircraft have never fired a shot or dropped a bomb on anybody or anything. Of the 11 above-listed countries, some have dropped out of the race so that as of 2010 only five still operate the ships.

In this respect as in so many other things, the country with the most interesting navy is China. Apart from an isolated period 500 years ago, when its ships reached as far as East Asia and brought back interesting cargoes, China has no history of projecting power or trying to extend its naval power beyond coastal waters. It was only during the 1990s that some efforts in this direction could be discerned as Beijing bought two old vessels from Russia; however, both have long since been decommissioned and one is said to be used as part of an amusement park. Since then many reports have claimed that China is becoming interested in building a blue-water navy capable of contesting the Pacific with the United States and that, as part of this effort, it is secretly building a new carrier from scratch.[8] Supposing the rumors are true, when the ship will be ready and what aircraft it will fly remain a mystery.[9] More doubt on this question is cast by the fact that the Chinese do not yet appear to have produced a first-rate combat aircraft suitable for carrier use.[10]

The technical details are no doubt intriguing, but what were the uses to which the ships in question were put? World War II witnessed many occasions on which surface vessels, including carriers, fought each other. Carriers also provided firepower during amphibious operations, escorted convoys, and played an extremely important role in anti-submarine warfare. But for the escort carriers, the Battle of the Atlantic in particular might have been lost. Since 1945, almost all of this has gone by the wind. The use of carriers and carrier aviation, and indeed of naval aviation as a whole, has been limited almost entirely to wars between, or against, third- and fourth-rate belligerents. Quite often those belligerents were not states but organizations of a different kind. In fact, the first to employ carriers in battle during this period were the French. Not having their own vessels, they leased or borrowed several old British and American ones and equipped them with surplus World War II fighters. Starting in 1947 the ships, cruising in the waters off the eastern coast of Vietnam, launched their aircraft against Viet Minh targets. Apart from anti-aircraft fire, which was intensive at times, there was no opposition, let alone any attempt by the enemy, who did not have aircraft of any kind, to strike back at the attackers.

Of all post-1945 wars, the one in which naval aviation played the greatest role was probably the one in Korea. Early in the war American and British carriers acted as substitutes for airfields, which, in Korea, were always scarce. Later, too, they saw fairly extensive service on both sides of the peninsula. Their aircraft reconnoitered, provided close support to the troops in the Pusan Perimeter, attacked communication lines behind the front, and helped blockade North Korea by sea. In doing all this they had the advantage that carrier aircraft such as the F-4U Corsair and A-1

Skyraider could carry much heavier loads of ordnance than the air force's P-51 Mustang and F-80 Shooting Star.[11] Later in the war naval helicopters joined the fray. They swept mines and flew search-and-rescue missions. The occasion when carriers played the largest role was probably in September 1950, when they helped cover the Inchon landings. Since the distance from Inchon to the Pusan Perimeter is about 200 miles, having the carriers close at hand presented a very important advantage. However, at that time the North Koreans, including their air force, had already been weakened almost to the vanishing point.

From this time on, the carriers' role declined. After China entered the war, naval aircraft often tangled with enemy jet fighters, only to learn that F-9F Panthers were no match for the MiG-15s (luckily for the Americans, their aircrafts' shortcomings were more than compensated for by the quality of their pilots). U.S. Navy aircraft were entrusted with the task of dealing with the North Korean- and Chinese-flown Po-2s, 1920s-vintage biplanes that were too slow for the air force's fighters to handle and that the GIs called "flying alarm clocks" because of their nuisance value. Some of these were rumored to be flown by women (Soviet women had in fact flown them in 1941–45), but the report appears to be unfounded.[12] Other navy aircraft sometimes escorted B-29s to their targets, this being another task for which many of their land-based opposite numbers were too fast. On one occasion American F-4U Corsair fighters operating from the carrier *Valley Forge* shot down a lonely Soviet Tupolev bomber that may have been on a reconnaissance mission.[13] With some exceptions, there was little in these missions that could not have been carried out, and was not carried out, by air force aircraft based either in Japan or in South Korea itself. To some extent, the two kinds were interchangeable, as is demonstrated by the fact that, on the one occasion when aircraft were used to drop torpedoes, the target did not consist of ships at sea but of a dam that was holding a water reservoir.[14]

The next time naval aviation saw action on any scale was during America's war in Vietnam. By this time the move away from propeller-driven aircraft toward the much more powerful jets had been completed. Carriers laid down from about 1950 on had angled decks, an arrangement that enabled them to simultaneously launch and recover their aircraft and thus shorten or eliminate the dangerous periods when the vessels were defenseless against attack. In July 1966, the former Israeli chief of staff and future minister of defense Moshe Dayan was taken to visit the carrier USS *Constellation*, the largest one serving in the East Asian theater at that time. Protected "from the air, the sea, the ground, outer space, and under water," the vessel made a "breath-taking impression" on him. Every 90 minutes, amid a numbing outburst of fire and noise, flights of combat aircraft took off to strike at targets in Vietnam. Recovery was an even more spectacular operation and one that often led to accidents. Significantly, though, when it came to specifying the precise nature of the targets Dayan's hosts refused to answer his questions.[15]

As in Korea, naval aircraft carried out a large variety of missions, including reconnaissance and interdiction. They also dropped mines into Haiphong Harbor in an effort to close it to Soviet shipping. As in Korea, they sometimes clashed with enemy aircraft, this time in the shape of MiG-21s, which proved to be tough and agile opponents. As in Korea, there was often little to choose between missions flown by carrier aircraft and those entrusted to their land-based air force counterparts. This was especially true because the air force had discovered that its F-105 Thunderchiefs, 1950s-vintage fighter-bombers designed to deliver tactical nuclear weapons, were ill-suited for conventional warfare. Instead it had to purchase the Navy's F-4 Phantoms, making the two services resemble one another even more.[16] Finally, as in Korea, perhaps the most outstanding characteristic of the naval air war was the fact that, though the enemy deployed powerful anti-aircraft defenses, the carriers did not come under attack even once. In this sense, indeed, it is hardly possible to speak of a war at all. The carriers represented factories whose output was firepower; no wonder there was a tendency to measure performance in terms of the number of sorties flown and tonnage of bombs dropped, rather than military impact.

Later wars in which naval aviation was involved, such as the 1991 Gulf War, the 2001 offensive against Afghanistan, and the Second Gulf War of

2003, saw a repetition of this pattern. The fact that, in each of these three wars, the enemy did not have nuclear weapons hardly requires mentioning. If Saddam Hussein had had them, almost certainly the wars against him would never have been fought. Moreover, in each of these three wars the enemy was, or turned out to be, extremely weak in conventional terms. To open the analysis with the second of these three wars, it is hardly worth mentioning that the Afghan Taliban did not have even a single aircraft. If they possessed any missiles at all, those were the short-range anti-aircraft Stingers the United States itself had provided them with during the 1980s. What had happened to them since then is not quite clear, but they do not seem to have influenced the conduct of the war in any way. Essentially a force of irregulars, unable to operate in more than company strength and possessing few technical skills, the Taliban were limited to personal arms, mortars, and machine guns. They also had a few captured, rather old, light anti-aircraft guns. This situation enabled the American carriers, which had taken up positions off the coast of Pakistan, to do pretty much as they pleased without any fear of being attacked in their turn.

In the case of Afghanistan, Pakistan's refusal to provide the United States with bases meant that the carriers were the only way U.S. tactical airpower could reach the enemy (the bombers, operating from the faraway British island of Diego Garcia, were another matter). Not so in the case of the two wars against Iraq, when air bases in Saudi Arabia, the Gulf countries, and Turkey (but only in the first war) were readily available. Still, Iraq was not the Taliban. In 1991 Saddam Hussein had both an air force—it could muster about 600 combat aircraft, many of them modern—and air-to-sea missiles. The latter were similar to those the Argentines had used to wreak havoc on the British at the Falklands nine years earlier.[17]

As far as naval aviation goes, the decisive fact that shaped the war was that Iraq's only outlet to the sea was located at the tip of a long tongue of the Indian Ocean, the Persian Gulf. Loath to risk its precious carriers in such narrow waters, the U.S. Navy opted to operate three of them inside the Gulf and three outside it, in the Red Sea. During the first weeks of the war even the three stationed in the Gulf were about 300 miles from their targets, and at no time did any of them get closer than 200 miles. Those in the Red Sea were positioned at up to 700 miles away, so that each mission flown from them took 3.7 hours on the average. Both the aircraft operating at 300 miles and those operating at 700 miles needed air-to-air refueling, the former on one leg of their journey and the latter on both. In other words, the prerequisite for operating the carriers was that they should stay safely out of reach of the Iraqi Air Force. But to stay out of reach of the Iraqi Air Force they had to be refueled by aircraft that could only be based on land. The entire procedure was complicated and expensive. Had the Iraqi Air Force been somewhat stronger and more adventurous than it was, surely it could not have been used.

Overall, carrier-based aircraft formed only less than a quarter of the U.S. total and less than a fifth of the Coalition one. Taking the war as a whole, each carrier only generated less than one sortie per aircraft per day on the average. Of those sorties, just one-quarter actually struck Iraqi land targets. All the rest performed a variety of other missions from counter-air (28 percent) to general support. The average daily amount of ordnance delivered per carrier per day was just 49 tons, much less for those that never left the Red Sea, considerably more for those that toward the end of the war dared come closer to the Iraqi coast.[18] The long flying distances apart, one reason for this was that none of the carriers was made to operate on a 24-hours-a-day basis. Instead all of them periodically suspended operations, some for shorter periods and some for longer ones. Apparently they were replenished more often than was strictly necessary. Overall, navy aircraft joined those of the air force in searching out and attacking suspected Scud missile bases (though without hitting a single Scud); suspected chemical, biological, and nuclear facilities; radar sites; command centers; and the like. Yet only 6 percent of all sorties flown by navy aircraft were directed against maritime targets. The rest could probably have been done equally well, or better, by land based aircraft;[19] as a matter of fact, some naval aircraft operated not from carriers but from makeshift airstrips along the Saudi shore.

Some observers went much further still. Perhaps the most interesting discussion came from Captain Steven Ramsdell, a naval historian who was sent out to report on the war:

> Many of the senior officers I spoke to pointed out that Desert Storm was not well suited to carrier operations. In their view the CVs [carriers] are suited to one-time raids similar to the Libyan action of 1986, but not to sustained campaigning. This opinion is widely held in the fleet. It ignores . . . the fact that our huge investment in carriers cannot be justified by such limited usefulness. In fact, the implication of this attitude is that carriers are little more than political instruments, not real war fighters.[20]

By 2003 Saddam's forces, having been defeated and subjected to years of sanctions, were only a shadow of their former selves, but they still existed. This time the U.S. high command judged the enemy sufficiently weak for two out of the four carriers that took part in the campaign—the *Abraham Lincoln*, the *Constellation*, the *Harry Truman*, and the *Kitty Hawk*—to be sent into the Gulf itself. Their Hornets, Intruders, and Harriers struck targets of opportunity throughout Iraq, including headquarters, communication sites, anti-aircraft missile sites, early warning radar sites, and the like. They also provided cover for some small amphibious landings—not that there were any Iraqi aircraft about to try to counter them—and provided close support to some marine units that were being gravely threatened by Iraqis who pretended to surrender but went on fighting instead. Thanks largely to the development of the Internet, which allowed the daily 800-page ATO (air tasking order) to be delivered to the carriers electronically instead of by hand, cooperation with the air force was much better than in 1991. Nor was the navy short of precision-guided weapons, as it had been on that occasion.[21] Yet some problems remained. Since carriers can only launch relatively small AWACS aircraft with limited range, the navy's fighter-bombers either had to rely on the air force for this purpose or had to do without. Apparently it preferred the latter, causing one commentator to refer to the missions it flew over Iraq in 2003 as "essentially a Hornet [F-18s] lovefest."[22]

The record of the use of naval aviation at sea, in anti-submarine warfare, or against opponents of its own kind is equally unimpressive. In fact, though there were some incidents and an occasional shot may have been exchanged, during the entire period since 1945 only rarely was naval airpower, whether land- or sea-based, employed in a real war against a real enemy able and willing to respond. The exception was the Falklands War between Argentina and Britain. Like most conventional warfare since 1945, the conflict was overshadowed by the dominant factor, nuclear weapons. In fact, there is reason to believe that the Argentines, who during the 1970s had a large and active nuclear program running, deliberately gave it up *because* they were thinking of ways to obtain—recover, as they saw it—the islands.[23] Conversely, had Argentina's ruler Leopoldo Galtieri possessed nuclear weapons in 1982, then almost certainly fear of escalation would have prevented him from opening hostilities in the first place, or so at least the fact that no two nuclear countries have fought each other since 1945 leads one to conclude.

Some British naval vessels involved in the war are said to have carried nuclear weapons in their holds.[24] If so, it did not make any difference since hostilities remained purely conventional. First satellite reconnaissance, kindly provided by the Americans, apparently helped the British, whose expeditionary force was coming from thousands of miles away, to reconnoiter the islands and locate their targets. Next a small number of Vulcan bombers, obsolescent but still in service, used air-to-air refueling to fly all the way from Ascension Island and drop bombs on the airstrip at Stanley. They were able to prevent the Argentines from basing fighters there, but the strip's use by transport aircraft and some others continued.[25] The core of the naval task force that left Portsmouth to retake the Falklands was formed by two carriers, HMS *Hermes* and HMS *Invincible*. Loaded, they only displaced 28,000 and 21,000 tons respectively. This made them comparable to the American and Japanese ones of the early years of World War II, except that the number of aircraft they carried was much smaller. On this occasion their complement consisted of Harrier "jump jets" of the Royal Navy and Air Force as well as helicopters equipped for anti-submarine warfare. Additional helicopters were carried aboard frigates and supply ships.

To repeat, the Harriers were hardly the world's best fighter aircraft. In providing them with a VTOL/STOL capability so they could operate from

Britain's small carriers, too much performance had to be sacrificed. Consequently the British carriers, considered too valuable to put at risk, had to operate sufficiently far to the east of the islands to stay out of range of the Argentine French-built Mirage, Nesher (an Israeli version of the Mirage, produced between 1970 and 1973), Skyhawk light bombers, and Super Étendard fighters. The last two were designed to be carrier-operated. In fact the Argentines did have a 20,000-ton carrier, the *Veinticinco de Mayo*. She had started life in 1942 as a British freighter, was converted into an escort carrier in 1943, and was handed over to the Dutch in 1946. She remained in service until 1968, when a fire all but demolished her. Purchased by the Argentine Navy, she was patched up. On May 1, 1982, she was about to launch a wave of five Skyhawks—all the operational aircraft of this kind that the Argentine Navy had—against the British task force, which was then about to invest the Falklands, when heavy seas prevented the aircraft from taking off. On the next day a British submarine sank the Argentine cruiser *General Belgrano* with heavy loss of life. Afraid lest the *Veinticinco de Mayo* might share the same fate, her commanders wisely decided to withdraw her to port.

The British task force commander was Admiral Sandy Woodward. He expected sea and air operations to last for about two weeks before the Argentine resistance in these two media would be broken, opening the way to an amphibious landing.[26] In fact it took three weeks of furious, albeit small-scale, fighting. During this period the British carrier-launched aircraft and sea-to-air Dart and Seawolf missiles fended off anti-shipping attacks by the Argentine land-based ones. With the exception of the Skyhawks, older and slower aircraft, the Argentine fighters, though hardly the most advanced of their kind in the world, were superior to the Harriers. This was especially true at high altitudes, where the latter's greater maneuverability counted for less and the greater speed and climbing ability of the Mirages, Neshers, and Super Étendards, for more. Nevertheless, since the Argentines' mission was to engage surface targets, their pilots were forced to fly low regardless of whether doing so was or was not tactically sound.

Most of the Argentine aircraft carried unguided bombs and were thus dependent solely on the pilots' training and courage to hit their targets.

Only the five available Super Étendards were armed with sophisticated French-built, air-to-sea Exocet missiles. So effective were they that they became the terror of the British Navy, some of whose personnel developed "Exocetitis." Yet in other ways the Argentine aircraft were at a disadvantage from the first. The nature of their mission meant that they had to carry ordnance for striking sea targets as well as for air-to-air combat, which reduced their maneuverability and speed. Even more problematic was the fact that they operated at extreme range. Over 500 miles separated their mainland bases at Tierra del Fuego from the Falklands. The Argentine Skyhawks could be refueled in the air—by land-based aircraft, needless to say—but only by carrying a reduced bomb load. Even so, they could only stay over target for a few minutes. The remaining aircraft had no air refueling capability at all.

The Argentine Navy having withdrawn from the conflict, superior British air-to-air missiles and pilot training won out over the other side's air force, but only by a hair's breadth. Had the Argentines succeeded in sinking one of the British carriers, as at one point they claimed to have done, then lack of air cover would have forced Woodward to bring the campaign to an end. Had one more supply ship been lost, then again operations would have had to cease. Even so, losses were heavy. Two British frigates, two destroyers, and a supply ship, the *Atlantic Conveyor,* were sunk, the last-named along with the helicopters she carried. Several other ships were damaged with heavy loss of life.

One British officer involved in these events was Captain Bill Canning, who commanded the frigate *Broadsword.* Here is his description of what coming under air attack was like:

> The first pair [of Argentine Skyhawks] came straight for us. . . . The aircraft were very low, so low that some of our look-outs could see the wake of their jet streams on the water—but Sea Wolf [ship-to-air missiles] can get down there. The system alerted itself as it does, automatically. . . . But the system did not engage at its best range—five to six kilometers—possibly because the two targets—wingtip to wingtip—confused the system. There was a frantic change to an

> alternate mode of operation. We took about three seconds; but that was two seconds too long . . . by the time it was done, they were over the top of us.
>
> There were four bombs. Three missed us, one hit. The one that hit bounced off the sea, came in through the starboard side of the ship aft, five feet above the waterline, and, as it was climbing upwards after bouncing, it came up through the flight deck, hitting the Lynx [helicopter] as it passed through, and carried on into the sea on the other side. The other three bombs fell—one ahead and two over the top of us, all very close. One of the look-outs said that, if he had stood up, he could have touched one of them.[27]

In fact, fully 60 percent of Argentine bombs dropped during the campaign failed to explode.[28]

The repeated attempts to stop the British from landing cost the Argentine Air Force dearly. After May 25, by which time they had lost 21 aircraft versus three British ones (all to noncombat causes), they had run out of resources. This left the British free to use their aircraft and helicopters for covering the landings, direct support—since the Argentine garrison took up fixed positions, there were hardly any lines of communication on the islands—as well as troop transport, casualty evacuation, and the like. The Vulcans again saw action, this time against Argentine positions near the capital of Stanley. To be sure, the aircraft on both sides were much more sophisticated than those of 1939–45 (though the Vulcans still carried the H2S targeting radar, first developed for bombing German cities during that period).[29] Yet apart from the fact that missiles had partly replaced cannon and iron bombs on air-to-air, ground-to-air, and air-to-ground missions, there was little that World War II naval commanders such as Britain's Dudley Pound, Japan's Isoroku Yamamoto, and America's Chester Nimitz would not have recognized. What *would* have surprised them was the small scale on which this "splendid little war"[30] was fought. Just 5,000 troops actually went ashore. At Iwo Jima in February 1945, the figure had been six times as large; at Okinawa in April of the same year, 12 times.

Whether the world will ever again see naval aviation used in the way, and as intensively, as it was at the Falklands, where both sides took and inflicted severe losses on one another, is anybody's guess. Almost certainly, if such an engagement does in fact take place it will be fought between nonnuclear states or by a nuclear state against a nonnuclear one; otherwise, given the small number of vessels so characteristic of modern navies and the spectacular nature of their loss, the danger of escalation may be too great. These facts in themselves are sufficient to guarantee that, on at least one side and quite probably on both, the navies and the aircraft deployed will be second- or even third-rate. Under such circumstances the overall number of machines engaged by each side is likely to be in the low dozens, if that. That which participates in any single operation will be much smaller still.

The United States apart, three nations are currently building carriers in an effort to join the five that already have them. Several of these eight have nuclear weapons or are capable of building them relatively quickly, but the carriers in question are not very large. Most of those either in service or under construction displace something between 30,000 and 40,000 tons. Some are much smaller still; furthermore, currently the only country besides the United States that has a nuclear-powered carrier is France. Small vessels imply suitably small air complements and/or that the aircraft will not be of the most advanced types. Other things being equal, they also mean that endurance at sea and operational range will be limited. For example, India's *Vikrant* will carry about 30 of the domestically produced modern fighters, the Hal Tejas.[31] Australia's *Canberra*, scheduled to be commissioned in 2012, will only carry helicopters. Thailand's Spanish-built carrier, the *Chakri Naruebet*, can carry six of the venerable Harriers and a similar number of light Seahawk helicopters. China's first carrier, said to be under active consideration, will probably carry no more than 15 aircraft.[32] Briefly, when it comes to carriers and carrier aviation, no country can even remotely compete with the United States. Any attempt to do so will surely require formidable financial resources as well as several decades' worth of work. But even the number of U.S. carriers is declining. As of 2010 there were only 11 left, with one more under construction, as against 26 at the end of World War II.[33]

With large carriers as expensive as they are, and with smaller ones unable to carry large numbers of the most powerful and equally expensive aircraft, no wonder many navies are following the example of air forces and armies but are turning their attention toward drones in the form of cruise missiles and UAVs instead. In spite of strong opposition from the naval air community, which feared that its own position was being undermined, cruise missiles such as the Harpoon and the Tomahawk started being mounted on surface vessels during the 1980s. They were first tried during the 1986 scrape with Libya, and the 1991 Gulf War saw them being used on a fairly extensive scale. The targets were anti-aircraft defenses and other installations, such as headquarters and communication centers, considered too dangerous for manned aircraft to tackle. Technically they seem to have worked about as well as their designers had hoped, but the Tomahawks, being non-reusable, carried a rather small bang for the buck (they had, of course, been designed for carrying nuclear warheads). Accordingly they only delivered a very small fraction of the total amount of ordnance that was dropped on Iraq from the air.

The naval use of UAVs was stimulated by an episode that took place at the end of 1983 off the shores of Beirut. In September of that year, the *New Jersey*, a World War II battleship that had been taken out of mothballs and reconstituted, arrived in the area. The intent was to shell positions held by a number of shadowy Lebanese militias that did not take kindly to the presence of American marines in their country. However, the fire of nine enormous 16-inch guns proved to be extremely inaccurate and little if anything was accomplished. Nor, incidentally, could the presence of the 45,000-ton vessel and its UAVs prevent two truck bombs from being driven into the Marine Corps headquarters in Beirut and exploded, killing 299 U.S. service personnel. In 1986–87, UAVs, intended to provide fire-direction, underwent a series of trials aboard the *New Jersey*'s sister ship, the USS *Iowa*. Following some teething troubles during which several of the early models were lost, they proved very successful.[34] Subsequently their use spread to other navies as well and they are currently being carried by many types of vessels from missile boats upward.

During the 1991 war, a Pioneer UAV was launched from the battleship *Wisconsin* and flew over Failaka Island off the Kuwaiti coast. By its mere appearance it caused the Iraqi troops stationed there to surrender, not necessarily because they were cowards but because they must have known that it would soon be followed by a rain of 16-inch shells. This particular machine is now on display at the National Air and Space Museum.[35] As is the case on land, one measure of the growing importance of UAVs at sea is that a separate career track for their operators is currently under consideration.[36] As is the case on land, too, their principal mission consists of surveillance and reconnaissance, tasks for which their relatively slow speed, considerable endurance, and low operating cost make them well suited. To use navy newspeak, they provide "cueing that is used by the operations personnel to station associated surface assets . . . [and] rapidly disseminate high quality imagery to our . . . partners, thereby improving overall mission effectiveness."[37] Another very important use consists of directing "over the horizon" anti-shipping missiles to their targets, a mission that would otherwise have to be carried out by more expensive, more vulnerable, helicopters.[38] Yet this is just the tip of the iceberg. In principle there is no reason why UAVs should not carry weapons too, and indeed the maritime environment is in some ways more suitable for their use than the one the land provides. In 2009 the U.S. Navy was utilizing Reapers, large UAVs with a 66-foot wingspan and a range of over 3,000 miles, to identify Somali pirates operating off Africa's east coast.[39] Given how small and widely dispersed the quarry is, undoubtedly this is the way to go.

Finally, in a volume whose subject is airpower little needs to be said about the question as to whether carriers and the naval aircraft that they carry remain viable at all. The Bikini series of tests in 1946, in which one carrier was sunk and another suffered such damage from blast and radiation that she had to be scuttled, cast some doubts on this issue.[40] However, those tests were broken off before they could provide a conclusive answer. Perhaps because they preferred acting the ostrich, in all the years since then neither the United States nor any other nation has held a similar series of trials. Yet the weapons used at Bikini only developed 21–23 kilotons of explosive power, less than 10 percent of that attributed to the warheads mounted on top of subsequent Soviet sea-to-sea missiles. At the height of the Cold War in 1978, the U.S. chief of naval operations, Admiral James Holloway, estimated that, in a *conventional* conflict between NATO and the Warsaw Pact, 30 to 40 percent of America's carriers would be lost.[41] What the figure might be in the not unlikely case the war went nuclear he did not bother to spell out.

Even when we limit the inquiry concerning the viability of carriers to conventional warfare, question marks, especially regarding the dangers posed by submarines, persist. In 1939–45, carrier-based aircraft often sank submarines and submarines often sank carriers. Since then such clashes have become very rare. One encounter took place in November 1971 when aircraft from the Indian carrier *Vikrant,* a predecessor of the current one, sank the Pakistani submarine *Ghazi.* Another occurred in 1982 when Skua air-to-sea missiles launched from a British Lynx helicopter disabled, but did not destroy, the Argentine submarine *Santa Fe.*[42] We have already noted how the submarine threat caused the Argentine carrier *Veinticinco de Mayo* to withdraw from the conflict. Probably it was a wise move.

This handful of real-life clashes has left both parties, the submariners and the naval aviators, free to argue that they alone ruled the seas and that the other was nothing but an auxiliary at best and a target at worst. Noting that no nation has lost a carrier in action from 1945 on, the aviators insist that, should an enemy submarine be so bold as to venture close and try to launch a torpedo at them and their escorts, it will surely be detected and sunk. Submarine commanders, to some of whom I have spoken in person, vehemently contest this claim. To them, the fact that no carrier has been sunk is due to the fact that the attempt has rarely been made. Much like Billy Mitchell in the 1920s, they always maintain that they could penetrate the defenses quite easily. Next, three or four torpedoes could sink a carrier or put it out of commission for a long time; however, the umpires who draw up the rules for the various exercises regularly twist them in such a way as to conceal that fact.

It is certainly true that, to avoid attacks by submarines inter alia, carriers in general and U.S. ones in particular do their best to stay away from coastal waters. In case the mission is to attack land targets, doing so means paying quite a heavy price in terms of the amount of firepower that can be delivered and the cost of doing so. Even so, it is claimed that Chinese submarines have got within torpedo range of a U.S. carrier during maneuvers.[43] Not that coming in close is always necessary. Instead of relying on torpedoes alone, some submarines also carry anti-shipping cruise missiles capable of being launched from under the water and of reaching their targets at a distance of several hundred miles.[44] With careers and tens of billions of dollars at stake, and with both sides sticking to their positions, as long as no actual war takes place the issue is unlikely to be resolved. One can only hope it will remain so for a long time to come.

CHAPTER 14

FROM KOREA TO THE SINAI

Though Korea was not the first post–World War II conventional conflict to see airpower in action, it was the first to witness its large-scale use. With both sides making use of jet fighters, Korea was also the most modern air war ever fought until that time. Another important innovation consisted of helicopters, considerable numbers of which were employed by the Americans on missions such as observation, liaison, casualty evacuation, and the like. Thus no account of air warfare since 1945 can afford to skip this conflict.

When the war broke out on June 27, 1950, North Korea already possessed a fledgling air force. It had been built up during the preceding four years and is said to have consisted of some 200 aircraft (132 combat), including Yak-3, Yak-7B, Yak-9, and La-7 fighters as well as Il-10 ground attack machines. All these were propeller-driven machines first introduced between 1941 and 1944. By Western standards they may have been somewhat crude, but this very crudeness made it possible to produce them by the thousands and operate them without an extensive infrastructure. Moreover, they did the job. Many if not most were flown by Soviet pilots, and indeed Soviet personnel formed the framework of the force as a whole.[1] To oppose them, the South Koreans had only eight light Piper Cub liaison planes (originally there had been nine, but one was lost in May 1949 when the pilot defected to the North) and three T-6 Texas trainers. Seven other T-6s were damaged during the first attack. At the time no U.S. forces were stationed in Korea, and indeed the day before the war broke out the Joint Chiefs of Staff in Washington, D.C., famously issued a statement that the peninsula was of no importance to America's defense.

Dominating the air—the South had hardly any anti-aircraft defenses—the North's air force provided effective close support to the advancing armored columns, helping them capture Seoul and push their enemies south. Yet this success was short-lived. As early as June 26, American P-51 Mustangs, F-82 twin Mustangs, and F-80 Shooting Stars—the last-named, jet engined—tangled with the North Koreans. Technological superiority soon made itself felt. To cite the most obvious fact only, a twin Mustang could reach 480 miles per hour and a Shooting Star, 600. But no machine available to the North Koreans at the time could do better than 420. With the Americans able to initiate and break off air combat almost at will, Kim Il Sung's aircraft were shot out of the sky; by the end of August those that still remained were able to offer no more than token resistance to the United States and its allies. U.S. control of the air in turn was very useful in assisting the Inchon landings and the subsequent advance to the Yalu. By the end of October, the North Koreans had lost nine-tenths of their territory and their army was on the verge of complete defeat. As to the North Korean Air Force, it never recovered. Though it received new aircraft, at the time the war ended in June 1953 it did not yet form a combat-ready force; some observers believed the Great Leader was deliberately husbanding his forces, preferring to fight the Americans to the last drop of Chinese and Soviet blood.[2]

The Chinese counteroffensive started on November 25, 1950, and quickly returned the boot to the other foot. Yet partly because Stalin had refused support and partly because the Chinese Air Force was not ready, initially at any rate it was conducted without the benefit of air cover and in the teeth of anything U.S. and allied aircraft could do. It was only in September 1951, long *after* the ground offensive had largely spent itself, that the Chinese Air Force, assisted by some Soviet pilots, was thrown into the battle.[3] With them came a new and superior aircraft, the jet-powered, swept-wing MiG-15. Faithful to the Russian tradition of scant regard for human life, it did not have an ejection seat, but in many other ways it was an outstanding aircraft, easily capable of outflying, outclimbing, outmaneuvering, and outfiring anything the U.S. Air Force had in the theater. The MiGs all but ended the B-29 daylight raids that had previously flown almost unopposed. To the Americans, their appearance came as a shock. It was simply inconceivable that any nation, least of all one committed to Godless Communism, could outperform them in what they had increasingly seen as their own domain. Indeed so impressed were the Americans with the Soviet aircraft that they dropped one million leaflets over North Korea, promising a $50,000 award and political asylum to any pilot who would defect. It worked; in September 1953, one arrived. However, by that time the war was over.[4]

In response to the MiGs, the Americans flew in three squadrons of F-86 Sabres, the only swept wing fighters in their inventory at the time. Yet even the Sabres only went so far to solve the problem. Both aircraft, the American and the Soviet one, came in several versions. Overall, though, the MiG had a higher ceiling than the Sabre did. Being smaller, its thrust-to-weight ratio was much higher. It also had a better turning radius at over 33,000 feet whereas its armament, consisting of two 21- and one 37-millimeter guns, was far superior to the Sabre's six 12.7-millimeter machine guns. The Sabre's own strong points were a smaller turning radius at less than 26,000 feet, an ability to roll faster, and a superior radar-ranging gunsight.[5] Another important advantage was a bubble canopy that provided the pilot with much better all-around visibility than the MiG's "Coca-Cola bottle view." Yet analyses done after the war's end concluded that what really mattered was not so much each parameter separately but the ability to shift rapidly from one to another. During the 1960s and 1970s, in the hands of the above-mentioned John Boyd, this idea was to become the basis for an entire theory; eventually it claimed to explain success not merely in war but in almost every other aspect of human life as well.

Arriving in Korea just three months before the war's end, Boyd was a junior fighter pilot. By the time he left the country, he had been credited with damaging one MiG. Subsequently he attended, and taught at, the Fighter Weapons School, the air force's predecessor to the navy's Top Gun course. There he became famous for his habit of betting $40 on his ability to beat all comers in mock air combat within less than 40 seconds and invariably winning the contest. Later, having graduated from Georgia Tech, he developed into something of an airpower theoretician. According to him, success in air combat depended not on superiority in this respect or that but on the relative speed at which both pilots could go through what he termed the OODA (observation, orientation, decision, action) loop.[6] In this respect the Sabre, with its bubble canopy, was far superior.

But how successful *were* American fighter aircraft in Korea? According to American data, Sabres shot down 792 MiGs while losing only 78 of their own, a ratio of 10:1. Taking all kinds of aircraft into account, the figure is said to be 14:1. Later, though, the MiG versus Sabre kills were revised to 379 and 103 respectively, giving a much less spectacular, though still very respectable, ratio of 3.7:1. Predictably, what few sources are available from the other side of the hill present a very different picture. While the Chinese admit that more MiGs were shot down by Sabres than the other way around, they claim that, during the entire war, the ratio of kills in air combat was only 1.142:1 in favor of the Americans.[7] Russian sources credit "Communist" aircraft with no fewer than 1,368 kills. By contrast, Communist losses are said to have amounted to 556 aircraft, though how many of those were shot down in air-to-air combat is not known.[8] Finding out which side was lying or, since war's first casualty is always truth, concocted the greater falsehoods is probably impossible; this is all the more the case because both sets of figures are almost certain to contain errors and are, in any case, not strictly comparable.

The real question is not how many points each side scored but what impact airpower had on the war as a whole. From June 1950 to March 1953 the U.S. Air Force lost about 2,000 aircraft, the navy and marines another 1,200. Of those losses, about half were due to enemy action.[9] This sacrifice, and that of the aircrews involved, enabled the United States and its allies to dominate the sky over North Korea to a growing extent, though they never had it entirely to themselves. The Communists on their part operated a force consisting almost entirely of interceptors. If only for that reason their mission was essentially defensive. Furthermore, just as U.S. aircraft never (well, almost never) crossed the Yalu, so Communist ones, acting tit for tat, stayed north of the 38th parallel. As a result, from the spring of 1951 to the end of the war more than two years later, allied lines of communication in South Korea were practically immune to attack; so were the critical maritime ones that linked South Korea to Japan, without which the war could not have been fought.

To follow the long-familiar division into strategic bombing, interdiction, and close support, Korea itself had hardly any industry and contained few if any strategic targets. A large-scale (1,254 sorties) bombing attack on Pyongyang carried out in July–August 1952 caused many casualties and great destruction. Though LeMay later boasted that SAC had "burned down just about every city in North and South Korea both" (and killed a million Koreans in the process), the effect on the North Koreans' determination and ability to pursue the war was limited at best.[10] Unlike Germany and Japan, North Korea could not be bombed back into the Stone Age because it was already there. This left, as a last resort, about 20 dams that controlled 75 percent of the water needed to irrigate the country's rice-producing fields. In May 1953 American aircraft struck five of the dams and breached them, causing widespread flooding. Yet whether similar attacks, carried out earlier in the war, would have caused the North to surrender is uncertain. Quite possibly its leaders would have responded by lowering water levels in the remaining dams, as they actually did, and asking their Chinese allies to ship over more food.

Thus the effectiveness of strategic bombing hinged on the Americans' willingness to hit targets in Manchuria, the Chinese province bordering on North Korea. However, Truman had put Manchuria off limits. This prohibition was later extended by Eisenhower. Much as they were later to do in Vietnam, U.S. Air Force commanders were always complaining that, though their pilots could see the MiG-15s taking off from airfields just across the Yalu, they were powerless to stop them. But would a change of policy have made a difference? Suppose the advanced Chinese airfields had been struck; surely the threat would have remained, only somewhat further back. As had happened in 1937–45, space was working for the Chinese. Barring the use of nuclear weapons, which seems to have been considered but, thankfully, was never approved, it is most unlikely that the United States could have forced China, which since 1949 was under the most effective government it had known for a century, to its knees. Briefly, extending operations into Manchuria would merely have widened the war, sinking the United States into a quagmire much larger even than Vietnam was later to become. To the Joint Chiefs of Staff, such a course of action was "foolhardy."[11]

Partly because of the risk involved, partly for institutional reasons, first the U.S. Army Air Forces and then the U.S. Air Force itself had never been very enthusiastic about providing the ground forces with close support. Perhaps the nearest they came was in France and Germany during the last ten months of World War II; by the end of that period, so weak had the Wehrmacht's anti-aircraft defenses become that Allied fighter-bombers could do much as they pleased. However, with the bomber generals again taking over the leadership during the postwar years, the art of close support was quickly forgotten. Besides, pilots did not have radio contact with the troops below so that the bomb line had to be defined with the aid of colored markers spread on the ground.[12] Particularly at the beginning of the campaign, the results were often disastrous as U.S. aircraft rained down ordnance on U.S. troops below. One U.S. officer working with South Korean troops claimed he had come under attack five times in a single day.[13]

This left interdiction as the principal method by which the air force could influence the conduct of the war. The most obvious targets were the 17 bridges that spanned the Yalu on which the ability of China and the Soviet Union to send troops and materiel into Korea depended. Lacking almost any other targets, Japan-based B-29s were often used on this mission. Here and there they were even employed against targets of opportunity, a gross misuse of resources if ever there was one. However, the bridges were well defended. By 1951, fully 75 percent of the Communist anti-aircraft defenses were committed to the lines of communication instead of the front.[14] Fear of incurring losses forced the U.S. bombers to fly at over 18,000 feet; at such altitudes they not only proved insufficiently accurate for the task but were easily picked off by the MiGs. Down below, gangs of Chinese and North Korean laborers carried out miracles of repair so that even such bridges as did receive hits seldom remained unserviceable for any length of time. Others were quickly replaced with the aid of pontoons or, in winter, the ice.[15]

The B-29s apart, the American workhorse during the later stages of the interdiction campaign in particular was the F-84 Thunderjet. It was a first-generation, straight-wing machine capable of delivering two tons of ordnance in the form of rockets or bombs.[16] Carrying such unaffectionate nicknames as "the iron sled" or "the groundhog," at higher altitudes it was no match for the faster, more maneuverable MiGs, which forced it to remain at comparatively low ones. In Korea, this meant that pilots' vision was frequently limited by mountains and the shadows they cast. Too often, just locating targets presented a major problem. Even if they could be found, many of them, such as bridges and tunnels, were located in narrow, winding valleys. Achieving a hit on them, assuming it could be done at all, required the pilots to perform complex and sometimes dangerous aerobatic feats. Targets were often camouflaged and well defended by anti-aircraft- and machine guns. Worst of all from the Allied point of view was the near-total lack of any night-vision capability. To be sure, living and fighting under the threat of fighter-bombers was dangerous, but the Chinese and North Koreans, like the Germans in Italy in 1943–45, were able to keep going by shifting operations into the hours of darkness.

A few figures will illustrate the extent of the problem facing those who tried to interdict the North's lines of supply. U.S. calculations indicated that aircraft flying at night hit no more than 0.262 vehicles per sortie—a number so low that one can only speak of a gross misuse of resources.[17] Daytime missions brought better results, but they also led to heavier losses at the hands of ground fire and enemy jet fighters. Except at times when it was engaged in heavy combat, a Chinese or North Korean division apparently required no more than 40 to 50 tons of supplies a day. For the estimated total of 60 divisions, just 2,400 tons were needed—just one-tenth of what an equal number of American divisions would have required during the last year of World War II.[18]

After the war, U.S. Air Force generals claimed that they had brought all but 4 or 5 percent of North Korea's railway traffic to a halt, but that unfortunately it was the rest that mattered. For the period July 1951–June 1953 alone, General Otto P. Weyland, commander of the Far Eastern Air Forces, put Chinese and North Korean losses at 75,000 motor vehicles, 1,000 locomotives, and 16,000 railroad cars. To these he added 2,000 bridges, 27,000 rail cuts, 600 barges and boats, 300 tanks, 12,000 gun positions, 15,000 bunkers, and no fewer than 28,000 troops.[19] Moreover, by the time the armistice was signed sustained attacks had put every North Korean airfield capable of launching jet aircraft out of action. Yet even if we assume that the data are correct, which may not have been the case, the fact is that China was able to mount its great offensive of 1950–51 without the benefit of airpower and in the teeth of everything that the Americans could do.

Later interdiction, extensively and often heroically carried out on a vast scale by the most modern, best-equipped, best-trained air force in history until then, failed to render the opposing ground forces less than battle-ready. Certainly the enemy, now again deployed roughly along the prewar border, suffered. His ability to mount large-scale offensives was impaired, contributing toward the stalemate that eventually developed. But he did not crack; indeed Mao Tse-tung is said to have come out of the conflict convinced that the power of military aviation to influence combat on the ground had been exaggerated.[20] The nature of the terrain, the inability of tactical airpower to find its targets by night, effective ground-based air defenses, the remarkable work of repair gangs, and the relatively small logistics needs of an army that marched and fought mainly on foot all contributed to this outcome.

All in all, it appears that the factors that determined the effectiveness of interdiction remained basically unchanged from what they had been during World War II.[21] For the same reason—that is, the fact that they brought little that was fundamentally new—it is unnecessary to describe the remaining conventional air campaigns of the 1950s and 1960s in any detail. Essentially there were two such campaigns: the one conducted by Israel, France, and Britain against Egypt in 1956 and the one India and Pakistan fought against each other nine years later. As far as conventional war is concerned, the Suez campaign was one of the last to see some propeller-driven combat aircraft in action. Either they took off from carriers, as the French Corsairs and the British Wyverns did, or else from land bases like the Israeli Mustangs and Mosquitoes. By way of their opening move, the Israelis sent some of their Mustangs to cut Egyptian telegraph wires with hooks attached to cables. When the cables snapped the pilots used their propellers and even their wings to carry out their mission, an almost foolhardy undertaking, to be sure, but one that apparently did achieve its objective of delaying the Egyptians' reaction. Another notable feature of the war in the air was the use of paratroopers—the French and British dropped one battalion each, and the Israelis also dropped a battalion. In all three cases men and equipment were widely scattered over the terrain, which detracted from their effectiveness. The British also launched a small-scale sea-to-land, heliborne assault.[22]

Taking off in response to the Israeli attack, Egyptian MiG-15s strafed Israeli columns in the Sinai, with some success, and Egyptian Il-28 light bombers tried to bomb Tel Aviv, without achieving any. The Israelis in turn operated British-built Meteors as well as French-built Ouragans and Mystère IVs. The former two had difficulty holding their own against the MiGs—"Come on, Dassault, give me another 2,000 lb of thrust," complained one Israeli Ouragan pilot—but the latter did not. Flown by well-trained and extremely determined personnel, they probably performed better than any other aircraft in this war. Just one was shot down, not in air-to-air combat but by ground fire.[23] With their air bases coming under

French and British attack, the Egyptian Air Force was all but forced to suspend operations. It ended by losing some 400 aircraft, two-thirds of them on the ground.[24] Within just six days the Israelis had achieved all their military objectives by overrunning most of the Sinai Peninsula. Thanks to American pressure that forced them to suspend the campaign, the French and the British, operating west of the Canal, achieved almost nothing. Yet it is likely that, had they been permitted to proceed, their initial success in annihilating the Egyptian Air Force would have availed them little. The campaign's objectives, namely to topple Nasser's government and reoccupy the Canal Zone, could only be achieved by fighting on the ground. For this they did not have the stomach—as is proved by the fact that, from start to finish, they suffered just 10 and 16 men killed, respectively.

In 1965 the Pakistanis flew British-built Canberras as well as American F-86s and F-104s. Their enemies, the Indians, had an odd assortment of machines, including the British-made Hawker Hunter and de Havilland Vampire, French-built Mystère IV, and MiG 21. Claiming to be a "martial race" in comparison with the supposedly pacifist Hindus, the Pakistanis opened the war with what they hoped would be a devastating, Luftwaffe-style, surprise attack on India's military airfields along the border. Thanks to the fact that the Indians did not have sophisticated radar the attackers enjoyed some success, destroying 35 aircraft on the ground. However, they did not paralyze the Indian Air Force, let alone render it hors de combat. In the battles that followed both sides claimed victory. The Pakistanis said that the overall score was 104 to 19 aircraft in their favor. The Indians said they had won by 73 to 35.[25] They also claimed that their loss rate, calculated on a per-sortie basis, was considerably lower than that of the Pakistanis. Unsurprisingly Pakistan's F-104 interceptors, designed to bring down bombers approaching the United States by way of the North Pole, did not prove very useful against the Indian fighters. At least one was shot down by a Mystère IV in a classic dogfight at low altitude. Surprisingly, some Pakistani Sabres were shot down by Folland Gnats, small, British-built, swept-wing, highly maneuverable subsonic trainers. They became known as Sabre slayers, though here again both sides accused each other of falsifying the numbers.

Early in the war India's aircraft outnumbered those of Pakistan three to one. As a result, after the Pakistani attempt to deliver a knockout blow at the outset had failed, it became clear that their objectives, essentially reducing the Indians to such a state that they would not be able to mount a counterattack, would not be met. Instead of focusing on Kashmir, as the Pakistanis had expected, the Indians opened a second front further south. While the aircraft of both sides were fairly advanced for the time, most were not very suitable for ground attack. Even the Pakistani-operated F-86s could only carry two tons of ordnance; the Indians' Mystère IVs and MiG-21s had a much smaller capability still. Neither belligerent had any experience in waging large-scale conventional war. In the end, neither was able to make much headway either in the air or on the ground. Yet neither had a military industry to speak of, and both believed that they themselves were running out of resources. Pakistan, indeed, begged other Muslim countries to provide it with spare aircraft. The final outcome was the so-called Spirit of Tashkent, after the Soviet city where a peace agreement was signed, that left both countries in possession of what had been theirs at the outset.

Looking back on these three wars, it is clear that airpower failed to bring a decision in any of them. In Korea and the 1965 Indo-Pakistani War, this was mainly because the initial surprise attacks did not achieve the hoped-for results (in Korea, this was only true by a hair's breadth). Instead, struggles of attrition resulted; in them airpower played an important, but far from dominant, part. The difference was that the belligerents in Korea could afford to bring in, and lose, thousands of aircraft and still keep going. On their part, neither India nor Pakistan had what it took to wage a war of attrition in the air. Having exhausted their resources, they too saw their quarrel end in a draw. The Israelis in 1956 did much better. Fighting an opponent who on paper was stronger than themselves, they took the enemy by surprise. Using paratroopers for the first move, they quickly established superiority in, if not command of, the air, and used their air force to assist the ground troops. Particularly important in this respect was the fortified position at Sharm el-Sheik, at the southern tip of the Sinai Peninsula, which was heavily bombed and strafed before it was captured by ground forces. Then as later, the Egyptian pilots proved no match for their enemies. However, much of the Israeli success was due not to their own efforts but to the fact that the Egyptians, specifically including the air force, were attacked in the rear by the French and the British. In turn, and regardless of what airpower could and could not do, those two too would probably have failed to achieve their war objectives even if political circumstances had allowed them to continue the campaign.

The June 1967 War, or the Six-Day War as Israelis call it, was very different. The Suez campaign had boosted Israeli self-confidence. To quote subsequent prime minister and president Shimon Peres, they persuaded themselves that future generations would put it on a par with the feats of Hannibal and Genghis Khan.[26] They went to work with a will; rarely did any nation strive so hard to improve its armed forces and its air force in particular. As the air force commander, Ezer Weizman, used to say in those pre–political correctness days: "the best [men] for flying, the best [women] for the pilots."

Before the 1956 war, so poor had the Israelis been that they bought some of their aircraft from scrap heaps, dismantling ten machines to build one. Even later they remained desperately poor by Western standards. Still the air force was able to do away with its propeller-driven combat aircraft. Instead it acquired new machines in the form of French-made Super-Frelon helicopters, Nord Noratlas transports, and the previously mentioned Super-Mystère fighters and Vautour light bombers. In 1964 they also received some U.S.-built Hawk anti-aircraft missiles. In 1967 terms this could be considered a reasonably modern, though not outstanding, order of battle. The crown of creation was the Dassault Mirage III. Others have noted the French tendency to come up with fighters "feline in profile, made up of smooth-compound curves with sleek flowing lines."[27] The Israelis also quickly fell in love with their "beautiful" Mach 2 fighter, going so far as to compose odes to it.

At that time nuclear weapons were not yet known to have reached the Middle East, meaning that the most important inhibiting factor was absent. The prevailing geopolitical circumstances led to a close resemblance between Israeli Air Force doctrine and that of the Luftwaffe in the 1930s. Like the Germans, the Israelis believed that they were superior to each of their enemies separately but unable to match them all in terms of numbers and staying power. Like the Germans, they hoped to solve the problem by using their internal lines to focus on one enemy after another. Like the Germans, their chosen method was a surprise attack designed to destroy the enemy air force on the ground. It was for this reason, too, that Weizman insisted on arming his Mirages with cannon instead of the air-to-air missiles the French wanted to equip them with. Air superiority having been achieved by this method, the air force would be free to intervene in the ground campaign, primarily by means of interdiction but also by providing close support where necessary and opportune. The outcome was a mean and lean—there were just 200 or so fighters—tactical force with no combat aircraft larger than light twin-engined bombers and almost no strategic capability whatsoever. Its purpose was to deliver the maximum possible firepower for a short time, not to engage in a prolonged war of attrition.

Planning and preparing Operation Moked (Focus) for breaking the Egyptian Air Force took years. Intelligence had to be gathered and numerous reconnaissance missions flown.[28] When the war broke out, the Israelis supposedly knew the name of every Egyptian pilot as well as that of his girlfriend. More important, they knew where to find every single Egyptian Air Force squadron as well as the routine according to which they operated. Additional runways were built to allow the necessary number of aircraft to take off simultaneously, and countless exercises held. Some exercises simulated the approach flights so as to discover the optimal combination of fuel and ordnance each type of aircraft could carry to which targets.[29] Others rehearsed the attacks themselves or were designed to take the measure of Egyptian radar and ensure that the pilots were sufficiently skilled to fly low to escape it. Other still brought the ground crews to a state of maximum efficiency so they took just ten minutes to refuel returning aircraft, rearm then, and turn them around. Compared with 1956, the number of sorties generated per aircraft per day increased fivefold. Serviceability went up from 30–40 percent to almost 100 percent.[30] Special bombs, slowed down by parachutes but then accelerated by rockets so as to bury themselves deep in the ground before exploding, were developed in order to block runways and prevent enemy aircraft from taking off and tackling the attackers.

At the time the Egyptian Air Force had some 500 aircraft of all kinds, the most modern ones being MiG-21 fighters, Sukhoi-7 fighter-bombers, and Tu-16 bombers. They were spread over 23 airfields, some located in the Sinai close to the Israeli border, others west of the Canal and well away from it. All the airfields were defended by anti-aircraft artillery and/or Soviet-supplied SA-2 missiles. These were of the kind that had shot down the American U-2 back in 1960, but they proved of no use against the Israelis. Early warning was provided, or supposed to be provided, by no fewer than 82 interlocking radar sets. However, the Israelis relied on electronic warfare to neutralize them.

On the morning of June 5, after having deceived the enemy by flying the normal morning patrols at 0645 hours, the Israeli fighters took off. At 0745 (0845 Egyptian time) hours, the first wave of attackers, having flown in at as low an altitude as 50 feet over sea and land and pulling up at the last moment, arrived at ten airfields simultaneously. So unprepared were the Egyptians that they had left their aircraft standing neatly on the runways where they formed ideal targets. During their first pass, the Israelis dropped their specially developed bombs, cratering the runways and rendering them unusable. Other bombs were fitted with delayed-action fuses, preventing immediate repairs from being made. Hardly any Egyptian fighters were able to get into the air. What anti-aircraft fire there was was sporadic, uncoordinated, and ineffective. Depending on how much fuel they had left, most of the attacking aircraft were able to make one or two additional passes, using their cannon for strafing. On the ground, the carnage was complete. As one Israeli pilot later wrote, his assigned target, Cairo West, "actually looked like hell. The great smoke pillars, and the shadows of the cloudy 'treetops' above, showed from far away like a huge, dark, jungle. . . . Kerosene fires belched red, sending black and white balloons among the bellows of the blacksmith's shop."[31] By 0900 hours the first wave had done its work. Meticulous planning and near-perfect execution led to 195 enemy machines being destroyed on the ground. Nine more were shot down in air-to-air combat.

The second wave took off at 0915 hours and struck some of the more remote airfields that had not been hit by the first one. The Egyptians had still not recovered from their surprise. Consequently another 100 of their aircraft were destroyed, almost all of them on the ground. So good were the results that the Israelis found themselves with more aircraft than they needed to carry out their mission. As one Egyptian pilot noted, "the planes [of the second wave] didn't shoot. They merely circled, their pilots surprised that the base was completely destroyed and that no enemies remained." Left defenseless, it was all the Egyptians could do to scurry about, try to take shelter, and shoot back with handguns.[32] Far from not having sufficient aircraft to accomplish the mission, which during the years of preparation had been the Israelis' greatest fear, they were able to divert some of them away to fight on other fronts. By 1035 the aircraft forming the second wave had also returned to base. At general headquarters Weizman, who at that time was serving as deputy chief of staff under Yitzhak Rabin, could be heard bellowing into the telephone telling his wife that the war had been won.[33]

Not only were the Egyptians taken by surprise, but the minister of defense, having ordered his subordinates not to disturb him, was fast asleep. President Nasser's deputy and his air force commander, along with a group of high-ranking officers, were absent on an inspection trip in the Sinai and could not be reached. On their return one of the two aircraft that carried them was shot up by the Israelis. Worst of all were the lies—the Egyptians claimed they had shot down no fewer than 86 Israeli aircraft, as well as an

American one, for the loss of two of their own. Apparently Nasser himself was left in the dark. One lie bred another, and the Egyptians were soon telling their Jordanian allies as well as the rest of the world that American and British aircraft had participated in the attack. As the early twentieth-century German chief of staff Alfred von Schlieffen wrote, for a really great victory to be won, the two sides, the victor and the loser, have to cooperate, each in his own way. If ever an operation met that condition, surely Focus was the one.

The day's operations cost the Israelis 16 aircraft, a little less than 10 percent of their order of battle. Most were lost not to air combat but to ground fire. The latter's relatively good performance was made possible mainly by the fact that the Israeli pilots often made several passes over each base they attacked, enabling the Egyptian gunners to recover from their initial shock. The Egyptian Air Force having been largely destroyed, the Israelis turned against their other enemies. The first to suffer was Syria. Responding to an urgent Egyptian call for help, the Syrians had sent a few of their aircraft to attack an Israeli petroleum-refining plant in Haifa, a vitally important strategic target. The Israeli defenses were weak; fully engaged against Egypt, they had left just 12 fighters to cover the homeland. The Hawk missiles were deployed far to the south where they protected the nuclear reactor at Dimona; all other anti-aircraft defenses were antiquated. Fortunately the ill-trained Syrian pilots proved to be unequal to the job, and no serious damage was done.

At 1200 hours on June 5, the Israelis struck back. Their targets were Damascus International Airport as well as four other airfields that defended the city from the south and east. The attacks came in two waves, each lasting two hours, with a two-hour interval between them. Though many enemy aircraft were destroyed on the ground, the Syrians proved to be a tougher nut to crack than the Egyptians. Unlike their allies, the Syrians had no surface-to-air missiles. They did, however, have a dense and fairly effective array of anti-aircraft guns as well as a functioning system for identifying and tracking incoming enemy aircraft. As a result the attack did not go as smoothly as it had in the south. So heavy was the fire that greeted Israeli aircraft targeting Damascus International Airport that the pilots had to withdraw, regroup over Lebanese territory, and fly in for a second time. The attack on another airfield had to be suspended until four Mirages could be sent to deal with the anti-aircraft defenses. By 1800 hours 53 Syrian aircraft, about half of the entire air force, had been destroyed for the loss of two Israeli aircraft. One airfield was put out of action, and four others were badly damaged.

At 1000 hours King Hussein of Jordan, having been misled by Nasser's lies, entered the war by shelling Jerusalem. He also sent 16 out of his 35 Hawker Hunters to attack Israeli targets, including an airfield north of Tel Aviv, where a transport aircraft was destroyed on the ground. Joining the Jordanians was a lone Iraqi Tu-16 bomber. Apparently its objective was to attack an Israeli Air Force base in the Valley of Esdraelon, but it missed its target and bombed a civilian settlement instead. On its way back it was brought down, crashing inside a military base and killing 16 Israeli soldiers.[34] In response, the Israelis lashed out at several Jordanian airfields as well as an Iraqi one. Hussein's pilots were much better trained than the remaining Arab ones. However, the balance of forces was completely lopsided; though they fought back fiercely and shot down two Israeli aircraft, the tiny Jordanian Air Force was wiped out. Most of the Iraqi bases were out of range for the Israelis, who were still some years away from acquiring an air-to-air refueling capability of their own. An attack on their nearest one, H-3 in western Iraq, led to the destruction of ten Iraqi aircraft, but the field itself was not put out of action.

With their 200 combat aircraft the Israelis were able to generate about 1,000 sorties. Of those, 750 were flown against Egypt and the rest against Syria, Jordan, and Iraq. Since the air force had only slightly more than one pilot per aircraft,[35] many pilots had to take off and fight as many as five times during a single day. These astonishing numbers formed a major factor behind the Israeli success. Closely paralleling the best that fighters and fighter-bombers had achieved during World War II, they also explain why both Nasser and Hussein apparently believed that Western aircraft were participating in the attack on their countries. This extremely rapid tempo was made possible partly by the pilots' own stamina and motivation, partly by the outstanding skill of the ground crews, and partly by the short distances that were often, though by no means always, involved.

Early the next day, having obtained near-absolute command of the air, the Israelis turned to the business of supporting their rapidly advancing ground forces. By that time the most important Egyptian-fortified perimeters defending the Sinai, the ones at Raffia in the north and at Abu Agheila in the center of the front respectively, had already fallen. In capturing the former, the armored columns were supported by some light Fouga Magister trainers that had been hastily equipped with machine guns and rockets; so rapid was the advance that a planned parachute drop on the town of El-Arish was canceled. The attack on Abu Agheila was assisted by a heliborne battalion that landed west of the fortified perimeter and cut it off. Though small in scale, this was one of the rare post-1945 occasions when vertical envelopment was tried and, thanks to the fact that the Egyptian Air Force was in no position to interfere, succeeded in achieving its objective.[36]

Operating all but undisturbed, the Israeli aircraft demolished a Jordanian armored brigade as it made its way to reinforce Jerusalem. Next they shot up another Jordanian brigade as it broke shelter while trying to mount a counterattack near Nablus. In the most important air supply operation of the war, transports dropped fuel to the armored brigade that had reached the Mitla Pass in the southern Sinai and blocked it. Trying to force their way through toward the Canal, the Egyptians, exposed in the open desert, were decimated by fighter-bombers roaring overhead. When the assault on the Golan Heights opened on June 9, it, too, was preceded by waves of fighter-bombers that dropped some 200 tons of ordnance—a large figure for those days—on the Syrian positions. Early next morning helicopters lifted another paratrooper battalion to the southern part of the Heights, only to find the area free of the enemy. Thus airpower played a key role, though not an exclusive one, on each one of the three fronts where the Israelis fought and won. Over the war as a whole, their own losses amounted to 37 aircraft destroyed plus another 19 made unserviceable, so that their force was reduced to about three-quarters of its original strength.

The reader may well ask why so much attention has been paid to this war in the present volume. After all, hostilities, though intensive, were comparatively small and brief. At the time Israel, and even more so its Arab enemies, were third- if not fourth-rate military powers. None of the belligerents had an aviation industry worth mentioning. Consequently all were absolutely dependent on their foreign supporters for all types of major hardware. Though the Israeli Mirages and Egyptian MiG-21s were modern for their time, on both sides many of the aircraft were obsolescent and some were obsolete. Though the Israelis certainly resorted to electronic warfare in their successful attempt to mislead the Egyptian radar in particular, neither side as yet possessed any kind of AWACS aircraft. Fighter-bombers operated largely on their own, without the vast fleet of escorts, consisting of other kinds of aircraft that were later to become routine. Technologically speaking, so backward was the Israeli military that the navy, the least important of its armed services, did not even possess its own radar set. Apparently that fact played a major role in making possible the USS *Liberty* incident when Israeli fighters mistakenly shot up an American intelligence ship. To complete the picture, the aircraft of neither side were equipped with air-to-air missiles, meaning that air combat took place at close range as it always had. Having been directed toward the enemy by radar, pilots relied on their eyes to identify him. Since recently developed computerized bombsights had not yet reached the Middle East, air-to-ground strikes were none too accurate and depended on the pilots taking risks by flying very low. Neither the belligerents in the Middle East nor anybody else had an effective nighttime capability for such missions. Though both sides deployed surface-to-air missiles, the Israeli SAMs never saw action. The Egyptian ones, immobile and designed to shoot down aircraft from high altitudes, proved ineffective.

Yet there was another side to the story. The period 1945–67 saw plenty of armed conflicts, but only a few occasions when airpower was used in conventional interstate war. Among such wars that amounted to more than mere skirmishes, such as regularly occurred in the Middle East among other places, the 1967 air campaign was the second largest after Korea. But whereas the Korean War and of course the 1965 Indo-Pakistani War ended in stalemate, the Six-Day War produced a spectacular victory. Experts understood it as a showcase for what a highly motivated, well-prepared, well-commanded air force could do if given the chance.[37] It was, moreover, an almost purely tactical/operational victory over the other side's deployed armies in the field; no attempt was made to strike civilian targets in the rear, nor did Israel possess the wherewithal to do so on any scale. Subsequent decades were to witness other air campaigns that brought victory, but none against an approximately equal enemy and none swifter or more decisive.

With the benefit of hindsight, it appears that the Israeli performance represented the swan song in an age that was already on the wane. That age had opened on September 1, 1939. On that day, airpower, proving its worth in what was quickly to turn into history's first Blitzkrieg, reached full maturity. Subsequently the combination of fighter-bomber cum tank, with wireless communications and forward observation officers forming the link between the two, became the most powerful instrument available to any commander who was planning to launch an offensive war on land and win a decisive victory. For several decades it became the highest ambition of every modern armed force in the world to emulate the Wehrmacht and improve upon it if possible. Countless billions were spent, and countless scenarios written, in an effort to prepare either for carrying out this scheme or for resisting it. However, throughout the period the most important countries were prevented by their nuclear arsenals from trying their hand at this game.

Under such circumstances, with nuclear weapons not yet having been introduced into the Middle East,[38] the Israeli Defense Force and Air Force were perhaps the only ones who succeeded. Not merely in the air but on the ground, too, in many ways the 1967 War looked as if it had been produced by some time machine coming straight out of the early years of World War II.[39] Yet appearances were illusory. To paraphrase Churchill's dictum on the Battle of El Alamein, in all these ways the war marked the end of the beginning as well as the beginning of the end.

CHAPTER 15

FROM THE SINAI TO TEHRAN

Great as it was, the 1967 Israeli triumph over the Arab states did not bring hostilities in the Middle East to an end. Border incidents involving the armed forces, including the air forces, of both sides were frequent. So were Israeli air strikes on terrorist targets first in Jordan and then in Lebanon too. Most of those were too small and too insignificant to be discussed in this chapter. But that is not true of the so-called War of Attrition that was launched by Nasser in March 1969 and lasted for 16 months until August of the next year.

The struggle along the 100 or so miles of the Suez Canal was highly asymmetric. To the west were the Egyptians with vast, if qualitatively inferior, ground forces. Their main strength consisted of as many as 1,000 Soviet-supplied artillery barrels. To the east were a relative handful of Israeli troops with not even one-tenth that number. It was to compensate for their inferiority that the Israelis activated their air force, without great success as we shall presently see. Drunk with victory, they underestimated their enemy's determination. At the same time they had to husband their forces because French president Charles de Gaulle refused to release 50 Mirage V fighter-bombers that had already been paid for. As a result of these two factors, at first most of Israel's air operations consisted of pinpricks. With some of their bases located in the Sinai, much closer to Egypt than previously, the Israelis were able to mount reconnaissance flights deep into the enemy's rear. They also sent planes to buzz Cairo and mounted heliborne raids against selected Egyptian targets.[1] Many of the raids were tactically very successful. Yet they failed to end the massive artillery bombardments coming from across the Canal.

Meanwhile the Soviets were rebuilding the Egyptian Air Force at top speed. Along with new aircraft, they brought in their own personnel to advise and train their clients. Learning from their mistakes, the latter concealed their aircraft in underground shelters. July 1969 saw the first air battles since 1967 fought above the Canal. By this time the Israeli order of battle had been strengthened by the addition of U.S.-built A-4 Skyhawks, light bombers capable of carrying more ordnance to a greater distance than anything they had operated before. By converting an old C-54 Stratocruiser, they even acquired an air refueling capability. Late in 1969 the Skyhawks were joined by the first F-4 Phantoms, which could fly over twice as fast and were even more powerful. Using smuggled blueprints the Israelis also started work on their own version of the Mirage V, but by the time those machines joined the order of battle, the War of Attrition had ended.

Facing these aircraft, as well as the older Mirages, Super Mystères, and Vautours, were advanced-model MiG-21s. Both sides now relied primarily on air-to-air missiles for air combat, though neither committed the American error of trying to make do without cannon. Indeed it was for fear of the guns that the Israeli Air Force commander at one point prohibited his Phantom pilots from engaging the MiGs, with their superior maneuverability, at close quarters.[2] Nevertheless, by carefully weighing their enemies' strength and weakness, in air combat the Israelis did better than ever before, shooting down 18 aircraft to one as against a ratio of only three to one in 1967.[3] Using their new aircraft to the full, they also rained down bombs on the Egyptian positions. Yet in spite of massive casualties, numbering hundreds of dead each month, the Egyptians kept coming.

But for Vietnam, about which more later, the air war over the Suez Canal was the most advanced in history until then. Gradually, the entire character of air combat started changing. On both sides, sophisticated radar enabled senior commanders on the ground to follow friendly and hostile aircraft throughout their missions. This meant that, instead of engaging in simple dogfights, whole groups of aircraft were sent up to confront each other. They worked, or were supposed to work, in well-coordinated teams. Some Israeli aircraft acted as bait, while others, flying low behind the hills of the western Sinai so as to avoid detection by Egyptian radar, waited in ambush for the right moment. Others still were vectored to the area even as the battle developed.[4] Increasingly, "shooters"—that is, fighters and fighter-bombers—came to work in close cooperation with reconnaissance aircraft and electronic warfare aircraft. Thus the modern "strike packages" were developed.[5]

As the role of centralized command and control grew, pilots lost some of their independence. On the whole these changes favored the Israelis, whose pilots were much better trained. Too, they had always emphasized this aspect of warfare; for example, when receiving new aircraft from the United States, they insisted that every one be equipped not with one but two radios even if it meant removing some other equipment. On the other side, the Egyptians continued to suffer from a shortage of qualified pilots. Though their population numbered in the tens of millions, so low was their level of socio-economic-cultural development that they found this problem very hard to correct, as they may still do.[6] Another difficulty was their tendency to vastly exaggerate the results they were achieving; after all, even the best system is only as good as the information that flows through it.

Soviet sources show that, during the second half of 1969, the Egyptians lost 41 aircraft to the Israelis and another 29 to accidents.[7] How many losses the Israelis took is unknown; however, clearly they dominated the air in the face of everything the Egyptian Air Force and air defenses could do. Still they saw no way to end the struggle. Week by week, their units manning the fortifications on the Canal took casualties from artillery fire and commando raids. Driven to near despair, they thought of switching from tactical strikes to deep strategic ones into the Egyptian rear; the arrival of the Phantoms, which could carry far more ordnance than any other fighter-bomber aircraft then available in the Middle East, seemed to provide the wherewithal to do so. The objective was "to bring the war home to the Egyptian people" and either make them force Nasser to call a halt to the war or topple him.[8] Though the Israelis did hit industrial manufacturing plants, air force supply dumps, and, on one occasion, a school that was targeted by mistake, in the end the idea turned out to be both foolish and dangerous. It was foolish because, like so many others before them, the Israelis vastly underestimated the effort and the time required to produce results;[9] initially, indeed, all they were able to commit to the offensive were four F-4s. It was dangerous because Nasser, who was often at his best when things were going badly, did not give in. Instead he called in the Soviets in much greater force than previously.

Egypt's anti-aircraft defense system consisted of thousands of anti-aircraft guns with calibers ranging from 12.5 to 100 millimeter. Also present were numerous SA-2 batteries. Up to that point the Israelis had been able to cope; in September 1969, in one of their more spectacular feats, some of their heliborne infantry had even succeeded in capturing, dismantling, and taking home a sophisticated P-12 Soviet radar set that both they and their American patrons wanted to take a close look at. There had long been Soviet "advisers" in Egypt, but in January 1970 they intervened in earnest. Soviet officers assumed command and Soviet personnel were integrated into the Egyptian forces down to battalion level, so that eventually their number reached 20,000. With the personnel came new weapons and weapon systems. Though the Soviets, probably because they feared the American reaction, refused to provide their Egyptian clients with bombers, they did send over batteries of mobile SA-3 missiles intended for medium-altitude work. Earlier these missiles had only been deployed around Moscow. In a single night, eight new batteries were added.[10] By the spring, the Soviet-Egyptian anti-aircraft defenses along the Canal had become the most powerful the world had ever seen and were still growing daily. Toward the end of the struggle the Israelis even found themselves trying to fight the new SA-6s, the first time these missiles were used outside the Soviet Union itself.

With the Soviet anti-aircraft defenses came some Soviet pilots who soon started flying patrols over the Canal Zone. As in Korea, they were prohibited from revealing their identity in case they were captured. Lacking combat experience, they were easy prey to the Israelis; on one occasion five were shot down. Politically, though, the prospect of a possible large-scale Soviet intervention in the conflict scared Israel witless. Indeed the need to consider Soviet reactions dominated the struggle from beginning to end. Meanwhile the duel with the anti-aircraft defenses continued. By this time the Israelis were using sophisticated electronic countermeasures, partly U.S.-supplied and partly home-produced, to try to defeat the missiles. Some of the equipment was mounted under the wings of the fighter-bombers themselves; the rest was installed aboard modified transport aircraft and helicopters. The objective was to warn pilots that they were being targeted and to interfere with the electromagnetic radiation emanating from the Egyptian radar sets as well as their communication system. By the time the war ended, the Israelis had also received American air-to-ground missiles originally developed for Vietnam.

A laser illuminated the target, which the missiles were guided to with the aid of a small joystick mounted in the cockpit. Depending on the altitude he was flying at, the pilot had to maintain the missiles in his sight for as much as a minute, a fact that greatly impeded his ability to carry out maneuvers of any kind. In Vietnam, the missiles had been used against stationary targets such as buildings, bridges, and gun-pits. U.S. pilots loudly sang their praise.[11] Along the Canal, where the opposing anti-aircraft system used similar weapons but was much denser, they proved dangerous to their operators and had to be withdrawn from service.[12] At the time, the U.S. arsenal already included more advanced, anti-radiation homing missiles, but Washington refused to sell them to the Israelis. Faute de mieux, the latter had to go on fighting as best they could. Though electronic warfare and evasive maneuvering meant that only one out of a hundred Egyptian missiles scored a hit, from November 1969 to August 1970 the Israelis admitted to losing five Phantoms. The Egyptians, of course, put the number much higher. Given how many thousands of sorties were flown, the Israeli losses, as reported by them, were not excessive. Yet the air battles left both the Israelis and their American advisers at their wits' end when it came to finding a way to deal with the constantly improving defenses.[13]

It is impossible to work out the relative importance of the factors that finally caused both sides to accept a cease-fire on August 7, 1970: the losses suffered in the fighting along the Canal, a general sense of exhaustion, or pressure from Washington and Moscow. On the one hand, the Israelis were not defeated. On the other, in sharp contrast to 1967, what many now saw as the world's best air force failed to overcome the most powerful anti-aircraft defenses. As General Weizman later wrote, "the missile had bent the aircraft's wing." In a way, that outcome was not surprising. After all, electronic warfare was something both sides could, and increasingly did, employ. Much the same technology developed to guide missiles from the air to the ground could be, and was, used to guide opposing ones from the ground to bring down targets in the air. Both sides could also engage in electronic warfare by interfering with the other's communications, misleading his radar, and so on.

Aside from the ongoing conflict in Vietnam, the following three years saw only one other large-scale war in which airpower played an important part, the 1971 one between India and Pakistan. Besides the old dispute over Kashmir, a major factor behind the war was Pakistani repression in its eastern province, later to be known as Bangladesh. As millions of refugees poured across the border into India, a crisis developed. The Indians saw the war as a repetition of the one that had been fought in 1965; the Pakistanis saw it as a deliberate Indian attempt to dismantle their country, and one that was ultimately successful.

After some fighting along the border between India and Bengal, the center of gravity shifted to the west. As in 1965, the Pakistanis opened the war by striking at Indian airfields, but the balance of forces was no longer what it had been. Whereas the Pakistanis still flew their F-104 interceptors and their now obsolescent F-86 fighter-bombers, the Indian order of battle had been reinforced by six squadrons of late-model MiG-21s. Once again the Pakistanis failed to neutralize the Indian Air Force, much of which had been deployed further to the rear and thus out of the Pakistanis' reach. Once again some Sabres were brought down by Folland Gnats, or so the Indians claimed. Another one of their claims is that, in all four recorded cases of combat between MiG-21s and F-104s, the former prevailed over the latter, one reason being that the Indians were flying a primitive AWACS aircraft whereas their opponents were not.[14] It is certainly true that the Indian Air Force supported the ground forces that were invading East Pakistan. Yet the decision in that theater was brought about less by regular warfare between the two countries than by the massive rebellion of the population and the obvious inability of the outnumbered Pakistanis to fight on two fronts at the same time. It is also true that the Indian Air Force, having survived the initial Pakistani attack, went on to gain air superiority over West Pakistan and again provided support to the ground forces by bombing and rocketing. The difference in attrition rates is said to have been much greater than in 1965. Even so, the Indian ground offensive was slow and hesitant and did not get very far.

Eventually East Pakistan was able to gain its independence and became Bangladesh, but the Indian Air Force only played a fairly small role in this development. Eventually the war in the west ended in a draw, as had happened six years earlier. Though the Indians have gone to some length to deny this,[15] possibly the fact that the U.S. carrier *Enterprise*, complete with its complement of nuclear-capable aircraft, appeared in the Bay of Bengal had something to do with their decision to evacuate the small slice of West Pakistan their troops had occupied. Tactically and operationally, airpower did play a role in the war, but its importance should not be exaggerated. Neither in the air nor on the ground did the Pakistanis have what it took to defeat India, an opponent much larger than themselves. To make things even worse for them, they were simultaneously trying to keep down their eastern province with its tens of millions of people.

In retrospect, the most important outcome of the war was that both sides decided to develop nuclear weapons and did so successfully. The Indians conducted their first "peaceful nuclear explosion" in 1974. Starting from a less developed industrial-scientific base, the Pakistanis took longer and probably acquired their own bomb during the mid- or late 1980s.[16] The outcome resembled the one that had developed in other places around the world; much as the two sides hated each other, large-scale warfare, air warfare specifically included, between them came to an end. In 1999 India used its air force to expel a battalion of Pakistani-supported irregulars who had crossed the border, but the scale of operations was very small.[17] Later both India and Pakistan followed the example of other nuclear countries. First they developed ballistic missiles to replace manned aircraft for nuclear weapon delivery; next, they started building or purchasing cruise missiles and UAVs.[18]

In October 1973 the fourth, or fifth (depending on how one counts), Arab-Israeli War broke out. By this time the United States had withdrawn from Vietnam, and its armed forces were eager to turn their attention back to "real," meaning conventional, warfare. The so-called Yom Kippur War provided them with a welcome opportunity to do just that, albeit only vicariously. During the War of Attrition, the United States, though it did provide the Israelis with Skyhawk and Phantom fighter-bombers, had withheld some of its most advanced offensive ground-attack weapons. After the August 1970 cease-fire had taken hold, they changed their attitude, and in any case the Israelis themselves were now producing a growing array of advanced weapons such as Shafrir air-to-air missiles. The Soviets on their part delivered SA-6 missiles to the Egyptians and Syrians, thus further strengthening their already formidable anti-aircraft defenses. The outcome was the most modern air war in history until then—one that was followed very closely by experts throughout the world.

This time it was the Israelis' turn to be taken by surprise. Both on the Golan Heights and over the Suez Canal, reconnaissance flights and other methods had revealed vast Syrian and Egyptian military buildups. However, Israeli intelligence did not believe there would be a war, claiming that no Arab leader would start one without first making sure his armed forces were able to obtain air superiority over the Israelis. Only on the morning of October 6, a few hours before the Arab offensive was due to begin, did it dawn on the Israelis that their "concept," as it was later known, had been wrong and that hostilities were imminent. With an army consisting largely of reservists, the Israelis had always planned to use their air force to hold back the attackers until those reservists could be mobilized and reach the front. To do so, it was necessary to have freedom of action in the air. Recalling the difficulties it had experienced during the War of Attrition, the air force had planned to launch large-scale preemptive strikes against the Syrians and Egyptians. Militarily such a strike, which had been carefully prepared and rehearsed, was the correct solution. The author of the most detailed account of the subject, who is himself a former Phantom pilot and squadron commander, claims that it would have been a great success; furthermore, it would still have left 80 Skyhawks free to participate in the ground battle.[19]

As more intelligence reports arrived during the night of October 5–6, the Israelis, with their ground forces on each of the two fronts outnumbered ten to one, hesitated. Apparently they were unable to decide which enemy, the Syrians or the Egyptians, they should hit first, and also whether their first target should be airfields, as in 1967, or the anti-aircraft missile defenses. What the air force commander did not know was that, as early as the morning of October 5, Prime Minister Golda Meir had promised Washington there would be no preemptive strike. Yet that news only reached the air force four hours before the attack got under way. Consequently there was nothing to do but throw doctrine to the wind, change plans, and focus on supporting the ground forces, especially on the northern front, where the danger appeared greater and more urgent.

Both the Syrians and the Egyptians opened their offensives with massive air strikes. The objectives of the former were limited; realizing that they would be unable to gain air superiority, they focused on close support and interdiction during the first hours of their offensive so as to exploit the effect of surprise. Except for a heliborne operation that captured a vital Israeli observation post on Mount Hermon, they were not successful. Israeli sources claim that 58 Syrian aircraft that were sent either on attack missions or to provide those missions with cover only destroyed a few vehicles, killed two soldiers, and injured six others. One Syrian MiG-21 was shot down by an Israeli Mirage and another was brought down by friendly anti-aircraft fire. Apparently feeling that it had shot its bolt, from that point on the Syrian Air Force played only a minor role in the war. It flew regular patrols over its own territory but hardly interfered with Israeli ground operations.[20]

The Egyptian plans were more ambitious and in some ways resembled those of the Israelis in 1967. Unable to reach their enemies' aircraft in their underground bunkers, they focused on Israeli military airfields as well as anti-aircraft defenses and every sort of command, control, and communications facility in the Sinai Peninsula. Except for one Kelt air-to-ground missile that was launched at Tel Aviv but never reached its destination, all targets were located in the Sinai. Simultaneously Egyptian helicopters were sent to land commando units along the main roads in the Sinai with the objective of slowing down the arrival of Israeli reinforcements. Some of the helicopters were intercepted by the Israeli aircraft in the air. Others were able to land safely and deliver their human cargoes, which, however, were mostly detected, surrounded, and destroyed on the ground. To that extent, the old concept of vertical envelopment was dealt another blow.

The attacks on air bases scored numerous hits on runways and other installations. Coming literally out of the blue, they caused considerable confusion and contributed to the fact that, early on, the Israeli response was uncharacteristically uncoordinated. Pilots took off in a hurry and tried to intercept whomever they could. Anti-aircraft missile battery commanders were simply told to shoot down whoever appeared on their radar screens without waiting for orders from above. Yet by the next morning most of the damage had been repaired. Thereafter the Egyptian Air Force played only a minor role in the fighting. Much later, it turned out that neither the Egyptians nor the Syrians had any intention to invade Israel. The former were planning to stay close to the Canal, under cover of their anti-aircraft missiles on the West Bank; the latter only intended to reoccupy the Golan Heights.

However, at the time the Israelis did not know this. As a result, early in the war they kept changing direction. Now the enemy's ground forces were the primary target, now his missile defenses. Now they focused on the northern front in an attempt to stop what looked like an invasion of Israel proper, now on the southern one where they targeted the Egyptian bridges over the Canal. On both fronts they attacked the enemy's anti-aircraft missiles, but on neither were operations pressed home. No sooner did any one of them show signs of success than it was interrupted by the need to carry out some other, seemingly more urgent, task. Another difficulty was the unexpected appearance on both fronts of highly mobile SA-6s—by the time fighter-bombers, properly configured for dealing with them, arrived on the scene, the missiles were often gone and had to be located all over again. Looking for them, let alone providing ground support before they had been knocked out, turned out to be extremely costly. Pilots who, with 1967 in mind, tried to evade the SAMs by flying low ran into the fire of radar-guided, quadruple-barrel ZSU-23 guns. Spitting out 4,000 rounds a minute, the latter literally chewed up the Israeli planes.

One Israeli pilot sent out to attack the Egyptian Army in the western Sinai later recalled:

> The sky was full of [our] aircraft, flying southwestward very low towards the Suez Canal. . . . I pull up slightly to 200 feet and see the war down on the ground: tanks and armored vehicles of all kinds driving about in all directions, firing, launching missiles and leaving luminescent streaks in the air. . . . It must be extremely crowded and noisy, yet to us, who cannot hear anything, it all looks like a silent movie. . . . I have only a few seconds to find my target. There it is . . . dense anti-aircraft fire is coming at us from all directions, even from behind. The Egyptians are good at this. . . . Pull the stick, switch on the afterburner to 4.5 G. With the nose pointing up, the horizon disappears and everything is blue. . . . Press the button to release the bombs. Wham! The Phantom leaps. Now the bombs are on their way to target. . . . I roll over and dive towards the ground, violently waving right and left to avoid the flak. . . . We cross the Canal. . . . the anti-aircraft fire grows less intensive. We are out of the danger zone.[21]

The air force did play a critical role in halting the Syrians, especially in the southern part of the Golan Heights, where, at one point, there were almost no ground forces left to oppose them, but the price was high. By the evening of October 7, out of 390 combat aircraft at the beginning of the war, 28—7 percent—had been lost and another 47 damaged, of which only 25 could be repaired.[22] Clearly such a rate was unsustainable. Over the next few days, the air force reduced the pace of operations to lick its wounds and take stock.

With the appointment of a former air chief of staff to command operations in the north, the air force was effectively split in two. While this arrangement violated the principle of concentration of force, it did achieve its objective of putting an end to the situation where operations were not pushed home and where many squadrons were permanently lost because the general staff could not decide on which front they should be employed first. Still it was mainly the ground forces, now arriving in growing numbers, which stopped the Syrians and later advanced to within 15 miles of Damascus, where they halted. Israeli ground support missions over the Golan Heights had to be flown at great altitudes where they were much less effective. Even so, aircraft continued to be lost throughout the war. In the Sinai things were worse still. When the Israelis mounted their first abortive counteroffensive on that front on October 8, they had to do so effectively without air support, because somebody at air force headquarters had insisted that the ground troops' forward air controllers be left out of the loop.[23]

During the rest of the war, which lasted until October 24, the Israeli Air Force bombed targets both in the Syrian port of Latakia and in the capital of Damascus itself. Yet when the Egyptians resumed their attack on October 13, it was Israeli tanks under Ariel Sharon, not the air force, that stopped the enemy in their tracks. Further to the south on the same day, the Egyptians at last broke anti-aircraft missile cover. This time the Israeli Air Force did intervene, and its intervention was effective. Throughout this period, the Egyptian anti-aircraft system still remained intact. Only during the last days of the war did the Israeli ground forces, which had crossed the Canal, finally begin tearing holes in it. The last few days of the war also saw the Egyptian Air Force going into action once again. As the Israelis threatened to surround the southernmost of the two Egyptian armies east of the Canal, Egyptian fighter-bombers flew what almost amounted to suicide missions in support, only to be shot down in considerable numbers by the resurgent Israelis.

The following figures will provide some idea of the scope of the fighting. In 1970 the Egyptians had 27 surface-to-air missile batteries; in 1973 they deployed no fewer than 146. The Syrian figures were six and 36 respectively. In 1973 the Israelis had 390 combat aircraft, Egypt and Syria 1,410. During the first critical 30 hours, 78 percent of sorties flown by Israeli aircraft were in support of the ground forces, 16 percent struck anti-aircraft defenses, and only 4 percent were directed against airfields. Over the entire 19-day war the Israelis shot down 277 enemy aircraft.[24] Given that, at the time it ended, the Egyptians and Syrians still had many hundreds of combat aircraft left, the small role their air forces took in the war is a remarkable tribute to the ability of the heavily outnumbered Israelis to dominate the skies. Of course these figures do not reflect all the activities of the Israeli Air Force in particular. It also provided their own ground forces with air cover, struck at enemy ground targets, flew numerous reconnaissance missions, and made heavy use of its helicopters and cargo aircraft. Heliborne commandos landed in Syria and blew up some bridges on the road from Baghdad to Damascus, delaying the arrival of a 60,000-strong Iraqi expeditionary force. Other heliborne forces attacked Egyptian communications east of the Canal. Yet on the whole, and mainly because Egyptian missile defenses were only breached toward the end of the war and the Syrian ones remained largely intact, its impact on the war was not nearly as great as it had been in 1967.

Another notable feature of the use of airpower during this war was the organization by both superpowers of massive airlifts to assist their respective clients. Apparently the Soviets flew in mainly replacement SAMs, most of which went to Syria rather than to Egypt. The Americans sent urgently needed Phantoms—which, refueled in midflight, reached Israel under their own power—Skyhawk spare parts, C-53 helicopters, ammunition, air-to-surface missiles more advanced than those the Israelis already had, and, by way of a demonstration of capability, a couple of M-60 tanks and 155-millimeter howitzers. Some of these supplies, particularly the air-to-surface missiles, arrived on time to play an important role during the war's last days; as this author can testify firsthand, the impact on Israeli morale was also very considerable.[25]

Almost nothing is known of the factors that induced the Egyptians and the Syrians to ask for assistance and the Soviet Union to provide it. As to the Israelis, clearly during the early days of the war they were close to despair. Foreign sources later claimed that they had threatened, or prepared, to use their nuclear weapons.[26] Possibly the preparations were deliberately made in such a way that the Americans would not fail to notice them. In other words, what really motivated the Americans was less the course of the war itself than not-so-subtle Israeli nuclear blackmail; in this way the dominant factor, entering through the back door, demonstrated its dominance once again. Needless to say, the transport aircraft flying in from both the United States and the Soviet Union were able to reach their destinations only because neither side, but especially the Israelis who, behind the front, were in almost full command of the air, dared fire a shot at them.

Even so, air transport on its own was unable to keep either Israel or its enemies fully supplied. Accordingly, both superpowers supplemented their airlifts with massive sealifts. The few available data show that, out of 75,000 or so tons of Soviet supplies that were sent to Syria, only 12,000 to 15,000 arrived by air.[27] The U.S. figures were 33,000 and 22,000 tons, respectively, but the figures are available only to October 30, the day the airlift was suspended. They thus exclude the supplies that went on reaching Israel by sea for several months after that date. By airlifting massive amounts of supplies over unprecedented distances, Operation Nickel Grass showed what air transport could do in respect to speed, flexibility, and range. The performance of the C-5 Galaxy, with its maximum payload of just over 80 tons, was especially remarkable.[28] Yet it also showed that there were limits to the quantity of supplies that could be lifted and that doing so was very costly indeed.

Something has already been said about the next Arab-Israeli War, which took part in Lebanon in 1982, and more will be said about it below.[29] Here we must focus on the major conflict of the 1980s, the Iran-Iraq War. In fact the name is a misnomer; it was Iraq that attacked Iran, not the other way around. In 1980 Iraq had 332 combat aircraft, Iran 445,[30] but after the Islamic Revolution of the previous year the latter country was in a situation of semi-chaos. This was an opportunity Iraq's Saddam Hussein hoped to exploit. Taking a leaf from the Israelis in 1967, on September 23, 1980, he opened hostilities with an air strike by MiG-23s and MiG-21s on numerous Iranian airfields as far away as Tehran. In fact, having been designed as interceptors and for high-level reconnaissance, neither aircraft was especially suitable for ground attack. Within a month Iraqi officers were full of complaints about the MiG-23s in particular.[31] Runways and fuel depots were hit, but many of the Iraqi bombs failed to explode. Most Iranian aircraft were housed in reinforced hangars and survived the attacks. Within hours the Ayatollah Khomeini's fighter-bombers took off in order to strike targets deep inside Iraq and not far from Baghdad itself.

Supported from the air, the Iraqis advanced 50 miles into Iran, but by early November they had become stuck. In June 1982, after an Iranian counterattack, they withdrew to the international border. From this point on, the struggle, in the air as well as on the ground, became one of attrition. Though it lasted much longer, in many ways it resembled World War I. Both sides built immense systems of fortified trenches. Trying to breach the other side's defenses or prevent their own from being overrun, from time to time they resorted to human-wave attacks and/or massive artillery bombardments including, on the Iraqi side, the use of poison gas. At first the advantage in the air tended to be on the side of the Iranians. Their main weapon was the F-14 Tomcat, a fourth-generation, variable-geometry aircraft. Originally developed for the U.S. Navy, it was bought by the Shah because it was the most sophisticated combat aircraft available at the time. Equipped with air-to-air missiles and, above all, a radar set capable of tracking eight targets simultaneously at a range of up to 60 miles, it was far superior to everything the Iraqis had.

In addition, the Iranians had F-4 Phantom fighter-bombers, light F-5 fighters, and some older Soviet aircraft. Relying on air refueling, they struck Iraqi airfields and oilfields as far as 500 miles from their own nearest bases.

Iranian pilots, some of whom had recently been released from jail, proved surprisingly competent. Profiting from their American training, which incorporated the lessons of Vietnam, they found it quite easy to overcome the Iraqi SA-2s and SA-3s, although the more modern SA-6 remained a problem. What did them in was the embargo under which Iran had been placed and under which, as a self-proclaimed Islamic state intent on exporting its revolution, it had to some extent placed itself. As the supply of spare parts dried up, the air force was gradually paralyzed. Midway through the war the Iranians had only 70 aircraft left versus 500 Iraqi ones.[32]

Unable to bring the war to an end, the Iraqis switched to attacks on Iranian oil installations and shipping in the Gulf. Early on, Iranian oil production fell by no less than 50 percent,[33] but a simultaneous rise in prices kept the country, and of course Iraq, afloat. Later things changed. Both sides engaged in the so-called tanker war, which went on intermittently until 1987. The Iraqis' main instrument consisted of some 40 French-built Mirage F-1 fighter-bombers. Best described as three-and-a-half-generation machines, they were effective warplanes, especially when carrying the now familiar Exocet missiles. The Iranians for their part received Chinese-made Silkworm air-to-sea missiles, but the weakness of their air force limited what they could do. Over a period of seven years, several hundred vessels sailing under the flags of many nations were hit. Some 3,000 crew members were killed, mostly by Iraqi aircraft. The amount of oil shipped out of the Gulf went down by 25 percent. Yet the Iraqis too were operating under constraints. Their allies, Saudi Arabia and the Gulf States, which played a large role in financing the war, repeatedly told them not to escalate the conflict.[34] Consequently the impact of the tanker war remained limited, as is shown by the fact that oil prices dropped consistently from 1982 on.[35]

Politically isolated, unable to import new equipment, the Iranians fell further and further behind. By contrast, Iraq kept receiving a steady flow of aircraft, spare parts to keep them flying, and sophisticated ordnance with which to arm them. Consequently the Iraqis were able to attack Iranian cities deep inside enemy territories whereas the Iranians were not. In repelling the Iranian ground assaults, the Iraqis also made extensive use of their helicopter gunships, which launched their missiles from behind the lines. Yet with Saddam Hussein's ground forces standing on the defensive for most of the time, his air force, for all the freedom of action it enjoyed, could not defeat Iran, a country much larger than Iraq and with three times its population. Iraqi air strikes at Iranian oil installations did reduce that country's oil exports, but since the Iranians were able to switch to other terminals located further to the south the decline never assumed critical proportions.

Throughout the war both sides had used their Soviet-built Scuds, medium-range ballistic missiles ultimately deriving from the World War II German V-2s, to launch an occasional strike. However, the numbers, spread over several years, were small. From 1982 to 1987 Iranian strikes totaled 117, or just under 20 a year. The Iraqis for their part launched some 160 missiles. Not only were the numbers far too small to have a real impact, but the missiles' inaccuracy meant that really important targets could only be hit by accident. In early 1988 this situation underwent limited change when the Iraqis introduced a modified Scud known as the al-Hussein.[36] Unlike its predecessor, the al-Hussein could reach Tehran as well as Khom, the holy city where Ayatollah Khomeini had taught and where the mullahs had the center of their power. To achieve this, the Iraqi engineers had to reduce the warhead to perhaps 500 to 1,000 pounds so that it was only one-quarter to one-half as large as the one carried by the V-2. Like its parent, the Scud, and its grandparent, the V-2, the al-Hussein was inaccurate, indeed erratic.

In the spring of 1988, about 200 of these dubious contraptions hit greater Tehran, killing some 2,000 people. That ratio is much higher than in any other war in which surface-to-surface missiles were used. For example, 39 similar missiles that struck Israel in 1991 killed only three people; this fact probably says something about the quality of the capital's buildings and also about that of the mullahs' civil defense organization. The outcome was to make as many as 30 percent of the capital's population, which numbered about 6,000,000, flee.[37] The total quantity of explosives dropped on the city was only a small fraction of what hit the smaller city of Hamburg in 1943. On that occasion the number of dead had been in the tens of thousands. Moreover, the Iraqi offensive was spread over a period of no fewer than seven weeks. These facts make one wonder whether the Iranians were really as committed to meeting the virgins in heaven as some commentators thought and, apparently, still think. Calculations pertaining to the number of Iranian casualties vis-à-vis the country's population lead one to the same conclusion.[38]

On April 20, a truce was called and the so-called war of the cities ended, but the war itself went on for another three months. During this period a series of major battles—including one called Majnun, which means "stark raving mad," after the island where it took place—were fought on the southern and central sectors of the 750-mile front. Taking the offensive and making liberal use of chemical weapons, the Iraqis routed their enemies.

Originally both sides had thought the war would be fought and decided mainly in the air.[39] In fact, this did not happen. Though they had seized the initiative and opened the war with an air strike against the opposing air force, the Iraqis failed to win a quick victory. After the first few months, aided and abetted by much of the world, they enjoyed considerable superiority in the air both at the front and deep into Iranian territory, where they struck at oil installations in particular. Yet they still had to fight a long and costly war of attrition, which, in 1982–83, brought them to the edge of defeat. From 1982 on, Iranian strategic attacks on Iraq amounted to mere pinpricks. Iraqi ones on Iranian targets were more effective, but political considerations prevented them from being pushed home to the point where they brought critical results. Iraqi surface-to-surface missiles fired at Tehran during the last months of the conflict helped demoralize the capital's inhabitants, but there are some indications that their morale had been low even earlier. In any case what decided the war were not the missiles but the battles that took the Iraqi ground troops across the Shatt al-Arab, the river that separates the two countries, into Iranian territory. Airpower certainly played a role in those battles, but it is impossible to say how large it was.

This chapter, dealing with the period from 1973 to 1988, should not be allowed to end without a brief mention of two other operations. Though small in scale, they made headlines around the world and provided spectacular demonstrations of what airpower could do. The first took place in July 1976 and rescued 105 Israeli and Jewish hostages aboard an Air France airliner hijacked by terrorists and forced to land in Entebbe, Uganda.[40] The operation, conducted at a distance of 2,500 miles from Israel's borders, involved four Israeli Air Force C-130 Hercules medium-transport aircraft. Like Superman the C-130s landed at Entebbe airport, discharged their commandos, took them in again along with the hostages, and flew off. Also involved were two Boeing 707s; one served as a flying command post, whereas the other landed at Nairobi, Kenya, with medical supplies onboard. During the return journey the C-130s also landed at Nairobi for refueling. In all this, the key question remains how the Israelis managed to avoid detection by Ugandan radar, thus preventing their enemies from sending up their MiG fighters or simply blocking the runways. Probably it is safe to assume that the air force, which had long devoted its full attention to electronic warfare and was to display the results of that attention in Lebanon in 1982, did not find it too hard to jam Ugandan radar either.

It was Israel, too, that launched the second operation. During the 1970s France had assisted Saddam Hussein in building a nuclear reactor. Early in the Iran-Iraq War it was bombed by Iranian F-4s, but without success. In June 1981 the Israelis, who saw the reactor as a critical danger to their country's existence, attacked.[41] This time the force consisted of eight F-16s and six F-15s tasked with covering them. The aircraft took off from a base near the southern port city of Elat and skimmed over Saudi territory at 30–60 feet. Maintaining strict radio silence, they apparently used electronic warfare to escape detection by any of the many radar sets in the area. Approaching the target they probably climbed to 1,500–2,000 feet, only to dive again as they were over it so as to achieve maximum accuracy. At the time there were all kinds of rumors concerning the kind of sophisticated air-to-ground missiles the Israelis used, but the truth seems to be that they relied on iron bombs and trusted to the pilots' training to place them on target. As it turned out, all 16 bombs dropped were direct hits. As the aircraft climbed toward greater altitudes on the first leg of their homeward flight, they were followed by anti-aircraft fire, which proved ineffective.

Both operations present perfect illustrations of the advantages of airpower: namely, its unique ability to strike distant targets at great speed without regard to geography and, nowadays, with great precision as well. Both came like bolts from the blue, which fact was probably *the* most important reason why they succeeded as well as they did. Neither the Ugandans nor the Iraqis were able to intercept the Israelis before they landed or dropped their bombs. The Entebbe operation was over in 53 minutes, the one over Baghdad in exactly two. After they had ended, neither opponent was in any position to respond in kind or in any other way. As countless cases mentioned on these pages show, usually the effect of air operations has to be evaluated as part of a much larger complex, a difficult and often all but impossible enterprise. In these two cases the operations stood on their own and hence succeeded entirely on their own. They were, to use a favorite expression, surgical. Yet it goes without saying that even under such circumstances success is by no means assured. The failure of the American attempt to rescue hostages in Tehran in April 1980 provides sufficient proof of that fact.[42] In the air, as everywhere else, human error or a little bad luck can turn even the best-conceived surgical operation into a mess.

CHAPTER 16

SPURIOUS VICTORIES?

Around 1990–91, a vast revolution swept over warfare—one that had been in the making for some time, but now appeared in its full force for all to see. In many ways it is still unfolding, and in many ways it is too early to assess its full implications. Probably the most important factor involved was the end of the Cold War and the collapse of the Soviet Union. Thus deprived of worthwhile opponents to match themselves against, the most powerful Western nations started questioning the very raison d'être of their countries' armed forces. Seeing their raison d'être questioned and their orders of battle cut, those forces started looking for new missions they could perform. Among them were expeditionary warfare in other parts of the world, operations other than war, peacekeeping, anti-drug policing, and many other kinds of more or less violent activities they had previously considered beneath their dignity. Without exception, all had in common that they were waged against nonnuclear opponents—in other words, those that did not threaten one's existence but only one's interests; quite often, they were unable to do even that.

The outcome was a fundamental change in attitudes. Traditionally war had been an activity in which people on both sides did their best to kill as many enemies, military and often civilian too, as was considered necessary to achieve victory. Very often they gloried in killing many more than were necessary for that end. In return they themselves expected to get killed and were killed, sometimes in numbers not far from those who died on the defeated side. Now, for the first time in history, it became a question of making sure that as few people as possible died on *both* sides. In part this was because birthrates in all the most advanced countries were falling very sharply. This made people far more reluctant to sacrifice their male offspring (on the other hand, since there was little danger anyhow, they were more prepared than ever to have women join the military, air forces specifically included).[1] Mostly, though, it was because, with their existence protected by their nuclear arsenals, the threat was small to nonexistent. Suffering many casualties, or killing large numbers of enemies, no longer appeared morally right and politically justifiable, and the greater the presence on or near the battlefield of the media, the truer this was.[2]

Under such circumstances, too, airpower became the instrument of choice by which post–Cold War conflicts were waged. There were several reasons for this. First, airpower could be quickly deployed to faraway countries that most people in the world's most powerful military nations could hardly even find on a map. Second, with a much higher tail-to-tooth ratio than any other service, airpower put very few friendly soldiers in harm's way. Even those few could only be engaged by means of extremely sophisticated technology that most nonnuclear countries, let alone guerrillas and insurgents of every kind, did not have. Third, thanks to the development from 1970 on of radar-, laser-, TV-, and GPS-guided weapons, as well as infrared night-vision equipment, airpower was now able to hit its targets much more precisely 24 hours per day. That, at any rate, was what air force commanders kept saying and what politicians and the public came to believe. Here it is necessary to add that, as a matter of fact, the attack aircraft of the 1980s and 1990s were *not* much more accurate than World War II fighter-bombers had been. Instead, what the new "precision-guided" munitions really did was to permit relatively small targets to be attacked from far greater altitudes than before; thus, the demand that there be few, if any, friendly casualties could be met.

The first country to get a taste of postmodern war, as it was often called, was Iraq. Three factors made the experiment possible. First and most important by far, at the time Saddam Hussein invaded Kuwait in August 1990 he was known not to have nuclear weapons. Had things been different, it is hardly conceivable that the war against him would have taken place. Second, his action, while threatening to the neighboring countries and touching on the interests of more remote ones, was very far from putting any of the latter in any kind of danger. Paradoxically the United States, which led the Coalition that was formed against him, was further removed from the scene and less vulnerable to any form of military attack than any of the rest. Third, the West's massive armed forces, built over several decades in order to deter the Soviet Union and fight it if necessary, had not yet been dismantled. In all these ways Saddam kindly gave his enemies an ideal opportunity to put themselves and their weapons to just the kind of test that, as long as the Cold War had lasted, they had only been able to prepare for, write doctrine for, and fantasize about.

A few facts will show what the war was all about. On one side was Iraq, a third-world country of 24 million that had just gone though a long and very costly war against its larger neighbor to the east. To make things worse still, a quarter of its population was not Iraqi and had been in more or less open revolt for three decades past. Facing Iraq was a coalition that included many of the most powerful countries on earth with a combined population of perhaps 450 million and economies to match. Whereas the Coalition was supported by almost every other state in the Middle East, Iraq did not have a single ally and was forced to keep a wary eye on Iran besides. Militarily at the point where it mattered, that is, the area between the northern tip of the Persian Gulf and Baghdad, the two sides were much more evenly matched; yet it was precisely in the air that the Coalition, with its 1,800 versus 600 combat planes, was at its greatest advantage. Since the Coalition also enjoyed overwhelming technological superiority, the real balance of forces was much more lopsided than a simple list of the aircraft on each side would lead one to believe.

Though technological superiority played a role in many of the air campaigns described in this volume, probably in none of them was it as pronounced as in this one.[3] As the very fact that World Wars I and II lasted as long as they did indicates, in both of them the belligerents were initially about equal. It is, however, true that, as World War II approached its end, the Japanese in particular found it harder and harder to keep up. In Korea the U.S. Air Force probably did have a technological edge, but it was not large enough to lead to a quick and decisive victory in the air or to enable airpower to decisively influence the war on the ground. During the various Israeli-Arab and Indo-Pakistani wars, the air forces on both sides, using equipment sold to them by the developed countries, were fairly evenly matched, technologically speaking. Indeed the Israelis in 1967 liked to boast that, had they themselves flown MiGs and their enemies, Mirages, the outcome would have been the same. In all these wars technological superiority, even if it existed, was but one factor among many, and frequently not the most important one at that.

In the Gulf in 1990–91, things were very different. At the time, Iraq's per-capita GDP was about one-tenth of that of the United States, its main enemy.[4] The discrepancy in industrial, technological, and scientific capabilities was much greater still. The United States had F-117 stealth aircraft, which were invisible to radar, and Iraq did not. The United States had B-52 heavy bombers capable of delivering vast amounts of ordnance from bases thousands of miles away, and Iraq did not. The United States had cruise missiles capable of being launched from the air, land, and sea, and Iraq did not. The United States had Patriot antiballistic missiles (although they did not work very well),[5] and Iraq did not. The United States had numerous reconnaissance and communications satellites, and Iraq did not. The United States had GPS for navigation and for accurately guiding bombs and missiles to their targets, and Iraq did not. The United States had JSTAR command-and-control aircraft capable of monitoring friendly and enemy movements both in the air and on the ground, and Iraq did not. This list could be extended indefinitely. The technological gap on the ground (Iraq hardly had a navy) was not quite as large. But even there it was considerable.

In fact, such was the magnitude of technological changes during the decade and a half before the war that many commentators spoke of a "revolution in military affairs" comparable to the one that the advent of tanks and aircraft had wrought in 1939–40.[6] Saddam Hussein found himself on the wrong side of this wave. Though he spent his oil money liberally enough, some of his efforts can only be described as pitiable. For example, so badly made were his Soviet-derived, 1950s-vintage, extended-range al-Hussein missiles that many of them never reached their targets but disintegrated in mid-course.[7] Looking back over the last few centuries, and excluding colonial wars between countries armed with modern European weapons and their non-European enemies, it would be hard to find *any* campaign in which one side enjoyed such a huge qualitative advantage over the other; to turn the argument around, Saddam's decision to face the strongest military power in history by conventional means can only be described as suicidal.

During World War II, practically all the troops and equipment deployed from one continent to another went by sea. In 1991, the vast majority of supplies and equipment (84 percent) still arrived by sea, but practically all the troops were flown in. Many of the flights were made by civilian airliners, a telling comment on Iraq's inability or unwillingness to interfere with them. Inside the theater, light transport aircraft and helicopters also helped position troops and equipment. However, even according to the air force historian, out of 200,000 troops that moved from east to west while preparing to carry out General Norman Schwarzkopf's "Hail Mary" maneuver, only 14,000 (and 9,000 tons of equipment) went by air.[8] The relative role of ground and air transport is perhaps best illustrated by the fact that, when the U.S. G-4 (quartermaster) wanted to cross a busy highway near the Saudi border that was serving as a key supply artery, he had to ride a helicopter to do so.[9] Air transport, in other words, had taken over when it came to transporting personnel, especially to airfields far enough behind the front to be safe from enemy interference. But when it came to delivering really large amounts of cargo it still could not compete with the much slower, but cheaper and more secure, sea and land transport.

As it turns out, the very first air operation in the war was launched by seven B-52 bombers. Having taken off from Louisiana, they spent two hours being refueled in the air over the Atlantic before making their way toward Iraq. Yet bases much closer to the theater of war were available to the Americans in Britain and Diego Garcia; thus the bombers' mission was largely a symbolic gesture intended to demonstrate a Cold War–vintage capability that had existed for many years but, unfortunately, could never be put to wartime use. With the bombers came air-, land-, and sea-launched cruise missiles. The arrival of these devices was carefully coordinated with sorties by hundreds upon hundreds of helicopters, strike aircraft, electronic warfare aircraft, and support aircraft of every kind.[10]

The American air component commander was General Charles Horner. For some reason he had refused to have Colonel John Warden, the most original air theoretician in a generation, at his headquarters and sent him back to the Pentagon as soon as he arrived in the theater,[11] but several of Warden's staff stayed behind and helped shape the planning process. The targets were selected with the aid of satellite photos and other technological methods that detected the electronic signature most of them generated. Broadly following Warden's "five ring" doctrine (see Chapter 12), the attackers all but ignored the Iraqi forces occupying Kuwait. Instead they focused on command, control, and communication centers; airfields; and anti-aircraft defenses.[12] Caught at a disadvantage every bit as great as that facing the Polish Air Force when it was attacked by the Luftwaffe early in World War II, the Iraqi Air Force was barely able to fight back. During the first few days, thanks largely to the fact that its ground-based command-and-control system had been destroyed, 35 of its aircraft were shot down in air combat. The rest fled.[13] Trying to fight, they faced annihilation. Staying put, they also faced annihilation by air-to-ground missiles that took out their underground shelters. Saddam's solution, probably the only logical one under the circumstances, was to order some 112 pilots to fly their aircraft to Iran, where they were interned. The rest took no further part in the war. By the time it ended, only about 300 aircraft were still available.[14]

Iraq's anti-aircraft defenses were estimated at about 7,000 guns, 7,000 radar-guided missiles, and 9,000 heat-seeking missiles. Served by a robust array of radar sets and a network of redundant optical fiber communications, they should have been a tough nut to crack.[15] In fact, performance fell far short of expectations. Some were hit by F-117 stealth aircraft, which, taking off from bases in Saudi Arabia and Turkey, were invisible to Iraqi radar. Not only did the F-117s dispense with elaborate "strike packages" to protect them, but their very presence was only revealed at the moment their missiles struck. Perhaps even more important was the fact that, as the Israelis in 1982 had proved, by this time the older Soviet SA-2s, SA-3s, and SA-6s had become well-known quantities. The same applied a fortiori to Iraq's Franco-German Roland SAMs and to some American Hawks that had been captured in Kuwait and that Saddam's engineers claimed had been made fully operational prior to the outbreak of hostilities. Their electronics could be, and were, subjected to all kinds of attack, from jamming to spoofing—thus illustrating the fact that, in modern air-to-ground and ground-to-air warfare, the gadgets on each side can be neutralized by those of the other. Iraq's anti-aircraft guns and shoulder-launched SA-7s were rendered inoperative simply by flying so high as to remain out of reach. Indeed one American pilot later explained that flak over Baghdad, the most heavily defended target, only reached an altitude of 3,000–4,000 feet.[16] One way or another, during the entire war only ten Coalition aircraft were brought down from the ground.

Making full use of command of the air, the Coalition also tried to target suspected Scud sites. Though the military value of Saddam's Scuds was negligible, their psychological impact was not. Above all, it was necessary to try to prevent them from being launched at Israel for fear that the latter country, by responding, might cause the coalition painstakingly assembled against Iraq to break up. The U.S. Air Force historian claims that, overall, just under 2,500 sorties were flown in an effort to find the Scuds. If true, then they formed only a little over 2 percent of the total. However, in his memoirs General Schwarzkopf wrote that "we . . . divert[ed] fully one third of the more than two thousand combat and support missions scheduled each day for the strategic air campaign to the Scud hunt."[17] Whatever the truth, subsequent investigations proved that not one mobile Scud launcher had been hit. The most that can be said is that, by their presence overhead, Coalition aircraft did make it much more difficult to launch the missiles.

With his air force destroyed or neutralized, Saddam's decision to shift the battle to the ground, where the forces on both sides were less imbalanced, turned out to be as suicidal as his conduct of the war as a whole. The three Iraqi brigades that took the offensive at Khafji at the end of January were detected by the JSTARs, which thus proved their worth for the first time. Almost immediately thereafter the Iraqis came under attack by U.S. Air Force B-52s, A-10s, and AC-130s; U.S. Navy F-18s and A-6s; and British Harriers and Jaguars. To these were added entire swarms of missile-firing U.S., British, and French attack helicopters. To this formidable array the Iraqis had no reply whatsoever. In fact, given how small the battlefield was and how vast the armada of Coalition aircraft swarming above it, day and night, the really surprising thing is that the number of casualties those aircraft inflicted on their own ground forces during the battle only amounted to seven.

By this time, so complete was the Coalition's control of the air that the Iraqis did not even detect two entire army corps moving from east to west right along their border with Saudi Arabia. Originally the air campaign had been supposed to last 30 days. In fact, due mainly to bad flying weather, it was stretched over 39. The closer the countdown to G-Day, the more the Coalition air commanders shifted their tender attention to the hapless Iraqi troops on the ground. They attacked supply dumps, bunkers, vehicles, artillery pieces, and tanks. If only because the desert areas of Kuwait and southern Iraq are among the flattest, most featureless areas on earth, there was simply nothing the Iraqis could do to avoid the storm of fire that was coming for them from the air. By the time the Coalition invaded Iraq and Kuwait on February 24, Saddam still had some 2,000 tanks and a similar number of other armored vehicles left;[18] however, their battered crews had lost any will to resist. As a result, instead of the ground war requiring three weeks to complete as Schwarzkopf had expected, it only lasted for 100 hours.[19]

During the months and weeks before the war, many Western commanders and commentators vastly exaggerated the capabilities of the Iraqi armed forces as well as the number of casualties that an attempt to defeat them would cost.[20] When these expectations were proved completely off the mark, most of them shifted gear. To celebrate their forces' achievement, they invented the above-mentioned "revolution in military affairs" and coined such terms as "hyperwar."[21] In one sense the hype was appropriate. Guided to their targets by satellites and AWACS, and making liberal use of precision-guided munitions, Coalition aircraft did play a decisive role in bringing the war to a successful end at minimum cost. In fact they appeared close to realizing Douhet's vision concerning a victory won almost entirely from the air. They also offered fresh proof, if proof was needed, that, without proper air cover, large-scale, conventional, ground operations are doomed to rapid defeat. Thanks to new technology in the form of FLIR (forward-looking, infrared) that had been incorporated into reconnaissance and combat aircraft during the 1980s, this was becoming almost as true by night as it had long been by day.

Perhaps even more important was the fact that, instead of targets being attacked more or less at random, they were selected in an intelligent way based on Warden's five rings.[22] Rather than trying to strike at the enemy's armored shell or trying to reduce his cities to smoldering ruins, precision-guided munitions made it possible to focus on the enemy's soft nerve system. Within days Saddam's headquarters became deaf and mute. Compared to the vast quantities of TNT dropped on Germany, Japan, and North Korea in 1939–45 and 1950–53, the amount used to attack Iraq was very small indeed. Even so, it was the 10 percent of ordnance that was "precision" guided that did most of the damage.

All these were notable achievements in which airpower might take pride. Still, it is easy to carry praise too far. As Horner later admitted, had it not been for the overwhelming resources at his disposal, things might have turned out very different from the way they did.[23] Especially notable was the near-complete failure of the Coalition to eliminate Iraq's surface-to-surface missile launchers, which in a world where such missiles are proliferating did not augur well. Taking a broader view, in many ways, what really took place in the Gulf was not so much a great triumph for airpower as a case of an elephant stamping on the worm that had provoked it. The fact that, during most of the campaign, only one side did any "fighting" at all makes this interpretation even more plausible. By way of a comparison, the number of Coalition aircraft that struck Iraq in 1991 was nine times as large as that which the Israelis used when they inflicted a crushing defeat on Egypt in 1967. On the ground, Saddam had fewer troops per mile of front than the Egyptians had. As a result, so widely dispersed were they that even cluster ammunition, which dispenses millions of razor-sharp spikes over large areas, had little effect on them.[24]

Commentators may debate the strength or weakness of Saddam's Iraq before the war. However, no such disagreement is possible in regard to Serbia in 1999. Like Iraq, Serbia had neither nuclear weapons nor the means to deliver them even over comparatively short distances, or else surely the war would never have been fought. But whereas Iraq is a country with a land area of 170,000 square miles and a population of 24 million, the corresponding figures for Serbia (including Montenegro, which was on the verge of breaking away) stood at 40,000 and 10 million respectively. Per-capita income was quite similar to that of Iraq, except that Serbia did not have oil. In 1991, the Iraqi armed forces were said to be the fifth largest in the world. Eight years later those of Serbia, representing the remnants of the once proud Yugoslav Army and only beginning to recover from their debilitating involvement in the Bosnian conflict, were rated 35th.

Serbia did have 238 combat aircraft,[25] but except for 15 MiG-29s all of them were obsolescent or obsolete. It also had Russian-made SA-2, SA-3, SA-6, and SA-9 missiles, but all of these dated to the 1970s or earlier. In fact they had been specifically designed to operate in combination with the ZSU 23-4s already familiar from Vietnam and the October 1973 war. The personnel manning the anti-aircraft defenses were known to be professional and competent.[26] They may have upgraded some of their equipment's electronics, but little information is available about this subject. That factor apart, the only reasonably modern anti-aircraft missile in the Serb inventory was the SA-13. Visually aimed, optical/infrared guided, and highly mobile, it is a low-altitude (up to 10,000 feet), short-range system. It can therefore be evaded simply by flying high enough.

This was the country, and this was the air force/air defense system, against which the mightiest alliance in history saw fit to measure itself. As in Iraq eight years earlier, its chosen instrument for this heroic project was airpower. Since Serbia did not present a threat to anything or anybody outside its own borders, President Clinton and the Joint Chiefs of Staff were even more worried about taking casualties than their predecessors had been. To make sure, they never allowed U.S. ground forces to be committed; later they apparently tried to pin the blame for this on the army chief of staff. Since those forces also included the attack helicopters, one of the most potent available weapons built up at vast cost and honed by means of constant exercises never saw action. Yet the decision may have been the correct one under the circumstances; had the Apaches been committed, then given NATO's inability to locate the Serb ground troops hiding in the mountains and forests of Kosovo, chances are that some, perhaps many, of them would have been shot down. In this as in other ways, America's NATO allies were only too happy to follow its example.

When preparations were complete and the air campaign opened on March 24, NATO aircraft committed to it numbered just under 400. Most were familiar, but newcomers to this formidable array were the B-1—which, during the war against Saddam Hussein, had been kept in reserve—and B-2 stealth bombers. The latter is a batlike stealth machine supposedly invisible to radar; both of these aircraft saw combat for the first time. While many NATO aircraft operated out of Italian bases, others started on their missions from bases as far away as Germany, France, Spain, Britain (whence the inevitable B-52s), and the continental United States (the B-2s). All these were far beyond the outgunned Serbs' reach. Even the nearby Italian airfields were never attacked. Still not content with its quantitative and qualitative advantage, NATO chose to open its attack by launching cruise missiles from U.S. surface ships as well as U.S. and British submarines.

NATO's commanders expected the campaign to be quick and easy, and its secretary general, Javier Solana, personally promised it would last "days, not months."[27] Since NATO suffered *no* casualties, it did indeed turn out to be easy, but it was anything but quick. Having lost three precious MiG-29s in air combat during the first days of the war, the Serb Air Force all but gave up the struggle against overwhelming odds. Serb anti-aircraft defenses did considerably better; playing a cat-and-mouse game by shifting from one position to another and turning their radar sets on and off, they shot down two NATO aircraft, one of them a stealth F-117 fighter-bomber that should have been invisible to radar but apparently wasn't. More important, they made NATO pilots stay above 15,000 feet, greatly reducing their ability to detect targets. In case they wanted to take a closer look, NATO commanders had to rely on UAVs. Bad flying weather, difficult terrain covered by extensive forests, and the need to coordinate each target with the defense minister of every one of the NATO countries that participated in the war did the rest. During the first 72 hours NATO succeeded in knocking out numerous fixed Serb military targets, including airfields and barracks (which, however, were later discovered to have been empty). Yet the damage they did to the Serb war effort as a whole was minimal; they succeeded neither in seriously impairing the capabilities of the Serb Army nor in preventing President Slobodan Milosevic from starting a campaign to cleanse Kosovo of its Muslim population.

A mere three days after the opening of hostilities, NATO was already beginning to run out of strictly military targets. Thereupon the U.S. commander, General Wesley Clark, was authorized to attack additional ones. Mostly they consisted of lines of communication, including railroads and marshaling yards, as well as depots of every kind. Yet the results were hardly better than before—indeed so bad was the weather that over half of the nightly strike sorties had to be aborted. Partly for that reason, during the first nine days of the campaign, NATO aircraft only managed to fly 0.75

sorties per day on the average. Of those just 15 percent were of the strike type.[28] While the list of targets kept being expanded, the Serbs, a proud people with a long martial tradition, proved tough and wily opponents. Like the feckless Iraqis, they were unable to do much by way of shooting back. Unlike them, they proved masters at dispersing and camouflaging their ground forces and in setting up dummy targets. Among other things they regularly substituted telegraph poles for anti-aircraft missiles and then watched NATO aircraft attacking them. Of course the terrain, which did not consist of desert, helped.

Whether because the size of the forces involved in the operation was initially much smaller or for other reasons, far less ordnance was dropped on Serbia than had been on Iraq eight years earlier. Meanwhile the number of NATO aircraft that participated in the campaign was gradually increased until it finally reached 1,000. Mindful of their commitments in other parts of the world, even Clark's superiors at the Pentagon were taken aback by the size of his requests. Yet, in the end they reluctantly approved them, which in turn meant that NATO had to ask for the right to use additional airfields in Hungary and Turkey. Still not content, Clark asked for the carrier *Enterprise* to join the *Eisenhower,* which was already taking part in the campaign. After some debate he got his wish, though the ship's 72-strong air wing was never actually put to use. So desperate was NATO that it finally turned its tender mercies to "command targets," by which Milosevic's private villa was meant. The villa was duly destroyed, but still the Serbs resisted.

One month into the campaign, 80 percent of all fixed targets attacked by NATO planes had already been hit at least once.[29] In spite of objections by various nations—for example, France did not want heavy attacks on power plants, whereas the Germans were worried lest strikes in downtown Belgrade would remind people of what the Luftwaffe had done there in April 1941—the list of targets kept being expanded.[30] Once infrastructure targets such as heavy industry came under attack, Serbia's economy began to suffer. Yet partly because there were few strategic targets in Kosovo, partly out of fear that striking at them would kill the very people NATO had come to protect, ethnic cleansing there went on almost as if NATO did not exist.[31] Above all, the Serb ground forces, most of which were safely concealed in the forests of the same province where they backed up the special units busily evicting Muslims across the border, remained almost intact in spite of a rain of bombs aimed at them by B-52 bombers, among other aircraft.

While no precise figures are available, certainly those that NATO commanders initially quoted concerning the destruction wrought on the Serbs were vastly exaggerated; had it not been so sad, watching the process whereby those figures were cut and cut would have been comical.[32] For example, whereas a NATO spokesman at one point claimed that Milosevic was losing 50 tanks a day (which if true, would have meant a total of almost 4,000, far more than he ever possessed), after everything was over exactly 14 wrecked tanks could be located on the ground. The situation in respect to armored personnel carriers and artillery barrels was no different.[33] Indeed it seems that only during the very last days, when Serb formations broke cover to cope with Albanian gangs coming from across the border, did they suffer any considerable damage at all. But at least the so-called Kosovo Liberation Army had the guts to try. Not so NATO; they never even attempted a ground campaign that might have led to casualties—which God forbid.

Over a decade later, the question why Milosevic finally surrendered after 78 days remains open.[34] Whatever the answer, insofar as no NATO ground or sea forces saw action, airpower did indeed prove decisive in this strange war. In the words of one commentator not normally inclined to overpraise the U.S. military, "the air war over Serbia was a masterful demonstration of airpower skill in terms of its military operational employment."[35] Even so, doubts remain. Why was the number of sorties carried out per NATO aircraft as low as it was? Since only about one-third of NATO's bombs and missiles were guided, did 99.6 percent of them really hit their target, as one American general claimed?[36] Since the Serbs with their upgraded 1970s-vintage technology succeeded in shooting down one stealth aircraft (an F-117), will others be able to do the same?[37] Given that, flying across the

Atlantic and back, the B-2s took 30 hours to deliver minuscule amounts (about 12 tons) of ordnance, were they really worth their cost of over half a billion dollars each?[38] Even during Operation Allied Force, as the war was known, the B-2s were escorted by electronic warfare aircraft. This led to a shortage of such aircraft and caused one of the B-2's most loudly touted advantages—the ability to fly missions without a "strike package" to accompany it—to be lost.[39] Yet these and other questions are dwarfed by the fact that, even more than in Iraq eight years earlier, a coalition made up of world's most powerful air forces deployed by the world's most powerful countries bombed and shot up the hapless armed forces of a hapless nation that did not have, and never could have, what was required to fight back. Even so, it took almost twice as long to make Milosevic give in than to force Saddam to do the same.

The last war we have to consider in this context is the one the United States and its allies fought against Iraq in 2003. Here a few words concerning the background are needed. In the United States, the 1991 Gulf War made it seem as if the so-called Vietnam Syndrome, which from 1975 on had undermined the self-confidence of the armed forces and hamstrung their operations, had finally been overcome.[40] The sobering experience of Kosovo notwithstanding, the Pentagon was full of talk about "defense transformation" and the "revolution in military affairs." Future wars would be very different from those of the past, even the recent past. Short, decisive, and waged with the aid of the existing forces rather than requiring mobilization, they would be over almost before they began. The place of massive ground forces would be taken by relatively small air forces. Relying on a combination of high-tech sensors and precision-guided munitions, they would strike directly at vital, if relatively small, targets of the kind Warden had envisaged. The result, which President George W. Bush's secretary of defense Donald Rumsfeld labeled "shock and awe," would be to quickly knock out entire countries with only moderate support from the ground.

At some time between 2001 and 2003, the decision was made to try this theory on Iraq. Even at best, Iraq had never been much more than a semi-industrialized country. By 2003 it had been subject to 13 years of sanctions.

To make things worse for Saddam, throughout the 1990s oil prices kept falling. Much of the revenue he still received from that source went not into his hands but into those of the UN. Per-capita income had shrunk to perhaps one-quarter of what it had been in 1990—without taking inflation into account. Whereas the U.S. defense budget alone stood at about $450 billion, Iraq's entire GDP was estimated at perhaps $15.5 billion.[41] Of the 600 modern combat aircraft with which Saddam had entered the 1991 war, and the 300 with which he had ended it, he only had some 235 left. Though he was unable to upgrade them as his enemies had, many of these aircraft were still reasonably modern. More problematic was the low state of readiness due to a shortage of spare parts caused by years of sanctions. Another problem was a lack of training that resulted from the extensive "no fly zones" imposed and guarded by the Allies. Some pilots flew 60 to 120 hours a year, but a great many only got 20.

Not having fought very much in 1991, the Iraqi Air Force seems to have retained a fair supply of air-to-air and ground-to-air munitions. However, the only new additions were some French-built, short-range Matra Magic 2 air-to-air missiles imported shortly after the war. As the failure to shoot down even one U.S. or British aircraft that enforced "no fly zones" during the previous decade shows, Iraq's anti-aircraft defense system was also in ruins. The few remaining high-altitude SAMs were obsolete. The most modern available low-altitude ones were the Soviet-built SA-13s of Kosovo fame, but even those dated back to the years before 1991. On the whole, one can only concur with the leading American expert on Middle Eastern military affairs who wrote that "in broad terms . . . the Iraqi [air] forces were obsolete to obsolescent, having never recovered from the Gulf War, and had suffered from further attacks between 1992 and 2003."[42]

To defeat this motley array, the Coalition created by President George W. Bush once again committed the most modern air forces ever deployed in war. The Cold War having ended, throughout the 1990s the erosion in the number of aircraft and orders of battle of all advanced countries, which had proceeded steadily from 1945 on, had continued. Partly for this reason, partly because the Iraqi armed forces were only a shadow of what they had been 12 years earlier, the number of combat aircraft used against them was also much smaller and only amounted to 786, three times as many as Saddam had. The total number of Coalition aircraft stood at 1,400, little more than half of those that had been available to Schwarzkopf in 1991. Over the first three weeks of the campaign, these assets generated 41,404 sorties, of which about half were made by combat aircraft. Though the calculation is somewhat crude owing to changing numbers of aircraft, this works out at little more than one sortie per aircraft per day.[43] The Iraqi Air Force generated no sorties at all. After the war was over, some of its aircraft were found disassembled and buried in the desert sand.[44] No doubt this was a highly innovative way of using airpower; a more telling comment on the real balance of forces would be hard to imagine.

As in 1991, a massive airlift to the Gulf preceded the beginning of the campaign. What proportion of all supplies went by air is not clear; probably it was somewhat higher than it had been in 1991. The major difference consisted in that, this time around, so weak had Iraq become that there was no fear of its armed forces trying to preempt their enemies by taking the offensive into Kuwait or Saudi Arabia. As in 1991, the war opened with a massive strike by cruise missiles—over 1,000 were launched from the air, from surface ships, and from submarines. Also as in 1991, this was a weapon the Iraqis did not have and could do almost nothing to counter. However, the mix of targets was very different. Three facts seem to account for the difference. First the Iraqi Air Force, which had already shown its weakness in 1991, was no longer a factor. As a result, only 7 percent of so-called sortie equivalents—a weighted measure the U.S. Air Force adopted to take account of the different capabilities of different aircraft and their ability to engage multiple targets—had to be devoted to obtaining and maintaining air superiority.[45] Second, ground operations were scheduled to start simultaneously with those in the air instead of much later. This caused the Coalition to focus much of its early efforts on Iraq's ground forces, the Republican Guard included, instead of postponing this kind of operation until later. Third, Iraq's infrastructure was hardly targeted—the reason being that the Coalition, bent on driving all the way to Baghdad, wanted it intact for its own use.

With the Iraqi Air Force hors de combat, it became possible to use 15 huge C-17s to drop 1,000 paratroopers over Bashur, a village and an airfield in northern Iraq, in what was the largest U.S. operation of its kind since World War II. Excluding accidents, what losses the Coalition air forces took were due solely to anti-aircraft fire and missiles. Over the war as a whole, Iraqi anti-aircraft guns are said to have opened fire 1,224 times. There were 1,660 reports of anti-aircraft missiles being launched and 436 cases when Iraqi radar emitters tried to lock on to coalition aircraft. Not many, considering that those aircraft flew over 40,000 sorties. Even these attempts at resistance were spread over 21 days, and a land area of 171,000 square miles. Many air defense targets had already been knocked out before the war got under way—from June 2001 to March 19, 2003, a total of 349 of them were attacked and a large fraction of those were destroyed.[46] In fact, so weak had Saddam's anti-aircraft forces become that, aside from Baghdad and a few major oil-producing areas, most of the country was simply left undefended.

Both the United States and Iraq had their military helicopters organized as part of their respective armies rather than of their air forces, as is the case in some other countries. Nevertheless, and given the objective of this study to be as comprehensive as space allows, this aspect of the matter must not be left out. Owing to an oversight on Schwarzkopf's part, Iraq's attack helicopters were not included in the no-fly zones established in the wake of the 1991 war. This enabled them to play a key role in helping Saddam put down the Kurdish and Shiite insurrections. Twelve years later he still had about a hundred of these machines left, although, like the rest of his forces, they were aging and suffered from a severe shortage of spare parts. Since the balance against them was only little more than three to one, in this particular case the Iraqi disadvantage did not consist primarily of numbers. Rather, the problem was that, since the Coalition enjoyed undisputed command of the air, they could not use their helicopters as they had done against the Iranians.

The rest of the story is quickly told. On paper Iraq still had impressive land forces, including 350,000 men, tanks, other armored vehicles, and artillery barrels. In reality, these forces turned out to suffer from the same problems as the air force did. Chief among them was obsolescent or obsolete equipment. For example, the 1991 war had provided conclusive proof that none of Iraq's Soviet-built tanks could stand up to the American Abrams with its 120-millimeter gun, laser fire controls, and rounds made of depleted uranium instead of the normal tungsten steel; in 2003 only three of the latter were lost, all of them to Kornet anti-tank missiles. There was also a shortage of spare parts, which translated into a lack of training. This in turn meant that any capability for conducting combined arms operations had long been lost. Finally, it quickly transpired that low morale would cause many troops to refuse to fight and to throw away their weapons.

These were the forces that found themselves under attack both from the air, where their enemies ruled supreme, and on the ground. Directed to their targets by means of satellites and JSTAR aircraft, using the most up-to-date equipment, the Coalition aircraft rained down air-to-ground missiles while also using their cannon for strafing. Under such circumstances it was hardly surprising that Iraqi resistance was sporadic. A good measure of the severity, or otherwise, of the fighting is the fact that the U.S. ground forces commander, Lieutenant General William Wallace, at one point became concerned about the fate of a company of marines that seemed to have been cut off by Iraqi troops.[47] Since commanders are supposed to think to levels down (and up), companies are for brigadiers to consider; yet here was an officer responsible for 100,000 men and women doing the same! Eventually the weather, which repeatedly produced sandstorms and all but brought operations to a halt, as well as the supply lines from Kuwait to Baghdad, which were the longest in any post-1945 campaign, played as much of a role in governing the pace of the advance, and thus the duration of the campaign, as the enemy did.

Looking back at the conventional part of the second war against Iraq, the conclusion is inescapable. To repeat: when an elephant steps on a worm, that worm gets crushed, especially if it has already been crushed before. The worm, moreover, turned out to be incompetent, creating what one analyst called a "permissive" environment for Coalition technology that a more skilled opponent elsewhere might have avoided.[48] From Korea to the Iran-Iraq War, the little wars discussed in the previous three chapters were fought between opponents who, if they were not always evenly matched, at any rate formed real threats to one another. That is not true of those discussed in the present chapter. Of the three, the last one was unquestionably the most spurious and the most unnecessary. It was, in plain words, the most foolish. Given the qualitative and quantitative imbalance of forces, perhaps all that can be learned from it is that, when Clausewitz said that "the best strategy is always to be very strong,"[49] he knew what he was talking about. Both Saddam Hussein and Milosevic violated this rule. In 1999 and 2003 they did so against their will; coming under attack, they had no choice. In 1991 Saddam probably acted out of sheer hubris.

The essential unimportance of the 2003 war in particular was brought out all the more strongly because "the end of major combat operations," to quote President Bush,[50] by no means marked the end of the conflict. As one commentator put it, the U.S. Air Force truly "rule[d] the sky." Allegedly its satellites could read vehicle license plates through clouds, smoke, rain, and fog, and its bombers and fighter-bombers could put GPS-guided missiles and bombs within feet of their intended targets.[51] Nevertheless, all the Coalition had achieved was to bring down Saddam's government. While its fall was hardly to be lamented, it quickly led to the breakdown of public order. What opponents were left, and there turned out to be many of them, were forced to disperse and flee. First they went into hiding and then they organized themselves. Soon they opened a years-long "war amongst the people"[52] far more difficult and bloody than anybody in Washington had anticipated. In that struggle, as in others of the same kind, airpower, in the form it had been used in all three wars, turned out to be almost irrelevant.

PART V

WAR AMONGST THE PEOPLE

1898–2010

At least since the German attack on Poland in 1939, and in many cases ever since Douhet published his masterpiece in 1921, one thing all the proponents of airpower had agreed on was that its first task is to tackle the enemy's air force. The preferred method for doing so was to attack its bases before it could ever get off the ground; should that not be possible, then the attempt to achieve command of the air should be made by means of air combat. By contrast, the conflicts discussed in this part of the present volume have this in common that, in practically all cases, the enemy did not have airpower of any kind. To the extent that he was able to respond at all, he did so exclusively by means of fire directed from the ground; quite often, as we shall see, he did not have the capability to do even that.

Had airpower been as dominant as some people have claimed, then the outcome ought to have been the rapid and complete defeat of the insurgents, guerrillas, bandits, terrorists, patriots, freedom fighters, partisans, or whatever else they were called or called themselves. In practice, things turned out rather differently. In this part of the present volume I will trace the use of airpower in what, in another work, I have called "non-trinitarian" war.[1] The most outstanding characteristic of such war is precisely that, instead of being waged by regular, uniformed, armed forces in "the field," it is fought "amongst the people." The latter are deliberately used by one side or the other in other to conceal himself. Under such circumstances very often combatants and noncombatants are extremely difficult if not impossible to distinguish from each other, and indeed they may switch roles at a moment's notice.[2] Contrary to both expectations and propaganda, the use of airpower in such wars has been the record of almost uninterrupted failure.

CHAPTER 17

THE FIRST FOUR DECADES

During the great period of colonial expansion from the early sixteenth to the late nineteenth centuries, no army or navy had an air force, of course. Long-range mobility was provided almost exclusively by ships, operational and tactical mobility by men moving on foot, assisted by pack animals and, here and there, a *very* small number of mounted men. Intelligence needed for campaigning was derived largely from local people enlisted with or against their will. Firepower was delivered almost entirely by small arms, first muskets and then, from the 1850s on, breechloaders, magazine rifles, and a handful of machine guns. To this was added an occasional light artillery piece that the conquerors had been able to bring along either by water, onboard gunboats, or by laboriously dragging it over largely roadless terrain. Yet it goes without saying that the powers' all but complete lack of airpower hardly ever prevented them from winning the wars in question. In fact, most of the time they got their way with so few casualties that it was simply no contest. Thus, especially between 1876 and 1914, they were able to add millions of square miles of land to their possessions.

One of the very first colonial wars in which airpower, in the form of a single balloon, was used was the Spanish-American one of 1898. As the reader will recall, how useful that balloon was at San Juan Hill is moot. Some credited it with opening the way to the U.S. victory in the battle. Others claimed that, by attracting fire, it was worse than useless. What is not in doubt is that, once the Spanish regulars had ceased to fight, the war changed its character and turned into a guerrilla struggle. As operations continued, it became clear that aerial reconnaissance, such as it was, was much easier to carry out over open, flat terrain than over hilly, vegetation-covered land,[1] which is precisely the kind that guerrillas of all times and places prefer.

Between 1900 and 1910, British soldiers and journalists in particular often speculated about the possibility of imitating Napoleon's attempt to use airpower to impress "European superiority on the enormous native population."[2] In fact, the first attempt in this direction proved almost as disappointing as Bonaparte's had been. As we saw, Italian aircraft and their crews reached Libya too late to participate in the bombardment and occupation of the most important coastal cities. Nevertheless, during the first weeks of their presence, when most of the fighting was still concentrated in the districts around those cities, they proved quite useful in reconnaissance and artillery spotting in particular. Later on, things became more difficult. Though airpower might be the only source of reliable intelligence the Italians had, it was also totally inadequate.

Much of the problem was due to the sheer size of the country. For all the bravery and commitment of individual pilots, the few available, primitive, aircraft could never hope to cover it. Though the terrain is almost entirely devoid of vegetation, much of it is very difficult. There are plenty of steep hills (some shaped like mushrooms owing to the wind) and deep, mostly waterless, wadis. It thus provides plenty of hiding places for fighters. The Arabs on their part quickly lost their fear of Italian airpower. They learned to disperse, camouflage themselves, and move only by night. They also fired back at their attackers. If, at the end of 1912, the war was brought to an official close, this fact had little to do with the Italian Army in Libya and even less with the handful of aircraft it deployed there.

That was not the end of the matter. By occupying Libya, the Italians also liberated its inhabitants from Ottoman control, which, in any case, had long been weak. Far from the coast, deep in the provinces of Cyrenaica and the Fezzan, guerrilla warfare, waged mainly by the Senoussi tribesmen, continued almost without interruption. Italy's entry into World War I diverted attention from Libya, but after 1922 the fighting intensified. By 1928 it had escalated to the point where it almost amounted to open warfare. To anyone familiar with the subsequent history of counterinsurgency, the outcome was not surprising. The Italian commander on the spot, General Pietro Badoglio, was kicked upstairs. His replacement, General Rodolfo Graziani, obtained Mussolini's permission to take any measures he thought fit. Yet only in 1934 did he finally bring operations to an end.

Needless to say, throughout the 23 years that the campaign lasted the rebels were at an even greater disadvantage in the air than on the ground. Not only were they never able to operate as much as a single aircraft, but their anti-aircraft defenses never consisted of much more than uncoordinated rifle fire. The insurgents' weakness left the Italian Air Force free to come and go practically as it pleased. Not surprisingly, it did just that. In addition to reconnaissance, always the strongest suit air forces held in counterinsurgency campaigns, it flew liaison missions, resupply missions in assistance of isolated columns and posts, and medical evacuation missions. However, probably its most important contribution consisted of bombing sorties (including ones that used poison gas) against defenseless Senoussi settlements with their miserable hovels and tents.

As we saw, Mussolini took a keen interest in military aviation. Thus many a fascist aviator gained his spurs while engaged in the above-mentioned glorious activities. Yet when it came to fighting the guerrillas, who by now had become thoroughly familiar with aircraft and the ways of countering them, his commanders found airpower to be largely useless. Only rarely were the tribesmen found. When they were found, often they could not be attacked. Either they had hidden in difficult terrain or they had dispersed. Unable to distinguish between combatants and noncombatants—not that they tried too hard—the Italian pilots often attacked the wrong people. In the end, Graziani's victory was won by moving 100,000 people, a third of the population, into concentration camps, where tens of thousands died of hunger and disease. Needless to say, his main instrument consisted of massive ground forces; to wit, 40,000 men pitted against 4,000, only half of whom had modern rifles. Graziani himself earned the title of the Butcher of Fezzan.

Whereas the Italian attempts to use airpower to pacify Libya have been largely forgotten, the British method of "air policing" has not. In fact, it is often used as an example of what can be done—illustrating the extraordinary British ability to keep a stiff upper lip and use their propaganda to cover up the inadequacy of their arms. Immediately after the end of World War I, against the background of demobilization and financial retrenchment, another large-scale war in Europe appeared remote. So deep were the cuts in the young Royal Air Force that its commander, our old acquaintance Trenchard, seriously feared that it might be reabsorbed by the army and navy. It was in order to ward off this frightful prospect that he and his subordinates first suggested air policing.

The underlying idea was that rebellious tribesmen in various parts of the empire could be policed much more easily and cheaply from the air, by strafing and bombing, than by ground troops engaging in laborious, and frequently futile, punitive expeditions. Politically speaking, the most important supporter of the concept was Winston Churchill. An aviation enthusiast, at various points during the 1920s he served as secretary of aviation, colonial secretary, and secretary of the treasury. Thus he was the ideal person to support the RAF. One area where the policy was applied was the northwestern frontier, the border area between today's Pakistan and Afghanistan, where it hardly proved more successful in securing lasting peace than previous methods had been. Another was British Somalia; there, thanks largely to the flat, treeless, desert terrain, it worked much better.

The success in Somalia encouraged the authorities in London to entrust responsibility for the security of the vast newly conquered territories in the Middle East—areas now known as Israel, the West Bank, Jordan, and Iraq—to the RAF. Later, operating from Aden, which had long been under British rule, it also took over in Yemen. In all these areas its aircraft, first what had been left over from World War I but then increasingly modern models coming into service, reconnoitered, bombed, strafed, and provided liaison over what were often very large distances. In addition Vickers Victoria light transports, the first ever to be used in war, flew troops in and out of combat areas.[3] To quote one historian, "in terms of saving British lives and treasure, the success of the new method was quite spectacular."[4] The War Office, he says, estimated that the army would need 20,000,000 pounds to quell the rebellion in Mesopotamia. The RAF did the job for just 8,000,000, and by the 1930s the cost of policing Iraq had fallen to a paltry 650,000 pounds a year. During the first 13 years of air policing the widely dispersed territories where the method was applied, the RAF only lost 26 men. Compared to the army's operations those of the RAF also resulted in far fewer enemy casualties, or so Trenchard, relying on his pilots' reports, claimed. Echoing Kipling, he even suggested that "the air is the greatest civilizing influence that these countries have ever known" and that similar methods might be suited for use in Ireland and England itself.[5]

Not everybody saw the results in such glowing terms. The army and navy resisted Trenchard's attempts to assume control. When it came to defending major colonies such as India and Singapore, they got their way. One critic was Field Marshal Henry Wilson, a onetime chief of the Imperial General Staff. Not only had he served in India, Burma, and South Africa, but immediately after World War I he commanded the forces in Northern Ireland; an officer more experienced in fighting terrorists and guerrillas would be hard to find. This was the man who, at one point, wrote that aircraft "appear[ed] from God knows where, dropp[ed] their bombs on God knows what, and [went] off again God knows where."[6] Others went much further. What one naval officer wrote in 1923 remains true today:

> In Mesopotamia, reconnaissance work was difficult on account of the nomadic habits of the Arabs, the continual obliteration of tracks and roads, and the general difficulties of observation. Offensive result against determined tribes was indifferent and against a faint-hearted enemy transitory. Pursuit, map-making, intercommunication and the transportation of supplies proved most useful. In Waziristan the demoralizing effect of the aeroplane was disappointing, on account of the difficulty of killing the enemy, that is, of effecting an ocular demonstration of power by brute force, one of the few things the hill tribes really understand. Villages offered poor targets, and both tactical reconnaissance and night flying were most difficult. In Somaliland, aircraft operations were much more successful. . . .
>
> In all these small war operations, the limitations which to us appear to be the most permanent are: the transitory influence of aircraft attack, due mainly to the shortness of time the aeroplane can remain in the air; its lack of power to occupy a disturbed district; the difficulty of providing it with landing grounds and the danger of indiscriminate slaughter of friend and foe, of women and children as well as armed men. Such slaughter is an action which does not harmonize with British traditions, and which ethically has again and again been proved to be unsound.[7]

The idea that "uncivilized," non-European people only understood force had many adherents at the time. At one point Harris himself said so in so many words,[8] and it certainly played a role in the adoption of "air control."[9] On the other hand, the term was misleading to some extent. Except on occasions when the mission was reconnaissance, and sometimes not even then, airpower did not operate on its own. Rather, air control simply meant that overall command was in the hands of the RAF rather than in those of the army. In almost all cases the outcome was that some ground forces, including infantry, mounted infantry, engineers, and armored cars, were commanded by air marshals whose main qualification was that they knew how to fly, fight, and organize aircraft. That such a system did not work very well is hardly surprising. Even so, as we shall see, normally it was joint operations by air and ground forces, not by the former alone, that brought results.

It was in Palestine, then a British Mandate, that these problems came to a head.[10] Palestine west of the Jordan is a small country comprising just 11,000 square miles. Much of the terrain is rugged and mountainous; thanks partly to a superior climate, partly to the incipient Zionist enterprise, it was also more urbanized than the rest of the Middle East. These facts made T. E. Lawrence, the "Arabian" expert whom Churchill had recruited as one of his advisers, question whether it was more suitable for air control than, say, Ireland and Britain.[11] Reality soon proved him right. When riots broke out in 1920–21, aircraft turned out to be quite useful in restoring order in the countryside. However, they could do little to quell the larger disturbances in the towns. Either they came too late, after the damage had already been done, or else they were useless against the Arab mobs roaming the narrow, twisting alleyways. In the end, the British high commissioner, Sir Herbert Samuel, had to call on both the army and the navy, which landed royal marines at Jaffa, to do the job. So poor was the performance of the British authorities, and specifically of air control, in dealing with the riots that the leaders of the Jewish community concluded that, in the future, they would have to look after their own defense.[12]

Later during the 1920s, a steady pattern emerged. Thanks to the nature of the terrain, almost pure desert, British air operations in Transjordan, where they engaged rebellious tribes, proved quite successful.[13] Even so, the RAF was hardly on its own, since it was backed up on the ground first by the so-called mobile force and then by the highly efficient Arab Legion. Not so in the much more populated country that lay to the west. To a certain extent it was the fault of others. In 1919, at Amritsar in India, army troops raised a storm by killing 400 unarmed demonstrators and injuring 1,200.[14] Thereupon the Air Ministry prohibited aircraft from participating in anti-riot activities in urban areas.[15] Thus, when another round of riots broke out in Palestine in August 1929, the RAF was only allowed to operate in the countryside. Even there strict regulations, aimed at preventing excessive casualties, limited what it could do. In the towns, which once again witnessed the first and largest riots, it hardly intervened at all. Only after ten days was order restored.

Back in Whitehall, the failure of air control to deal with the disturbances did not escape notice. A committee of inquiry was set up. To forestall the possibility that it might rule against the RAF, Trenchard sent out Air Marshal Hugh Dowding, the officer who was later to head Fighter Command during the Battle of Britain, to investigate what had happened. He also had his staff issue a series of memoranda aimed at showing that the RAF had never believed the country could be secured from the air alone. His point was taken; once the situation had been stabilized, the army in Palestine was reinforced. The authorities in Palestine now disposed of two full infantry battalions as well as two squads of armored cars.[16] Nevertheless, overall responsibility still continued to rest in the hands of the Royal Air Force.

In April 1936, when the next uprising got under way in Jaffa, the Royal Air Force found itself in a similar situation. Several days passed during which the Arab Revolt, as it was called, spread to other towns as well as the countryside, before its aircraft were permitted to intervene on any scale. From this point on, the RAF played a very active part in the attempts to reestablish order. Aircraft patrolled the borders in search of bands trying to cross them and flew over the interior while looking for troublemakers. As Arab gangs set up roadblocks and shot up vehicles that ran into them, aircraft were sent to provide convoys with overhead escort. When groups of rebels were located, aircraft were sent to strafe and bomb them. Others were used for liaison, and still others helped bring in additional troops from Egypt and Transjordan. For all this to be possible an infrastructure had to be built first, much of which was later to fall into Israeli hands. Still, when it came to combat, they were often unsuccessful. Their attempts to prevent additional fighters from entering Palestine were frustrated when the Arabs learned to take cover during the day and move only at night. Called in to attack rebels at specific spots, aircraft often arrived too late. Used against guerrillas in the mountains of Samaria and Judea, they found it hard to hit the insurgents who hid in the valleys, inside olive groves, and among the rocks.

In 1929 the rebels had been afraid of the British aircraft and would often run as soon as one or two of them appeared on the scene. By 1936, though, they had become sufficiently familiar with them to stand their ground. Often they fired back with their rifles—outside the towns, practically every adult male had one at home. Occasionally they scored a hit, forcing pilots and other crew members (many of the aircraft were two-seaters and carried a machine gunner with his face to the rear) to make an emergency landing or injuring or killing them. At times even one of airpower's greatest advantages, its speed, turned into a problem. Arriving on the scene, aircraft often fired their machine guns and dropped their bombs, then returned to base. They thus caused bands to disperse before the army could bring its superior firepower to bear against them—a problem, as we shall see later on, that was by no means limited to Palestine during the 1930s.

If aircraft refrained from bombing villages, as they usually did, then the guerrillas would use them to take shelter. If they did drop bombs on them, then the outcome would be large numbers of noncombatant casualties. A compromise solution, often used by others as well, was to drop leaflets that warned the inhabitants of the coming attack. However, since this meant that few people would be around when the aircraft arrived, it was not very satisfactory either. Then as later, the British were well aware of the counterproductive effects that too many dead civilians might produce. In fact, whether or not aircraft should be allowed to bomb villages quickly became a major bone of contention between the RAF, whose pilots acted as Wilson had described, and the army, which saw the results on the ground. This was all the more the case because the British had to consider public opinion in the neighboring Arab countries. So insoluble did these problems appear that, as early as June 5, less than two months after the revolt had broken out, no less a figure than the chief of the air staff, Air Chief Marshal Edward Ellington, was questioning whether Palestine was the sort of country in which air control could be effective at all.[17]

Once the chief of the air staff in London had begun to doubt the capability of his own organization it was only a matter of time before the government stepped in. In Palestine, July 1936 was relatively quiet. However, during the second week of August terrorist activity resumed on an even greater scale, especially in the all but roadless mountains of Galilee. On September 2, the cabinet met. Responsibility for the security of Palestine was taken away from the RAF and entrusted to the army, which of course also meant that overall authority passed from the hands of the Ministry of Aviation to those of the War Office. Soon large contingents of ground forces started arriving. Ultimately their number was to reach 20,000, complete with artillery, armored cars, and even a few tanks. An indication of the seriousness with which the government took the matter is provided by the fact that two of the officers who commanded the troops, General John Dill and General Bernard Montgomery, later rose to the position of chief of the Imperial General Staff.

By that time even an officer such as Air Commodore Charles Portal, who was destined to command the RAF during most of World War II, had come over to the view that, in a country such as Palestine, the main burden of police work should fall on the army. At best, his own service could act as a junior partner in the enterprise.[18] In the summer of 1939, after the British had killed over 5,000 people (most of whom fell victim to the army's forces, though the latter were often assisted from the air), injured perhaps 15,000 more, blown up thousands of homes (including much of the ancient city of Jaffa), and all but brought the country's economic life to a halt, the Arab Revolt finally petered out. Appearances notwithstanding, this was hardly a triumph of military power of any kind. Instead, the government had given in to most of the rebels' political demands. Those included draconian restrictions on Jewish immigration and settlement as well as a promise of "evolution towards independence" within ten years. As a result, within a few years the British were to face a Jewish Revolt that was to drive them out of the country.

No other imperial power of the interwar period seems to have followed the British in entrusting overall responsibility for security in certain colonies to the air force. Several, indeed, could not have done so even if they had wanted to, given that their air forces were part of the other services. For example, in the 1920s, Nicaragua became the stamping ground of the U.S. Marines, who, not for the last time, found themselves fighting the left-wing supporters of Augusto Sandino, known as Sandinistas. Nicaragua is a relatively small country, having but 10 percent of the area of Italian Libya. However, the mountainous nature of its eastern regions as well as the absence of roads made much of it inaccessible. Under such circumstances, airpower, in the form of reconnaissance, liaison, resupply, and medical evacuation, was vital. Had the various contingents and strong points scattered over much of the country not been supported from the air, they could never have survived.[19] Compared with the U.S. Army the marines had the advantage that, being very few in number, they were much less interested in large-scale wars and thus in strategic air operations. Instead they were prepared to do whatever it took to assist their own on the ground—including, if necessary, flying that most hated kind of mission, close air support.

Under such circumstances airpower could also play an important role in preventing the second phase—to use Maoist terminology—of guerrilla warfare, which is building a territorial sanctuary that the guerrillas can hold, from maturing into the third, which is open, regular warfare. On the few occasions when the Sandinistas massed in the open to attack some town, marine aircraft appeared overhead and made short shrift of them. The same happened when the rebels took up fortified positions and tried to hold them against all comers. Thus the marines once again demonstrated airpower's greatest advantages—its range, speed, ability to take the opponent by surprise, and the ability to bring concentrated firepower to bear against selected opponents. However, events in Nicaragua resembled those in Libya and Palestine in the sense that the guerrillas did not take long to learn what their flying opponents could *not* do. Dispersing, adopting camouflage, and taking care to move only at night, for several additional years they survived and even prospered. The conflict was only ended by a former and future secretary of war, Henry Stimson, whom President Calvin Coolidge sent to the area in 1927 and who, after five years of talks, was able to negotiate an agreement between the sides. Early in 1933, the last U.S. Marines left the country.[20]

At about the same time as the marines used aircraft in Nicaragua, the Spanish and French armies used them to put down the Riff uprising in Morocco. Like Libya, much of Morocco consists of empty desert. More than Libya, much of the terrain is not only difficult but covered by wild, inaccessible mountains characterized by deep, rocky valleys. Except for the absence, in many areas, of vegetation to cover the bare hillsides, a more suitable arena for waging guerrilla warfare would be hard to find. At peak during the early 1920s, the Riff forces, ably commanded by a former schoolteacher in the Spanish colonial service by the name of Abd el-Krim, probably consisted of perhaps 30,000 well-armed regulars—though "well-armed" meant no more than that they had modern rifles and, later, a few machine guns taken from the enemy—and twice as many tribal fighters.

To combat the Riff, the Spaniards and French added forces until they totaled over 300,000 men. These vast forces came complete with artillery, light tanks, armored cars, motorized supply columns—in the desert, horses caused more trouble than they were worth—and, of course, airpower. Only a few years having passed since the end of World War I, and with no fresh conflict in Europe in sight, the number of available aircraft was practically unlimited. It is true that, against the background of tumultuous technical progress, they were fast becoming obsolescent. Certainly the vast majority of them could not have been used in a major war between modern countries. However, against premodern opponents possessed of no airpower and very few heavy weapons of any kind they served well enough; Abd el-Krim, of course, never even had a single aircraft.

Not surprisingly, events followed a pattern somewhat similar to the ones in Libya. When it came to missions involving intelligence, liaison, supply, and medical evacuation, airpower, consisting of about 150 aircraft of various kinds, proved extremely useful. Aircraft were also used to drop bombs on villages in the hope of intimidating the civilian population.[21] On the other hand, then as later the question often presented itself whether such bombardment, by virtue of its inaccuracy and its tendency to hit people who wanted nothing but the quiet life, did not do more harm than good. Meanwhile, as had happened in Libya, missions flown against the guerrillas themselves, to the extent that they could be located, seldom yielded any real results. For the Riff, hardy and courageous fighters who were intimately familiar with the terrain, to find shelter in the rocky hills was not difficult. Not only were their casualties limited, but they did not hesitate to fire back at their flying attackers. Four years of massive ground operations by massive ground forces were needed before the rebels were finally brought to heel. Abd el-Krim himself was captured and exiled. In all this airpower played an important role, but perhaps more as an auxiliary than in any other capacity.

During the decades after World War II, the failure of many counterinsurgency campaigns has often been blamed on the unwillingness of those in charge, civilian or military, to take the necessary ruthless measures. Hence it is important to note that the failure to achieve swift victory over the Riff was not the result of any faintheartedness on the French and Spanish side. In fact, making use of their respective foreign legions—which, at that time, had not yet acquired the nickname "the White SS"—commanders of both countries committed countless atrocities of every kind, including the destruction of entire villages. The Third Geneva Convention had not been signed and the International Court in The Hague not yet established. Like the British, the French and the Spaniards looked at colonial peoples as savages against whom almost anything was permissible and permitted.

The same was even more true of the German occupation forces in World War II. As we saw, the Luftwaffe played an extremely important role in the Wehrmacht's early victories. Whereas resistance in the occupied countries of the west never grew to the point that it required the Germans to bring their airpower to bear, the situation in the east, that is, the Soviet Union, as well as the southeast, that is, Yugoslavia and Greece, was entirely different. In those regions what the Germans called banditry and their opponents, guerrilla warfare got under way almost immediately. In time it assumed massive proportions, involving tens and even hundreds of thousands of partisans and freedom fighters. It is true that, in proportion to the vast extent of occupied territory in the Soviet Union in particular, the amount of resources that the Germans were able to throw into the antipartisan struggle was strictly limited. Suffice it to say that, on the ground, each security division was responsible for 4,500 square miles on the average, and that some were responsible for 12,000 and more.[22] It is also true that, at the time, the Luftwaffe was fully occupied by a world war. Fighting it absorbed the lion's share of resources. For example, after March 1944 the Luftwaffe in Yugoslavia had only some reconnaissance aircraft and lighter bombers left. These facts explain why, in many of the major histories of the Luftwaffe written after the war, its role in counterinsurgency operations is hardly mentioned.

As one might expect, when it came to "anti-bandit" operations, the most important role airpower played consisted of surveillance and reconnaissance, including photoreconnaissance. The larger the operation and the less accessible the terrain, the more true this was.[23] Especially in the Soviet Union, the larger operations might also involve artillery. Here again aircraft, used for spotting, came in handy.[24] On the whole, the results were mixed. Frequently there was a vast discrepancy between the huge number of people whom the Germans killed and the small number of captured weapons, indicating that most casualties had been civilians.[25] One reason why many operations were relatively ineffective was that air reconnaissance was a double-edged sword, since the presence of Luftwaffe machines overhead could very well alert the partisans to the fact that something was afoot. Another was that neither the swamps and forests of Byelorussia nor the mountains of central and southern Yugoslavia represented the kind of terrain over which air reconnaissance could be used to the greatest advantage. In fact it has been claimed that, especially in Yugoslavia, the most successful operations were the smaller ones.[26] In many of those, directed against only a handful of partisans, airpower was not involved at all.

Once air reconnaissance and other forms of intelligence gathering had done their share, the operations themselves were conducted on the ground by men riding vehicles or else proceeding on foot. The objective was always to surround the partisans and eliminate them, but since they usually knew the terrain better than the Germans did, many of them got away.[27] As early as April 1943, the idea of using paratroopers against the Yugoslav partisans was raised at the Oberkommando der Wehrmacht (OKW). In December of the same year, following the failure of yet another large-scale sweep known as *Kugelblitz* (hail of bullets), Hitler himself called the attention of General Alfred Jodl, deputy commander of that organization and his chief strategic adviser, to this possibility. He wanted each security division in Yugoslavia to be provided with a battalion of paratroopers;[28] their task, as he saw it, would be to land at the right place at the right moment so as to seal off escape routes. However, at this point in the war resources were strained to the utmost. As it turned out, on only one occasion did Hitler's vision come true.

The operation in question was called *Rösselsprung* (knight's move), and it took place in May–June 1944.[29] The objective was to smash the enemy by means of a direct attack on Marshal Josip Tito's headquarters at Drvar in western Bosnia. First there came the bombers whose mission was both to kill and destroy and to keep the enemy from reacting to what followed. Their sorties were coordinated with those of transport aircraft assembled from as far away as France. They dropped paratroopers and towed gliders to the area. The number of German troops, either airborne or ones who made their way to the battlefield by land, was about 3,500, including men from such elite formations as the Waffen SS as well as the Brandenburg commando division. They were supported by several thousand locally recruited Serb and Croat militiamen. As it turned out, the secrecy of the operation was compromised, something that, in a war amongst the people, was and remains hard to prevent. Most partisans left the town in good time. The 60 or so who stayed delayed the Germans for long enough to enable Tito and the foreign guests at his headquarters to flee.

On May 25, the first day of the operation, the Luftwaffe flew no fewer than 440 sorties in support; after that, however, it all but disappeared from the skies. Operating from the airfields in southern Italy that decades later were to accommodate NATO aircraft in their attack on Serbia, Allied aircraft had created a situation where the Luftwaffe commander in Croatia was forced to prohibit his pilots from taking off.[30] Most of the time, one of the outstanding characteristics of insurgencies of every kind is that the insurgents must manage without air assets of any kind. Not so on this occasion, when they not only enjoyed air cover but were partly dependent on air supply. British aircraft provided the partisans with weapons, equipment, and medicines. With the supplies came foreign experts who provided liaison and advised Tito. Later during the summer, this assistance helped strengthen the partisans to the point where their operations became regular in all but name.

To return to *Rösselsprung*, once the initial move had failed it degenerated into a series of confused shoot-outs. German records, which when it comes to their own actions are probably reliable, indicate that they lost about 1,000 men killed and injured. That was a larger number than in 1941, when they had beaten the 800,000-strong Yugoslav Army and overrun the country. As usual, both sides agree that the number of casualties on the other side was considerably larger, though it is not clear by how much. As usual, many and perhaps most of the Yugoslavs who died were noncombatants. In principle, from the German point of view, killing lots of people from the air or in any other way might have served some useful purpose in intimidating the rest. However, after over three years of intermittent "anti-bandit" operations, noncombatant deaths, even in large numbers, hardly impressed the population. Whatever else, the Germans did not achieve either their most important objective, capturing Tito or killing him, or the wider one, inflicting at least a local defeat on the partisans. Just a few months later they found themselves in full retreat from Yugoslavia, which thus became the only country in Europe that did not have to wait for allied armies, Western or Soviet, for its liberation.[31]

Present-day advocates of airpower will undoubtedly argue that, compared to what came later, the aircraft that took part in these and other campaigns were small, unreliable, and plainly primitive. All this is true enough, not only for the interwar period but also in regard to the Luftwaffe. Until the end of 1942 partisans usually operated in groups that were too small for airpower to play an important part in combating them. Later Goering's overburdened commanders were unable to use their most advanced aircraft on the eastern and southeastern fronts. Even what units were deployed to those two fronts hardly saw anti-partisan warfare as their principal task and were neither organized nor trained with that purpose in mind. Yet it is equally true that, compared to the aircraft that came later, pre-1945 models enjoyed some important advantages. They were simple, cheap, extremely maneuverable—an important quality, when it came to attacking guerrillas who often took shelter in difficult terrain—and easy to maintain and repair under field conditions.

Though the aircrafts' ranges were short, when it came to fighting "wars without fronts," that factor did not matter much. Though the payloads they could carry were comparatively small, the same aircraft could take off and fly many missions in a single day. Most of the ammunition expended consisted of machine gun bullets and small unguided bombs. Both could be made available in practically unlimited quantities. There was no question of huge air bases operated and maintained by equally huge logistic, administrative, and technical services; in other words, the disproportion between what it cost to maintain a guerrilla or a terrorist and the price tag attached to the aircraft operating against him was not nearly as great as it was to become later during the jet age. Even the fact that aircraft were slow assisted, rather than hindered, their operations. Nor did these advantages go unnoticed by airmen whose mission it was to combat guerrillas in the post-1945 period. As late as Vietnam, the U.S. Air Force, the world's leading force with the most advanced technology at its disposal, was still making use of some piston-engined aircraft.

Summing up, right from the beginning—even before the beginning, if we include the extremely limited U.S. "airpower" brought to bear in Cuba—aircraft did not perform as well in counterinsurgency as they did in regular warfare. Remarkably, this applied even though no insurgents except those in Yugoslavia were protected by airpower of any sort; resistance, if any, could only come in the form of active and passive measures taken on the ground. While circumstances varied, the size of the countries in question, the nature of the terrain that guerrillas of every kind prefer, and the frequent difficulty of locating them from the air all contributed to this outcome. Other important factors were the aircrafts' own limitations. Early on these included inadequate air-to-ground communications, which often forced pilots to drop messages or pick them up after having landed. Others were limited ability to loiter over the battlefield and limited ability to carry and aim ordnance. Perhaps worst of all was the near-total lack of night reconnaissance and combat capabilities. Even if these problems could be overcome, airpower lacked any ability to hold ground and defend it. As the Italians had discovered, until stressed monoplanes replaced biplanes during the late 1930s, those engaged on anti-guerrilla operations also proved quite vulnerable even to rifle fire directed at them from the ground.

Out of all the counterinsurgency campaigns waged by various armed forces around the world between 1919 and 1939, aircraft probably proved most useful in Nicaragua. The reason was that, in this war, the Sandinistas on a few occasions got to the point where they switched, or tried to switch, from guerrilla to regular attacks on cities. As they did so they had to concentrate. As they concentrated, they presented convenient targets. Hence Marine Corps aircraft, used to support their comrades on the ground rather than to go after Douhet-like targets in the deep rear (targets that, in counterinsurgency campaigns, hardly existed in any case), were able to intervene most effectively. In most other cases the insurgents never got to that point. There could be no question of Palestinian rebels throwing the British out of Jerusalem, Jaffa, or Nablus, or of Soviet or Yugoslav partisans doing the same to the Germans in any occupied city or town. No doubt this was due partly to airpower, which tracked their moves. On the other hand, that airpower on its own hardly ever enabled its owners to suppress rebellion. That was done, to the extent that it was done, mainly by ground forces, often after hostilities that lasted for years.

By 1945, a situation had long been established where, both on land and at sea, no major military operation could take place in the face of hostile airpower. That, however, did not apply to most kinds of irregular operations, whatever they were called. In those cases the use of airpower was much more problematic and its impact not nearly as great. As aircraft continued to become more powerful and more sophisticated during the decades after 1945, the gap between the usefulness of airpower in the two different forms of war grew wider still. It was, indeed, to play a critically important role in shaping the world during the decades that followed.

CHAPTER 18

LOSE AND LEAVE

Whereas German anti-partisan operations had shown how much less effective airpower was in this kind of warfare than against regular forces, the lesson was not taken up. Instead the victors—the losers, as usual, had no say in the matter—tended to attribute the German inability to put down the various insurgencies to the singularly ferocious nature of the occupation; the latter, they claimed, merely caused resistance to increase. Having thus paid tribute to their own heroism and that of their allies, they went on to consider each other as their most important enemies. In the air as elsewhere, the outcome was a technological race between the great powers of the time. To repeat what has been said above, within 20 years after 1945 the maximum speed of combat aircraft had gone up from well under Mach 1 to well over Mach 2. However, since their maneuverability and ability to stay over target declined in proportion, on the whole they were less suited for dealing with insurgencies than their predecessors of the period 1911–45 had been.

After World War II, the first large-scale insurgency in which airpower was used was the Greek Civil War. Even before the German-Italian invasion of 1941, Greece had been an extremely poor country. Four years of occupation, when it was cut off from the world, reduced its population to near famine. The most important resistance movement during those years had been the Greek People's Liberation Army (ELAS). Communist in its inspiration and objectives, and feeling excluded from the right-wing government that was set up after the war, it launched a guerrilla campaign for which the country's mountainous terrain made it well suited. As if to emphasize this fact, the attack generally seen as marking the beginning of the campaign, on March 30, 1946, was directed against a garrison on Mount Olympus. Though the guerrillas did receive supplies from Yugoslavia, it goes without saying that they had no airpower of any kind. By contrast, the government, supported first by Britain and then by the United States, was able to use it on an ever-growing scale.

Having just emerged from World War II and occupation, initially the Greek Air Force could do little in support of counterinsurgency operations. This meant that the British had to carry the main burden. As in Burma during World War II, aircraft kept in touch with deep-penetration commando operations on the ground, resupplied them, and evacuated their wounded.[1] Trained by the British and having received a number of Harvard light trainers (which were used for reconnaissance), Spitfire fighters, and C-47 transports, over time the Royal Greek Air Force took a growing role in the hostilities. Yet the strength of the rebels kept on growing. In January 1947, perhaps because they felt that things were not going well for them, the British suddenly decided to withdraw from active participation in the conflict. From then on they were content to resupply, train, and advise their clients. The less involved they became, the more they stressed the need for the maximum use of airpower. This, the chiefs of staff in London claimed, represented "a significant shift in high-level British thinking about counterguerrilla warfare."[2]

Soon thereafter the Americans took over. With their much deeper pockets, they greatly expanded and re-equipped the Greek Army, its air component included. They provided the Greek Air Force with its first proper ground support aircraft, a squadron of Curtiss SB2C Helldivers. Originally designed for carrier operations and known as the "beasts," their maximum speed was only 300 miles per hour.[3] Under Alexander Papagos, who took over as the Greek commander in chief, a new strategy was worked out. Essentially it consisted of reconquering the country stage by stage and securing it by moving the population into camps; eventually at least 800,000 and perhaps a million people suffered this fate. As in Libya, the main instrument in the counterinsurgents' hands consisted of massive ground forces. At peak they numbered 170,000 men complete with a corps organization, artillery, and armored cars; the ratio of regulars to guerrillas stood at approximately seven to one.[4] As in Libya, the regulars were assisted by airpower.

Initially the most important tasks of the Greek Air Force were to provide intelligence and logistical support. Later, as more American advisers arrived and took the place of the British ones, things changed. Reinforced, the Greek Air Force added direct fire support and interdiction—isolating battlefields so as to prevent the enemy from escaping—to its tasks. It also flew independent missions against guerrilla targets. Yet the real reasons why the Greek armed forces, and of course their air component, were ultimately successful were entirely different. First, the Greek Democratic Army (GDA), as ELAS now called itself, overestimated itself. In the summer of 1948 it tried to turn from guerrilla to conventional warfare; this move provided the Royal Army and Air Force with targets and led to a series of heavy defeats at Mount Gramos and elsewhere. Second and even more important, at the time the conflict between Stalin and Tito broke out, the leaders of the GDA unwisely decided to side with the former. As a result, the supply of weapons and equipment from Yugoslavia quickly dried up and the border between it and Greece was closed. Against this background Papagos's forces were finally able to bring the war to an end; in this process the air force played an important, but far from decisive, role.

The Greek Civil War was precisely that, a civil war. There was no question of the loser evacuating the country and leaving it to the enemy. Instead, the concentration camps were filled—ultimately they held as many as 100,000 former GDA members and supporters. The situation in the numerous colonial conflicts that followed during the 1950s was entirely different. In all of them the European nations, mistaking the conditions that prevailed after 1945 for those that had existed before 1939, were initially determined to stay put. In all of them without exception, they failed in their purpose. The fact that in no case did the insurgents have any airpower at all made no difference. Used by the counterinsurgents, the best airpower could do was to postpone defeat.

The most celebrated defeat was the one the British suffered in Malaya. As we saw, like no other nation Britain during the interwar period put its faith in air policing, sometimes with success, sometimes without. Even where air policing was successful, though, this hardly meant that aircraft operated on their own without assistance from troops on the ground. These facts were recognized even by some RAF officers. As one group captain wrote in 1946, "since the essence of occupation is the presence of troops in the territory, it is probable that the greatest contribution which the air force can make is to carry the Army around the country. In this way, it will be possible to combine the speed and penetration of the air force with the discriminatory action of troops on the ground." Aircraft could also keep ground troops supplied.[5]

From 1942 to 1945, the Malaysian Communist Party (MCP) had waged a guerrilla campaign against the Japanese occupation. In 1948, after the British return, it resumed the struggle. Though it was largely confined to the 20 percent or so of the population that were Chinese, it could not be contained. Malaya is a country with an area of a little under 130,000 miles. Some two-thirds of this territory is covered by a jungle that is as impenetrable as any in the world. In 1948 communications to the west of the central mountain ridge that runs from north to south were reasonably good. However, to the east of it they barely existed. To make things even harder for the RAF, most of its major bases were located in the extreme south of the peninsula, that is, on the island of Singapore. Just to reach out to where the rebels were took up valuable fuel and flying time.

British strategy in Malaya is perhaps best described as a three-headed effort. The first consisted of what the Americans in Vietnam later described as search-and-destroy missions. However, thanks largely to the fact that resources were insufficient, the scale on which they were conducted was limited. The second consisted of surrounding entire villages and removing their population into camps so as to deny the guerrillas food and shelter; the third, of political reforms aimed at making the government more acceptable to the people. Airpower, of course, could be of assistance only in the first of these tasks. Principally it was used in two ways, indirect and direct. Indirect action consisted of the usual surveillance and reconnaissance flights as well as the insertion of small units of paratroopers and other airmobile troops into the jungle where they spent their time hunting guerrillas or trying to ambush them. It also included evacuating their wounded and extricating them either when necessary or else after their mission had been completed.

Direct support, often carried out in assistance of those units and following their request, consisted of strafing and bombing real or suspected guerrilla targets. When it came to analyzing the war, the British proudly claimed that, in comparison with some others, they only used little firepower. That is true; however, it is also true that they did not hesitate to use the most powerful aircraft at their disposal. These were heavy piston-engined Avro Lincoln bombers, the last of their kind, which had entered service in 1944. Each carried well over six tons of bombs. One historian has claimed that, of the two types of mission just mentioned, the direct and the indirect, the former were much the most effective. In providing ground troops with high mobility and enabling them to stay in action for much longer than they would have been if only supplied from the ground, airpower acted as a force multiplier.[6] On the other hand, British officers at the time understood that the jungle did not lend itself to direct support. Not only did the terrain and the vegetation make it all but impossible to determine how many rebels were hit, if any, but there were numerous incidents when British ground troops were caught by their own bombs. More than one of them felt that the direct use of airpower created more problems than it solved.[7] The faster the aircraft—Malaya was the first counterinsurgency to see jets in action—the greater the difficulties; like others coming after them, the British discovered that the machines most suitable for strike missions were older, slower, propeller-driven ones.[8]

Yet the situation continued to go from bad to worse. On October 6, 1951, the first British commander in Malaya, General Harold Briggs, was replaced (one month earlier, his civilian counterpart, High Commissioner Henry Gurney, had been killed in an ambush). The turning point, when it came, had little to do with military power of any kind. As early as 1950, the Labour government had determined that Britain's position in Malaya was untenable.[9] A year later, on October 25, 1951, elections were held, and the Conservatives, led by Winston Churchill, were returned to power. Not long thereafter the British administration gave the Chinese minority equal rights with the Malayan majority, thus removing a major bone of contention. It was left to General (later Field Marshal Lord) Gerald Templer, who replaced both Briggs and Gurney, to supervise the transition. From that moment on military activities on both sides started declining; after all, if the outcome is a foregone conclusion, why fight and die? Whereas the RAF's activities went on much as before, its order of battle, which at peak in 1951–53 had consisted of some 200 aircraft, could be progressively cut down. By 1957, the year when Malaya became an independent country (later renaming itself Malaysia) and joined the Commonwealth, British operations on the ground and in the air had all but ended. Thus not even a victory, if such it was, could alter the pattern of lose and leave.

Further to the east, the French, who did not have as powerful and as clever a politician as Churchill at their head, fared much worse. As in Malaya, the driving force in Vietnam was the Communist Party, which had fought the Japanese and went on fighting the French on the return of the latter. Not only is the territory of the two countries almost exactly the same, but both have plenty of mountains and jungles (though the percentage of the land they cover is smaller in Vietnam than in Malaysia). However, the differences are equally important. Malaya is a peninsula jutting into the Indian Ocean, whereas Vietnam is bordered by several neighbors to the west. It also has a common frontier with China. Though there are several good ports, the land transportation system was underdeveloped. These facts were destined to play a large role during the struggles that ensued.

Under French rule, Vietnam was a unified country with its capital at Hanoi in the northeast. The idea of dividing it into a northern and a southern part seems to have been raised for the first time by the French in 1948; however, the Viet Minh movement, led by Ho Chi Minh, balked at it. Next, overestimating their power, the Communists tried to defeat the French by launching a conventional offensive in the north. At one point, 1,200 men even attempted to seize Hanoi by a coup de main, only to be easily defeated. Rather than giving up, they reverted to guerrilla warfare. The objective was to bring the countryside, where some 90 percent of the population lived, under control by persuasion or force. The outcome, to speak with the author of a famous book of the time, was "a street without joy." Whereas the southern part of the country remained relatively calm, in the north and center, French outposts were attacked and overrun. French convoys were shot up, which was one reason why they tried to use air transport as much as possible, and French-appointed officials were assassinated. There was also much random violence in the form of bombings that struck the cities in particular, killing and injuring innocent people and proving that the French administration was no longer capable of providing security.

By the beginning of 1947, less than two years after the end of World War II, the French had approximately 115,000 troops in Indochina. Eventually their number reached no fewer than 600,000, of whom a little over two-thirds were locally recruited auxiliaries. On the other side of the hill, the Viet Minh never had more than half this figure.[10] At first the French only had some old Ju-52 German transports left over from World War II. Later they received much more modern American C-47s and C-119s (the so-called Flying Boxcars, used, among other things, to drop napalm on the Viet Minh)[11] as well as reconnaissance aircraft and F8F fighters. Overcoming their doubts, the Joint Chiefs of Staff even agreed to divert 21 light twin-engine B-26 bombers already on their way to Korea to assist the French.[12] Subsequently their number was increased to 47. At peak the French operated 275 aircraft. This was considerably more than the British ever used in Malaya and comprised almost half of their entire air force.[13]

Over two-thirds of all the aircraft were American built. The United States also provided some mechanics to maintain them.

As usual, the most important types of mission flown were reconnaissance, strategic mobility, close support, liaison, and medical evacuation. On one or two occasions French aircraft even bombed their own capital of Hanoi to eliminate guerrillas who had penetrated it, though this was never done on a large scale.[14] Yet there were severe limits on what could be done. As always since airpower was first used in the counterinsurgency role, commanders complained that the available forces did not suffice—what commander in history ever had enough? The weather was not always cooperative, and Viet Minh guerrillas in the mountains made such effective use of the terrain and the vegetation that they could rarely be struck from the air. Those, probably the majority, known to live and operate in or near the villages could be and were, but, given the large number of civilian casualties the results were often counterproductive.

In October 1950 the U.S. ambassador, Donald Heath, informed his superiors that the Viet Minh would soon "be able to hurl tank-led plane-covered assault[s]" against the populous areas of northern Vietnam, but his prediction never came true.[15] Until 1953 they did not have anti-aircraft artillery either; even later, though the French did register a few cases when their aircraft received hits, they did not consider such artillery a serious problem until events taught them differently. Besides shooting back where possible, the Viet Minh soon learned the usual tricks of the trade, including extensive use of camouflage and confining their movements to nighttime wherever possible. Each evening the jungle paths woke up as tens of thousands of coolies started pushing their bicycles along. They also constructed huge underground complexes that could not be detected from the air and which they used to store supplies. A cook by the name of Hoang Tram even became a sort of national hero for inventing a stove that enabled hot meals to be prepared without producing telltale smoke.[16] Try as they might, French air and ground forces could not prevent the enemy, commanded by master strategist Vo Nguyen Giap, from building up his conventional forces in the north of the country.

These were the years when, on both sides of the Atlantic, enthusiasm for anything "airborne" was at its peak. In particular, commandos and paratroopers, who could easily be distinguished by the color of their berets, caught the imagination of the military as well as the general public: as the song went, "fighting soldiers from the sky,/fearless men who jump and die."[17] France, too, had them, and indeed the time soon came when the "Mythe Para," exemplified by men who had cut their teeth in Indochina and were later to play a leading part in the Algerian War as well, cast its spell over the country. That fact was probably one reason, and even a fairly important reason, behind the French attempts to use them in a different way, and on a larger scale, than others. Whereas the Germans in Yugoslavia had used paratroopers in attempts to block the escape routes of Tito's partisans, and whereas the British in Malaysia inserted teams of airborne commandoes into guerrilla-infested areas and kept them supplied from the air, the French chose to employ entire battalions and even regiments.

Relying on surprise, the paratroopers were dropped onto supposedly strategic locations deep in enemy territory. There they quickly organized for all-round defense and waited for the Viet Minh to attack them. Once that happened, they were able to use their superior firepower on the ground and in the air without fear of what was later to become known as collateral damage. Some of the descents proved to be blows in the air, but here and there the system seemed to work. One occasion on which it did work, or so the French high command in Indochina thought, was at Na San late in 1952 when a regiment of paratroopers was dropped west of Hanoi and subsequently repulsed all the attempts to dislodge it.[18] Even so, since Na San was evacuated in August 1953, it is not clear what the French achieved. An American team, sent by the commander in chief, Pacific (CINCPAC), to evaluate the situation, called it "an inconclusive battle in a mountain wilderness."[19]

However that might be, it is clear that the French never succeeded in preventing Giap's forces from receiving their supplies from China. As the war went on without an end in sight, French morale deteriorated. Nothing is more indicative of this than the fact that, during the first seven years after

1945, no fewer than six commanders in chief—many of them carrying fancy aristocratic names—replaced each other. Each one, it seemed, only hoped to wait out his time and go home before his reputation was irreparably damaged. Of course it was not their fault alone; in Paris during the same years, no fewer than 19 different governments took power and were forced to relinquish it. When commander number seven, Henri Navarre, was appointed in 1953, he found nothing but despair. Determined to change this state of affairs, he decided on yet another airborne operation—the largest of all—at a godforsaken place called Dien Bien Phu.

By late 1953, Giap's forces had become strong enough to prepare to invade Laos. This fact itself is a telling comment on the French forces' failure, both on the ground and from the air, to prevent the growth of what, less than ten years previously, had been nothing but small bands of ill-organized, ill-equipped guerrillas. Operation Castor, as it was called, opened on November 20. Flying in relays, 60 C-47s dropped 3,000 paratroopers during the first day alone. Aided by a bulldozer, engineers restored a former Japanese airstrip in the area, allowing supplies too delicate to be dropped to be brought in as well. Eventually the total number of troops the high command committed to the battle reached 16,000, complete with artillery and ten light tanks. They built a number of strongholds, all of them named after women, and prepared to defend a rough perimeter 30 miles long.

Confronting the French were four times as many Viet Minh. By this time they were operating in division-sized formations under strict centralized control. What made the battle different from the one of Na San was that the former commanded the high ground—not so Dien Bien Phu, which is a valley surrounded by mountains. Working by night in the face of everything French airpower could do, Giap's troops hauled their artillery into the mountains, put it in position, and carefully camouflaged it so it could not be identified from either the ground or the air. On March 13, 1954, it opened fire. Infantry attacks designed to isolate and overrun individual strongholds soon followed. First the Japanese-built landing strip the French used was overrun. With it went their ability to fly in many kinds of supplies. Next anti-aircraft artillery fire interfered with their attempts to supply the garrison by parachute. A few aircraft were shot down, and the rest were forced to fly at 8,000 feet instead of 2,000 as previously. They also had to take evasive action, causing them to drop their loads inaccurately so that many of them fell into Giap's hands. For example, on May 6, the cargoes of 19 out of 25 C-119s never reached their destination.[20]

The most important French airfields were located in the Tonkin Delta far from the battlefield. They were attacked by guerrillas who destroyed no fewer than 78 aircraft, mostly transports. Meanwhile, at Dien Bien Phu, the defensive perimeter shrank as one stronghold after another fell. At one point there was talk of sending in 100 American B-29s. However, the U.S. Air Force general who would have commanded the operation, Joseph Caldara, claimed that there were "no true B-29 targets" in the area,[21] and in the end, President Eisenhower put the matter on ice.[22] After weeks of ferocious fighting, some of it hand to hand, 11,000 survivors, half of them wounded and running out of supplies, surrendered.

So bad was the French defeat at Dien Bien Phu that it became something of a bogey. From then to the present, in spite of endless talk about the advantages of vertical envelopment and air mobility, no military has dared launch an airborne operation on anything like this scale either to deal with an insurgency or for any other purpose. The last U.S. commander in Vietnam, General Creighton Abrams, is reported to have blown his top whenever his subordinates dared authorize their use.[23] Whatever else may be said about the battle, it cannot be classified as "war amongst the people." Instead it was a regular engagement, fought between uniformed forces in a thinly populated area by large formations (approximately one division against four), with plenty of heavy weapons on the Vietnamese side in particular. If it is nevertheless included in this part of the volume, that is because it came at the tail end of a long conflict of the aforementioned kind.

When we look back at this struggle, the bottom line is that the French, for all their numerous shortcomings, had airpower whereas their opponents did not. Long before the Battle of Dien Bien Phu was joined, that airpower had been unable to prevent the transition from Mao's second stage to the third. Though a few of Giap's attempts in this direction, the most important of which was Na San, were frustrated, in the end he managed to make the shift. In part, of course, it was due to the exceptionally difficult nature of the country; in effect, the border between China and northern Vietnam was obliterated, enabling the flow of material to proceed almost without interruption. But suppose the French had interdicted Giap's lines of supply, forcing him to remain in the second stage? Judging by almost every other struggle of the same kind from 1945 on, the French, with or without the support of airpower, would still not have been able to force their enemies to give up. An even longer conflict would have ensued, and almost certainly the final outcome would have been very similar to what it was. American officers, wiser when reporting on the activities of others than they were to prove when they themselves fought in the same country later, reached that conclusion as early as 1952.[24]

No sooner had the French lost Indochina than they engaged in another colonial struggle much closer to home. Of all the numerous anticolonial wars waged in various parts of the world before the Americans entered Vietnam, Algeria was the largest by far. Thanks to the utter determination displayed by both sides, it also turned into one of the most ferocious. Large-scale violence broke out for the first time on May 8, 1945, when VE Day was being celebrated. Riots in the town of Sétif, east of Algiers, caused the deaths of 104 *colons,* or colonists, also called *pieds-noirs,* many women and children included. This was long before postmodern war arrived on the scene and took over; the French response was savage, leading to the death of between 1,020 (the French say) and 45,000 (according to the Algerians) people, though 6,000 is probably a more reasonable estimate.[25] Many of the deaths were caused by three U.S.-provided Douglas Dauntless dive-bombers used to bombard about 40 villages in the region. On the surface, calm was restored, but underneath, the ferment continued. After many complicated political struggles that need not concern us here, the Front de Libération Nationale (FLN) was founded. On November 1, 1954, it led the nation into what was very soon to turn into a full-scale rebellion.

Algeria is a very large country, covering a territory of over 930,000 square miles. Some 800,000 of those consist of desert, practically unpopulated and hence not very suitable for guerrilla warfare; yet even the strip of inhabited territory that stretches from east to west along the Mediterranean, which is estimated at 115,000 square miles, is more than large enough for that purpose. Topographically speaking the region in question consists of hills, mountains, valleys, and plateaus. Parts of it are wooded, others cut by deep wadis capable of providing plenty of shelter, and others still either cultivated or urbanized. To the west lies Morocco, to the east, Tunisia. Both countries gained their independence in 1956. Tunisia in particular became a major venue through which weapons originating in Egypt were smuggled into Algeria. As we shall see, one of the principal uses of airpower during the war, which lasted until 1962, was to try to stop the flow. A major difference between the war in Algeria and other colonial conflicts was that the country was legally part of France, though only the *pieds-noirs* were represented in the French Parliament. This meant that not only volunteers but conscripts too could be sent to fight there.

Small as it was, the FLN opened its fight for independence with a series of what today would be called terrorist attacks. Initially military personnel and installations were targeted. Things, however, soon changed. On August 20, 1955, armed bands set upon the French inhabitants of Philippeville and the neighboring townships, massacring perhaps 130 people of all ages. When French forces arrived, they retaliated by killing anywhere between 1,300 (they say) and 12,000 (the FLN said) Algerians.[26] After that, little if anything remained out of bounds. The FLN struck at the infrastructure—electricity poles, pipelines, and bridges. They targeted places, such as coffeehouses, shops, and public squares, where civilians met or assembled. As so often was the case elsewhere, Algerian nationals who worked for the French and refused to leave their posts or collaborate with the FLN were threatened and, if they did not respond, mutilated or assassinated.

Owing to the insurgents' inexperience, many early attacks were unsuccessful and only caused a few casualties or none at all. The outcome was to mislead the authorities into a false sense of security. Yet the incidents, instead of ceasing, expanded and became increasingly frequent, forcing the French to bring in reinforcements. By 1957 the number of French troops had risen to 400,000, remaining at this level during the rest of the war. For six years on end, the struggle in Algeria was given absolute priority over France's other military commitments, those pertaining to NATO included. As in Indochina, the French also raised so-called *harkis,* local auxiliaries, whose number eventually reached no fewer than 170,000. On the other side, the number of full-time *fellaghas* (fighters) probably never exceeded 30,000–40,000. Most sources agree that, out of a Muslim population of about nine million, many more might have been recruited, but the FLN never had enough weapons to equip them. At any one time perhaps 50 to 60 percent of the guerrillas operated inside Algeria. The rest trained or rested in the neighboring countries.

With the French troops came their air force. By this time France was rapidly recovering from the results of defeat and occupation during World War II; its aviation industry was flourishing. These facts, as well as Algeria's geographical proximity to the mother country, enabled large air force contingents to be based there. Following lessons learned in Indochina, they were made to operate in a decentralized manner. Along the coast, control was in the hands of three tactical headquarters, each one corresponding with, but not subordinate to, the army corps in that area; two other air force headquarters operated in the Sahara, which was practically empty of French troops. The number of aircraft, which stood at just under 155 at the beginning of 1955, went up to no fewer than 686 three years later. Out of those, nota bene, about 120 were operated not by the air force but by the army.[27] The aircraft included the most modern available fighters and fighter-bombers, the transsonic F-86 Sabres and Dassault Mystère IVs already mentioned more than once in these pages. Still the French soon learned that they were not very suitable for the purpose. Preference was given to older, slower, more maneuverable machines. Among them were T-6 and T-28 trainers, P-47 fighters, A-1 (Douglas Skyraider) ground attack aircraft, and B-26 light bombers. These aircraft were supplemented by light machines used for reconnaissance, artillery spotting, and liaison as well as transport aircraft in the form of the obsolete Ju-52s, the indispensable C-47s, and the heavier Noratlases. All were piston engined, and all but the last-named dated to World War II.

Ultimately the number of French Air Force personnel reached over 30,000.[28] Such a force required a huge investment in ground facilities. The outcome was a massive infrastructure consisting of no fewer than 30 airfields and several hundred airstrips suitable for light aircraft.[29] To this were added command-and-control facilities, radio direction-finding stations to locate bands of rebels trying to communicate among themselves, and logistic centers. Consumption of aviation fuel increased from 4,000,000 gallons in 1954 to almost 10,000,000 in 1956.[30] The payoff consisted of about 250,000 sorties flown in 1958–59 alone, of which about a third were for reconnaissance.[31] On the one hand, 75 percent of all French intelligence was the result of air reconnaissance without which they would have been deaf and blind. On the other, only about two-thirds of the intelligence thus obtained turned out to be accurate and useful. Pilots' mistakes, as well as photo-interpreters' errors, often sent the forces that depended on them on wild goose chases. Another problem was that the population soon learned how to deal with reconnaissance aircraft. Instead of hiding, as they initially did, they continued their normal activities, thus making it impossible for the pilots and observers to draw any useful conclusions. Even much of the intelligence that *was* accurate and *could* have been useful failed in its purpose. For all the superior technology and airpower at their disposal, the French often failed to go through the OODA (observation, orientation, decision, action) loops—to use Colonel John Boyd's terminology—as fast as they should. Presumably one reason for this was that, whereas most anti-guerrilla operations involved army units, air reconnaissance was largely the responsibility of the Armée le l'Air; later, a similar problem was to bedevil U.S. operations in South Vietnam.[32]

Even when the intelligence was accurate and timely, the use of airpower to follow it up often gave rise to other problems. Unlike the Viet Minh, the FLN was never in a position to deploy anti-aircraft artillery. This fact rendered its fighters helpless against the combat aircraft that attacked them; however, they could and did use their small arms to shoot at light aircraft and helicopters, occasionally bringing down one of them. In Algeria as elsewhere, each such feat helped boost the insurgents' morale. When French troops succeeded in cornering their enemies on the ground, they would habitually call for air support in order to finish the job. Arriving on the scene, the pilots in turn would often ask the troops to put up signs to mark their positions and thus avoid friendly casualties, with the result that the signs also enabled the *fellaghas* to see where their enemies were. Perhaps worst of all were the occasions when airpower, in the form of bombers, was used on a relatively large scale against villages suspected of harboring guerrillas and proved as inaccurate as it had always been. It has been claimed that, during the entire conflict, no single operation did more to raise hatred against the French and play into the FLN's hands than the one that struck the Tunisian village of Sakiet on February 8, 1958, killing about 80 civilians.[33] Yet Sakiet was no more than the tip of the iceberg. Almost from beginning to end, the French applied the principle of collective responsibility, which meant that they routinely sent in aircraft to bomb villages from which terrorists had allegedly come.

Not only the air force, but the navy too played a role in the struggle. Like its sister service, the navy relied principally on World War II–vintage, piston-engined aircraft. Among them were American-built Catalina flying boats, Consolidated-Vultee Privateer medium bombers, Grumman Avenger torpedo aircraft, and Grumman Goose light transports—the last-named equipped with powerful radar sets—as well as British-built Avro Lancaster bombers. From 1958 on these aircraft were joined, then largely replaced, by much more modern, turboprop-powered P-2 Lockheed Neptunes originally developed for anti-submarine warfare. Much the most important task of naval airpower was to conduct maritime surveillance so as to prevent men and weapons from reaching the FLN by sea. Since the sea presents a much simpler environment than the land, and since there are no bothersome civilians around, in carrying out this mission the navy's aircraft were quite successful. One ship alone, the *Athos,* was found to carry 72 mortars, 40 machine guns, 74 automatic rifles, 240 submachine guns, 2,300 rifles, 2,900 mortar rounds, and 600,000 cartridges. It is said that, throughout the conflict, no large quantities of supplies reached Algeria directly by sea; instead they came overland by way of the neighboring countries.[34]

Of all the innovations the war witnessed, none seemed to hold a greater promise than the increase in the number of helicopters. Both the British in Malaysia and the French in Indochina had deployed them. In counterinsurgency as in regular operations helicopters proved much more expensive and much more vulnerable than other aircraft. Those in service at the time were also relatively small, weak, and primitive. Though they proved extremely useful in tasks such as observation, liaison, small-scale troop transport, resupply, and casualty evacuation, in the end the available numbers were too small to make much of a difference. As the production of helicopters rose during the mid- and late 1950s, and as the machines themselves became more powerful, the military of many countries expected to use them in precisely the kind of struggle "amongst the people" that was now becoming almost the norm in many countries around the world. One former German officer, whose credentials as a counterinsurgency expert went back to the occupation of the Soviet Union in 1941–44, even claimed that, had he and his comrades possessed helicopters during that period, they could and would have defeated the partisans.[35]

Between 1957 and 1960 the number of French helicopters in Algeria increased from 82 to 400. Some machines were operated by the air force, others by the army, and others still by the navy. They included Sikorsky S-55s and S-58s and Bell H-13 light transports as well as a twin-rotor Piaceski H-21 "flying bananas," all of them American made. France's own light Alouette IIs, two-seater, extremely maneuverable machines best described as the flying equivalent of the contemporary Citroën Deux Chevaux car, were also used.[36] Clearly, in the kind of struggle the French were waging, fixed-wing aircraft were becoming less useful, rotary ones more so. Light helicopters were used for liaison, observation, casualty evacuation, and as flying command posts. Others served to relay radio transmissions from one ground station to another. Medium ones transported troops both operationally and tactically. One out of six helicopters was equipped either with light cannon or with rockets and served as a gunship, the first time such machines were employed in any war.

One outcome of this process was a notable decline in the use of paratroopers, who had played a prominent role during the Indochina War. Commanded by such figures as General Jacques Massu and Major Marcel Bigeard, both of whom were later to serve as models for the heroes of Jean

Lartéguy's 1960 novel *The Centurions,* French paratroopers in Algeria acquired quite a reputation both for their military effectiveness and for their brutality. They stood guard, they marched, they fought, they massacred, and they tortured—but they did not jump from aircraft into combat. Only once during the war was a descent into Moroccan territory planned, but it was canceled at the last moment. Judging by the memoirs of one young paratrooper, almost all their operational movements were made by truck or else by arduous marches on foot.[37] From time to time they, as well as other troops, would be lifted to their objectives by helicopters. The latter could deliver them in a much more concentrated manner, and much more accurately than aircraft could.

In every way—command and control, the amount of resources committed, and the sheer number of aircraft and helicopters used—French airpower in Algeria was stronger by far than anything ever used in counterinsurgency operations until then. Since then, too, it has rarely been equaled. Airpower seems to have played a particularly important role during the early stages of the war, before the *fellaghas* and the civilian population that supported them got used to dealing with it, and also during the final years from about 1958 on. At that time, perhaps its greatest success consisted in that, whereas Giap and the Viet Minh had gradually been able to build up entire divisions of troops, the FLN rarely put together anything larger than companies. Nor were the rebels ever able to obtain and use heavy weapons to match the ones the French habitually brought to bear against them.

Geographically speaking, the areas where airpower was most useful were the sea and the Sahara Desert (where there were few guerrillas anyhow). Over the open terrain to the east, through which ran the border between Algeria and Tunisia, it also worked quite well. Here the French built an elaborate barrier consisting of an electrified fence, and swept patrol roads, mines, and numerous interconnected observation points. The intent was to cut off the flow of reinforcements and deny the FLN its much needed refuge. The entire civilian population was evacuated, the whole area was declared a free-fire zone, and it was patrolled 24 hours a day with airpower playing a dominant role. From time to time bands of guerrillas were caught and annihilated as they tried to cross in either direction. While the barrier did not completely isolate the theater of operations from the outside world, unlike similar American attempts in Vietnam it largely fulfilled its purpose.

In October 1956, a combination of brilliant intelligence, adroit deception, and an extraordinary disregard for international law enabled the French Air Force commanders in Algeria to mount a real coup. With their superiors turning a blind eye, they sent fighters over the Mediterranean to intercept a Moroccan DC-3 airliner on its way to Tunis, forcing it to land in Algeria. Inside were five of the FLN's principal leaders, including Ahmed Ben Bella, the most important of all; it was as if the Americans in Vietnam had captured Ho Chi Minh, Giap, and some other members of the Politburo in one sweep. Still the struggle went on as before. One very important reason for this was that, when it came to fighting in the cities, airpower was almost entirely useless. There was no way it could be used to locate, trap, or kill terrorists operating in the streets, let alone the winding, often covered, alleyways of the Kasbahs. Whether the paratroopers did in fact win the Battle of Algiers, as has often been asserted, will not be discussed here.[38] Nor does it matter whether, had French public opinion not become disgusted with the conflict and the politicians thrown up their hands in despair, that battle could have brought the war to some sort of victorious conclusion. The point is rather that, as Massu's men fought the battle, there was little if anything airpower could do to assist them. In the end it was police work, accompanied by torture, that did the job, not aircraft of any kind.

Perhaps the best way to sum up this chapter is to turn to David Galula (1919–67). Galula was a 1939 graduate of the French military academy at Saint-Cyr who spent World War II fighting with Charles de Gaulle. He spent the years from 1945 to 1949 at the French Embassy in Beijing, where he was an eyewitness to the struggle that led to the victory of Mao Tse-tung and the Communists over the forces of Chiang Kai-shek. Posted to Algeria, where he eventually reached the rank of lieutenant colonel, he served first as company and then as deputy battalion commander. In 1963 and 1964 he published two books about his experiences, as many others, Massu included, also did. Yet unlike them he was not forgotten. The U.S. campaigns in Afghanistan and Iraq during the first decade of the twenty-first century led to a revival of interest in the man and his methods.[39] So much so, in fact, that the leading academic American expert on terrorism, Bruce Hoffman of RAND, wrote that *Pacification in Algeria,* the second of Galula's two volumes, has "a remarkable, almost timeless, resonance" almost 50 years after being committed to paper.[40]

Like anyone who has ever studied modern counterinsurgency, Galula was puzzled by the fact that, even though the French had *"a truly enormous material superiority over the rebels"* (emphasis in the original),[41] they ended up by losing the war and leaving the country. Recognizing that his own side had committed errors, he has numerous important lessons to offer. There are chapters on controlling the population and on the best ways to gain its support. There are chapters on strategy, on the French lack of a proper counterinsurgency doctrine, on operations at the sector level, and on contacts between the military and the population it is supposed to control and pacify. Other chapters deal with clearing guerrilla-infested areas, mobilizing the population for self-defense, and the treatment to be meted out to prisoners and suspects (he thought they should be well treated so as to induce their comrades to surrender too). There is even a chapter on how to capitalize on the Algerians' alleged discrimination against, and mistreatment of, the 50 percent of the population who were female. From start to finish, the objective was to protect the population, isolate it from the rebels, control it, and move it politically in the desired direction.[42]

Pacification in Algeria ends with two lists: "Major Factors in the Algerian War" and "Basic Principles of Counterinsurgency Warfare." Neither in that book nor in its companion volume does airpower take up more than a sentence or two.

CHAPTER 19

A WAR TOO FAR

While the French and Algerians were waging a savage war against each other, another struggle of the same kind was brewing in Vietnam. Following their defeat at Dien Bien Phu, the French decided to pull out. Subsequently an international conference held in Geneva in May–July 1954 agreed to temporarily divide the country into two halves, a northern one and a southern one, pending the holding of free elections in the entire country in July 1956. As it turned out, the elections never took place. Instead two separate administrations emerged, a Communist one under Ho Chi Minh in the north and a supposedly free and democratic one under Ngo Dinh Diem in the south. Seeking to reunify the country under Communist control, Ho Chi Minh, along with his supporters in the South, launched what was to become the largest struggle of its kind in the entire twentieth century.

American personnel, both military and civilian, had been involved in Vietnam ever since the Japanese had evacuated it in 1945. As the war there expanded, increasingly they provided the French with funding, logistic support, weapons, and advice. They also sent back a flow of reports that were often highly critical of what the French were doing; in 1954 the staff of the Air University studied the war, concluding that airpower had done precious little to help the French.[1] With SAC and the bomber generals firmly in control, the United States had little patience for a subconventional war fought in a small, remote country such as Vietnam. Some commanders, the vice air chief of staff in Washington, D.C., included, may even have thought that it could be dealt with simply by dropping a few nuclear weapons, though they did concede that, in that case, it would be necessary to warn America's allies first.[2] Besides, these were the 1950s. Whereas most countries were still trying to repair the damage resulting from World War II, the United States was going from strength to strength; there seemed to be no limit either to its resources or to its power.

During the last years of their rule the French in South Vietnam had sought to build some kind of an army, including a rudimentary air force.[3] Later the Americans undertook to ensure that South Vietnam would not fall to communism as the North had done. As the fashionable domino theory of the time had it, that would have led to the "loss" first of the rest of Indochina, then of Thailand and Burma, and finally of India as well.[4] American advisers arrived in the country to help organize the Army of South Vietnam (ARVN), train it, and arm it.[5] They also supported an air force that was rapidly making the transition from infancy into youth. Eventually that air force was to operate many kinds of contemporary aircraft, including light machines for observation, liaison, and training (O-1, O-2, T-6, T-41, and U-17); light and medium transports (C-7, C-47, C-119, C-123, and C-130); light bombers (B-57); light and medium helicopters (H-19, H-34, CH-34, CH-47, and French Allouettes); and light fighters (A-1, A-37, F8F, and T-28).[6]

Except for the fighters, some of which came out of World War II whereas others were converted trainers, all these machines were reasonably modern for their time. In 1961, a U.S. Army general even cited the "terrific firepower" of the modified A-1. It could, he said, provide the South Vietnamese ground forces with mobile, accurate, and massive support.[7] Such was the confidence, not to say hubris, of the air force that, early on, it tried to scare the Viet Cong simply by flying some of its aircraft over their heads. On the other hand, though the Americans did much to augment the logistic and technical expertise of the South Vietnamese Air Force, throughout the conflict they remained keenly aware of their allies' limitations in these fields. Hence the Vietnamese never received the most advanced jet combat aircraft such as fighters and bombers, but those would have been useless in counterinsurgency warfare anyhow. As a result, the only jets in South Vietnamese hands were F-5 light fighters similar to the ones other developing countries got.

As usual in struggles of this kind, those on the receiving end of these forces, in this case, the Viet Cong, had no air force at all. At first they did not have anti-aircraft defenses either. For several years hostilities assumed their normal form. Starting from very small beginnings—the distribution of propaganda leaflets here, an act of sabotage there—the Viet Cong, aided and abetted by the North, mounted hit-and-run attacks on all sorts of military and civilian targets. The objective was to demonstrate the government's inability to protect and control the population and bring about its collapse. By 1958, an estimated 20 percent of all village heads had been assassinated.[8] Saigon responded by expanding its armed forces until, in 1964, they probably outnumbered the Viet Cong ten to one.[9] They were used to guard all sorts of critical installations, gathering intelligence and striking back at the guerrillas wherever and whenever they could be found. As so often was the case from the Italo-Turkish War on, aircraft played a considerable role in these operations. They flew countless reconnaissance missions, transported troops to where they were needed, strafed and bombed Viet Cong targets, and provided services such as liaison and medical evacuation.

Under President Eisenhower, the U.S. involvement in Vietnam remained limited. But this does not necessarily mean that, had he been the one to face the growing insurgency after 1961, he would have refrained from doing what his successors eventually did.[10] A similar argument could be made concerning John F. Kennedy; whether, had he lived, he would have expanded America's effort in Vietnam as Lyndon Johnson did or allowed the country to fall to the Viet Cong and Ho Chi Minh must remain anybody's guess. What is certain is that the effort grew from just 2,000 men when Eisenhower left office to 16,500 when Johnson entered it in late 1963. Of those, some 3,000 were air force personnel, including pilots, technicians, forward observers, and others. Initially the air force, in the belief that taking on the Vietnam mission would divert resources away from the most modern bombers and fighters, resisted it as best it could.[11] Later, pressed by Kennedy, and worried lest he would turn to the army instead, the air force expanded, or pretended to expand, its capabilities for waging subconventional warfare. To this end it formed a force of air commandos, named after a U.S. Army Air Forces unit that had operated against the Japanese in Southeast Asia during World War II. Equipped with aircraft broadly similar to those the French had used, the commandos were taught to strafe, rocket, and drop napalm before being deployed to Vietnam at the end of 1961.[12]

Originally their mission was to train, assist, and advise the South Vietnamese Air Force. With or without their superiors' permission, though, before long they took a hand in combat. Flying aircraft painted in Vietnamese colors, either along with the Vietnamese crews or, increasingly, on their own, they undertook reconnaissance and close support missions. Nor was this all; as early as the spring of 1962, the first F-102 Delta Daggers arrived. To the impartial observer, sending supersonic fighters to combat insurgents might seem like a strange idea. It was, however, typical of the way in which, given the ever present struggle for resources, each element of the U.S. armed forces did what it could to carve out a role for itself. The planes' stated mission was to intercept North Vietnamese Il-28 light bomber aircraft supposedly flying into Vietnam from Cambodia and Laos. Later they also fired air-to-ground rockets, a mission for which they were anything but well suited. Early on, attempts were made to pretend that they were operated by South Vietnamese pilots, but few people were fooled. To this day, it remains unclear whether the Il-28s were real—apparently none was brought down—or a figment of some radar operator's imagination. What was definitely *not* a figment of the imagination was a Viet Cong attack on the air base at Bien Hoa, near Saigon, on November 1, 1963, which destroyed many U.S. and South Vietnamese aircraft, including 13 B-57s and six A-18s.

This and other setbacks notwithstanding, the U.S. Air Force presence in South Vietnam continued to expand. Counting both the air force and the army's Special Forces, in 1963 alone some 300,000 sorties were flown.[13] Even this massive number did not include the small but growing South Vietnamese Air Force. Nevertheless, the war continued to go from bad to worse. Not even Operation Ranch Hand, which began in 1962 and under which aircraft sprayed toxic chemicals to defoliate huge swaths of jungle and destroy crops deemed useful to the Viet Cong, seemed to produce results.[14] One indication of this fact was the growth of the enemy's anti-aircraft capability. By the end of 1963, a total of 114 U.S. aircraft, including 54 helicopters, had been shot down and many others damaged.

As so often was the case, pilots' response to anti-aircraft fire was to fly at higher altitudes. Doing so they paid a price in terms of their ability to identify targets and hit them. Secretary of Defense Robert McNamara, Secretary of State Dean Rusk, and his assistant for Far Eastern Affairs, Averell Harriman, all tried to convince the air force that the war was mainly political by nature and that causing large numbers of civilian casualties would be counterproductive, to no avail. In fact the opposite happened: early in 1964, the rules governing air support were relaxed so as to allow greater firepower to be used. As President Johnson, who had succeeded Kennedy in November 1963, was later to complain, throughout the conflict the air force generals' one response to the failure of bombing seemed to be to demand more of it. As part of the growing effort, the air commandos' old propeller-driven aircraft, which were nearing the end of their operational life and could not meet all demands, began to be phased out. Their place was taken by faster, less maneuverable, and therefore less accurate F-100s and F-105s.

Throughout the previous half-century, almost every time airpower was used to combat insurgencies, commanders had complained about the shortage of aircraft, pilots, and every other resource from airfields to fuel and ammunition. American ones during the Vietnam War did the same, but with infinitely less justification. The America that Kennedy and Johnson led was not post-1945 Britain, nor was it France of the Fourth or even the Fifth Republic. It was the richest, economically most successful nation in the whole of history at the peak of its industrial might, which no other could even remotely match. The military resources that poured into the

Southeast Asian Theater between 1965 and 1969 were the largest by far deployed by any nation in any armed conflict since 1945. At peak, in 1968–69, the number of American troops in the Southeast Asian Theater reached 550,000. Including the South Vietnamese Army, the total number of those fighting, trying to fight, or pretending to fight, the Viet Cong and the North Vietnamese Army exceeded a million and a half men—which gave them a four-to-one advantage over the enemy.

Not the least important of the resources in question were thousands upon thousands of aircraft as well as the vast infrastructure needed to maintain them, operate them, and guard them against guerrilla attack. During the war as a whole, air operations, whether conducted by the air force, the army, the navy, or the marines, are said to have counted for over half of the hundreds of billions of dollars spent.[15] There were, however, some differences among the services. Both the air force and the navy relied very largely on fixed-wing aircraft. Not so the marines, which also used helicopters, and the army, which flew them almost to the exclusion of anything else. Of all the ordnance dropped in the Southeast Asian Theater between 1963 and 1975, the air force accounted for about 80 percent. It therefore seems safe to ignore the navy, given that something has already been said about its operations and also that it did little that could not have been done by its sister service too. It is also important to emphasize that, of some eight million tons of bombs the United States and its allies dropped over Indochina in 1964–75, only about 643,000 struck North Vietnam. All the rest hit South Vietnam, Cambodia, and Laos.[16] To this extent, the decision to discuss the conflict under the rubric "War Amongst the People" seems justified.

As U.S. Army divisions and even entire corps—eventually there were to be three—began arriving in South Vietnam from mid-1965 on, helicopters came to play a far greater role in the conflict. During the 1950s, helicopters, like everything else that could fly, were widely acclaimed as the glamorous wave of the future. Both the army and the marines relied on them for command and control—the tendency of each firefight to attract commanders' helicopters as a trash can attracts flies became notorious[17]—reconnaissance, transport, medical evacuation, and, more and more, to act as gunships.[18]

Most spectacular was the creation of the First Air Cavalry Division. Originally it was intended for conducting conventional warfare in a theater dominated by nuclear weapons. However, after it was activated in July 1965, it began to be deployed to Vietnam. Thanks to several hundred helicopters in its table of organization, it became the world's first major formation that relied principally on these machines for tactical and operational mobility.

Linked by an intricate net of electronic communications, helicopters provided the U.S. and South Vietnamese ground forces with an entirely new kind of mobility. This was due to their ability to land troops and equipment—some even carried light vehicles and artillery—accurately on their objectives and, which was equally important, extract them after they had completed their mission. In theory, and to some extent in practice, they were thus able to act as force multipliers; better lift troops to their destinations than have them drive or walk over what was often difficult, often roadless, enemy-infested terrain. Equipped with machine guns and, toward the end of the conflict, anti-tank guided weapons (ATGWs), helicopters were also made to serve as gunships—this being a role for which their relatively low speed, extreme maneuverability, and ability to hover in place made them well suited and which they increasingly took over from fixed-wing aircraft.

Initially the promise of the new units appeared very great. To return to Moshe Dayan who, on McNamara's own express orders, was allowed to see "everything": the division could land an entire battalion within four hours of the order being given. "Incredible!" he went on—"there are no restrictions. They land on mountaintops, on steep hillsides, whatever." If necessary they even brought along small bulldozers. Operations were characterized by a certain degree of informality that enabled anyone with a mission to perform to simply grab an available machine and take off very quickly. The crews' skill in flying and maneuvering their machines could only be called admirable. So was the division's efficiency in rapidly deploying its weapons and using them.[19]

Nevertheless, the helicopters were no more successful than fixed-wing aircraft had been. One very important reason for this was lack of intelligence.

Too often, the air cavalry's blows hit empty air; on other occasions a helicopter costing hundreds of thousands of dollars would be kept busy chasing a sandal-wearing youngster armed with an assault rifle. Another problem was the Viet Cong tactic of keeping close to vegetation-covered areas. By the time the helicopters arrived, the enemy, forewarned by the noise (normally the helicopters would be preceded by an intense air or artillery bombardment, the objective being to carve out landing zones in the jungle), would melt away. Unless strict discipline was maintained, any attempt to disembark or embark was likely to turn into a somewhat wild melee as the men shoved each other in an effort to be the first to get out or in. Once all the troops were safely on the ground, they would move toward the tree line in search of the enemy. Provided the latter did not simply choose to melt away, the outcome was almost certainly an encounter, in which the Americans and their South Vietnamese allies were at no particular advantage; furthermore, owing to the close quarters at which combat took place, they were unable to use their superior firepower.

Though the helicopters did provide mobility and did act as a force multiplier, there was a high price to be paid. The air cavalry needed 1,500 men to perform maintenance operations and another 1,000 to guard its bases. Thus a considerable part of its forces was permanently lost. Worst of all, everything the troops needed, water included, was provided by air. Each follow-up sortie gave the Viet Cong another opportunity to bring the helicopters down.[20] Unless they flew very high or low, helicopters proved extremely vulnerable to every kind of ground fire. Particularly dangerous were shoulder-held anti-aircraft missiles and, above all, heavy 12.7-millimeter machine guns. Helicopters trying to land or take off could also be hit by anti-tank rockets (RPGs). Given the noise their machines generated, and unless they could see the muzzle flashes, often the crews did not even know they were under fire until they were hit. A hit by an anti-aircraft missile or anti-tank rocket was usually fatal. But even a single lucky bullet fired from an assault rifle might pierce a pipe containing fuel or hydraulic fluid, forcing the pilot to withdraw from the action and/or carry out an emergency landing. Hits on the rotor, whose complex mechanism and blades represent a helicopter's most vulnerable part, were also often fatal. The total number of helicopters that saw service in Vietnam was about 12,000. Of these, 5,086 were lost either to combat or to accidents. Helicopters were hit no fewer than 22,000 times.[21] Almost all these losses took place in airspace that, except for anti-aircraft fire of the kind just described, was completely dominated by the United States and its allies. No country, no nation, no armed force is likely to match these figures in any kind of foreseeable future.

As so often happens in counterinsurgency campaigns, the U.S. commanders in the field blamed their failure to win the war on the country beyond the border, North Vietnam. The latter, they claimed, no doubt correctly, was providing the Viet Cong with tremendous support in terms of troops and war materiel of every kind.[22] To intercept the flow and persuade North Vietnam to cease hostilities, Operation Rolling Thunder was initiated in February 1965. From beginning to end it was a pure air campaign—though the possibility of supplementing it by a ground invasion was often discussed in Washington, D.C., nothing ever came of the idea. Had it been realized, then almost certainly the outcome would have been an even larger and less controllable insurgency. Initially supposed to last for eight weeks, Rolling Thunder was to go on for three and a half years. It thus became the longest operation in the history of the U.S. Air Force.

At the time, fashionable strategic theories recommended the use of military power, airpower included, primarily as an instrument with which to signal one's political intentions to the adversary.[23] Partly for this reason, partly because of a very real and perhaps well-founded fear of Korea-style Chinese intervention, Operation Rolling Thunder did not launch a single powerful blow against key targets in North Vietnam. Instead it was conducted in a piecemeal, graduated manner. No decision made during the war proved more controversial. At the time and later, there were numerous complaints that Johnson and McNamara, plus a handful of other men who sat in the targeting group that met in the White House every Tuesday, tried to run the war by remote control. One pilot felt that that he and his comrades "were hopelessly misdirected and restricted . . . woefully misused by a chain of stagnant high-level . . . leadership that didn't have the balls to fight the war that they ineptly micromanaged."[24] Out of an initial list of 94 targets, most of them bridges, rail marshaling yards, docks (North Vietnam was receiving a large part of its supplies by sea, from the Soviet Union), barracks, and supply dumps that the Joint Chiefs of Staff had prepared, just a few were approved. Even those were limited to the region south of the nineteenth parallel, which meant that Hanoi and the port of Haiphong remained out of bounds, and each one had to be cleared with the secretary of defense personally.

Much of this is true—but it is also true that the air force commanders, happily using the most recent communications that technology had put at their disposal, were no less inclined to micromanage their pilots than Johnson and McNamara were. Nor were they necessarily more inclined to listen to what their subordinates, who did the actual fighting, had to say.[25] Probably an even more important problem was the frequent lack of hard data to serve as a yardstick by which performance could be measured. Consequently there was a strong temptation to calculate in terms of the number of sorties flown and tons of ordnance expended while estimating, instead of counting, enemy losses they might have inflicted. The outcome, a managerial ethos that looks at war in terms of capabilities and output rather than effectiveness vis-à-vis the enemy at hand, took decades to shake off.[26]

Initially most of the attacks hit the southern panhandle of North Vietnam, that is, the area that borders on the South. However, much of the area was covered by thick jungles. They provided supply convoys, some using trucks and others bicycles, with all the cover they needed; various technological devices, including ones specially developed for the purpose, that the Americans used to locate them proved only partly successful. In any case, if the attacks on this area became too intensive, the North Vietnamese always had the option of shifting their supply lines westward into Laos and Cambodia. Doing just that, they created the vast complex of jungle roads known as the Ho Chi Minh Trail. When attacks on transportation targets failed to bring the desired results, the Americans switched to POL (petrol, oil lubricants). The main storage facilities were indeed destroyed. However, since the North Vietnamese, anticipating the campaign, had placed their POL supplies in 50-gallon barrels and dispersed them, the impact on their war effort was very small. Much the same applied to other energy-related targets such as electric power-generating stations and grids. Having very little industry, North Vietnam at the time was simply not the kind of country where attacks of this kind could achieve much.

In any case gradualism, the attempt to influence the enemy's behavior rather than break his will as traditional U.S. Air Force doctrine would dictate, was only one of the many things that went wrong with Operation Rolling Thunder. To quote one very experienced pilot, "the odds of [unguided iron bombs hitting their target] are not high. A bewildering number of fundamental errors infest the . . . system. Our bombs' impact point in relation to the target will be affected by unforeseen winds, natural ballistic bomb dispersion, inherent radar tracking inaccuracies, my limited ability to fly the jet precisely, target location uncertainty, map errors, computer settling time, my reaction time on the pickle button, the rotation of the earth, and gravity."[27] This problem became even worse after the Americans, for lack of fixed targets (most of which had either been destroyed or made to disperse or camouflaged), switched to smaller, more mobile ones. Under a procedure known as "armed reconnaissance," small formations of aircraft patrolled highways, railroads, and rivers while looking for targets of opportunity. Eventually such sorties made up three-quarters of the bombing effort;[28] given how large and expensive the aircraft and how small and elusive the targets were, a less effective use of airpower is hard to imagine.

Another problem was the complicated, convoluted command system in use. Most of the sorties were flown from the west, that is, Thailand, where control over them was divided between the Seventh and 13th Air Forces. Others came from the east, that is, from carriers cruising off the coast of North Vietnam, and came under the authority of the commander in chief, Pacific Command (CINCPAC), Admiral U. S. Sharp, whose headquarters was far away in Hawaii. Army general William Westmoreland, as head of the Military Assistance Command, Vietnam (MACV), had no influence over the air campaign that was supposed to help him do his job.

The discrepancies, not to say absurdities, went on and on; as Henry Kissinger later said, it was a perfect example of the bizarre way the Pentagon functioned.[29]

The air force's principal fighter-bomber at the time was the F-105 Thunderchief. Capable of reaching Mach 2, it was designed for delivering tactical nuclear weapons from low altitudes. Yet both the accuracy with which it could hit its targets and, even more important, its ability to defend itself in combat proved problematic. The F-4 Phantoms and F-111 Aardvarks, which largely took its place later in the war, represented some improvement but nevertheless suffered from similar problems. Like the F-105, both were powerful, fast, relatively heavy, and hard-to-maneuver machines. While the F-111 could carry 14 tons of ordnance, no less, like the Phantom it was hard to control at the low speeds most suitable for bombing. As long as they operated over South Vietnam, U.S. and allied jets, if not slower aircraft and helicopters, were pretty invulnerable. Not so over North Vietnam, where the enemy quickly became much more dangerous than anybody in Washington had anticipated.

North Vietnamese fighters, first MiG-17s and then the faster but almost equally agile MiG-21s, started engaging the Americans almost from the beginning of Rolling Thunder. Thanks to Israel's Mossad, which had induced an Iraqi pilot to desert, the U.S. Air Force did have an opportunity to take a close look at the latter aircraft; nevertheless, the air force was ill prepared to face the MiG-21s in combat. American fighter pilots at the time were under strict orders to refrain from practicing air-to-air combat against any aircraft different from the ones they themselves were flying; thus, instead of trying to bring down light F-5s as the closest U.S. equivalent to the MiG 21, F-4 "fought" F-4 and F-111, F-111. Training exercises, held over Death Valley, California, consisted of two similar aircraft coming at each other from opposite directions like some lance-wielding medieval knights, launching their missiles, and turning away. Probably the intention was to silence critics, such as John Boyd, who were claiming that Soviet fighters were better than American ones.[30] The procedure did little if anything to prepare pilots for the ordeal they were about to face; having reached Vietnam, some were "jumped" by MiGs and shot down before they knew what was happening to them.[31] To make things worse, both MiG-17s and MiG-21s presented small targets for the American fighters' radar sets, whereas the MiG-17's high tail location made it hard for infrared missiles launched from above and behind, the classic positions, to home in on it. During the Rolling Thunder years both sides' losses in air combat were about equal. But whereas the North Vietnamese regarded that ratio as acceptable, given that it denied their enemies full command of the air, the Americans did not.

Douhet and others, including America's own bomber generals, had long held that, in air warfare, the offense was inherently stronger than the defense. However, events over North Vietnam soon proved that this was not necessarily the case. Whereas U.S. warplanes were armed with Sidewinder, Sparrow, and Falcon air-to-air missiles, the MiGs carried guns and plenty of them. Taking off from Chinese airfields that were immune to attack, and relying on their superior maneuverability to get close to their enemies, they found themselves at a distinct advantage. By Christmas Day 1965, Rolling Thunder aircraft had flown almost 54,000 sorties and dropped just over 40,000 tons of bombs. As usual, calculated on a per-sortie basis, naval aircraft, most of whose targets were located near North Vietnam's eastern coast, contributed less than those of the air force did. The price was 170 American and a few South Vietnamese aircraft lost.[32] Still there was no sign that the campaign was having any impact on North Vietnam's will and ability to continue the struggle.

Worse still was to follow. At the time Rolling Thunder got under way North Vietnam was said to be defended by 1,500 anti-aircraft guns. Within the year, their number had trebled. North Vietnam also received SA-2 and SA-3 missiles. Though neither missile was particularly good—aircraft equipped with warning devices did not find it too difficult to avoid the larger, less maneuverable SA-2s in particular—they forced the Americans to fly high and take evasive action. Either they would miss their targets or else they would jettison their loads altogether in order to defend themselves. The climate did not help either; during eight months a year, the weather in Southeast Asia is atrocious for flying, making it very hard for pilots to locate their targets. Radar-equipped B-52s, which were flying from Guam, might have provided a partial solution to the problem. However, at this time they were only utilized over the southernmost part of North Vietnam. In part, the decision to restrict them in this way grew out of political considerations; in part, though, it was because the air force itself worried about possible losses.[33]

Down below, the North Vietnamese, in an astonishing display of ingenuity and determination, put into place a vast series of active and passive measures meant to reduce the impact of the campaign. Supplies and equipment of every kind were dispersed and camouflaged. Part of the population was evacuated from the towns into the countryside, and the rest made to dig shelters and get into them as soon as the alarm was sounded. Effective medical, civil defense, and civil assistance organizations did what they could to assist the wounded and help those whose homes had been destroyed. In principle there was nothing new in any of these measures. Thanks largely to the predominantly rural character of the country, though, they were probably more effective than any others of their kind.

Estimates of North Vietnamese civilians killed by Rolling Thunder range from 52,000 to 180,000. The material damage inflicted was incalculable. Nevertheless, in 1967–68, with no sign yet that the campaign was achieving its objective of forcing the North to suspend or reduce its assistance to the guerrillas in the South, the character of the campaign changed. Except for Hanoi and Haiphong, which remained off limits, by then most of the targets the Joint Chiefs of Staff had originally suggested had been knocked out. With only a few left, the campaign concentrated on interdicting roads and the supply convoys that kept moving along them. Still, as the tactically problematic, but strategically decisive, Tet Offensive proved, the Americans were getting no closer to winning the war.

By the time Johnson officially brought Rolling Thunder to an end in November 1968, U.S. Air Force, Navy, and Marine Corps aircraft had flown no fewer than 300,000 attack sorties against North Vietnam. Like so much else pertaining to this monstrous war, such a figure would be utterly unimaginable today.[34] Not only were the most powerful available aircraft, the F-4 in particular, used in the thousands, but the campaign also saw the first-time introduction of a whole series of new technologies that have become standard since. Among them were B-52 heavy bombers employed in the conventional role, converted cargo planes that could deliver fire at a rate never exceeded before or since, various kinds of air-to-air and air-to-ground missiles, all sorts of electronic countermeasures (ECMs) designed to interfere with enemy radar, Grumman E-1 and E-2 AWACS aircraft, drones, satellite communications (useful because both the navy's aircraft and the B-52s were commanded from headquarters located very far away indeed), and air-dropped sensors that were supposed to identify and locate targets in the jungle. Indeed one could argue that most of the technologies successfully employed against Iraq in 1991 were already present, at least in embryonic form, during the last years of the Vietnam War. The difference, of course, was that the Iraqi terrain was ideal for waging air warfare whereas Vietnam was anything but; if anything saved the North Vietnamese from defeat, it was the jungle and their own extraordinary ability to use it for their own purposes.

After Nixon took over the White House in January 1969, the character of the war changed. Previously the objective had been to force the Viet Cong to suspend its campaign and the North to stop supporting it. Now, as U.S. forces were gradually taken out of the country, it became one of withdrawal with as much honor as could be saved. By April 1972 there were only 69,000 troops left. U.S. aircraft, including both fighter-bombers and B-52s, continued operating over South Vietnam, southern North Vietnam, Cambodia, and Laos. The last named became the second most heavily bombed country in history after South Vietnam.[35] The waste involved can only be called staggering. A typical mission against a suspected truck park and supply dump hidden in the jungle might involve 16 F-4s (12 to drop bombs, four to guard them against MiGs), eight F-105 "Wild Weasels" to suppress enemy anti-aircraft fire, and another camera-equipped F-4, a total of 25.[36] Yet what evidence exists tends to show that the attacks largely failed to achieve their purpose. The performance of the sensors in the extremely complex terrain proved disappointing, and there was still no proper night-vision technology. Indeed the Viet Cong and North Vietnamese could often mislead their would-be tormentors simply by filling a metal barrel with oil, soaking it with fuel, and setting it alight.

Until 1969 the Viet Cong in the South had operated almost exclusively in the guerrilla mode. Now, with the U.S. presence weakening fast, this was less and less the case. Joined by regular North Vietnamese units, it gradually changed to conventional warfare. To supply and reinforce the forces, the length of all-weather roads inside North Vietnam was increased from 1,070 miles in 1965 to eight times that figure in 1972, itself a clear indication that the interdiction campaign had failed.[37] Entire divisions, complete with artillery and tanks, started taking up positions in South Vietnam. By March 1972 Giap felt strong enough to order a major invasion of South Vietnam. In terms of the number of participating troops it was the largest operation the world had seen since Korea. By this time the number of U.S. Air Force aircraft in South Vietnam had fallen to just 76—three-quarters of which consisted of F-4s and the rest the old, trustworthy T-37s. About a hundred other jet fighters operated out of Thailand, whereas B-52s continued to be based on Guam. Thanks to Nixon's policy of Vietnamization, the South Vietnamese Air Force had considerably more combat aircraft and helicopters than the U.S. forces did; however, it was still afflicted by lack of technical capability as well as fighting morale.

On March 29, 1972, three North Vietnamese divisions, with as many as 200 tanks among them, finally did what the Americans had always prevented them from doing: they concentrated on preparation for a major offensive. Entering South Vietnam, they immediately encountered South Vietnamese Army forces, but those were easily brushed aside. Later the North Vietnamese were reinforced until they reached 14 divisions and 600 tanks, Viet Cong units not included. By this time the United States had hardly any ground forces left in the theater. All it could do was to bring in additional aircraft, and this was duly done. Yet in the face of this magnificent target, old habits proved hard to break; when the air force generals first presented Nixon with the plans for Operation Linebacker I, as it was called, he considered them too timid. To address the problem he called on

Alexander Haig, an army general who was then serving as deputy assistant for national security, for advice. The latter came up with what the president thought he needed.[38] Possibly there is an indication here that, for all the complaints about McNamara's gradualism and its ill effects, the air force commanders themselves were not always as ready to put their money where their mouths were as they later claimed.

By the end of May 1972, F-4s had been moved back to South Vietnam and Thailand. The number of B-52s at Guam was increased to 210, which represented the largest number of aircraft of this kind ever assembled on one base.[39] The bombers alone could deliver almost three times as many bombs as LeMay had used to devastate Tokyo a quarter of a century earlier. By this time more laser-guided bombs were becoming available; their ability to take out vital point targets such as bridges at comparatively low cost was soon to become legendary. In fact, the claims made on behalf of these weapons are somewhat misleading. The real difference was not that fewer sorties were needed to destroy a bridge, or oil storage tank, or similar targets than had been the case during World War II. Rather, it consisted of the fact that, thanks to laser guidance, pilots could now achieve this feat from a comparatively great altitude without worrying too much about the SA-7 Strella shoulder-launched, heat-seeking missiles that the Americans encountered for the first time. In any case the competition between aircraft and air defenses was far from over—as the October 1973 war was soon to prove for the entire world to see.

Complete figures concerning the amount of ordnance delivered are unavailable, but clearly the total was awesome. The North alone received 150,000 tons, and loads dropped on North Vietnamese Army units inside South Vietnam increased that figure by tens of thousands more.[40] For the first time in the war, Haiphong Harbor was mined in order to close it to Soviet supply-carrying vessels. Later it was estimated that, by September, North Vietnam's imports had been reduced by anywhere from a third to a half.[41] Hundreds of bridges in North Vietnam were destroyed, and hundreds of roads cut. Often targets were selected in such a way that the bombs started landslides, making the roads, many of which ran through mountainous country, hard to repair. Fuel depots, vehicle repair shops, and the like were also struck. A total of 134 aircraft were lost, which given the vast number of sorties was considered an acceptable figure. American sources claim that North Vietnam lost about half as many—including some shot down by the B-52s' tail gunners.[42] Though the figures may be approximately correct, they ignore the fact that American aircraft cost far more than the MiGs; one analyst of the time, Alain Enthoven, estimated that for every dollar of damage Rolling Thunder inflicted on North Vietnam it cost the United States ten.[43]

By the time Linebacker I ended in late October 1972, it had smashed Hanoi's all-out effort to switch from guerrilla to large-scale conventional warfare and end the war. However, it neither caused hostilities inside South Vietnam to cease—the North Vietnamese troops simply melted into the jungle, as they had so often done before—nor forced the North Vietnamese leadership to sign the peace agreement then being worked out in Paris. Meanwhile Congress was preparing to legislate the United States out of the war. Aware that time was running out fast, Nixon ordered Operation Linebacker II to start on December 18. Targets consisted of Haiphong Harbor, which was mined for the second time; airfields and warehouses around Hanoi; and the usual railway marshaling yards, though how any of the latter managed to survive the pounding they had just received is hard to determine. The operation was originally planned to last just three days, and its real objective was intimidation.[44]

When Christmas 1972 arrived there was still no sign of its having the desired political effect. During Linebacker I, when most sorties had been flown by daylight, the main threat had come from the MiGs that took off to meet them. But when the Americans changed their tactics and started flying by night, as during Linebacker II, improved missile defenses took a toll on the hitherto all but invulnerable heavy bombers. Determined to retain their command of the air at all cost, the Americans switched to attacking the missile batteries. F-111s, F-4s, and the navy's A-6 Intruders all participated in the effort, using new tactics and launching their homing and laser-guided missiles at the radar sets and SAMs on the ground. By the time the operation ended, 11 days after it had begun, North Vietnam's most important military airfields had been reduced to heaps of rubble and the largest anti-aircraft missile assembly plant demolished. For the first time during the war, Giap had run out of missiles. This meant that the huge bombers with their 30-ton cargoes could pretty much do what they pleased, including the destruction of the dams on which North Vietnam depended for feeding its population; yet whether such an operation would have led to the desired results (as the wrecking of some dams in Korea had not) remains uncertain. Whereas bombing operations beyond the twentieth parallel were suspended, those further to the south continued for a few more days until, on January 9, 1973, Kissinger and North Vietnam's Le Duc Tho signed a peace agreement. America's longest war, one that was initially waged against a handful of guerrillas attired in funny conical hats and "Ho Chi Minh" sandals made of old tires, was finally over.

The American air war in Southeast Asia has been called the most extravagant ever waged, and with very good reason.[45] From 1965 to 1972, the total number of combat sorties amounted to 3.4 million. Exclusive of accidents, the war cost the United States 3,034 aircrew killed or missing as well as 2,257 aircraft.[46] Operationally, Linebacker I and II showed airpower at its horrendous best. Displaying a sort of grim determination—no thanks to the air force generals, if Nixon may be believed—that had too often been lacking in earlier years, the Americans rained down a deluge of bombs. No question, this time, of waging "war amongst the people," or anti-guerrilla warfare, or counterinsurgency. Essentially it was a question of knocking out some very powerful anti-aircraft defenses, where they existed, and then smashing whatever targets were considered relevant to North Vietnam's military effort, though in fact the order in which these missions were carried out was somewhat different from the one Douhet and others had recommended. Precision-guided weapons, many of them used for the first time, played a key role in the effort. Particularly impressive was the attack on Thanh Hoa Bridge in May 1972—everybody seems to cite it[47]—when 14 fighter-bombers did what 871 earlier sorties had failed to accomplish. Even so, what really took place was not so much a revolution as a technical correction. In many ways it brought the balance between air offense and ground-based defense back to what it had been during the last years of World War II, albeit only by using infinitely more complex and more expensive aircraft and munitions. Furthermore, if the advocates of airpower are right in claiming that precision-guided weapons made a decisive contribution to the outcome, then it is equally true that Linebacker I and II could not have been mounted earlier than they were for the simple reason that those weapons had not yet become available.

Operationally and politically Linebacker I and II did two things. First, they wrecked Hanoi's effort to end the war by means of a conventional offensive. To this extent, they reconfirmed the old lesson, which had been demonstrated so often since 1939 as to become axiomatic, that no large-scale conventional campaign is feasible in the teeth of enemy command of the air. Since Giap had no way to interfere with U.S. air operations over the South (his anti-aircraft missile batteries were stationary and could not follow the field units), none of this should have come as a surprise to him. Perhaps, after years during which his guerrillas had learned to cope with anything airpower could do, he forgot the difference between that kind of war and regular operations; or perhaps he simply assumed that, since most U.S. aircraft had left the country, he was at last free to do as he pleased.[48] Second, they showed that airpower, used on its own and on an unprecedented scale, could achieve political results—albeit only against what was, after all, a very small and very undeveloped country, and only in a war that, as the impending congressional vote and subsequent events proved, had already been lost years before and was going to be lost anyhow. Since the United States had already let Hanoi know that it would not insist on the latter's forces leaving South Vietnam, and since the agreements also obliged the United States to withdraw its forces from that country, all the Paris agreements really did was to grant Washington and its client a respite. Thus one must agree with those who claim that airpower did not break the will of North Vietnam.[49] Rather, it had been the United States whose will had been broken some time before, presumably in the days, weeks, and months after the Tet Offensive in early 1968, leaving it to Nixon to use airpower, as the form of armed force least costly in terms of American lives, to try to conceal that fact and obtain the best possible terms.

On the other hand, the even larger quantity of ordnance dropped on South Vietnam from 1964 to the spring of 1972, as well as the thousands upon thousands of helicopters that were used and lost, did little or nothing to win the guerrilla war inside that unfortunate country. The fact that the Viet Cong operated in small, dispersed groups, that it probably only needed 100 tons of supplies—capable of being transported by just 50 trucks—per day, and, above all, the American airmen's near-complete inability to distinguish between combatants and noncombatants all contributed to this outcome. Airpower, whether used in the direct or indirect mode, was able to prevent the guerrillas from switching from Mao's second stage to the third. In fact, this ability had already been demonstrated in 1968 when a ferocious bombardment had destroyed the Viet Cong and North Vietnamese forces that were trying to take Khe Sanh.[50] However, that was about all it could achieve; some observers believe that airpower in the South, by virtue of the indiscriminate way in which it was used, did more harm than good.[51] For all the immense quantitative and qualitative growth that had taken place since airpower was formed in the early 1900s, in many ways the war in Vietnam simply repeated the lessons that had been steadily accumulating almost from the first day when it had been used in war. It was, however, a lesson that was not learned and, to a large extent, still has not been learned.

CHAPTER 20

AFTER VIETNAM

As if to confirm the late historian Barbara Tuchman's argument in *The March of Folly* (1985), the almost incalculable cost of the use of airpower in Vietnam, and its ultimate failure to bring the hoped-for decisive results, did not deter others from trying their hands at the game. It is true that, in terms of sheer size, nothing like Vietnam has taken place again or is likely to take place again. But this is not to say that others coming after the Americans in 1961–75 were less deluded concerning what could and could not be achieved.

The first campaign we have to consider in this context is the one that ultimately led to the transformation of British Southern Rhodesia into today's Zimbabwe. In point of scale it was among the smallest described in the present volume. Since the number of white settlers was only just over 200,000, and since Rhodesia had no heavy industry of any kind, there were strict limits to the size of the counterinsurgency effort that the country's rulers were able to put together. Nevertheless, thanks in large part to the fact that this was not an attempt by outsiders trying to hold down natives but a struggle between two different population groups equally committed to, and familiar with, the country, that effort was among the best-run, tactically and operationally most successful, of its kind.

The war opened in July 1964 against the background of the white 5 percent of the population refusing to share power with the 95 percent who were black on the basis of one person, one vote. In 1965–66, after Southern Rhodesia had declared unilateral independence from Britain, it escalated. Two guerrilla groups were mainly involved, ZIPRA (Zimbabwe People's Revolutionary Army) and ZANLA (Zimbabwe African National Liberation Army). Originally ZIPRA was the larger of the two, but later it was ZANLA under its leader Robert Mugabe that played the major role and ruled the country after it had achieved its independence. Both groups were based in the neighboring countries, primarily Mozambique. Zambia, though already independent, depended on Rhodesia for much of its electricity and also for the railway through which it exported its main product, copper; consequently it never provided much assistance to the rebels.

Both ZIPRA and ZANLA opened hostilities by attempting to infiltrate men and equipment into Rhodesia. For several years most infiltrators returned to base without having achieved anything, or were caught, or were killed, or gave themselves up to the authorities. The few who did not fail in their mission in one of those ways murdered civilians on remote farms, tried to sabotage all kinds of installations, and sought to indoctrinate and incite the black population to revolt. Originally the combined membership of ZIPRA and ZANLA was in the low hundreds, if that. So limited were funds that leaders could not pay their telephone bills; the insurgents had neither organization nor military experience. They had to learn their craft, often at a high cost in blood.

In 1964, the Rhodesian armed forces, exclusive of the police, consisted of approximately 3,600 regulars organized in two small brigades. They also had about 6,500 reservists who formed territorial units that could defend their home provinces but were not available for mobile operations throughout the country.[1] Preparing for the conflict, the Rhodesian armed forces originally thought in terms of a conventional war. They worried about a possible British airborne descent on the capital of Salisbury aimed to undo the unilateral declaration of independence, and also about a communist-instigated, armor-supported invasion from one or more of the neighboring countries. Accordingly they planned to set up a regular force complete with artillery and light tanks. Fortunately for them, they lacked the necessary manpower, financial resources, and logistic infrastructure. Instead of buying advanced heavy weapons that would have been largely useless in a counterinsurgency campaign, they used their limited assets to the best possible effect.

With a land area of approximately 150,000 miles, Southern Rhodesia was somewhat larger than either Malaysia or Vietnam. Given the small size of the security forces, inevitably airpower played a large role in the conflict. Compared with what the British and French had brought to bear, their forces were minuscule. All they had was a squadron of C-47 transports, as well as Alouette III (larger successor to the Alouette II of Algerian War fame) and Bell-205 (the civilian version of the UH-1) helicopters. Some helicopters received 20-millimeter cannon and were converted into gunships; later they were also equipped with countermeasures (flares) to defend against Strella anti-aircraft missiles. They were supplemented by Cessna Skymasters, light piston-engined utility aircraft equipped with machine guns, rockets, and napalm bombs. Three squadrons of light Vampire and Hawker Hunter jet fighters, plus a squadron of Canberras, completed the picture.

Light and slow, these aircraft were much more suited for counterinsurgency than the heavier, faster jets the Americans had used in many of their operations in Vietnam. Rhodesian aircrews were highly motivated and exceedingly well trained. Given how few they were, special attention was paid to make sure many of them should be qualified to fly as many different kinds of aircraft as possible. The terrain was very varied and included villages, bush, and areas covered by huge boulders. Still, much of it was dry, flat, and open. These qualities made it hard for the guerrillas to travel and to hide. Conversely, the air force was almost ideally suited to the mission at hand; if it had a weakness it consisted of the fact that, like the rest of the Rhodesian armed forces, it suffered from international economic sanctions that had been imposed on the country in 1966. As time went on, obtaining spare parts and replacing outworn equipment became increasingly difficult.[2]

Initially the only available airborne unit was a company of SAS (Special Air Service) modeled on the redoubtable British commando force of that name.[3] Later, the principal force with which the Rhodesians waged the war was the so-called Fire Force, also known as the Incredibles or the Saints. Expanding to form a full battalion, they consisted of men recruited from many English-speaking nations and trained and equipped as light infantry. These forces reached the peak of their efficiency, as well as effectiveness, from 1974 on. Normally the presence of guerrillas was reported by the police, army units on the ground, or, until the early 1970s, local (black) villagers who evidently feared the insurgents more than the security forces. Thereupon the commandos, armed with automatic rifles, light machine guns, and shoulder-fired anti-tank weapons, were flown to the scene in C-47s and helicopters. Various means, such as hiding behind ridges and flying against the wind, were used to disguise their presence for as long as possible. The first to arrive were always the helicopters with commandos and weapons aboard. Next in line came the troop carriers. As far as intelligence allowed, the men were dropped (Rhodesian paratroops were trained as sportsmen are, that is, to free-fall and open their own parachutes, which made for much more accurate descents) or, in the majority of cases, landed in small teams all around the guerrillas. As bombing and strafing from the air forced the latter to disperse, they ran straight into the surrounding Rhodesians. Provided only the terrain was reasonably open, their chances of getting away were slim.

But for airpower, which provided them with mobility and acted as a true force multiplier, the security forces could never have confronted their enemies. The exchange rate—the number of personnel on both sides who were killed in these operations—was always extremely favorable to the Rhodesians.[4] Furthermore, whereas the guerrillas were often operating far from base and were forced to give themselves up if wounded or running out of supplies, such limitations did not affect the counterinsurgents. Not content with this, on several occasions the Rhodesians used their airpower to bomb and raid guerrilla bases in Zambia and Mozambique. These operations, which came literally out of the blue, were very successful; the raiders killed hundreds while losing very few men themselves.[5]

Rhodesian airpower certainly killed civilians on occasion. Still, excellent training and the use of relatively light, extremely maneuverable, and highly accurate aircraft and weapons helped minimize the number of casualties. The inhabitants of many guerrilla-infested areas were evacuated into protected areas. While this procedure did not exactly endear the authorities to the population, at least it helped minimize the number of dead and injured. In the end, what caused the defeat of the white minority was the 1974 coup in Portugal that toppled the dictator Marcelo Caetano, resulting in the collapse of Portuguese rule in Mozambique. With the guerrillas free to operate openly on the other side of the 800-mile border, the security forces could not prevent as many as 12,000 men from crossing it. The guerrillas mined roads, engaged in sabotage, and assassinated both white and black civilians. Occasionally they also shot down Rhodesian helicopters and aircraft, including a civilian one with all its passengers. As the war progressed, the number of incidents increased, though the guerrillas were never able to penetrate the cities. Meanwhile white emigration from Rhodesia grew to 2,000 a month, severely straining the country's very limited manpower resources and economy. In other words, the Rhodesians ended up by being swamped by guerrillas who, in terms of quality, were never any match for them. In this respect they differed sharply from counterinsurgents in places such as Indochina, Algeria, Vietnam, and, later, Western-occupied Iraq and Afghanistan, in all of which the counterinsurgents enjoyed a considerable numerical advantage.

December 1979, the month that marked a cease-fire in Rhodesia, also saw the beginning of what was ultimately to become a nine-year Soviet effort to combat guerrillas in Afghanistan. Afghanistan is a large country that takes up 249,000 square miles. Much of the terrain is extremely mountainous, and large parts of it are practically inaccessible to any kind of mechanized transport. Prompted by a request from the pro-Soviet president, Hafizullah Amin, who had seized power from his predecessor but was unable to put down an insurgency, a Soviet Guards Airborne Division was sent to occupy Kabul. First a battalion of paratroopers was dropped on each of the two nearby airfields. These were soon followed by the rest of the division. Success was due partly to surprise, partly to the fact that numerous Soviet personnel acting as advisers were already in place, and partly to the absence of any organized opposition. As all key installations fell into Soviet hands, the 40th Army, counting some 52,000 men and divided into two heads, moved into the country in two separate arms, forming a ring around most of it until they met at Kandahar in the south. Rarely in history had such a large country been overrun so quickly.[6]

At the time the Red Army was at the peak of its power, and many considered it the mightiest fighting machine history had ever seen.[7] Invading Afghanistan, it brought along hundreds of tanks, thousands of armored personnel carriers, artillery, and even anti-aircraft units to counter a nonexistent Afghan air force. However, following decades of peace interrupted only by small-scale clashes such as the ones in Somalia in 1977–78, very few commanders or troops had any combat experience, let alone of the specialized kind needed to combat guerrillas. Leonid Brezhnev, the man who ordered the invasion, did not run a democratic country. He and his paladins neither had to consider public opinion nor shared many of whatever moral inhibitions the Americans, fighting in Vietnam, may have felt. For nine years on end they did what they thought had to be done, even if that meant ruthlessly bombing villages known or suspected of harboring mujahideen, and even if it meant killing hundreds of thousands and turning millions into refugees.[8]

Nevertheless, within a few months the Soviets found themselves vainly trying to cope with an uprising that kept growing larger and more dangerous. Driven by a mixture of nationalism and religious fanaticism, making excellent use of the difficult terrain, and supplied and equipped by the United States by way of Pakistan, the insurgents proved tough and wily opponents. Besides mounting rocket attacks on all kinds of Soviet installations, they made a specialty of attacking road convoys, often allowing the armored spearhead to pass before firing at the logistic support vehicles that followed.[9] On the one hand, they never learned how to operate in units larger than companies. On the other, like similar fighters elsewhere they enjoyed the inestimable advantage of being able to melt into the civilian population almost whenever they wanted. This ability was perhaps even more important in the towns, where Soviet airpower was of limited if any use, than it was in the countryside. Indeed in this uprising, as in many of those that preceded it and followed it, one of the main drawbacks of airpower was its inability to operate in complex, crowded, urban environments.

At peak the Soviet forces in Afghanistan consisted of 120,000 men. Given how dangerous ground transport was soon to become, many of them were brought into the country, as well as shifted from province to province within it, by means of air transport. The maximum number of aircraft and helicopters available at any one time is said to have been 500;[10] the number of those that saw action at one time or another must have been considerably larger. Given the size of the country and the nature of the terrain, inevitably airpower played a large role in counterinsurgency operations right from the start. As always the most important mission was reconnaissance. While air reconnaissance is not without problems, on the whole intelligence is gathered faster, and at less risk, from the air than in any other way. Next in line came close air support for troops on the ground. It could be delivered either by Mi-8 and M-24 helicopters or by Su-25 fighter-bombers. Entering Afghanistan a decade and a half after the Americans got involved in Vietnam, the Soviets no longer had older, propeller-driven aircraft in their inventories. Yet the Su-25s were well suited for the purpose, being well armored and capable of flying relatively slowly and low.

Others types of missions carried out either by the air force or by army aviation consisted of landing troops, either by helicopter or, less frequently, by parachute, on, near, or around mujahideen units and positions; inserting small numbers of troops deep into enemy territory in order to ambush convoys, gather intelligence, and capture prisoners; and securing mountain passes through which Soviet convoys were supposed to drive ahead of time. Given mujahideen expertise in mountain warfare, the last-named kind of operation was particularly important. One Soviet specialty, which few others seem to have developed, was the use of low-flying helicopters for dropping masses of antipersonnel mines from the air. The objective was to obstruct the movements of the mujahideen, but inevitably large numbers of civilians were killed and wounded as well; that this was hardly the way to win the population's hearts and minds does not require saying.

Soviet airborne units, which included a high percentage of Spetnatz (special operations) forces, were much better equipped than the infantry.[11] Particularly noteworthy was the BMD-1, a tracked, lightly armored reconnaissance vehicle. Specially designed with air mobility in mind, it carried a powerful, 73-millimeter, automatic cannon.[12] Many Soviet helicopters were larger and more powerful than their U.S. opposite numbers. Though they had to operate in mountainous terrain, where the thin air reduced the lift the rotors could provide, they were still able to carry not only troops but vehicles as well. Having disembarked, U.S. heliborne forces would invariably make their way on foot; by contrast, Soviet ones often did so by vehicle. They were thus able to land at some distance from the enemy, which in turn meant less exposure and a lower risk of casualties.

Initially all the mujahideen had to defend themselves against Soviet airpower were heavy machine guns and some 20-millimeter rapid-fire guns smuggled into the country from Pakistan. Later, the picture changed. Like everybody else the Soviets used flares to mislead heat-seeking anti-aircraft missiles such as the Redeye. However, the Stingers the mujahideen started receiving during the early 1980s were something else entirely.[13] Equipped with both infrared and ultraviolet seekers, they were much harder to counter. Capable of being launched by a single soldier—officially, two were needed—and effective at any altitude from 600 to 12,500 feet, they proved extremely dangerous to helicopters in particular. The standard Soviet/Russian volume on the war in Afghanistan admits that the missiles forced commanders to "severely limit" the use of these machines, especially during daylight.[14] Yet the Stingers do not seem to have greatly increased losses; what they did was to make pilots adopt more cautious tactics, often at the cost of reduced effectiveness.

Not surprisingly, the Soviets discovered that their aviation assets, whether fixed-wing or rotary, were particularly vulnerable during takeoff and landing. Accordingly, one favorite mujahideen tactic consisted of setting up "air ambushes," small parties of men who, concealing themselves, took up position near the air bases. The best positions were located at the end of runways or, when the terrain allowed, on high ground overlooking them. As in Vietnam, the need to protect the bases against this and other forms of ground attack, from rockets to men who infiltrated on foot, represented a heavy drain on manpower. To some extent it canceled out the ability of airpower to act as a force multiplier.

Soviet officials put the number of their own killed during the ten-year campaign at 13,000, but the real figure was probably twice that. The most recent source claims that the war also cost the Soviet Union at least 118 fixed-wing aircraft as well as 338 helicopters, thus reconfirming how vulnerable the latter are in a war without fronts as opposed to one in which they can fly in relative safety behind the lines.[15] Practically every one of the many different models in service appears on the list; it even includes a lone MiG-23, the variable-wing, high-altitude fighter capable of climbing to 47,000 feet in just one minute and with a maximum speed of Mach 2.4. Yet as the Iraqis also learned, the Flogger, to use its NATO code name, is hardly suitable for the ground attack role, least of all against small, elusive guerrilla targets. Hence one can only assume that it was flying a reconnaissance mission, a role in which it is known to have been used at least since 1967.

While the Soviets were losing their war in Afghanistan, the United States was involved in a much smaller counterinsurgency operation in El Salvador. In 1989, after nine years of war, the government forces outnumbered the guerrillas by better than four to one. Financed, equipped, and trained by the United States, they also had an air force consisting of 18 Ouragan and A-37 light fighter aircraft, two AC-47 gunships, 11 O-2 reconnaissance aircraft, eight transports, and 67 helicopters—to all of which, of course, the guerrillas had no answer whatsoever. Yet in November of that year this preponderance of force, especially in the air, did not prevent the Farabundo Martí National Liberation Front (FMLN) from launching a country-wide offensive that, at peak, caused the entire northern part of El Salvador to fall into their hands. While this particular offensive ended up by being repulsed, more or less, a new threat quickly emerged: the insurgents started receiving shoulder-fired SAM anti-aircraft missiles. In 1990 the FMLN forces inflicted 2,000 casualties on the Salvadoran armed forces, an almost 5 percent casualty rate. No wonder that, in the next year, the government gave up. A cease-fire was agreed on and a compromise peace concluded.[16]

As so often was the case, one of the most controversial aspects of the war in El Salvador was the bombing of civilians by the Salvadoran Air Force. In undeveloped regions such as Guazapa and Chalatenango, bombing was almost the only way the government was able to put pressure on the guerrillas. As usual there were conflicting claims. Some vastly exaggerated the number of civilians killed; others claimed, even less credibly, that very few if any civilians had been killed in strikes by fighter aircraft and gunships. According to two authors who have studied the subject,[17] the truth probably lay somewhere in between—if only because civilians in the free-fire zones imitated the guerrillas and learned to adapt to air strikes by camouflaging their homes and taking cover as soon as the aircraft appeared. These strikes probably harassed the guerrillas to some extent. However, their effect may have been more than counterbalanced by the moral and propaganda benefits that the guerrillas derived both in attracting new supporters and among bystanders.

Both the Soviets and the Americans could console themselves with the thought that, relative to the size of the forces, airpower was not used very extensively and only represented a relatively small fraction of the vast resources at their disposal. The same cannot be said of the Israelis in Lebanon. We last met the Israeli Air Force on June 9, 1982, when, thanks to a combination of highly innovative technology and brilliant planning and execution, it heavily defeated the Syrian one. To do so it made use of drones—as already described—as well as some of the most advanced combat aircraft available to any country at the time. Using AWACS aircraft to coordinate their moves, the Israelis made short shrift of their opponents, claiming to have shot down a hundred of them for the loss of just one in what was the largest air combat—some 150 aircraft on both sides—of the entire jet age. The victory confirmed the reputation of the Israeli Air Force as perhaps the best in the world. During the three decades that have passed since then, neither the Syrians nor any other Arab air force has dared put its supremacy to the test.

At the time the Israeli Air Force order of battle consisted of some 640 combat aircraft—F-15s, F-16s, Kfirs,[18] and older but still serviceable Skyhawks.[19] The last-named ones were admittedly slow, but their stability and maneuverability made them at least as useful for air-to-ground action as their faster, more modern brothers in arms. Furthermore, Israel is a very small country and Lebanon is located right next door to it. Accordingly, though it was always necessary to remain on guard against what other Arab countries might do, a much larger percentage of the available air assets could be thrown into the struggle than had been the case either in Vietnam or in Afghanistan. Once the Syrian missile batteries had been destroyed, opposition from the ground, mainly in the form of the ubiquitous Strella missiles, was always extremely weak. These advantages notwithstanding, Israeli command of the air, achieved by dint of years of concentrated effort and at the price of disclosing the existence of many new weapons and techniques that would otherwise have remained secret, did not result in victory on the ground as well.

The limits of airpower became clear even during the first week of the campaign. Though its command of the air was absolute, the air force failed to prevent the guerrillas of the Palestine Liberation Organization (PLO) from escaping the Israeli ground forces that were advancing along the coast in the direction of Beirut. Nor did they succeed in preventing the Syrian Army from withdrawing from Lebanon in good order; in the words of one Israeli Air Force general, the victory, while soothing to the pride that had been bruised in 1973, did not bring significant military or political benefits.[20] As so often was the case in the annals of air warfare, Israeli aircraft struck their own units and inflicted casualties. Once the ground forces had reached the northern edge of their advance, the Beirut–Damascus road, it took the air force weeks of heavy bombing before the PLO finally agreed to evacuate the Lebanese capital. Even then, this achievement was due in equal measure to the units that besieged it on the ground as well as all kinds of international pressure.

Much worse was to follow. The departure from the scene of PLO leader Yasser Arafat and several thousand of his fighters did not end the campaign, as the Israelis had hoped. To the contrary, it quickly led to a "war amongst the people" as protracted and as vicious as any of its kind. In many ways Lebanon is as well suited for this kind of war as the Israelis, who were almost totally inexperienced in the matter, were vulnerable to it. The Lebanese countryside is mountainous and covered by vegetation, much of it consisting of woods and the rest of orange groves and the like. Considerable parts of it are taken up by sprawling hillside villages ideal for serving as guerrilla bases; the even more densely inhabited Palestinian refugee camps along the coast are, if anything, even better suited for the purpose. Israeli convoys on their way to the Beirut–Damascus road, 60 miles north of their own border, had to pass through this terrain. No wonder they soon came under attack, first by the PLO and a Shiite militia called Amal, and then by the much more formidable one whose name, Hezbollah, was almost to turn into a household word.

For 18 years on end, from 1982 until 2000, the Israelis did what they could to combat Hezbollah in particular. To gather intelligence and conduct surveillance, increasingly sophisticated UAVs, an Israeli specialty in which they had and have few competitors, were used. Over the years the number of sorties they flew rose into the thousands if not more. The most advanced fighters, fighter-bombers, and attack helicopters—each costing tens of millions of dollars—also flew countless sorties, striking at all kinds of guerrilla targets. The technology employed was as good as any and better than most; whereas in 1991, nine out of ten bombs the Americans dropped on Iraq were still of the old iron type, by that time the Israelis had completed the shift to guided ones.

After each and every strike, according to the standard formulae used by the Israel Defense Forces (IDF) spokesman, "all our aircraft returned safely to base," a phrase that was repeated so often that it became something of a standing joke. Invariably the pilots "reported good hits." Engaging their enemies on the ground as well, the Israelis relied on helicopters to support and supply their troops. Operating in classical counterinsurgency fashion, from time to time they also mounted heliborne commando operations deep into Lebanon. Over the years some helicopters were hit, but apparently none was shot down. Yet for all the often ludicrous disproportion between the cost of the means used and that of the targets struck—tens of millions of dollars versus a few hundred or thousand—nothing worked. Guerrilla operations, instead of subsiding, increased. By the time they finally gave up, the Israelis had lost about 1,500 dead. Considering the size of the population, on a year-by-year basis this figure is larger than the American one in Vietnam.

Yet the withdrawal, which took place in May 2000, did not end the agony and, along with it, the seeming inability of the Israeli Air Force to deal with it. Six years later, after many minor skirmishes, the fighting along the Israeli-Lebanese border resumed. Called into action once again, in one sense the air force performed magnificently. On July 13, in a prepared operation that relied on intelligence provided by UAVs and other sources, it took just 34 minutes to locate and destroy 59 of Hezbollah's Iranian-supplied, long-range ("long-range" meaning, in this case, anything above 60 miles) rocket launchers.[21] The magnitude of the achievement is highlighted by the fact that, back in 1991, General Horner's aircraft had spent several weeks and thousands of sorties hunting for mobile Iraqi Scud launchers. As the post-action investigation was to reveal, however, they failed to destroy even one. Once hostilities had come to an end, Hezbollah leader Hassan Nasrallah personally expressed his shock and dismay at these results; had he known how strong the Israeli reaction would be, he said, he would never have started the war.[22]

That, of course, was an extraordinary feat. It may explain why, except for one occasion, the Hezbollah never used whatever al-Fajr (Dawn) and Zilzal (Earthquake) rockets it still had left; one source goes so far as to claim that the Israelis destroyed not only launchers but most of the 200 or so Zilzal rockets in storage.[23] No doubt encouraged by its success, the Israeli

Air Force continued operations. Over the war as a whole it flew 12,000 fighter sorties. The total number of sorties was 19,000.[24] Yet success was mediocre at best. The attacks on transportation targets did not prevent Hezbollah from receiving a fresh flow of weapons from Syria. Above all, the air force did not end the salvoes of short-range (four to 25 miles) Katyusha and Grad rockets that kept hitting northern Israel every single day of the five-week war. On August 1 and 2 alone, 400 rockets landed, one reaching as far as Hadera 40 miles north of Tel Aviv. It was not the Israeli Air Force's fault; the Katyushas in particular were small, mobile, and numbered in the thousands. They and their larger cousins had been concealed inside concrete bunkers dug into the earth and all but buried under the vegetation. When the orders to launch arrived, they were raised to the surface with the aid of hydraulic levers. Such targets are very hard to locate and hit from the air, the more so because, to avoid Hezbollah's ground-to-air missiles, pilots stayed at high altitudes. Helicopters, operating over southern Lebanon while exercising extreme and, as it turned out, justifiable caution, did no better than the fighters. Though they flew hundreds of attack sorties and expended hundreds upon hundreds of expensive Hellfire missiles, their impact on the fighting was disappointingly small.[25]

To be fair, the ground forces did no better. In marked contrast to the Israeli style of war at its best, as in 1956, 1967, and 1973, they were used piecemeal without a proper center of gravity. The overriding objective was to avoid casualties. At times it looked as if the High Command had no idea of what it was doing. It kept sending in now one unit, now another, in all kinds of unspecified directions on all kinds of unspecified missions.[26] Repeatedly formations were ordered to enter Lebanon, withdrawn, and sent in again at some other sector or with some other mission. In the end the war was won, to the extent that it was won, by sheer persistence. Contrary to what Nasrallah had promised his followers, the Israelis proved that they were prepared to take casualties and carry on. As they did so, they made massive use of their air force to wreck an entire Hezbollah-infested Beirut neighborhood as well as much of Lebanon's transportation infrastructure. Although Nasrallah, with Syrian and Iranian aid, was able to quickly rearm his movement, he seems to have got the message. Since then the border has been almost perfectly quiet. True, the *very* occasional rocket continues to be launched; yet each time this happens, Hezbollah, obviously afraid of the possible consequences, hastens to disclaim responsibility.

This brings us to the final two "wars amongst the people" to be considered in the present volume, the ones in Afghanistan and Iraq. Both campaigns were masterminded by that great proponent of high-tech airpower, U.S. secretary of defense Donald Rumsfeld. By virtue of the distance between the most important centers of power and the theaters of war, both made extensive use of air transport—in the case of Afghanistan, which is a landlocked country, had it not been for such transport waging the war it would not have been possible at all. To ferry equipment into Uzbekistan, 67 C-17 sorties were needed.[27] Both campaigns were specifically designed to make the utmost use of the most powerful, most advanced air force seen in history until they got under way. The immediate objective was to deliver the most powerful possible blow—this was known as "shock and awe," a term first used by analysts back in 1996[28]—at minimum cost, the long-term one, to demonstrate that "military transformation" was indeed feasible.

The 2001 attack on Afghanistan was launched almost entirely from the air. The only U.S. forces on the ground consisted of some teams of Special Forces that were flown in by helicopter in order to help guide the bombs and missiles to their targets by means of their laser designators.[29] First, targets were identified by means of satellite imagery and other types of space-based sensors. Next, employing the now customary mixture of aircraft (for lack of land bases, all but the B-52s had to take off from carriers cruising off the Pakistani coast) and cruise missiles, the Americans quickly smashed the most important Taliban positions. The task of mopping up was entrusted to the so-called Northern Alliance, loosely organized groups of Afghan warriors. Serving under their tribal chiefs, they were hastily equipped with former Soviet weapons supplied by Uzbekistan. Meeting little resistance, they captured the most important urban centers. Two years later in Iraq, airpower, this time used along with about 100,000 ground troops, played a major role in the defeat of Saddam's army and the occupation of Baghdad as already described. Both air campaigns, it must be repeated, hit extremely weak opponents so much so that the Taliban in Afghanistan did not have any means of striking back at all.

The initial operations in both countries having been completed without much difficulty, the Americans and their allies soon followed the Israelis in Lebanon in being taught the limits of airpower in a "war amongst the people." In Afghanistan, the way the offensive was conducted enabled most of the Taliban to avoid death or capture. This included not just rank-and-file fighters but the most important leaders, the Taliban's Mullah Omar and al-Qaeda's Osama bin Laden, as well. Years later a report, submitted to the U.S. Senate, specifically blamed the latter's escape on the absence of boots on the ground.[30] In fact, all the Americans did was to repeat the error they had committed in Vietnam; there, too, before Giap changed the rules of the game in 1972, their immense airpower had forced the Viet Cong to disperse, with the result that it could not be brought to battle either. Though the Taliban were forced to run in all directions, most made their way through the thin dragnet Rumsfeld had put in place to catch them. Having reached the parts of the country—most of it, in fact—that remained free of American and allied operations, it was only a question of time before they regrouped and engaged in the kind of guerrilla warfare in which Afghans have long been masters. Doing so, naturally they enjoyed all the advantages the country had offered their predecessors from the time of Alexander the Great on.

Afghanistan is one of the poorest countries on earth. Nevertheless, thanks in large part to the drug trade, which the Americans and their allies have vainly tried to suppress, money to wage the war has never been lacking. Neither airpower nor any other kind of armed force could prevent the Taliban from acquiring the usual assortment of guerrilla weapons: small automatic arms, machine guns, mortars, light anti-tank and anti-aircraft weapons, short-range rockets, and mines. They also made extensive use of easy-to-operate, but quite secure, radio sets. Almost a decade after the war started, all these seem to be available in practically unlimited quantities. This fact, of course, is one indication of the failure of airpower, which is responsible for interdiction, to do its job. Inexplicably, one weapon the Taliban have *not* used is the Stinger anti-aircraft missile, which the Americans themselves provided to the mujahideen during the mid- to late 1980s. Possibly those left over from the Soviet invasion have all been sold to third parties; had things been different, then air operations in Afghanistan would be much more difficult than they are.[31]

American and allied airpower in Afghanistan is being utilized very much in the usual manner. Long-range transport aircraft, many of them rented or leased from civilian companies and too large and expensive to be put at risk,[32] regularly bring troops and equipment into one of the neighboring countries that have agreed to cooperate. From there smaller military transports take over, lifting them into Afghanistan proper in what are often quite dangerous trips. On their way back they fly out casualties and troops whose tours of duty have ended. Satellite imagery and reconnaissance aircraft such as the German Tornados provide enemy intelligence. The latter is then acted upon by fighter-bombers—that is, until General Stanley McChrystal in 2009 all but banned their use as counterproductive.[33] Helicopters perform the usual operational and tactical missions, providing liaison, acting as flying command posts, and transporting troops and supplies. Along with some converted cargo aircraft, they also provide fire support in their role as gunships. A very important role is being played by the now ubiquitous UAVs whose great endurance, low operating cost, and risk-taking ability (in case one is shot down or otherwise lost, there is no need to worry about the pilot) make them especially suitable for intelligence gathering. As described above, some UAVs are also being equipped with missiles and used on attack missions. To that extent, the age of the automated battlefield has truly arrived.

As of mid-2010, nine years after it got under way, the outcome of the Afghan adventure was still very much in doubt. Rumsfeld's plan of combining airpower and a few Special Forces on the ground to win a quick, cheap victory had gone up in smoke. Instead, over 100,000 military personnel of many nations, backed up by tens of thousands of Afghan troops and disposing of the most modern airpower ever used in war, are trying to combat loose groups of irregular fighters whose number certainly does not exceed 25,000. Yet even that number, representing as it does a mere fraction of allied strength, is probably between two and five times the one the Taliban could muster when Operation Enduring Freedom started in late 2001.[34] Obviously those groups are far too weak to escalate the struggle and reach Mao's third stage. Most of the time they operate on the border between the first (terrorism) and the second (guerrilla). Yet the Taliban seem to have time working for them; precisely because they remain dispersed and well able to conceal themselves among both the rural and the urban populations, there appears to be scant chance of defeating them by means of airpower or any other form of modern military force. As in Vietnam, a core element of the chosen "exit strategy"—a term that speaks for itself—consists of increasing the Afghan Army from 90,000 to 134,000 men. As in Vietnam, too, probably the best the United States and its allies can do is to leave with their main mission unaccomplished but with their honor more or less intact.[35] Now that hostilities have spread into neighboring Pakistan, if anything the outlook is even bleaker than before.

Until the summer of 2006, it looked as if the war in Iraq was going even worse than the one in Afghanistan; of the two, it certainly took up the greater resources by far. Like the preliminary attack on Afghanistan in 2001, the one on Iraq made heavy use of the most advanced forms of airpower that the world's only superpower and its allies could field. No sooner had Baghdad been occupied than both soldiers and civilian analysts started heaping praise on what it had accomplished. Yet we have seen that, in terms of the number of missions flown (which is one factor that governs the amount of ordnance expended), precision, and—quite often—timeliness, it was no great improvement over the swarms of World War II fighter-bombers that roamed the skies of Tunisia, Italy, France, and Germany in 1943–45. As a result, when major combat operations died down and terrorism took their place, the emperor was found to be naked, or almost.

Though the northern districts of Iraq are mountainous, they are inhabited by the Kurdish people. They had no incentive to rise against the American-led occupation and can safely be ignored. Much of the remaining countryside consists of open, featureless desert where guerrillas find it hard to operate and where there are few targets for both sides. The major exception is Mesopotamia, the irrigated district that runs from northwest to southeast, where all the large cities have historically been located. Thanks to the vegetation that covers parts of it and its dense population, it is as well suited to terrorist and guerrilla operations as any other in the world. Ever since the British left Iraq in 1947, the country's government had been extremely centralized, but underneath the relatively modern state bureaucracy, tribes and clans continued to be as influential as before. Once Saddam and his paladins were gone, these conditions created a decentralized, indeed at times anarchic, society. Since Saddam's armed forces, various popular militias included, had numbered about a million people, members of that society who chose to fight either the occupation forces or each other never lacked either weapons or expertise in using them.

Though he had been warned many times,[36] Rumsfeld seems to have been surprised by the growth of armed resistance and the extremely violent forms it soon assumed. As in all counterinsurgency campaigns, it quickly turned out that the larger and the more powerful the available aircraft, the less useful they were and the higher the cost of using the relatively few available ones. It was a question of using sledgehammers, some of them valued at tens of millions of dollars, in order to locate and destroy mice. Indeed the very fact that F-16 fighters were employed more than once to bomb bridges over the Euphrates in the very heart of Baghdad showed how weak U.S. control over a country it had supposedly defeated and conquered was. Yet these strikes and others like them only formed a very small part of the airpower employed; in outline, the way the latter was used for counterinsurgency in Iraq differed little from similar campaigns elsewhere.

Having resolutely refused to face reality from the time of Vietnam on, the U.S. Air Force entered the war without a counterinsurgency doctrine of any sort.[37] With the army, things worked out differently. In 2006, the year when it issued its new counterinsurgency manual over the signature of General David Petraeus, it relegated airpower to an appendix that only took up five pages out of almost 200. Moreover, it was Petraeus's belief that airpower in counterinsurgency is best employed in the indirect rather than direct role. Hence he explicitly recommended that the use of the most powerful combat aircraft be discontinued; the rest were to be placed under the command of tactical commanders who were most familiar with the situation and best able to direct its use.[38]

To meet the growing demand for light transports, helicopters, and UAVs, the air force began setting up new squadrons consisting of all sorts of light propeller-driven machines long considered obsolete but now purchased in a hurry and equipped with the most up-to-date electronic equipment.[39] Thanks to the fact that there is almost no ground-to-air opposition, they were able to fly, and as of the time of writing continue to fly, all over the country. They provide liaison, move troops and supplies, gather intelligence, strike at ground targets, and evacuate the wounded. In particular, UAVs, used to escort and cover convoys on the ground, have helped reduce the number of bombs that caused many casualties among the U.S. troops. Other UAVs patrolled pipelines with considerable success.

Still the ground troops were not satisfied with the support they got. Too often it was a question of too late, too little (or too much); some claims made by air force proponents—for example, that the sound of jet engines overhead was a good method to win hearts and minds—were clearly ridiculous.[40] Losing patience, the army, with the apparent support of Defense Secretary Robert Gates, started establishing its own aviation units parallel to those of the air force. As one might expect, they too consisted of helicopters, light aircraft, and UAVs, all tied together by the most advanced sensors and communications. The idea is to have this force, known as Odin, on call for all commanders at the level of brigade and under.[41] Even as counterinsurgency operations are making the army extend its reach into the air, the air force is compelled to do more on the ground. A growing number of its personnel operate UAVs and act as forward observers. Others simply guard air bases against guerrilla attacks, a factor that does not have to be considered in regular warfare but of which, speaking of Iraq, there were 1,500 in 2003–6 alone. A single air base might require as many as 1,200 personnel for this purpose, and even then it hardly needs to be said that complete security cannot be guaranteed.[42] Thus counterinsurgency, besides placing a large question mark on whether airpower was really as effective a force multiplier as has sometimes been claimed, was actually beginning to erode the distinction between air and ground forces as it had been understood for decades past.

U.S. personnel killed in action during the conventional phase of Operation Iraqi Freedom numbered 137. Even if Iraq's military weakness is taken into account, that is a very low figure indeed. However, by the end of 2009, the total had risen to no fewer than 4,367. In other words, the number of those who lost their lives in counterinsurgency operations of every kind exceeded those killed by Saddam Hussein's army by a factor of almost 32 to one.[43] Excluded are nonmilitary personnel, some of them American and others foreigners, who lost their lives while in the employ of the numerous security firms the Pentagon has engaged to carry out all sorts of duties in the country. Clearly the advocates of airpower cannot have it both ways. If it is true, as it undoubtedly is, that the successful use of superior airpower made a huge contribution and was one reason why casualties during the first three weeks of the war were minimal, then it is equally true that the failure of airpower in the counterinsurgency role must be held at least partly accountable for what followed later on. On balance, reflecting on the growing number and importance of counterinsurgency campaigns and on what the air force had achieved and not achieved in them, some observers started wondering whether it should not be abolished.[44]

CONCLUSIONS: GOING DOWN, 1945–?

We now know where airpower has come from, how it has developed, and what it has achieved in the many wars, large and small, in which it has participated; but where may it be going? Most authors, surveying its history as the youngest and in many ways most dynamic form of military might, believe that it has a great future before it and that the sky's the limit. *Per arduu ad astra*, by way of hardship to the stars, as the motto of the Royal Air Force, the oldest and still claiming to be one of the most important of the lot, proudly puts it.

This study has followed a different path. One reason why it has been able to do so is that it has adopted a wider perspective than most: embracing fields such as naval aviation, heliborne operations, and space operations that are not always considered an integral part of the subject. Conventional, nuclear, and subconventional war have all been covered. Furthermore, instead of celebrating airpower's rapid technological progress and steadily growing capabilities, both of them fascinating subjects that have caused many authors to be carried away, it has tried to focus on military effectiveness—both compared with the remaining services *and against the enemy*—as the one factor that ultimately matters.

Starting from very humble beginnings, airpower took off like a rocket. It withstood the test of World War I, developed very rapidly from 1919 to 1939, and reached the peak of its effectiveness in 1939–45. This effectiveness manifested itself in two main ways. First, starting with the German campaign in Poland and ending with Operation Olympus, the planned American invasion of Japan, during those years no large-scale military operation that did not enjoy adequate air cover stood any chance of success. While some forms of war—the defense—and some types of terrain—mountains in particular—were less favorable to airpower than others, on the whole this was as true in Norway as in the North African desert, in the Pacific as in Europe. If anything, it was even more true at sea than over land. Second, though some authors have argued that airpower, in the form of strategic bombing, has never succeeded in breaking any government's determination to carry on the fight,[1] its ability to thoroughly wreck entire countries was demonstrated beyond doubt. To convince oneself of that fact, it is enough to look at photographs of Hamburg, Dresden, Berlin, and of course Tokyo and Hiroshima and Nagasaki.

Even so, there were definite limits to what airpower could and did achieve. Contrary to the visions of some of its early advocates, armies and navies did not disappear. Nor is there any real proof that their role in warfare as a whole underwent some dramatic decline. While it is true that both were very dependent on airpower and, when unsupported by it, often all but powerless against it, it is also true that they retained some unique capabilities that airpower did not, and still does not, possess. Armies had the ability to conquer enemy territory, pacify it, and hold it against all comers; navies could transport very heavy and bulky loads over long distances at reasonable cost as well as project military power overseas without any need for land bases. It was navies assisted by airpower that ruled the high oceans, not the other way around. Thus the presence of boots on the ground, as well as command of the sea, remained as important as they had ever been.

Since then, far from growing, the power of airpower has undergone a slow, but steady, decline. Admittedly, change was anything but smooth and simple. No large-scale historical or even physical-climatological process—I am, of course, thinking of the oft-mentioned phenomenon of global warming—is. Long after 1945, airpower continued to play a World War II–like role in some of what I have called "little wars" between or against countries that did not yet have nuclear weapons. This was especially true in the Middle East, and especially of the 1967 war. Though the fact could never be publicly acknowledged, the latter was in many ways a copy of the *Blitzfeldzuege* of 1940–41; it was as if General Heinz Guderian and Co. had mounted a time machine and gone out to fight the Arab armies.

As is almost always the case, cause and effect are hard to separate. Nevertheless, a good starting point is a simple look at the numbers—given that, from the beginning of history, numerical superiority has always been a critically important factor that made for victory in war. As we saw, when World War I got under way the aircraft operated by each of the major belligerents numbered in the low hundreds. From that point on the logistic curve followed its usual course, culminating in 1940–45 when the five most important belligerents—the United States, the Soviet Union, the British Empire, Germany, and Japan—built a total of no fewer than 785,000 aircraft. The peak year was 1944, when the United States alone built almost 100,000 of them.[2] The number of pilots and aircrew who completed their training and took off to fight was in proportion. So, of course, was the overall number of uniformed personnel, the number of bases, and the size of the industry that built the aircraft as well as everything they needed to fly and operate against the enemy.

A few figures will illustrate what happened from that point on.[3] When Curtis LeMay left SAC in 1957, it consisted of 224,000 airmen, close to 2,000 heavy bombers, and nearly 800 tankers. Fifty years later there were only a little over 200 heavy bombers and a proportional number of tankers left; meanwhile, of course, SAC itself had been abolished. Between 1950 and the early 1970s, a total of 15,948 fighters—F-86s, F-100s, F-101s, F-104s, F-105s, F-106s, and F-111s—were built for use by either the U.S. Air Force or others. The corresponding number for 1975–2009, including both F-15s and F-16s, is only about one-third of that figure. During the 1970s and 1980s, the United States purchased an average of 262 aircraft per year. Since then the number had been cut by three-fourths—and this in spite of the fact that the air force, as the primary customer, has been spending up to 90 percent of its entire procurement budget on aircraft as opposed to everything else.[4]

The story does not end there. The original intention had been to buy 750 F-22s with production starting in 1994. However, in 1990 the figure was lowered to 648 and the start of production delayed by two years. Later it was cut to 442, 339, and 277 until Secretary Robert Gates ended the agony by ordering the production lines shut after just 187 had been built.[5] And this is the country that spends as much on defense as the next 15 combined! The fate of the Eurofighter has been similar; ten years after the countries that produce it agreed to buy 620 aircraft among them, the number in service stood at 137. As if to emphasize how absurd the situation has become, it flew its first "operational" mission in February 2006 when it covered the Turin Winter Olympics[6]—a strange thing for any combat aircraft to do, considering that al-Qaeda does not have an air force. Examining the data in *The Military Balance,* the authoritative series published by the London-based International Institute for Strategic Studies, I discovered that, between 1996 and 2008, the order of battle of almost every one of the world's leading air forces went down by about one-third, even though they did not go through major wars in which many combat aircraft were lost.

The decline in naval aviation, carrier aviation included, has been greater still. True, the number of carrier-owning nations has grown (as has that of nations themselves). However, most of the vessels in question are only half carriers flying half aircraft, by which are meant STOL/VTOL machines that fall far short of modern fourth-generation fighters in point of weight, power, speed, ordnance-carrying capability, and other characteristics. Attempting to take on a full-sized American carrier, all they can expect is a short, exciting life. The largest American carriers can take almost as many aircraft as their World War II predecessors could; however, their own number is going nowhere but down.

Most important of all, war at sea has declined even more than war on land. Only once, at the Falklands in 1982, was the role played by carriers absolutely essential. Had one of them been sunk, the campaign would have had to be abandoned. Though some carrier aircraft have been used against land targets, such occasions have been far apart and relatively unimportant. Neither in Korea nor in Indochina nor in Vietnam nor in Iraq did they do very much to decide the outcome. This has led some analysts to question whether the huge American carriers, with their insatiable logistic requirements, are suitable for sustained operations of war.[7] As to other nations' ships, one may perhaps quote the Jewish Talmud: If the cedars are consumed by fire, what should the moss on the wall say?

As noted earlier, probably the key factor that drove the process was nuclear proliferation—in plain words, the introduction of bombs so powerful that a relative handful of them could turn even the mightiest states into radioactive deserts. In the absence of a credible defense, meaning one that has been tested a thousand times under realistic conditions and found to work each time, every time, the outcome was threefold. First, the men—very occasionally, the women—who ruled those states took every precaution to ensure that any hostilities that might break out between them should be limited in scale and/or waged by proxy. Second, without exception they proceeded to emasculate the generals—with the air force generals at their head—so as to make sure they would be in no position to launch an unauthorized war or an accidental war. Though the process was not simple, inevitably the outcome was a very great decline in the order of battle. Third, whereas nonnuclear states continued to fight each other as before, as far as nuclear ones were concerned, war only remained possible against opponents that, not possessing nuclear weapons, were often so weak as to raise the question why they should be fought at all.

Another very important factor is cost. Calculating in constant 1985 dollars, the F-100 Super Sabre of 1954 cost just over $2 million. The 1962 F-4 Phantom of 1962 cost over $6 million, whereas the F-15 Eagle of 1974 cost $25 million.[8] During the first three and a half decades after World War II the real annual cost of maintaining armed forces on land and at sea grew by 2.9 and 6.4 percent respectively. In the case of airpower the figure stood at 7.1 percent; indeed John Boyd's biographer says that he once calculated that, to arrive at the true cost of any aircraft, the initial estimate should be multiplied by pi (3.14).[9] Aircraft operating costs, calculated on a per-sortie basis, showed an even greater increase.[10] Each time a cost overrun was incurred—since 1970, there has been hardly any Western military aircraft production program that did *not* do so—treasuries and parliaments were tempted to compensate by extending development periods and cutting numbers. As numbers decreased, research and development costs had to be spread over fewer aircraft. This in turn caused per-unit prices to go up, creating a vicious cycle. The upshot was that, in the end, nobody had any idea what the "real" cost of any aircraft was.

Ours is often hailed as an age of unprecedented rapid technical change. That may very well be true as far as computers and some other fields are concerned, but in the field of military aviation it is definitely not. Back in World War I any aircraft that was over a year old was obsolescent or obsolete. Consequently it would be relegated to a secondary theater—including, in some cases, the maritime theater—second-line duties, or training duties. Throughout the 1920s and 1930s, flight records were broken almost weekly. Bringing the German Me-109 from the drawing board to serial production took just two and a half years.[11] Doing the same with the British Spitfire took even less. During the six years that World War II lasted, both aircraft went through no fewer than nine model changes. Constantly comparing notes by examining each other's downed aircraft, the engineers who worked on them ended by doubling engine output from 1,000 to 2,000 horsepower. It was a process of creative destruction; the very fact that countless aircraft were being lost in combat or to other causes ensured that the stream of innovations would never stop.

During the 1950s, as one pilot noted,[12] excitement was in the air as almost every week brought something new. Since then things have changed. The extreme reluctance of advanced countries to fight each other has led to a sharp drop in the number of losses, both in absolute terms and per sortie flown;[13] if only for that reason, the air forces of those countries tend to stretch the life of the machines they already have. Again taking the U.S. Air Force as our example, at no time has the inventory of aircraft been older than it is right now. Its average age is 38 years, far more than that of most of the pilots who fly them. Conversely, as one air force chief of staff once put it to me, the men, and perhaps a few women, who will fly the next generation of combat aircraft—in the unlikely event that there *will* be a next generation, one may add—are still wearing their diapers.

Given how stretched-out production plans have become, some have not yet been born. Some aircraft, notably the famous B-52 bombers and the KC-135 tankers that support them, are 40 and 50 years old. Current plans are to keep some F-15s flying until they reach a similar age. Too often the pace of innovation, far from accelerating, has slowed until it is barely perceptible. In the meantime, the number of repairs, and with them the percentage of aircraft that are unavailable for operations at any given moment, is going nowhere but up and up.[14] Keeping an aircraft fit to fly can be enormously expensive; for example, whereas a new longeron (a thin strip of metal to which the skin is attached) for an F-15 can be had for $12,000, the labor cost for installing it is 20 times as high.[15]

Proponents of airpower will no doubt object that, though airframes remain the same or almost so, many of them are being steadily upgraded by adding new electronics, new missiles, and so on. Occasionally an aircraft is even provided with a new engine that improves its performance and extends its operational life. That is true, but it does not prove that, compared to the past, technological development is indeed accelerating. When Nelson won the Battle of Trafalgar in 1805, his flagship, the *Victory*, had been upgraded several times (and at great cost).[16] But that does not mean that it was not fully 40 years old.

To make things worse, or better depending on one's point of view, fear of nuclear escalation is everywhere. It has led to a situation where conventional war between state-owned armed forces is being rapidly replaced by subconventional war, or irregular war, or war amongst the people, or guerrilla war, or terrorism, or whatever it may be called. As Part V of the present volume has shown in some detail, right from the beginning the use of airpower—indeed of conventional military power in general—in conflicts of this kind has been problematic. First, they tended to make a mockery of the primary mission of any air force, which is to gain and maintain command of the air. In this way they rendered the most capable, and most expensive, aircraft superfluous. Second, aircraft were unable to spend time loitering over the battlefield or deliver sustained firepower. Consequently their impact on the fighting was like that of throwing a stone onto an anthill. A disturbance is created, but things quickly return to normal; often the faster and the more modern the aircraft, the greater the problems in this respect. Above all, the speed of combat aircraft, their relative lack of maneuverability, and, too often, their inability to deliver ordnance accurately meant that they were often used in an indiscriminate manner. The last-named quality was carried to the point where, in more than one campaign, airpower was judged to be counterproductive.[17] Nor was it simply a question of pilots being compelled to heed all sorts of political and humanitarian considerations and made to fight "with one arm tied behind one's back." One needs to look no further than the record of the Luftwaffe in Yugoslavia and of the Soviet Air Force in Afghanistan to realize that this was not the case.

In many ways, the real turning point has been the Vietnam War. The most important air forces of the 1960s were much smaller than those of 20 years before. Nevertheless, as that war rather dramatically showed, aircraft were still sufficiently cheap and numerous to allow their owners to use them and lose them if necessary. Used and lost they were, by the thousands; yet this being for the most part a war amongst the people, the results were not what they should have been. It was during the 1970s, against the background of dramatically improving airframes, engines, electronics, and weapons, that orders of battle really started shrinking. The process unfolded in the West before it reached the Soviet Union; in fact one could argue that it was by refusing to change in time that the Soviet Union bankrupted itself. Countries that did not join the trend, such as China, were stuck with huge numbers of obsolescent aircraft. But did it matter? Since China has acquired a reasonable number of nuclear weapons, nobody in his or her right mind has seriously thought of engaging it in a serious war; thus the number and quality of aircraft in its order of battle, as in those of other countries, has become largely irrelevant.

Since Vietnam, and even more so in the wake of more recent wars in the Gulf, much has been made of the fact that modern military aircraft are far more capable than their predecessors so that smaller numbers are needed. This argument has been touched upon several times, so all we have to do at this point is to recall the reasons why it is wrong. First, there is no sign that, on a one-against-one or even squadron-against-squadron basis, modern aircraft are more capable than their predecessors 60 or even 90 years ago. Second, the claim that today's aircraft can deliver ordnance much more accurately than their World War II predecessors is misleading, sometimes deliberately so.[18] The reason why it is misleading is that it compares bombers with fighter-bombers. Comparing fighter-bombers of both periods, it turns out that a Stuka was quite as capable of knocking out a World War II tank as an A-10 Warthog is of doing the same to a present-day one. Similarly, P-47 Thunderbolts in 1944–45 did not take many more sorties to bring down a bridge or hit a locomotive than an F-16 did six and a half decades later. The main difference is that the Stukas sometimes flew so low that they went right through the blast created by the exploding tank, whereas the F-16, faced by much stronger anti-aircraft defenses, must stay above 15,000 feet or risk being shot down. Should it be shot down, then the loss, in terms of replacement cost, will be incomparably greater than it was in 1944–45.

It is true that a single B-52, delivering joint direct attack munitions (JDAM), can do some things it would have taken many B-17s or B-29s to do, even at night, and even through cloud cover as operations in Kosovo showed. However, so vulnerable are these aircraft that they can only be used in theaters where opposition is negligible or absent, and then only with the aid of massive "strike packages." Plus, so costly are they to purchase and operate that only one country still has them or their equivalents, with no replacement in sight.

Much has been said about the ability of modern information technology to tighten the "kill chain" between "sensors" and "shooters," enabling airpower to respond more quickly to events on the battlefield.[19] Many of these claims are exaggerated if not deliberately misleading. Less than a year before Operation Iraqi Freedom was launched, the army chief of staff, General Eric Shinseki, told Congress that field units normally had to wait about 25 minutes for air support.[20] That only represented a marginal improvement on what the RAF in Egypt had achieved in the Western Desert during the second half of 1942 and was four times (!) as long as in Palestine during the Arab Revolt of 1936–39.[21] Nor are the reasons for this situation hard to find: whereas there is no question but that technology has been steadily improving,[22] timeliness is governed by several other factors as well. Among the most important are the size of the theater of war and the number of aircraft available to operate over it; the distance from airfield to target; the number of sorties each aircraft can fly per day; and the state of readiness and training. In three out of those four respects, the Americans in Afghanistan and Iraq were no better off than their grandparents in Italy and Western Europe had been—if anything, they are indeed worse off.

For example, on April 3, 2003, the Third Battalion, Fourth Marine Brigade, hit a well-planned Iraqi ambush at Al Kut. Air support was asked for, but when the skirmish ended after 20 minutes it still had not arrived. Had it done so, then on a "battlefield" measuring just 60 acres it might still not have been of much use. Another excellent example of the way things work comes from the Israeli Army. It is said that, whereas during the 2006 war in Lebanon response time was 60–90 seconds, during Operation Cast Lead of December 2008–January 2009 it had been reduced to just 30.[23] Does this mean that was how long it took an Apache helicopter to take off, fly to Gaza, position itself, and launch its missiles? Obviously, though the distances involved are very small, the answer is negative. Or does the figure refer to helicopters already flying over the Strip? If so, how many helicopters are needed to keep up round-the-clock surveillance? For how long can they stay airborne until others must take their place, how long can the exercise be kept up, and how much will it cost? Suppose the Strip's area had taken up 1,000 square miles instead of 139, how would the figure change? And what if the terrorists, instead of being completely helpless, had possessed heavy machine guns and shoulder-held anti-aircraft missiles?

Two other factors must be mentioned here. First, while it is true that many advanced fighters and fighter-bombers are capable of striking numerous targets in a single pass, when it comes to counterinsurgency, where the opponent is dispersed and concealed, such targets are unlikely to present themselves. Second, the more precise the munitions aircraft use, the better the intelligence required, a condition that is anything but easy to meet. In fact a real danger exists that, in the era of the so-called strategic corporal, the new technology will be used to centralize command. Technically, already today it is possible to have a head of state peering over the shoulder of each pilot. The outcome will be to slow down the pace of operations, as happened in Vietnam.[24] However, the opposite danger cannot be ignored either. The faster the available aircraft can respond, the greater the temptation to use them as flying artillery and disperse them, thus negating airpower's greatest advantage, its ability to concentrate its forces at a single point.

On top of this, the argument concerning timeliness commits the worst of all possible military sins—namely, it focuses on the performance of one side while blithely ignoring any moves the enemy may make. Even the prescient John Warden, who has been quoted as saying that *any* modern nation contains roughly 500 targets and 3,000 aiming points as Iraq did and can therefore be knocked out by means of a "surgical" strike from the air similar to the one used against Saddam, appears to be guilty in this respect.[25] If ever there has been a faulty, though unfortunately very common, way of looking at war it is this one. It is an error to which the air forces of advanced Western nations, few if any of which have fought an equal enemy during the last decades, are especially prone.

Finally, there are historical grounds for suspecting that the combination of very high quality and very small numbers is a typical sign of military degeneration.[26] A good example of the process is the development of ancient Greek warships. As the term indicates, the Athenian triremes that ruled the sea at the time of Pericles had three banks of oars each. Later more were added until some Hellenistic vessels had ten and more.[27] So few, expensive, and cumbersome were these ships that they could never be used in battle; faced by smaller, but more numerous, opponents, they must have been helpless. Some are known to have ended up being captured in port by the Roman legions, which, needless to say, advanced by land. Similarly, by about 1525 full suits of armor had become so heavy, so elaborate, and so expensive that only a handful of knights were still able to afford them. On campaign even those few had to be escorted by infantrymen whose function was in many ways like that of today's strike packages; this fact caused them to become even more expensive and even less useful. By 1550, the process of shortening, lightening, and simplifying armor got under way. Two hundred years later it had been all but completed, leaving cuirassiers as the only troops who still wore any at all.

Perhaps an even better example of the way things work is offered by naval history from about 1860 to 1945.[28] As steam engines took the place of sails, ships of the line with their multiple rows of guns on both sides were gradually transformed into modern battleships. As battleships developed and their guns grew more powerful, they became much larger and more expensive whereas their numbers went into a steep decline. As the number of vessels went down, fleet commanders surrounded them by all sorts of smaller ships to act as scouts and protect them against emerging threats such as torpedoes, submarines, and finally aircraft. The outcome was the creation of the naval equivalent of strike packages, also known as task forces. By 1939 the floating steel castles were at their last gasp. Over the next six years quite a few on both sides were actually sunk or damaged by aircraft, submarines, or manned torpedoes before they were able to raise steam and leave port. After 1945, they all but disappeared.

During the early years of airpower its advocates were always explaining that so-and-so many aircraft could have been had for the cost of a single warship. However, by now the point has been reached where aircraft are almost as precious as naval vessels. The combination of growing cost, the slowing down of technological innovation, and declining usefulness in the most common (and often most dangerous) types of war is proving deadly to the future of combat aircraft in particular.[29] At the same time, as the number of such aircraft declined, they also started to be overtaken by a whole variety of other "systems," to use a fashionable term. Among the earliest were surface-to-surface ballistic missiles. Entering service from about 1955 on, within less than a decade they got to the point where they were able to reach from practically any point on earth to any other; had anyone seen much point in doing so, they could even lift hydrogen bombs into earth-circling orbits. The larger the number of missiles, the longer their range, and the greater their accuracy, the more serious the threat they posed to manned aircraft of various types.

As usual during the Cold War, the first to introduce ballistic missiles were the superpowers. First developed countries, then less developed ones, soon followed. By the last decades of the twentieth century the relevant technologies had proliferated to the point where countries such as Pakistan, North Korea, and Iran no longer saw any need to develop manned combat aircraft for delivering nuclear weapons. In the United States, proponents of "transformation" often spoke of skipping over an entire technological stage,[30] but it was the above-mentioned countries that, in their own modest way, actually did so, going straight for missiles and cruise missiles. The outcome was a force that was in some—not all—ways more capable and less vulnerable. To say nothing of the fortunes saved.

Other post-1945 innovations included sensor-carrying satellites to substitute for reconnaissance aircraft; UAVs to act as rapidly developing "maids for everything," as the saying goes; and helicopters to replace gliders and paratroopers in transporting, landing, and extracting commanders, troops, and supplies over short distances in particular. Naturally conditions, requirements, and strategies differ from one state to another. A single solution applicable to all of them is neither conceivable nor necessary. Nevertheless, taking a broad view of the future, there can be no doubt that satellites of every kind—regardless of whether their mission is weather forecasting, navigation, communication, surveillance, or reconnaissance—should be grouped with ICBMs in some kind of a unified space service; after all, a satellite launcher is nothing but a modified ICBM, and the other way around. Yet is it really true that the service in question should be part of the air force? Or should there be a single space service to control long-range surface-to-surface missiles as well as meeting the requirements of air, land, and sea forces?[31] Precedents are not lacking; after all it was the German Army, not the Luftwaffe, that successfully built and operated the first ballistic missiles. Following World War II, neither the former Soviet Union nor present-day China adopted the American system whereby ICBMs and satellites form part of a unified, independent air force.

Referring to the termination of the F-22 fighter program, one writer quite correctly attributed it to the "attack of the drones."[32] To the extent that UAVs serve the army and the navy on various missions, logically speaking all except the longest-range systems of this kind—I am thinking of Global Hawk and its equivalents—should be developed by, and under the control of, those services. The same applies to helicopters. Their mission is to lift a variety of loads, be they commanders or troops or supplies or the wounded, for the army and the navy, from the places where they are assembled to the ones they have to reach. They can also serve as highly mobile gunships and anti-tank platforms, though as tanks disappear—and they are disappearing fast—the latter mission has lost much of its importance. Logically they should form part of the services they are supposed to support, especially when it is a question of striking at tactical and operational targets. In fact this solution has often been applied, and is already being applied, by various armed forces around the world. As the transfer some years ago of helicopters from the Royal Australian Air Force to the Australian Army, for example, indicates, their number is growing.

That leaves air transport. Owing to the need for large, powerful aircraft to carry troops and supplies, chronologically speaking transport was among the last missions for which airpower was used. In fact most of the earliest transports were converted bombers, and in some instances this continued to be the case until bombers started to disappear during the 1970s. First employed soon after World War I in order to move troops in "air policing" operations, air transport vividly displayed its potential during the opening weeks of the Spanish Civil War. Since then its importance, though it has often been obscured by the more glamorous combat arms, has kept growing. At a time when war among developed countries has almost disappeared and most such countries only engage in expeditionary warfare far from home, air transport is absolutely indispensable. In terms of sheer speed, as well as its ability to reach landlocked countries such as Afghanistan and the Congo, its superiority over all other available means is undisputable and undisputed.

However, there are serious problems. Many of the aircraft in question require fairly extensive ground facilities and are extremely vulnerable both in flight and during takeoff or landing. One needs only imagine the outcry that will follow if a fully laden C-17 long-range transport is shot down together with its full complement of 134 troops onboard; such aircraft, in other words, can only be used in places where there is hardly an enemy to speak of. As this example also shows, military transports cannot carry nearly as many troops as civilian airliners can. To this must be added the problem of cost. The price tag, which is around $200,000,000, is about the same as that of a commercial airliner of similar size. But fuel, maintenance, and depreciation costs are much higher. As a result, so far not one civilian operator has purchased it. Hence it is understandable that many air forces also prefer civilian aircraft for their long-range missions, switching to smaller military machines or helicopters to complete the last leg of the journey if necessary.

As with helicopters and UAVs, a very good case could be made for putting short- and perhaps medium-range transport aircraft under the command of those whose needs they serve. To repeat the obvious, there is no single solution that will satisfy every requirement of every country. Very probably it is not even possible to find a single solution that will satisfy every requirement of any country. Yet with warbirds, that is, manned combat aircraft, apparently heading toward extinction and with the role of other machines growing, in many cases what is left of air forces may well be facing death by a thousand cuts.

Meanwhile the decline of airpower has already wrought vast changes in the culture with which it has traditionally been associated. Right from the beginning flying has been linked to technological skill, mastery, speed, and, perhaps most important of all, audacity. Transcending the differences between democracies on one hand and fascist and communist dictatorships on the other, in many ways it was the embodiment of the twentieth-century dream of modernity and progress. As Trenchard and many other senior commanders understood very well, all of these are qualities that air forces cannot simply command. Instead they must be carefully nurtured with the aid of what, in another work, I have called the culture of war, including forms of behavior, uniforms, insignia, decorations, standards, ceremonies, monuments, and much more. Though selection is obviously needed and was practiced from the first, in the final analysis all air forces must rely on those who step forward and ask to be counted. That is all the more the case because, once a pilot is in the air, there is little to prevent him or her from doing whatever he or she pleases.

As the English-Irish poet, William Butler Yeats, commemorating the pilot son of a lady friend who had been killed in action, wrote in 1919:

> *Nor law, nor duty bade me fight,*
> *Nor public men, nor cheering crowds,*
> *A lonely impulse of delight*
> *Drove to this tumult in the clouds . . .*[33]

Good military pilots, fighter jocks above all, were expected to be bright, aggressive, self-confident, and even cocky. They also had to be prepared to take calculated risks while trying to squeeze the maximum performance out of their aircraft. Partly because pilots' skills had been expensively imparted and were hard to replace, partly to compensate for extreme risks taken and losses suffered, discipline between missions tended to be on the lax side. Men such as Hans-Ulrich Rudel, the Stuka ace who never drank anything but milk, were very much the exception. Often the outcome was a raucous lifestyle with heavy drinking and womanizing. Ernst Udet was not the only pilot who, aware of the risks he was taking, refused to get married. Not surprisingly, this kind of thing reached its apogee during the world wars when death was looking aircrews in the face day in, day out. In the words of General Spaatz, of World War II fame: "I guess we considered ourselves a different breed of cat. . . . We flew through the air and other people walked on the ground. It was as simple as that."[34]

Change got under way during the 1980s. Probably the most important factor involved was the growing realization that, with nuclear weapons proliferating and nuclear stalemate prevailing, large-scale conventional warfare and preparation for it were increasingly turning into exercises in make-believe. As part of this process, aces—meaning, pilots who shot down more than five enemy aircraft—have all disappeared. Indeed as early as the Vietnam War, as attention inside and outside the military shifted to the prisoners held at the Hanoi Hilton, they were no longer the celebrities they used to be.[35] Thus there seemed to be less justification for giving pilots, and by no means only pilots, their head.

In fourth- and fifth-generation aircraft, functions such as threat prioritization and identification are normally performed by computer-linked radar. So is weapons release, which, in a less politically correct age, pilots sometimes compared to orgasm. Instead of flying their aircraft, pilots are literally incorporated into them. Hoses enable them to breathe, wires to hear and speak, lap belts and shoulder harness to remain in their seats, and calf garters to prevent their legs from flailing about. Much of the time, losing sight of the external world, they depend solely on instruments and have not the slightest idea of where they are. Most sorties are now planned second by second before they ever get under way, a tendency that long periods of peace tend to accentuate even more. All this has gone a long way to erode the exhilarating sense of freedom and mastery that flying used to impart. Since most kills now take place beyond visual range and are only registered in the form of blips disappearing from a screen, even the "pleasing, beautiful sight" of an opponent exploding in midair is no longer what it used to be.[36] Demonstrative action of any sort tends to be frowned upon. The more expensive the aircraft and the fewer their number, the truer this is; indeed in many cases pilots have been replaced by UAV operators on one hand and "silent silo sitters" (Curtis LeMay) on the other.[37]

Yet another factor was the entry into the military, air forces included, of women.[38] Right from the beginning of aviation, a few women were caught up in the excitement and got involved in the action. During the 1920s and

1930s women of various nations set numerous world records. Yet since they did not fly the vastly more powerful and vastly more dangerous aircraft men operated, they did so almost exclusively in their own class. Between 1939 and 1945 tens of thousands of women served in various air forces and performed any number of tasks from typing to operating searchlights. Some British and American women ferried aircraft behind the front; one of them, Jacqueline Cochran, the holder of numerous flight records, was described by "Bomber" Harris as a "blonde bombshell" when she walked into his office.[39] Some Soviet women even flew in combat, though compared to their male comrades their number was insignificant.[40] One reason for that was that combat flying in the unpressurized aircraft of the time, which did not have hydraulically or electronically operated controls, could be very hard work; in fact, looking back on their experience, some female pilots concluded that combat flying was not for women. In all that pertains to the treatment of women, Nazi Germany has acquired a particularly bad reputation. Yet as far as I know, it was the only country where women test-flew combat aircraft.[41]

After 1945 women all but disappeared from most militaries, air forces included. The few remaining ones either filled the usual administrative and medical slots or served decorative purposes by accompanying senior officers to meetings, etc.[42] Change, brought about partly by the feminist movement and partly by the growing reluctance of men to serve, started around 1970. Since then, in all countries that allowed women to join their militaries, air forces received more than their fair share of them, the reason being that those forces have a much higher tail-to-teeth ratio (most women prefer to serve in the tails, where they are far less likely to get killed) than the other armed services.[43] Even today, though one in six U.S. Air Force personnel is female, only one in 50 pilots is.

Yet the presence of women, even in limited numbers and even in the relatively low ranks that most of them occupied, was a cardinal reason why the entire culture of air forces started being toned down and assumes less extravagant, kinder, gentler forms. The place of drinking and carousing was taken by weightlifting and dieting. In the United States and elsewhere, previously officer clubs had routinely hosted wild parties complete with strippers and wet T-shirt contests;[44] now such occasions have become literally unthinkable. Claims of sexual harassment have created a situation where a pilot is more likely to be cashiered for talking to, or even looking at, the "wrong" members of the opposite sex (to say nothing of members of the same sex) in the "wrong" way than to be shot down in combat. Those who did not get the message, like those unfortunate enough to be caught up in the 1991 Tailhook scandal at Las Vegas, had to learn it the hard way. The outcome was said to be the worst defeat of the U.S. Navy, and its air community in particular, since Pearl Harbor.[45]

By one story Admiral Ernest King, who commanded the U.S. Navy during the greatest and most ferocious war of all times, once said that, whenever the enemy stands at the gates, the sons-of-bitches are sent for.[46] It now begins to look as if, for good or ill, in most of the world's air forces, the sons-of-bitches are going home.

NOTES

PREFACE

1. *On War*, Princeton, Princeton University Press, 1976, p. 97.

Part I: Into the Blue, 1900–1939

1. ANTECEDENTS AND BEGINNINGS

1. C. Flammarion, *Mes voyages aériens*, Paris, Flammarion, 1894, pp. 90–91.

2. Quoted in H. Schmitthenner, *Die Luftfahrer*, Bergen, Mueller & Kiepenheuer, 1956, p. 110 (my translation).

3. According to L. Winter and G. Degner, *Minute Epics of Flight*, New York, Grosset & Dunlap, 1933, pp. 26–27.

4. Thomas Jefferson, *The Writings*, H. A. Washington, ed., Washington D.C., Taylor & Maury, 1853, vol. i, pp. 445–46.

5. See on this period in Zeppelin's life G. de Syon, *Zeppelin!: Germany and the Airship, 1900–1939*, Baltimore, Johns Hopkins University Press, 2001, p. 15.

6. L. P. Mouillard, *L'Empire de l'air*, 1881, quoted in E. M. Emme, ed., *The Impact of Airpower*, Princeton, van Nostrand, 1959, p. 19.

7. Letter to the *Journal de Paris*, quoted in S. Poleskie, "A Brief History of Ballooning," 2006, at http://journals.aol.com/spoleski/WhereisStephenStevePoleskieNow/entries/2006/11.

8. S. Moreh, ed., *Al Jabarti's Chronicle of the First Seven Months of the French Occupation of Egypt*, Leiden, Brill, 1975, pp. 112–13.

9. The best source for this entire episode is "RPAV, Remotely Piloted Aerial Vehicles: An Anthology," 2003, at http://www.ctie.monash.edu/hargrave/rpav_home.html. See also R. Gentile, *Storia dell'Aeronautica delle origine ai giorni nostri*, Florence, Scuola di Guerra Aerea, 1967, p. 60.

10. A. Robida, *La Guerre en vingtième siècle*, Paris, Tallandier, 1991 [1883].

11. I. F. Clarke, *The Pattern of Expectation, 1644–2001*, New York, Basic Books, 1979, p. 105.

12. See on him the excellent Wikipedia article at http://en.wikipedia.org/wiki/Thaddeus_Lowe.

13. J. A. Hennessy, *The United States Army Air Arm, April 1861 to April 1917*, Honolulu, University Press of the Pacific, 1985, p. 9.

14. See, for a detailed description of balloon operations during the siege, D. Cameron, *The Balloonists: The History of the Aeronauts*, Phoenix Mill, Sutton, 2006 [1956], pp. 172–78.

15. Temple Lecture, quoted in *The Aeronautical Journal*, v, 20, vol. 1901, p. 55.

16. Hennessy, *The United States Army Air Arm*, p. 13.

17. T. Roosevelt, *The Rough Riders*, New York, Da Capo, 1990 [1902], p. 119.

18. I. B. Holley, *Ideas and Weapons*, Washington, D.C., Office of Air Force History, 1983 [1953], p. 25.

19. J. Scott, ed., *Proceedings of the Hague Peace Conferences, The Conference of 1899*, New York, UNIFO, 1975 [1921], p. 353.

20. A. Harris, *Bomber Offensive*, New York, Macmillan, 1947, p. 177.

21. H. G. Wells, *The War in the Air*, London, Nelson, 1914 [1907–8], p. 149.

22. Ibid., pp. 201–2.

23. Ibid., p. 242.

24. Ibid., p. 196.

25. See on this below, pp. 139–140.

26. Details in O. Groehler, *Geschichte des Luftkrieges 1910 bis 1980*, Berlin (East), Militaerverlag, 1981, p. 19.

27. See J. M. Hormannn, *Zeppeline, Marineluftschiffe und Marineflieger*, Hamburg, Mittler, n.d., p. 54.

28. W. Cross, *Zeppelins of World War I*, Lincoln, NE, Authors' Guild, 2001 [1991], p. 17.

29. A. M. Gollin, *No Longer an Island: Britain and the Wright Brothers, 1902–1909*, Stanford, Stanford University Press, 1989, p. 196.

30. Quoted in M. Brown, "100 Years of Maxim's Killing Machine," *New York Times*, 26.11.985.

31. See on these maneuvers H. Driver, *The Birth of Military Aviation: Britain, 1903–1904*, Woodbridge, Boydell Press, 1997, p. 254.

32. Quoted in Groehler, *Geschichte des Luftkrieges*, p. 15.

33. Ibid., pp. 13–14.

34. See, for the technical details, "Blériot XI," at http://en.wikipedia.org/wiki/Bl%C3%A9riot_XI.

35. See on this J. L. Schlim, *Ludwigs Traum vom Fliegen*, Oberhaching, Aviatic Verlag, 2000, p. 69.

36. See, for what follows, e.g. L. Kennett, *The First Air War, 1914–1918*, New York, Free Press, 1991, p. 114 ff.

37. F. Sykes, *From Many Angles: An Autobiography*, London, Harrap, 1942, p. 114.

38. D. Grinnell-Milne, *Wind in the Wires*, London, Mayflower, 1966, quoted in J. E. Lewis, *The Mammoth Book of Fighter Pilots*, New York, Carroll & Graf, 2004, p. 14.

39. Grinnell-Milne, *Wind in the Wires*, quoted in Lewis, *The Mammoth Book*, p. 33.

40. The most important one is G. Alegi, "Nei cieli della Libia—Colonialismo e i primi impieghi dell'aeroplano," in R. H. Rainero and P. Alberini, eds., *Le forze armate italiane e la nazione italiana (1861–1914)*, Rome, Commissione italiana di storia militare, 2003, pp. 247–63, kindly put at my disposal by the author.

41. See, for a general account, D. C. Herrmann, "The Paralysis of Italian Strategy in the Italian-Turkish War, 1911–1912," *English Historical Review*, 104, 411, 1989, pp. 332–56.

42. W. H. Beehler, *The Italian-Turkish War*, Annapolis, MD, The Advertiser Republican, 1913, p. 27. The entire book is available at http://www.archive.org/stream/historyofitalianoobeehiala and reference is made to that edition.

43. *Ufficio storico, I primi voli di guerra nel mondo: Libia, 1911*, Rome, Ministero Difesa-Aeronautica, 1952, p. 49.

44. F. Pedriali, "Aerei italiani in Libia (1911–1912)," *Storia Militare*, 170, November 2007, p. 40.

45. *Ufficio storico, I primi voli*, p. 53.

46. E. N. Bennett, *With the Turks in Tripoli*, London, Methuen, 1912, p. 25.

47. Ibid., pp. 142–43.

48. *Times*, 12.8.1912.

2. TEST PASSED

1. See A. M. Gollin, *The Impact of Airpower on the British People and Their Government, 1909–1914*, Stanford, Stanford University Press, 1989, pp. 198–99.

2. The most detailed account of these events is contained in B. W. Tuchman, *The Guns of August*, New York, 1962, pp. 447–59.

3. Quoted in Kennett, *The First Air War*, p. 31.

4. M. Hoffmann, *War Diaries and Other Papers*, London, Secker, 1929, pp. 265–68; see also Tuchman, *The Guns of August*, pp. 326–27.

5. See for a blow-by-blow account T. C. Treadwell and A. C. Wood, *The First Air War*, London, Brassey's, 1996, pp. 38–43.

6. See on this pp. 426 and 439 below.

7. See the table in G. W. Hooper, "The Progress of Aircraft," *Naval Review*, 8, 3, August 1920, p. 410.

8. Kennett, *The First Air War*, p. 179.

9. C. Lewis, "Sagittarius Rising," in Lewis, ed., *The Mammoth Book*, p. 84.

10. M. von Richthofen, *Der rote Kampfflieger: Die persoenlichen Aufzeichnungen des Roten Barons*, Hamburg, Gema, 1990 [1917], p. 143.

11. M. J. Grider, "Crashes and Cocktails," in Lewis, ed., *The Mammoth Book*, p. 189.

12. Richthofen, *Der rote Kampfflieger*, pp. 79–80.

13. R. Fonck, *Mes combats*, Paris, Flammarion, 1920, p. 133.

14. E. Boehme, *Briefe eines deutschen Kampffliegers an ein junges Maedchen*, J. Werner, ed., Leipzig, Koehler, 1930, pp. 66–67.

15. E. Udet, "Death Flies Faster," in Lewis, ed., *The Mammoth Book*, pp. 166–67.

16. Kennett, *The First Air War*, p. 179.

17. See on this E. von Hoeppner, *Germany's War in the Air*, Nashville, Battery Press, 1994 [1921], p. 61.

18. E. Angelucci, *The Rand McNally Encyclopedia of Military Aircraft, 1914 to the Present*, New York, Gallery Books, 1990, p. 29, plate 7.

19. According to G. Neumann, *Die deutschen Luftsreitkraefte im Weltkrieg*, Berlin, Mittler, 1921, pp. 268–69.

20. According to J. Morrow, *The Great War in the Air*, Washington, D.C., Smithsonian, 1993, p. 309.

21. Figures based on Angelucci, *The Rand McNally Encyclopedia of Military Aircraft*, p. 29, plate 7.

22. Bishop, "Blue Nose," in Lewis, ed., *The Mammoth Book*, p. 65.

23. 10.8.1917; memo quoted in B. Greenhouse, "Evolution of a Close Ground-Support Role for Aircraft in World War I," *Military Affairs*, 39, February 1975, p. 23.

24. W. S. Douglas, *Years of Combat*, London, Collins, 1963, p. 240.

25. See on this Greenhouse, "Evolution of Close Ground Support Role," pp. 26–27.

26. Lt. Col. Tubeuf, "Stellungskampf bei Montdidier" (1932), quoted in J. F. Williams, *Corporal Hitler and the Great War, 1914–1918*, London, Cass, 2005, p. 190.

27. Hoeppner, *Germany's War in the Air*, p. 149. See also J. Castan, *Der Rote Baron*, Stuttgart, Klett-Cotta, 2007, pp. 241–43.

28. E.g., C. Grahame-White, "Aircraft in the War," *Fortnightly Review*, 96, 1 October 1914, pp. 667–77.

29. Quoted in N. Jones, *The Origins of Strategic Bombing*, London, Kimber, 1973, p. 64.

30. According to H. Montgomery Hyde, *British Air Policy Between the Wars, 1918–1939*, London, Heinemann, 1976, p. 46.

31. See, for much of what follows, W. Cross, *Zeppelins of World War I*, Lincoln, NE, Authors' Guild, 2001, *passim*.

32. According to J. M. Hormannn, *Zeppeline, Marineluftschiffe und Marineflieger*, Hamburg, Mittler, n.d., p. 28.

33. P. Padfield, *Aim Straight: A Biography of Admiral Sir Percy Scott*, London, Hodder & Stoughton, 1966, p. 244.

34. Hoeppner, *Germany's War in the Air*, p. 160.

35. See on this B. D. Powers, *Strategy Without Slide Rule*, London, Croom Helm, 1978, pp. 37–42.

36. See J. Ferris, "Fighter Defense Before Fighter Command: The Rise of Strategic Air Defense in Great Britain, 1917–1934," *Journal of Military History*, 63, 1999, pp. 853–54.

37. See on this Anon, *Quest for Performance: The Evolution of Modern Aircraft*, chapter 2: Fighter Aircraft, at http://www.hq.nasa.gov/office/pao/History/SP-468/ch2-2.htm.

38. J. Ferris, "Airbandit: C3 I and Strategic Air Defense During the First Battle of Britain, 1915–1918," in M. Dockrill and D. French, eds., *Strategy and Intelligence: British Policy During the First World War*, London, Hambledon, 1996, pp. 52–60.

39. See the graphs in Groehler, *Geschichte des Luftkrieges 1910 bis 1980*, p. 92.

40. Jones, *The Origins of Strategic Bombing*, p. 209.

41. I. J. Muraccioli, *L'Aéronautique navale des origines à 1918*, Paris, Plon, 1985, p. 17.

42. Air Historical Branch, *The Royal Air Force in the Great War*, London, Imperial War Museum, 1936, p. 18.

43. Quoted in R. S. Churchill, *Winston Churchill*, Boston, Houghton Mifflin, 1966, vol. ii, p. 660.

44. See for them Wikipedia, en.wikipedia.org/wiki/HMS_Ark_Royal_(91) and en.wikipedia.org/wiki/HMS_Ark_Royal_(R07).

45. P. Beesley, *Room 40: British Naval Intelligence, 1914–1918*, London, Hamilton, 1982, pp. 151–68.

46. C. Barnett, *The Swordbearers*, London, Eyre & Spottiswoode, 1963, p. 139.

47. H. H. Frost, *The Battle of Jutland*, Annapolis, Naval Institute Press, 1964 [1936], p. 171.

48. R. Scheer, *Deutschlands Hochseeflotte in Weltkrieg*, Berlin, Scherl, 1927, p. 151.

49. Frost, *The Battle of Jutland*, p. 143.

50. Scheer, *Deutschlands Hochseeflotte*, p. 158.

51. Ibid., pp. 181–82.

52. Printed in J. F. C. Fuller, "The Development of the Submarine and Aerial Warfare in the Future," *Naval Review*, 10, 1, February 1922, p. 86.

53. P. G. Halpern, *A Naval History of World War I*, London, Routledge, 1994, p. 426.

54. C. Manfroni, *Storia della Marina Italiana durante la Guerra Mondiale, 1914–1918*, Bologna, Zanichelli, 1925, p. 14.

55. See, for a contemporary list, Anon, "Naval Air Requirements," *Naval Review*, 7, 3, August 1919, p. 305.

56. See J. S. Corbett and H. Newbolt, *History of the Great War: Naval Operations*, London, Longmans, 1920–31, vol. 5, p. 347.

57. *Diary*, Capt. Ph. W. Dumas, 31.1.1918, printed in P. G. Halpern, ed., *The Royal Navy in the Mediterranean 1915–1918*, London, Navy Records Society, 1987, p. 378.

58. Hooper, "The Progress of Aircraft," *Naval Review*, 8, 3, August 1920, p. 416.

59. S. Roskill, *Documents Relating to the Naval Air Service*, Cambridge, Navy Records Society, 1969, vol. 1, p. 530.

60. See on this W. Murray, *War in the Air, 1914–1945*, London, Cassell, 2002, p. 62.

61. These and subsequent figures from Angelucci, *The Rand McNally Encyclopedia of Military Aircraft*, p. 29, plate 7.

62. 1913 figure: P. Kennedy, *The Rise and Fall of the Great Powers*, New York, Vintage, 1987, p. 201, table 17.

63. Angelucci, *The Rand McNally Encyclopedia of Military Aircraft*, p. 29, plate 7.

64. Air Ministry, *Handbook of German Military and Naval Aviation (War), 1914–1918*, London, Imperial War Museum, 1995 [1918], p. 95.

65. According to Groehler, *Geschichte des Luftkrieges*, pp. 83, 85.

66. E. Ludendorff, *The General Staff and Its Problems*, New York, Dutton, n.d., vol. 2, p. 452; W. Robertson, *From Private to Field Marshal*, Boston, Houghton Mifflin, 1921, p. 349.

67. Ferris, "Fighter Defense," p. 854.

68. W. Raleigh and H. A. Jones, *The War in the Air*, Oxford, Clarendon, 1922, vol. iv, p. 154.

69. Kennedy, *The Rise and Fall of the Great Powers*, p. 200, table 15.

70. Groehler, *Geschichte des Luftkrieges*, p. 85.

71. See D. Divine, *The Broken Wing: A Study in the British Exercise of Air Power*, London, Hutchinson, 1966, p. 143.

72. Groehler, *Geschichte des Luftkrieges*, p. 85; Jones, *The Origins of Strategic Bombing*, pp. 197–98.

3. VISIONS, ORGANIZATIONS, AND MACHINES

1. See, on these aspects of war, M. van Creveld, *The Culture of War*, New York, Ballantine, 2008, *passim*.

2. R. Wohl, *The Spectacle of Flight: Aviation and the Western Imagination, 1920–1950*, New Haven, Yale University Press, 2005, p. 29. My discussion of the cultural aspects of airpower owes a lot to this splendid work.

3. See M. L. Siegel, *The Moral Disarmament of France: Education, Pacifism, and Patriotism*, Cambridge, Cambridge University Press, 2004.

4. Quoted by G. L. Mosse, *Masses and Man: Nationalist and Fascist Perceptions of Reality*, Detroit, Wayne State University Press, 1987, pp. 230–31.

5. G. Ciano, *Diary*, New York, Fertig, 1946, pp. 260–65, entries for 4.6–17.6.1940.

6. H. Bruce Franklin, *War Stars: The Superweapon and the American Imagination*, New York, Oxford University Press, 1988, pp. 19–53.

7. S. S. Montefiore, *Stalin: The Court of the Red Tsar*, New York, Vintage, 2005, p. 157.

8. Quotes from S. W. Palmer, *Dictatorship of the Air: Aviation Culture and the Fate of Modern Russia*, Cambridge, Cambridge University Press, 2006, p. 238.

9. Quoted in B. E. Bailes, "Technology and Legitimacy: Soviet Aviation and Stalinism in the 1930s," *Technology and Culture*, 17, 1, January 1976, p. 61.

10. L. E. O. Charleton, *The Menace of the Clouds*, London, Hodge, 1937, p. 13.

11. See, on him, M. Smith, *British Air Strategy Between the Wars*, Oxford, Clarendon, 1984, especially pp. 74–75, 101, 137–38.

12. Quoted in Montgomery Hyde, *British Air Policy*, p. 57.

13. Speech of April 13, 1923, quoted in P. S. Meilinger, "Trenchard, Slessor, and Royal Air Force Doctrine Before World War II," in P. S. Meilinger, ed., *The Paths of Heaven: The Evolution of Airpower Theory*, Maxwell AFB, AL, Air University Press, 1997, p. 75.

14. See, for the role he played on that occasion, S. Budiansky, *Air Power: The Men, Machines, and Ideas That Revolutionized War, from Kitty Hawk to Gulf War II*, New York, Viking, 2004, pp. 115–17.

15. W. Mitchell, *Winged Defense: The Development and Possibilities of Modern Air Power, Economic and Military*, Mineola, Dover, 1988 [1925], pp. 3–6.

16. Thanks to Dr. Grant Hammond for pointing this out to me.

17. See R. Weigley, *The American Way of War*, New York, Macmillan, 1973, p. 237.

18. See on airpower doctrine as developed at Maxwell C. H. Builder, *The Icarus Syndrome*, New Brunswick, NJ, Transaction, 1994, pp. 75–85.

19. See, for this and the following quotes, G. Douhet, *The Command of the Air*, Washington, D.C., Office of Air Force History, 1983 [1921], pp. 4, 5, 6, 9, 10, 11, 12, 17, 24, 35, 57, 58.

20. See on Alksnis, T. Alison and Von Hardesty, "Aviation and the Transformation of Combined Arms Warfare, 1941–45," in R. Higham and others, eds., *Russian Aviation and Air Power in the Twentieth Century*, London, Routledge, 1998, pp. 44, 92.

21. See M. Sterrett, *Soviet Air Theory, 1918–1945*, London, Routledge, 2007, pp. 54–55, 86–126.

22. See W. Wever, "Doctrine of the German Air Force," in E. Emme, ed., 1935, *The Impact of Air Power: National Security and World Politics*, Princeton, van Nostrand 1959, pp. 182–85; and W. Murray, *Strategy for Defeat: The Luftwaffe 1933–1945*, Washington, D.C., Government Printing Office, 1983, pp. 7–9.

23. See on this M. Cooper, *The German Army*, London, McDonald & Janes, 1978, pp. 131–38.

24. A. and J. Seaton, *The Soviet Army, 1918 to the Present*, New York, New American Library, 1986, p. 80; M. Hickey, *Out of the Sky: A History of Airborne Warfare*, New York, Scribner's, 1979, p. 14.

25. See on them J. Corum, *The Luftwaffe: Creating the Operational Air War, 1918–1940*, Lawrence, University Press of Kansas, 1997, pp. 235–38; also J. Lucas, *Storming Eagles: German Airborne Forces in World War II*, London, Cassell, 1988, pp. 14–24.

26. Anon, "The Fiends of the Air," *Naval Review*, 11, 1, February 1923, pp. 94–95.

27. Smith, *British Air Strategy Between the Wars*, p. 47. Some of what follows is based on this work.

28. *House of Commons Debates*, vol. 270, c. f632., available at airminded.org/2007/11/10the-bomber-will-always-get-through.

29. See on this T. Aldgate, "British Newsreels and the Spanish Civil War," *History*, 1958, 1973, pp. 60–65.

30. See, for the growth and impact of what can only be called the Guernica myth, G. van Hensbergen, *Guernica: The Biography of a Twentieth-Century Icon*, New York, Bloomsbury, 2004.

31. Protocol of meeting of September 24; quoted in U. Bialer, *The Shadow of the Bomber: Fear of Air Attack and British Politics, 1932–1939*, London, Royal Historical Society, 1980, p. 157.

32. *House of Commons Debates*, vol. 339, 6.10.1938.

33. See M. P. Sorlin, "Les Perspectives aéronautiques dans la crise tchecoslovaque de 1938," *Forces Aériennes Françaises*, November 1958, pp. 601–35.

34. First speech in the House of Lords, 9.4.1930, *Parliamentary Debates, House of Lords, Hansard*, vol. 77, cols. 22–62.

35. See B. R. Sullivan, "The Downfall of the Regia Aeronautica," in R. Higham and S. J. Harris, eds., *Why Air Forces Fail: The Anatomy of Defeat*, Lexington, University Press of Kentucky, 2006, pp. 136–37; A. C. Cain, "L'Armée de l'air, 1933–1940: Drifting

Towards Defeat," in ibid., p. 48; and Air Ministry, *The Rise and Fall of the German Air Force*, Richmond, National Archives, 1948, pp. 3–6.

36. See R. Bernotti, *Storia della Guerra nel Mediterraneo*, Rome, Bianco, 1960, pp. 60–64.

37. See on these problems S. Neitzel, "Kriegsmarine and Luftwaffe Cooperation in the War Against Britain, 1939–1945," *War in History*, 10, 4, November 2003, pp. 4–5.

38. E. Raeder, *Mein Leben, Tuebingen, Schlichtenmeyer*, 1957, pp. 91–105; K. Doenitz, *Memoirs: Ten Years and Twenty Days*, New York, Belmont, 1957, pp. 30–32; F. Ruge, *Der Seekrieg 1939–1945*, Stuttgart, Koehler, 1954, pp. 36–38, 89, 100, 124–27, 232.

39. Hormann, *Zeppeline*, p. 71.

40. See, on what Stalin allegedly did to Soviet airpower, V. Suvorov, *The Chief Culprit: Stalin's Grand Design to Start World War II*, Annapolis, MD, Naval Institute Press, 2008, pp. 32–40.

41. See R. J. Overy, *The Air War 1939–1945*, London, Europa, 1980, p. 71.

42. A. Boyd, *The Soviet Air Force Since 1918*, New York, Stein and Day, 1977, p. 141.

43. Quoted in M. van Creveld and others, *Air Power and Maneuver Warfare*, Maxwell AFB, AL, Air University Press, 1994, p. 48.

44. See, on the way it worked, ibid., pp. 21–101.

45. Overy, *The Air War*, p. 23, table 2.

46. Sullivan, "The Downfall of the Regia Aeronautica," pp. 159–60.

47. The figures and other details are from Schneider Trophy Races, www.schneider-cup.com.

48. Data from R. Higham, *Air Power: A Concise History*, London, MacDonald, 1972, pp. 78–80.

49. Groehler, *Geschichte des Luftkrieges*, p. 111.

50. C. Fayette Taylor, *Aircraft Propulsion: A Review of the Evolution of Aircraft Piston Engines*, Washington, D.C., Smithsonian, 1971, p. 88, table 1.

51. Most of these data were taken from Angelucci, *The Rand McNally Encyclopedia of Military Aircraft.*

52. See, for as detailed an account as anyone could wish for, A. L. Pardini, *The Legendary Secret Norden Bombsight*, Atglen, PA, Schiffer, 1999.

53. See, on this chef d'oeuvre of espionage, L. Farago, *The Game of the Foxes: The Untold Story of German Espionage in the United States and Great Britain During World War II*, New York, McKay, 1971, pp. 47–62.

54. D. R. Jones, "From Disaster to Recovery: Russia's Air Forces in Two World Wars," in R. Higham and S. J. Harris, eds., *Why Air Forces Fail: The Anatomy of Defeat*, Lexington, University Press of Kentucky, 2006, p. 277.

55. Douhet, *Command of the Air*, Part II (1926), p. 141; Part III (1928), pp. 218, 219–20, 286–87.

56. Quoted in Padfield, *Aim Straight*, pp. 283–84.

57. See on all this G. Till, "Airpower and the Battleship in the 1920s," in B. Ranft, ed., *Technical Change and British Naval Policy, 1860–1939*, London, Hodder & Stoughton, 1977, p. 112.

58. J. H. Belote and W. M. Belote, *Titans of the Sea: The Development and Operations of Japanese and American Carrier Task Forces During World War II*, New York, Harper & Row, 1975, pp. 18–19.

59. See A. J. Marder, *Old Friends, New Enemies: The Royal Navy and the Imperial Japanese Navy*, Oxford, Clarendon, 1981, pp. 22–75; E. S. Miller, *War Plan Orange: The U.S. Strategy to Defeat Japan, 1897–1945*, Annapolis, MD, Naval Institute Press, 1991; and D. C. Evans and M. A. Peattie, *Kaigun: Strategy, Tactics, and Technology in the Imperial Japanese Navy, 1887–1941*, Annapolis, MD, Naval Institute Press, pp. 447–86.

60. A. Stephens, "The True Believers: Air Power Between the Wars," in A. Stephens, ed., *The War in the Air, 1914–1945*, Fairbairn, ACT, Air Power Studies Center, 1994, pp. 47–80.

61. Marder, *Old Friends, New Enemies*, pp. 305–6.

62. J. Corbett, *Some Principles of Naval Strategy*, London, Longman, 1911, pp. 157–311.

63. See on this Smith, *British Air Strategy*, pp. 96–97.

64. See, for the order of battle, Royal Navy Home Page, at www.naval-history.net/WWW2CampaignRoyalNavy.htm.

65. N. Baynes, ed., *The Speeches of Adolf Hitler, 1922–1939*, London, Oxford University Press, 1942, vol. II, p. 1650.

66. J. H. Belote and W. H. Belote, *Titans of the Seas: The Development and Operations of Japanese and American Carrier Task Forces During World War II*, New York, Harper & Row, 1975, p. 30.

67. M. R. Peattie, *Sunburst: The Rise of Japanese Naval Air Power, 1909–1941*, Annapolis, MD, Naval Institute Press, 2001, p. 130; Marder, *Old Friends, New Enemies*, pp. 293, 305.

68. See A. D. Harvey, "Army, Air Force and Navy Air Force: Japanese Aviation and the Opening Phase of the War in the Far East," *War in History*, 6, 2, April 1999, p. 81.

69. Douhet, *Command of the Air*, Part III, pp. 184, 199.

70. M. H. C. Young, "Aircraft Attack or Gunfire Against Ships," *Journal of the Royal United Services Institute*, 1936, pp. 340–46.

4. FROM WAR TO WAR

1. M. van Creveld, *The Changing Face of War*, New York, Ballantine, 2007, pp. 108–17.

2. Groehler, *Geschichte des Luftkrieges*, p. 103.

3. Boyd, *The Soviet Air Force*, pp. 4–5.

4. Eighty-six percent were caused by accidents; Groehler, *Geschichte des Luftkrieges*, p. 107.

5. See, on the origins of German air support to Franco, Budiansky, *Air Power*, pp. 200–4.

6. Details of the orders of battle of the German and Italian contingents are from W. Beumelberg, *Kampf um Spanien*, Berlin, Stalling, 1939, p. 56, and J. Coverdale, *Italian Intervention in the Spanish Civil War*, Princeton, Princeton University Press, 1975, pp. 393–96, respectively.

7. Beumelberg, *Kampf um Spanien*, p. 61.

8. "Air Lessons from Current Wars," *US Air Services*, May 1938, p. 17.

9. Montgomery Hyde, *British Air Policy Between the Wars*, p. 486.

10. See below pp. 100–102.

11. See W. Cornelius and T. Short, *Ding Hao: America's Air War in China*, Gretna, Pelican, 1980, p. 84.

12. See, on all this, A. D. Harvey, "Army Air Forces and Navy Air Force: Japanese Aviation and the Opening Phase of the War in the Far East," *War in History*, 6, 2, April 1999, especially pp. 183–87.

13. See A. Sella, "Khalkin Gol: the Forgotten War," *Journal of Contemporary History*, 18, 4, October 1983, pp. 674–75.

14. According to Boyd, *The Soviet Air Force*, p. 86.

15. W. R. Trotter, *A Frozen Hell: The Russo-Finish Winter War of 1939–1940*, Chapel Hill, NC, Algonquin, 1991, pp. 188, 189.

16. R. Pennington, "From Chaos to the Eve of the Great Patriotic War, 1922–41," in Higham and others, eds., *Russian Aviation*, p. 51.

17. See, for some figures on the Soviet order of battle, C. van Dyke, *The Soviet Invasion of Finland, 1939–40*, London, Cass, 1997, p. 137.

18. Ibid., pp. 147, 201.

Part II: The Greatest War of All, 1939–1945

5. FROM TRIUMPH TO STALEMATE

1. See on this M. van Creveld, *Supplying War: Logistics from Wallenstein to Patton*, Cambridge, Cambridge University Press, 1978, pp. 111–12, 116.

2. Richthofen's VIII. Fliegerkorps alone had 11 of the latter; H. von Rohden, "Die Plannung und Vorbereitung des Kuftkrieges gegen Polen 1939," *Luftkrieg*, 5, 1946, appendix 6.

3. Generalstab der Luftwaffe, "Der Einsatz der operative Luftwaffe gegen Polen," 23.7.1944, German Military Records, National Archives, Washington, D.C., reel T-971/19/75.

4. Van Creveld and others, *Airpower and Maneuver Warfare*, pp. 36–38.

5. Air Ministry, *The Rise and Fall of the German Air Force*, p. 63.

6. Ibid., p. 64.

7. See the detailed analysis in K.-H. Friesner, *Blitzkrieg-Legende: Der Westfeldzug 1940*, Munich, Oldenbourg, 1995, pp. 52–58.

8. See P. Cot, "En 40 où étaient nos avions?" *Icare*, 59, spring–summer 1971, pp. 35–57.

9. See Angelucci, *Rand McNally Encyclopedia of Military Aircraft*, p. 189, plate 88.

10. Lucas, *Storming Eagles*, pp. 48–55.

11. H. R. Trevor Roper, ed., *Hitler's War Directives*, London, Pan, 1964, p. 65.

12. The most detailed discussion, which is by no means universally accepted, is Lt. Gen. Lackne, "Bericht Einsatz des KG 54. auf Rotterdam," Bundesarchiv/Militärarchiv, Freiburg i. B, 1954.

13. See, for a graphic description of the crossing of the Meuse, A. Horne, *To Lose a Battle: France, 1940*, London, Macmillan, 1969, p. 189.

14. See Friesner, *Blitzkrieg-Legende*, pp. 343–58.

15. See, on the nature of "trinitarian" war, M. van Creveld, *The Transformation of War*, New York, Free Press, 1991, pp. 35–42.

16. See, on the origins of radar, A. Beyerchen, "From Radio to Radar: Interwar Military Adaptation to Technological Change in Germany, the United Kingdom, and the United States," in W. Murray and A. R. Millett, eds., *Military Innovation in the Interwar Period*, Cambridge, Cambridge University Press, 1996, pp. 265–99.

17. See Montgomery Hyde, *British Air Policy Between the Wars*, pp. 405–25.

18. 15,000 versus 10,000: Overy, *The Air War*, p. 33, table 3, and p. 150, table 12.

19. Directive No. 17, 1.8.1940, in Trevor Roper, ed., *Hitler's War Directives*, p. 79.

20. See D. Zimmerman, *Britain's Shield: Radar and the Defeat of the Luftwaffe*, Phoenix Mill, Sutton, 2001, pp. 204–8.

21. The scene is described in W. Shirer, *Berlin Diary*, New York, Knopf, 1941, p. 369.

22. See on these dramatic days R. Overy, *The Battle of Britain*, London, Penguin, 2000, pp. 78–80; also the older account by B. Collier, *The Battle of Britain*, New York, Macmillan, 1962, pp. 123–39.

23. A. Milward, *War, Economy and Society, 1939–1945*, Berkeley, University of California Press, 1979, p. 91, table 1, and p. 167.

24. Montgomery Hyde, *British Air Policy Between the Wars*, pp. 449–52.

25. See on this entire subject R. A. Pape, *Bombing to Win: Air Power and Coercion in War*, Ithaca, NY, Cornell University Press, 1996.

26. See J. Terraine, *The Right of the Line: The Royal Air Force in the European War, 1939–1945*, London, Hodder & Stoughton, 1985, pp. 311, 315.

27. Ciano, *The Diaries*, p. 275 entry for 13.7.1940.

28. Sullivan, "Downfall of the Regia Aeronautica," p. 162.

29. Trevor Roper, ed., *Hitler's War Directives*, p. 90.

30. F. Halder, *Kriegstagebuch*, Stuttgart, Kohlhammer, 1962, vol. 2, p. 375.

31. The most detailed account remains A. Clark, *The Fall of Crete*, London, Cassell, 2004 [1962].

32. Wells, *The War in the Air*, p. 238.

33. See on this R. Hallion, *Strike from the Sky: The History of Battlefield Air Attack*, Washington, D.C., Smithsonian, 1989, p. 160.

34. See below, pp. 123.

35. See, for the order of battle, H. Boog and others, eds., *Das Deutsche Reich und der Zweite Weltkrieg*, Stuttgart, Deutsche Verlags-Anstalt, 1983, vol. 4, pp. 307–9.

36. Murray, *Strategy for Defeat*, p. 80, table 12.

37. Figures from H. Plocher, *The German Air Force Versus Russia, 1941*, USAF Historical Study No. 153, Maxwell AFB, AL, Air University Press, 1965, p. 41; also Jones, "From Disaster to Recovery," pp. 272–73.

38. See for all this van Creveld and others, *Airpower and Maneuver Warfare*, p. 71.

39. Murray, *Strategy for Defeat*, p. 84.

40. See H.-U. Rudel, *Stuka Pilot*, New York, Bantam, 1984 [1952].

41. See, on them, van Creveld, *Supplying War*, pp. 166–74.

42. See on this E. Ziemke, "Franz Halder at Orsha," *Military Affairs*, 39, 4, December 1975, pp. 173–76.

43. See, however, Boyd, *The Soviet Air Force*, pp. 108–39.

44. Suvorov, *The Chief Culprit, passim*.

45. J. T. Greenwood, "Soviet Frontal Aviation During the Great Patriotic War," in Highham and others, eds., *Russian Aviation*, p. 67.

46. Overy, *The Air War*, p. 150, table 12.

6. WAR OF FACTORIES, WAR OF WITS

1. Calculated on the basis of Kennedy, *The Rise and Fall of the Great Powers*, p. 201, table 17.

2. Overy, *The Air War*, p. 21, table 1.

3. Sullivan, "Downfall of the Regia Aeronautica," pp. 151, 152–53.

4. Overy, *The Air War*, p. 150, table 12.

5. Milward, *War, Economy and Society*, p. 188.

6. Quoted in G. M. Gilbert, *Nuremberg Diary*, New York, Da Capo, 1995 (1947), p. 115.

7. Overy, *The Air War*, p. 77, table 5.

8. See W. Maer, *Hitler*, London, Allen Lane, 1973, pp. 132–36; A. Speer, *Inside the Third Reich*, London, Macmillan, 1970, pp. 230–37; R. Overy, *War and Economy in the Third Reich*, Oxford, Oxford University Press, 1994, p. 72.

9. H. Herlin, *Der Teufels Flieger: Ernst Udet und die Geschichte seiner Zeit*, Munich, Heyne, 1974, p. 246.

10. E. L. Homze, *Arming the Luftwaffe: The Reich Air Ministry and the German Aircraft Industry, 1919–39*, Lincoln, University of Nebraska Press, 1976, pp. 262–67.

11. W. Johnen, *Duell unter den Sternen*, Friedberg, Pallas, 1956, pp. 126–28.

12. See M. J. Neufeld, *The Rocket and the Reich*, New York, Free Press, 1995, pp. 267–75.

13. Overy, *The Air War*, p. 171, table 16; Boyd, *Soviet Air Force*, p. 116.

14. Smith, *British Air Strategy*, pp. 253–67.

15. C. C. Lovett, "Russian and Soviet Naval Aviation, 1908–96," in Higham, ed., *Russian Aviation and Airpower*, especially pp. 116–19.

16. See Angelucci, *The Rand McNally Encyclopedia of Military Aircraft*, p. 271, plate 133.

17. Soviet aircraft production figures from J. T. Greenwood, "The Aviation Industry, 1917–97," in Higham and others, eds., *Russian Aviation and Air Power*, p. 146, table 6.4, and p. 147, table. 6.5.

18. A. N. Vozhnesenskii, *The Economy of the USSR in War and Reconstruction*, Washington, D.C., Public Affairs Press, 1948, p. 68.

19. G. Q. Flynn, *The Mess in Washington: Manpower Mobilization in World War II*, Westport, CT, Greenwood, 1979. The references are to pp. 39, 65, and 66–67.

20. Overy, *The Air War*, p. 153.

21. Flynn, *The Mess in Washington*, p. 40.

22. Overy, *The Air War*, pp. 169–71.

23. See W. K. Wark, "British Intelligence on the German Air Force and Aircraft Industry," *Historical Journal*, 25, 3, September 1983, pp. 627–48.

24. See B. H. Liddell Hart, *History of the Second World War*, London, Pan, 1971, pp. 474–75.

25. For an account of the origins of proximity fuses by one of its inventors, see R. B. Baldwin, *The Deadly Fuse*, London, Janes, 1980.

26. See on this D. Van der Vat, *The Atlantic Campaign*, New York, Harper & Row, 1988, pp. 329, 333, 349–50.

27. See J. McCarthy, "Did the Bomber Always Get Through?" in Stephens, ed., *The War in the Air*, pp. 81–94.

28. R. V. Jones, *The Wizard War: British Scientific Intelligence, 1939–1945*, New York, Coward, McCann & Geoghegan, 1978, pp. 92–105, 135–45.

29. See, for the development of the Leigh Light (after its inventor), B. Johnson, *The Secret War*, New York, Methuen, 1978, pp. 216–17.

30. Quoted in Terraine, *The Right of the Line*, p. 403.

31. See on this problem I. Gooderson, *Air Power at the Battlefront: Allied Close Air Support in Europe, 1943–1945*, London, Routledge, 1998, pp. 12–14.

32. Quoted in H. Probert, *Bomber Harris: His Life and Times*, London, Greenhill, 2001, pp. 291–92.

33. Speer, *Inside the Third Reich*, pp. 227–28.

7. CLOSING THE RING

1. Van der Vat, *The Atlantic Campaign*, p. 266.

2. J. Buckley, "Air Power and the Battle of the Atlantic, 1939–1945," *Journal of Contemporary History*, 28, 1, January 1993, p. 159.

3. Quoted in D. Richards and H. Saunders, *The Royal Air Force 1939–1945*, London, HMSO, 1974, vol. ii, p. 106.

4. See D. Wragg, *The Escort Carrier in World War II*, Barnsley, Pen & Sword, 2005, pp. 12–24.

5. See A. Price, *Instruments of Darkness*, London, Kimber, 1967, pp. 113–14.

6. See on this Budiansky, *Air Power*, pp. 137–39.

7. The best study of the raid on Schweinfurt, as well as its consequences, remains F. Goluecke, *Schweinfurt und der Strategische Luftkrieg 1943*, Paderborn, Schoeningen, 1980.

8. See S. L. McFarland, "The Evolution of the American Strategic Fighter in Europe," *Journal of Strategic Studies*, 10, 2, June 1998, pp. 189–208.

9. See, for the organization of the German defenses, D. Caldwell and R. Mueller, *The Luftwaffe over Germany: Defense of the Reich*, London, Greenhill, 2007, pp. 69–72, 103–7, 118–23.

10. Johnen, *Duell unter den Sternen*, *passim*; H. Knoke, *I Flew for the Fuehrer*, London, Cassell, 2003 [1953], *passim*; A. Galland, *The First and the Last*, New York, Holt, 1954, *passim*.

11. E.g., J. E. Johnson, *Wing Leader*, New York, Ballantine, 1956, *passim*.

12. Quoted in I. L. Hawkins, ed., *B-17s over Berlin*, Washington D.C., Brassey's, 1990, p. 72.

13. Overy, *The Air War*, p. 120, table 10.

14. Pape, *Bombing to Win*, pp. 258–60, 265, 268–80.

15. Figures from Probert, *Bomber Harris*, p. 335.

16. Anonyma, *Eine Frau in Berlin*, Frankfurt/Main, BtB, 2002, p. 236.

17. Knoke, *I Flew for the Fuehrer*, p. 105, entry for 25.7.1943.

18. Dieter Borkowski as quoted in C. Hartmann and J. Huerter, *Die Letzten 100 Tage des Zweiten Weltkrieges*, Munich, Droemer, 2005, entry for 1.2.1945.

19. See on this G. J. DeGroot, "Whose Finger on the Trigger? Mixed Anti-Aircraft Batteries and the Female Combat Taboo," *War in History*, 4, 4, November 1997, pp. 434–53.

20. E. B. Westermann, *Flak: German Anti-Aircraft Defense, 1914–1945*, Lawrence, University Press of Kansas, 2001, p. 177, table 6.2.

21. Ibid., p. 184, table 7.1.

22. W. F. Craven and J. L. Cate, *Official History of the Army Air Forces in World War II*, Washington, D.C., OAFCH, 1981, vol. ii, p. 51; see also J. Parton, *Air Force Spoken Here: The Life of General Eaker*, Bethesda, MD, Adler & Adler, 1986, p. 324.

23. See, e.g., R. A. Pape, "The True Worth of Air Power," *Foreign Affairs*, March/April 2004, pp. 116–30.

24. Ibid.

25. R. von Pohl, "Antiair Protection of German Supply Routes in Italy," *Military Affairs*, 17, 3, autumn 1953, p. 133.

26. E. Mark, "A New Look at Operation STRANGLE," *Military Affairs*, 52, 4, October 1988, pp. 176–84. See also the older account by F. M. Sallagar, *Operation "STRANGLE,"* Santa Monica, CA, RAND, 1972.

27. F. Morgan, *Overture to Overlord*, London, Hodder & Stoughton, 1950, p. 132.

28. S. E. Ambrose, *Eisenhower: Soldier and President*, New York, Simon & Schuster, 1990, p. 127.

29. See Budiansky, *Air Power*, pp. 301–2.

30. Quoted in M. Shulman, *Defeat in the West*, London, Secker & Warburg, 1947, p. 148.

31. See on this entire question Gooderson, *Air Power at the Battlefront*, especially pp. 199–247.

32. T. A. Hughes, *Overlord: General Pete Quesada and the Triumph of Tactical Air Power in World War II*, New York, Free Press, 1991, p. 130.

33. Gooderson, *Air Power at the Battlefront*, p. 191.

34. Air Ministry, *The Rise and Fall of the German Air Force*, p. 217.

35. Groehler, *Geschichte der Luftkrieg*, p. 353.

36. Greenwood, "Soviet Frontal Aviation," pp. 76–77.

37. Ibid., p. 85.

38. Montefiore, *Stalin*, 536.

39. Greenwood, "Soviet Frontal Aviation," p. 86.

40. Figures from J. Warren, *Airborne Operations in World War II, European Theater*, Maxwell AFB, AL, Air University Press, 1956, pp. 226–27.

8. FROM CARRIER WAR TO GRANDE FINALE

1. See, for the creation of the unit, D. Ford, *Flying Tigers: Claire Chennault and the American Volunteer Group*, Washington, D.C., Smithsonian, 1991, pp. 28–70.

2. This story is taken from M. Dayan, *Vietnam Diary*, Tel Aviv, Dvir, 1977 [Hebrew], p. 20. Dayan met Montgomery in 1966.

3. See, on Wingate and his Chindits, S. Bidwell, *The Chindit War: The Campaigns in Burma*, 1944, London, Hodder & Stoughton, 1979.

4. See J. W. Dower, *War Without Mercy: Race and Power in the Pacific War*, New York, Pantheon, 1986, pp. 102–3.

5. G. W. Prange and others, *At Dawn We Slept*, New York, McGraw-Hill, 1981, p. 500.

6. Quoted in D. M. Goldstein and K. V. Dillon, *The Pearl Harbor Papers: Inside the Japanese Plans*, New York, Brassey's, 1993, p. 114.

7. See "Midway Order of Battle" at en.wikipedia.org/wiki/Midway_order_of_battle.

8. Quoted in G. Astor, *Wings of Gold: The U.S. Naval Air Campaign in World War II*, New York, Presidio, 2005, p. 300.

9. According to D. Gillison, *The Royal Australian Air Force in World War II*, Canberra, ACT, 1962, vol. 1, pp. 523–34.

10. See G. Bennett, *Naval Battles of World War Two*, Barnsley, Pen & Sword, 2003, pp. 221–45.

11. Akira Hara, "Japan: Guns Before Rice," in M. Harrison, ed., *The Economics of World War II*, Cambridge, Cambridge University Press, 1998, p. 262; H. van der Wee, *Prosperity and Upheaval: The World Economy, 1945–1980*, Harmondsworth, Penguin, 1986, p. 30.

12. One detailed list of ships said to have been sunk by kamikaze attacks is available at wgordon.web.wesleyan.edu/kamikaze/background/ships-sunk.htm.

13. Probably the best work on the kamikaze operations remains D. Warner and Sadao Seno, *The Sacred Warriors: Japan's Suicide Legions*, New York, van Nostrand, 1982.

14. See on this story J. McPhee, "Balloons of War," *New Yorker*, 29.1.1996, pp. 52–60.

15. See G. P. Gentile, *How Effective Is Strategic Bombing?* New York, New York University Press, 2001, pp. 80, 82.

16. The most recent detailed account of the raid is C. K. S. Chun, *The Doolittle Raid 1942: America's First Strike Back at Japan*, Oxford, Osprey, 2006; also J. Doolittle, *I Could Never Be So Lucky Again*, New York, Bantam, 1991.

17. See, on its development, C. Berger, *B-29: The Superfortress*, New York, Bantam, 1970.

18. According to L. Kennett, *A History of Strategic Bombing*, New York, Scribner, 1982, p. 369.

19. K. P. Werrell, *Blankets of Fire*, Washington, D.C., Smithsonian, 1996, p. 140.

20. See, for a short account of LeMay's reasoning, B. Tillman, *LeMay*, New York, Palgrave Macmillan, 2007, pp. 58–60.

21. See C. C. Crane, *Bombs, Cities and Civilians: American Airpower Strategy During World War II*, Lawrence, University Press of Kansas, 1993, pp. 125, 129, 131.

22. W. W. Sinclair, *The Big Brothers: The Story of the B-29*, San Francisco, Naylor, 1972, p. 89.

23. Tillman, *LeMay*, p. 70.

24. According to S. E. Ambrose, *The Victors: Eisenhower and His Boys: The Men of World War II*, New York, Simon & Schuster, 1999, p. 40.

25. P. Wyden, *Day One: Before Hiroshima and After*, New York, Simon & Schuster, 1984, p. 324.

26. See, for a brief examination of these questions, Pape, *Bombing to Win*, pp. 100, 104, 114, 126–135.

Part III: The War That Never Was, 1945–1991

1. *Proverbs*, 27.24.

9. THE DOMINANT FACTOR

1. M. J. Armitage and R. A. Mason, *Airpower in the Nuclear Age*, Urbana, University of Illinois Press, 1983, pp. 1–19.

2. Quoted in Gentile, *How Effective Is Strategic Bombing?*, p. 112.

3. See on this fascinating story J. G. Barlow, *Revolt of the Admirals*, Washington, D.C., Brassey's, 1998.

4. See on their capture D. Cadbury, *Space Race: The Battle to Rule the Heavens*, New York, HarperCollins, 2006, pp. 37–62.

5. See W. von Braun, "The Redstone, Jupiter and Juno," *Technology and Culture*, autumn 1963, pp. 452–86.

6. B. Brodie, ed., *The Absolute Weapon*, Princeton, Princeton University Press, 1946, pp. 24, 28, 46, 52, 63. I wish to take this opportunity to remember my late friend and colleague, Prof. Michael Handel, who reprinted this essay in one of his textbooks from which I have taken it.

7. The definition is based on Clausewitz, *On War*, book I.

8. See T. V. Paul, *The Absolute Weapon Revisited: Nuclear Weapons and the Emerging International Order*, Ann Arbor, University of Michigan Press, 2000; also S. D. Sagan and K. N. Waltz, *The Spread of Nuclear Weapons: A Debate*, New York, Norton, 1995.

9. T. S. Schelling, *Arms and Influence*, New Haven, Yale University Press, 1966, chapter 1; see also R. Jervis, *The Meaning of the Nuclear Revolution*, Ithaca, NY, Cornell University Press, 1989, pp. 6–8.

10. Quoted in E. Goldman, *The Crucial Debate—and After: America, 1845–1960*, New York, Vintage, 1960, p. 100.

11. McG. Bundy, *Danger and Survival: The Political History of the Nuclear Weapon*, New York, Random House, 1988, p. 616.

12. See, for the questions raised during the 1950s, A. Wohlstetter, "The Delicate Balance of Terror," *Foreign Affairs*, 37, 2, January 1959, pp. 211–34; for the 1960s, Freedman, *The Evolution of Nuclear Doctrine*, pp. 31–59; for more recent ones, K. A. Lieber and D. G. Press, "The End of MAD? The Nuclear Dimension of U.S. Primacy," *Foreign Policy*, 30, 4, spring 2006, pp. 7–44.

13. M. Trachtenberg, "A 'Wasting Asset': American Strategy and the Shifting Nuclear Balance, 1949–1954," *International Security*, 3, 3, winter 1988/89, especially pp. 4–7.

14. T. B. Allen, *War Games*, New York, McGraw-Hill, 1987, pp. 99–101, 177–78.

15. 1970 article in *Kommunist*, quoted in D. R. Herspring, *The Soviet High Command, 1967–1989*, Princeton, Princeton University Press, 1990, p. 62.

16. See on this R. L. Garthoff, *Soviet Strategy in the Nuclear Age*, New York, Praeger, 1962, pp. 184–85, and, in much greater detail, L. Goure and others, *The Role of Nuclear Forces in Current Soviet Strategy*, Miami, University of Miami Press, 1974, pp. 25–37.

17. See on this possibility D. K. Simes, "The Death of Détente?," *International Security*, 5, 1, summer 1980, pp. 3–25.

18. See, for Britain, France, and China, J. Hopkins and Weixing Hu, eds., *From the Second Tier: The Nuclear Weapons Policies of France, Britain and China*, La Jolla, University of California Press, 1994; for India, S. J. Ismat, "Strategy for Total Defence: A Conceptual Nuclear Doctrine," *Defence Journal*, 2000, at http://www.defencejournal.com/2000/mar/doctrine.htm; for Pakistan, P. Cotta-Ramusino and M. Martellini, "Nuclear Safety, Nuclear Stability and Nuclear Strategy in Pakistan," 2002, at http://www.pugwash.org/september11/pakistan-nuclear.htm.

19. R. Rajagopalan, "The Dangerous Dilution of Nuclear Deterrence," in J. Singh, ed., *Asia's New Dawn: The Challenges to Peace and Security*, New Delhi, ICW, 2000, pp. 181–93.

20. J. L. Gaddis and others, eds., *Cold War Statesmen Confront the Bomb: Nuclear Diplomacy Since 1945*, Oxford, Oxford University Press, 1999, pp. 171–93 (Churchill), 39–61 (Stalin), and 194–215 (Mao).

21. See R. M. Basrur, *South Asia's Cold War: Nuclear Weapons and Conflict in Comparative Perspective*, London, Routledge, 2008, pp. 55–57.

22. See A. O. Ghebhardt and others, "The Soviet Air Force High Command," *Air University Review*, 34, 1, May–June 1973, pp. 75–83.

23. P. Podvig, ed., *Russian Strategic Nuclear Forces*, Cambridge, MA, MIT Press, 2001, p. 352.

24. Memo of 21.6.1947, quoted in M. Trachtenberg, "'A Wasting Asset': American Strategy and the Shifting Nuclear Balance, 1949–1954," *International Security*, 3, 3, winter 1988/89, p. 5.

25. Ambrose, *Eisenhower: Soldier and President*, p. 224.

26. See, for what follows, P. D. Feaver, *Guarding the Guardians: Civilian Control of Nuclear Weapons in the United States*, Ithaca, NY, Cornell University Press, 1992, pp. 89–111.

27. See on this episode L. Groves, *Now It Can Be Told: The Story of the Manhattan Project*, New York, Harper & Brothers, 1962, pp. 367–72.

28. *The Journals of David E. Lilienthal*, H. S. Commager, ed., New York, Harper & Row, 1964, vol. 2, p. 374.

29. Quoted in D. G. McCullough, *Truman*, New York, Simon & Schuster, 1992, pp. 649–50.

30. *The Journals of David E. Lilienthal*, vol. 2, p. 391.

31. Truman Memo, Department of State, *Foreign Relations of the United States*, Washington, D.C., GPO, 1983, vol. 1, p. 33.

32. See on this Freedman, *The Evolution of Nuclear Strategy*, pp. 123–26.

33. *The Journals of David E. Lilienthal*, vol. 2, pp. 616–17.

34. Lecture of 1.6.1950, letter of 30.6.1950, both quoted in P. J. Roman, "Curtis LeMay and the Origins of NATO Atomic Targeting," *Journal of Strategic Studies*, 16, 1, March 1993, pp. 49, 53.

35. R. H. Krohn and J. P. Hanrahan, "U.S. Strategic Air Power, 1948–1967," *International Security*, 1, 4, spring 1988, p. 83.

36. R. G. Hewlett and O. E. Anderson, *A History of the United States Atomic Energy Commission*, University Park, Pennsylvania State University Press, 1962, vol. 1, pp. 137–38, 150–52, 159–61, 181–83; R. M. Anders, ed., *Forging the Atomic Shield: Excerpts from the Office Diary of Gordon E. Dean*, Chapel Hill, University of North Carolina Press, 1987, p. 23.

37. See on this episode Hewlett and Anderson, *A History of the United States Atomic Energy Commission*, p. 137.

38. See P. Stein and P. Feaver, *Assuring Control of Nuclear Weapons: The Evolution of Permissive Action Links*, Boston, Harvard Center for Science and International Affairs, 1987, p. 42, table 1.

39. The critical document, NSC 162-2 of October 30, 1953, is printed in M. Gravel, ed., *The Pentagon Papers*, Boston, Beacon, 1971, vol. 1, pp. 412–29.

40. Feaver, *Guarding the Guardians*, pp. 155, 160, 164.

41. According to N. Friedman, *The Fifty-Year War: Conflict and Strategy in the Cold War*, Annapolis, MD, *Naval Institute Press*, 2000, p. 148.

42. See Ambrose, *Eisenhower*, p. 403.

43. Interview with General Goodpaster, 17.8.1989, in Feaver, *Guarding the Guardians*, p. 171.

44. *Washington Post*, 8.9.1964.

45. See P. Stein and P. Feaver, *Assuring Control of Nuclear Weapons: The Evolution of Permissive Action Links*, Boston, Harvard Center for Science and International Affairs, 1987, pp. 18, 38.

46. Ibid., p. 47.

47. According to A. Cockburn, *The Threat: Inside the Soviet Military Machine*, New York, Random House, 1983, p. 189; see also Podvig, ed., *Russian Strategic Nuclear Forces*, pp. 38–43.

48. See J. D. Steinbrunner, "Nuclear Decapitation," *Foreign Policy*, winter 1981–82, p. 19.

49. See A. F. Woolf, "Nuclear Weapons in the Former Soviet Union: Location, Command, and Control," Congressional Report Service Issue Brief No. 91144,

27.11.1996, pp. 3–12. The report is available at http://www.fas.org/spp/starwars/crs/91-144.htm.

50. S. Gregory, *The Command and Control of British Nuclear Weapons*, Bradford, University of Bradford, 1986, p. 24; D. Caldwell, "Permissive Action Links: A Description and Proposal," *Survival*, 29, 3, May–June 1987, p. 227.

51. See, for India, G. Kanwal, "Command and Control of Nuclear Weapons in India," *Strategic Analysis*, 25, 10, January 2000, pp. 1707–31; for Pakistan, Z. Cheena, "Pakistan's Nuclear Use Doctrine and Command and Control," in P. Lavoy and others, *Planning the Unthinkable: How New Powers Will Use Nuclear, Biological and Chemical Weapons*, Ithaca, NY, Cornell University Press, 2000, p. 130.

52. Basrur, *South Asia's Cold War*, p. 103.

53. See on these difficulties B. G. Blair, *Strategic Command and Control: Redefining the Nuclear Threat*, Washington, D.C., Brookings, 1985.

54. See, for this entire subject, James Martin Center for Nonproliferation Studies, "Israel," April 2006, at http://cns.miis.edu/wmdme/israel.htm. Some sources put the number of Israeli warheads at 400, but others consider this unlikely.

55. Podvig, ed., *Russian Strategic Nuclear Forces*, p. 352.

56. According to S. McLean, ed., *How Nuclear Weapons Decisions Are Made*, London, Macmillan, 1986, pp. 13, 16.

10. THE JET AND THE HELICOPTER

1. Data from "B-36," en.wikipedia.org/wiki.Convair_B-36.

2. See M. S. Knaack, *Encyclopedia of the U.S. Air Force, Aircraft and Missiles*, Washington, D.C., Office of Air Power History, 1988, vol. 1, p. 39.

3. Air Force Secretary Donald Charles, 1956, quoted in Tillman, *LeMay*, p. 117. For a good description of the aircraft see "B-52," en.wikipedia.org./wiki/B-52_Stratofortress.

4. This was the Joint Chiefs of Staff's estimate for 1961; *International Herald Tribune*, 9.5.1978.

5. D. Hopper, "Upgraded B-52 Still on Cutting Edge," 31.3.2008, at www.af.mil/newsstory.asp?id=123092368.

6. "B-58," en.wikipedia.org/wiki/B-58_Hustler.

7. "B-70 Valkyrie Cancellation," no date, at GlobalSecurity.com, http://www.globalsecurity.org/wmd/systems/b-70-can.htm.

8. Tillman, *LeMay*, p. 190.

9. "Tu-95," en.wikipedia.org/wiki.Tu-95.

10. "Tu-160," en.wikipedia.org.wiki.Tu-160.

11. Figures from T. Gervasi, *The Myth of Soviet Military Supremacy*, New York, Harper & Row, 1986, p. 412.

12. See, for this aircraft, "Mirage IV," en.wikipedia.org/wiki/Dassault_Mirage_IV.

13. See, for a description of the experience, J. Broughton, *Rupert Red Two: A Fighter Pilot's Life*, New York, Zenith, 2008, p. 189.

14. R. D. Goartz, "An Analysis of Air-to-Air Missile Capability in Southeast Asia," Montgomery, AL, Maxwell AFB, June 1968, pp. 1–2.

15. See G. T. Hammond, *The Mind of War: John Boyd and American Security*, Washington, D.C., Smithsonian, 2001, pp. 55–61.

16. E.g., P. Meilinger, *Airwar: Essays on Its Theory and Practice*, London, Cass, 2003, p. 170.

17. D. Gates, *Sky Wars: A History of Military Aerospace Power*, London, Reaktion, 2003, p. 22.

18. See, for an extended treatment of this subject, van Creveld, *The Culture of War*, pp. 228–31.

19. F. Rolfsen, "Report: F-22 Pilot Affected by Maneuvers," *Air Force Times*, 4.8.2009.

20. http://www.f22-raptor.com/technology/stealth.html.

21. See, e.g., J. P. Stevenson, "F-22 Fighter Performance," June 2006, at http://www.cdi.org/pdfs/Stevenson%20F-22%20Brief.pdf.

22. W. Matthews, "Senate Blocks Funds for More F-22s, but Battle Not Over," *Defense News*, 21.7.2009.

23. Figures from *Defense Procurement Daily*, 2.8.2009, at defenseindustrydaily.com/f22-raptor-procurement-events-updated-02908, and from Secretary of Defense Robert Gates's speech to the Economic Club of Chicago, 16.7.2009, at http://www.defenselink.mil/speeches/speech.aspx?speechid=1369.

24. "F-35 Program Review May Raise Costs," Military.com, 15.8.2009, at http://www.military.com/news/article/f35-program-review-may-raise-costs.html; C. Drew, "Gates Tries to Get F-35 Program Back on Course," *New York Times*, 3.2.2010, at http://finance.yahoo.com/banking-budgeting/article/108749/gates-tries-to-get-f35-program-back-on-course.

25. See B. J. Bernstein, "Eclipsed by Hiroshima and Nagasaki: Early Thinking About Tactical Nuclear Weapons," *International Security*, 15, 4, spring 1991, pp. 149–73.

26. S. Sandler, *The Korean War: No Victors, No Vanquished*, Lexington, University Press of Kentucky, 1999, p. 185.

27. See J. Lanxade, "L'Opération Turquoise," *Défense nationale*, 2.2. 1995, pp. 9–11.

28. D. Goure and C. M. Szara, eds., *Air and Space Power in the New Millennium*, Washington, D.C., CSIS, 1997.

29. H. Reitsch, *Fliegen—Mein Leben*, Munich, Lehmans, 1972, pp. 221–23.

30. See, e.g., H. G. Spurgeon and S. C. Crist, "Armor in the Twenty-First Century," *Armor*, January–February 1994, pp. 12–14.

31. R. Simpkin, *Race to the Swift: Thoughts on Twenty-First Century Warfare*, London, Brassey's, 1985, pp. 3–18, 117–32.

32. See S. Trimble, "General: Deep Strike, Urban Tactics for Helicopters May Need Review," *Aviation Week*, 30.7.2003, at http://www.aviationweek.com/aw/generic/story_generic.jsp?channel=aerospacedaily&id=news/urb07303.xml.

33. According to M. Armitage, *Unmanned Aircraft*, London, Brassey's, 1988, p. 100.

34. "B-2 Spirit," Wikipedia, at http://en.wikipedia.org/wiki/B-2_Spirit.

35. T. Capaccio, "The B-2's Stealthy Skins Need Tender, Lengthy Care," *Defense Week*, May 27, 1997, p. 1.

36. According to the *Washington Post*, 10.7.2009.

37. P. Sprey and J. Stevenson, "Is the F-22 Worth the Money?," Center for Defense Information, 2006, slide no. 50, http://www.cdi.org/program/document.cfm?DocumentID=3389&from_page.

11. MISSILES, SATELLITES, AND DRONES

1. N. Friedman, *The Fifty-Year War,* p. xvii.

2. M. J. Neufeld, *The Rocket and the Reich: Peenemünde and the Coming of the Ballistic Missile Era,* New York, Free Press, 1993, pp. 172–75.

3. H. Trenchard, "Air Power and National Security," in Emme, ed., *The Impact of Air Power,* p. 194.

4. Gervasi, *The Myth of Soviet Military Supremacy,* p. 129.

5. D. Ball, *Politics and Force Levels,* Berkeley, University of California Press, 1980, p. 130, table 12.

6. A very good overview of these missiles is provided in "R-36" at http://en.wikipedia.org/wiki/SS-18 and in "LGM-118 Peacemaker" at http://en.wikipedia.org/wiki/MX_missile.

7. See, most recently, U.S. Army Center of Military History, *History of Strategic Air and Missile Defense,* Washington, D.C., GPO, 2009.

8. For the most recent developments concerning the U.S., see Missile Defense Agency Press Release, "Successful Missile Defense Intercept Test Takes Place off Hawaii," 25.6.2008, at http://www.mda.mil/mdalink/pdf/08news0071.pdf; for Russia, "Russia Tests Anti-Ballistic Missile," PressTV, 31.10.2007, at http://www.presstv.ir/detail.aspx?id=29246§ionid=351020602; for Israel, "Israel to Test Anti-Ballistic Missile in US Waters," *Haaretz,* 18.8.2009, at http://www.haaretz.com/hasen/pages/ShArt.jhtml?itemNo=1100297&contrassID=2&subContrassID=1; for India, S. Dikshit, "India Developing New Missile Towards Destroying New Missiles," *The Hindu,* 3.12.2006, http://www.hindu.com/2006/12/03/stories/2006120312940100.htm; for Japan, "Japan Plans Tokyo Missile Shield," BBC News, 15.1.2008; http://news.bbc.co.uk/2/hi/asia-pacific/7188698.stm.

9. "General Says Russia Will Counter U.S. Missile Defense Plans," *USA Today,* 27.5.2008.

10. "Arrow," Y-Encyclopedia, 31.8.2009, at http://www.ynet.co.il/yaan/0.7340,L-168285-MTY4Mjg1XzlxMjg3MzQ2N18xNDg2.

11. CNN, "Radar Problems Foil Missile Test," 1.2.2010, at http://www.cnn.com/2010/US/02/01/missile.defense.test/index.html.

12. M. Burrows, "Ballistic Missile Defense: The Illusion of Security," *Foreign Affairs,* 62, 4, spring 1984, pp. 843–56.

13. T. Maliq, "Air Force: X-37 B Space Plane Not a Weapon," Space.com, 23.4.2010, at http://www.space.com/businesstechnology/x-37b-spacecraft-space-weapons-100423.html; for the debate, M. Moore, *Twilight War: The Folly of U.S. Space Dominance,* Oakland, CA, Independent Institute, 2008.

14. Y. Rabin, *Diary,* Tel Aviv, Maariv, 1979 [Hebrew], vol. 2, pp. 497–98.

15. See, for the meaning of the concept, Lambeth, *Mastering the Ultimate High Ground,* pp. 101–3.

16. *The Report of the Commission to Assess United States National Security Space Management and Organization,* 2001, p. 25. It is available at http://www.fas.org/spp/military/commission/report/htm.

17. See, on this entire subject, Moore, *Twilight War,* pp. 96–101.

18. See, for the U.S., Vought Corporation, ASAT, at http://www.voughtaircraft.com/heritage/products/html/asat.html, and, for China, D. Engber, "How to Blow Up a Satellite," *Slate,* 15.2.2008, at http://www.slate.com/id/2184555/.

19. RussianSpaceWeb, 24.2.2008, at http://www.russianspaceweb.com/is.html.

20. See J. Farquharson, "Interwar British Experiments with Pilotless Aircraft," *War in History,* 9, 2, April 2002, pp. 197–218.

21. See Reitsch, *Fliegen—Mein Leben,* pp. 306–23.

22. "V-1 Flying Bomb," at http://en.wikipedia.org/wiki/V-1_flying_bomb.

23. "P-5 Pyatyorka," at http://en.wikipedia.org/wiki/SS-N-3.

24. See R. K. Betts, "Introduction," in R. K. Betts, ed., *Cruise Missiles: Technology, Strategy, Politics,* Washington, D.C., Brookings, 1981, pp. 1–30, and J. C. Toomey, "Technical Characteristics," in Betts, ed., *Cruise Missiles,* pp. 31–51.

25. U.S. Navy, "Weapons—Airborne Weapons—AGM-84E SLAM/SLAM-ER/SLAM-ER+Standoff Land-Attack Missile," at http://www.chinfo.navy.mil/navpalib/policy/vision/vis98/vis-p09.html.

26. See www.scifitoday.com/story/2003/1/4/7149/84188.

27. D. Ivri, "How We Destroyed the SAM Array in SHELEG War," in Maarachot, ed., *Forty Years Since the Six Days' War and Fifteen Years Since the Lebanon War,* Tel Aviv, Maarachot, 2004 [Hebrew], pp. 23–29; M. Tlas, "The Israeli Invasion of Lebanon," Damascus, Tishrin, 1983 [Arabic], pp. 189–90.

28. See, for some details, "R-Q 4 Global Hawk," at http://en.wikipedia.org/wiki/Global_Hawk.

29. R. Merle, "Price of Global Hawk Surveillance Program Rises," *Washington Post,* 7.12.2004, page A-17.

30. "Attack of the Drones," *Economist,* 5.9.2009, Technology Section, p. 22.

31. See, e.g., O. Franchi, "Iranian-Made Ababil-T UAV Shot Down by Israeli Fighter in Lebanon Crisis," FlightGlobl, 15.8.2006, at http://www.flightglobal.com/articles/2006/08/15/208400/iranian-made-ababil-t-hezbollah-uav-shot-down-by-israeli-fighter-in-lebanon.html.

32. "UAV Operators Headed for Extinction," *Strategy Page,* 9.2.2006, at http://www.strategypage.com/htmw/htairfo/articles/20061209.aspx. Something seems to have gone wrong with the title of this article, which says just the opposite of what the text does.

33. See on this "Women's Work," *Strategy Page,* at http://www.strategypage.com/htmw/htlead/articles/20090104.aspx (referring to Israeli women).

34. "General Arnold's Sad Legacy," *Strategy Page,* 25.5.2009, at http://www.strategypage.com/htmw/htlead/articles/20090525.aspx.

35. Report for Congress, "Unmanned Aerial Vehicles: Background and Issues," 25.4.2003, at http://74.6.239.67/search/cache?ei=UTF-8&p=uav+cost&fr=yfp-t-203

&u=www.fas.org/irp/crs/RL31872.pdf&w=uav+%22unmanned+aerial+vehicles%22+cost+costing+costs&d=KgrmmBlMTTIR&icp=1&.intl=us.

36. A. Mulrine, "UAV Pilots," AirForce-Magazine.com, January 2009, at http://www.airforce-magazine.com/MagazineArchive/Pages/2009/January%202009/0109UAV.aspx.

37. Basrur, *South Asia's Cold War*, p. 62.

12. PAPER WARS

1. See on this van Creveld, *The Changing Face of War*, pp. 205–12.

2. J. P. McConnell, "Air Superiority," Office of the Chief of Staff, USAF, 3.5.1964, quoted in J. P. Stevenson, *The Pentagon Paradox: The Development of the F-18 Hornet*, Annapolis, MD, Naval Institute Press, 1993, pp. 26–27.

3. AAP-6(V), NATO Glossary of Terms and Definitions.

4. G. B. McClellan, *Regulations and Instructions for the Field Service of the U.S. Cavalry in Time of War*, Philadelphia, Lippincott, 1862, pp. 126, 128.

5. See, for the evolution of HAPDB, P. R. Faber, "Interwar U.S. Army Aviation and the Air Corps Tactical School: Incubators of American Airpower," in Meilinger, ed., *The Paths of Heaven*, pp. 211–21, as well as P. McCoy Smith, *The Air Force Plans for Peace, 1943–1945*, Baltimore, Johns Hopkins University Press, 1970, pp. 22, 23.

6. C. F. Ziemke quoted in Builder, *The Icarus Syndrome*, p. 186

7. Quoted in J. T. Greenwood, "The Atomic Bomb—Early Air Force Thinking and the Strategic Air Force, August 1945–March 1946," *Aerospace Historian*, September 1987, p. 161.

8. K. P. Mueller, "Strategic Airpower and Nuclear Strategy," in Meilinger, ed., *The Paths of Heaven*, p. 381.

9. Wm. R. Johnston, "Multimegaton Weapons: The Largest Nuclear Weapons," 6.4.2009, at http://www.johnstonsarchive.net/nuclear/multimeg.html.

10. See, for the details, M. G. McKinzie and others, *The U.S. Nuclear War Plan: A Time for Change*, New York, National Resources Defense Council, 2001, pp. 5–6, at http://holtz.org/Library/Social%20Science/Political%20Science/US%20Nuclear%20War%20Plan%20-%20NRDC%202001.pdf.

11. See D. Ford, *The Button: The Pentagon's Strategic Command and Control System*, New York, Simon & Schuster, 1985, pp. 90–93.

12. "Single Integrated Operations Plan," at http://en.wikipedia.org/wiki/Single_Integrated_Operational_Plan.

13. Quoted in McKinzie and others, *The U.S. Nuclear War Plan*, p. 8.

14. *White House Report*, 4.12.1996, at http://www.usembassy-israel.org.il/publish/press/whouse/archive/december/wh11205.htm.

15. See, for the commanders' background, "Chief of the United States Air Force," at http://en.wikipedia.org/wiki/Chief_of_Staff_of_the_United_States_Air_Force. It is only fair to add that, until 1982, most chiefs of staff had started their careers as bomber pilots.

16. See J. Olsen, *John Warden and the Renaissance of American Air Power*, Washington, D.C., Potomac Books, 2007, pp. 102–103.

17. General Jay Kelley, quoted in ibid., p. 265.

18. Quoted in ibid., p. 286.

19. See, on this topic, D. S. Fadok, "John Boyd and John Warden: Airpower's Quest for Strategic Paralysis," in Meilinger, ed., *The Paths of Heaven*, pp. 370–81.

20. See, for a contemporary description of what such a campaign might be like, P. H. Vigor, *Soviet Blitzkrieg Theory*, New York, St. Martin's, 1983.

21. See on these issues V. D. Sokolovsky, *Soviet Military Strategy*, 3rd ed., London, MacDonald, 1975, as well as H. M. Catudal, *Soviet Nuclear Strategy from Stalin to Gorbachev*, Atlantic Highlands, NJ, Humanities Press, 1989, pp. 132–34.

22. See Ford, *The Button*, p. 109; D. Ball, "U.S. Strategic Forces: How Would They Be Used?" *International Security*, 7, 3, winter 1982, pp. 31–60.

23. J. A. Warden, *The Air Campaign: Planning for Combat*, Washington, D.C., National Defense University Press, 1988, p. xvii.

24. Simpkin, *Race to the Swift*, pp. 167, 168.

25. Ibid., p. 189.

26. Ibid., p. 304.

27. See on this P. O. White, "The Role of the Army Tactical Missile System in Joint Warfare," research paper, Carlisle Barracks, PA, 1993, pp. 6–7. The paper is available at http://209.85.129.132/search?q=cache:rwq40V60Y1EJ:handle.dtic.mil/100.2/ADA264044+%22USAF+Bid+To+Take+Over+Air+Defense%22&cd=1&hl=iw&ct=clnk&gl=il.

28. See J. Baylis, "NATO's Strategy: The Case for a New Strategic Concept," *International Affairs*, 64, 1, winter 1987, p. 44.

29. Franklin, *War Stars*, pp. 155–61.

30. J. Hackett, *The Third World War: August 1985*, London, Sphere, 1985, pp. 8–9.

31. Ibid., p. 245.

32. Ibid., p. 289.

33. Ibid., pp. 369–70, 371–72, 375.

34. Quotes from T. Clancy, *Red Storm Rising*, London, Fontana, 1987, pp. 203, 211.

35. The words in quotation marks are from W. Scott et al., *Space Wars: The First Six Hours of World War III*, New York, Doherty, 2007, pp. 94, 199, 315.

36. Ibid., p. 258.

37. Ibid., p. 332.

38. 2008 figures from *CIA World Factbook*, at https://www.cia.gov/library/publications/the-world-factbook/.

39. Scott et al., *Space Wars*, p. 250.

40. Ibid., pp. 312–13.

Part IV: Little Wars, 1945–2010

13. THE TWILIGHT OF NAVAL AVIATION

1. See, for a list of the countries that flew the Phantom, "F-4 Phantom II," at http://en.wikipedia.org/wiki/F-4_Phantom.

2. See, for the evolution of Soviet thought on this subject, C. C. Petersen, "Aircraft Carriers in Soviet Naval Theory from 1960 to the Falklands War," Center for Naval Analyses, Professional Paper No. 405, January 1984, at http://web.archive.org/web/20061212225857/http://www.nwc.navy.mil/press/Review/2004/Winter/art6-w04.htm.

3. Quoted in G. Till, *Maritime Strategy and the Nuclear Age*, London, Palgrave, 1984, p. 182.

4. Lovett, "Russian and Soviet Naval Aviation, 1908–96," pp. 123–25.

5. "List of Aircraft Carriers of Russia and the Soviet Union," at http://en.wikipedia.org/wiki/List_of_aircraft_carriers_of_Russia_and_the_Soviet_Union.

6. See "List of Aircraft Carriers by Country," at http://en.wikipedia.org/wiki/List_of_aircraft_carriers_by_country.

7. "Never Trust a Used Carrier Salesman," Strategy Page, 29.9.2009, at http://www.strategypage.com/htmw/htnavai/articles/20090929.aspx.

8. See N. Polmar, "Is China Building Aircraft Carriers?," DefenseTech.org, 23.5.2008, at http://www.defensetech.org/archives/004195.html.

9. See I. Story and You Ji, "China's Aircraft Carrier Ambitions: Seeking Truth from Rumors," *Naval War College Review*, 57, 1, winter 2004, pp. 77–93.

10. See, for a detailed list of aircraft they have produced, "Multirole Combat Aircraft," at http://en.wikipedia.org/wiki/Multirole_combat_aircraft.

11. See, on the role of naval aviation in Korea, J. R. Bruning, *Crimson Sky: The Air Battle for Korea*, Washington, D.C., Potomac, 2005, pp. 22–40.

12. V. Morozov and S. Uskov, "On Guard for Peace and Labor: A Short Observation on the PRPK Air Forces from 1948 to 1996," at http://www.korean-war.com/DPRK.html, p. 2.

13. See on this episode C. G. Hearn, *Carriers in Combat: The Air War at Sea*, Mechanicsburg, PA, Stackpole, 2006, p. 234.

14. Ibid., p. 239.

15. Dayan, *Vietnam Diary*, p. 56.

16. See, for the memoirs of one USAF Phantom pilot in Vietnam, E. Cobleigh, *War for the Hell of It*, New York, Berkley Caliber, 2005.

17. See, for the Iraqi order of battle, R. P. Hallion, *Air Power and the Gulf War*, Washington, D.C., Smithsonian, 1992, pp. 124–32.

18. See GAO/NSIAD, "Cost-Effectiveness of Conventional and Nuclear-Powered Aircraft Carriers," 1.8.1998, at http://www.fas.org/man/gao/nsiad98001/a5.htm; also R. P. Hallion, *Storm over Iraq*, p. 255 and table 8.1.

19. Hallion, *Storm over Iraq*, p. 255 and table 8.1.

20. Quoted in ibid., p. 259.

21. See, on the use of naval airpower during the Second Gulf War, A. H. Cordesman, *The Iraq War: Strategy, Tactics, and Military Lessons*, Washington, D.C., CSIS, 2003, pp. 399–404.

22. Strategy Page, 23.11.2004, at http://www.strategypage.com/militaryforums/6-9693.aspx.

23. See, for Argentina's nuclear capability, R. W. Jones and M. G. Mcdonough, "Argentina," Non-Proliferation, 1998, available at http://www.ceip.org/programs/npp/nppargn.htm, and, for the way its rulers see nuclear weapons in relation to the Falklands, VOA News, "Argentina Reasserts Claim to Falkland Islands," 3.1.2007, at http://www.voanews.com/english/archive/2007-01/2007-01-03-voa29.cfm?CFID=47093395&CFTOKEN=93208398.

24. "Argentina Seeks Nuclear Apology," BBC News, 7.12.2003, at http://news.bbc.co.uk/2/hi/americas/3297805.stm.

25. See on this operation R. White, *Vulcan 607*, London, Bantam, 2006.

26. See, for the Falkland War as it was waged at sea, M. Middlebrook, *Task Force: The Falklands War, 1982*, Harmondsworth, Middlesex, Penguin, 1987, pp. 126–30, 132–38, 146–47, 155–63, 238–42.

27. Quoted in Middlebrook, *Task Force*, p. 241.

28. According to R. de la Peraja, "The Argentine Air Force Versus Britain in the Falkland Islands," in Higham and Stephens, eds., *Why Air Forces Fail*, p. 253.

29. See, for this radar, "H2S radar," at http://en.wikipedia.org/wiki/H2S_radar.

30. "A Second Falklands?," *Washington Times*, 8.6.2007, at http://www.washingtontimes.com/news/2007/jun/08/a-second-falklands/.

31. "Vikrant Class Aircraft Carrier," at http://en.wikipedia.org/wiki/Vikrant_class_aircraft_carrier.

32. See, on China's ambitions in this regard, "Chinese Navy Working Towards Aircraft Carrier Capabilities," *Marport*, 15.5.2009, at http://blog.marport.com/2009/05/15/875/.

33. Figures from "The Carriers," Navy.mil, at http://www.navy.mil/navydata/ships/carriers/cv-list.asp.

34. Dave's Web Harbor, "USS Iowa," n.d., at http://www.combie.net/webharbor/museum/bb61-1.html.

35. See the museum's inventory at http://www.nasm.si.edu/collections/objectsondisplay.cfm.

36. A. Tilghman, "New Rating Considered for UAV Operators," *NavyTimes*, 4.11.2008, at http://www.navytimes.com/news/2008/11/navy_uav2_110208w/.

37. M. K. Hilley, "Mahan UAV at Forefront of 21st Century Readiness," Navy.mil, 24.2.2009, at http://www.navy.mil/search/display.asp?story_id=42801.

38. O. E. Fitch, "Naval UAV Overview Brief," Naval UAV Executive Steering Group, n.d., at http://www.dtic.mil/ndia/targets/fitch.pdf.

39. M. Thompson, "The US Navy's Newest Weapon in the War Against Pirates," *Time*, 4.9.2010, at http://news.yahoo.com/s/time/20090904/us_time/08599192045900.

40. See, for an excellent article on the tests, "Operation Crossroads," at http://en.wikipedia.org/wiki/Operation_Crossroads.

41. Quoted in J. L. George, ed., *Problems of Seapower as We Approach the Twenty-First Century*, Washington, D.C., American Enterprise Institute, 1978, p. 302.

42. See on these episodes "PNS Ghazi," at http://en.wikipedia.org/wiki/PNS_Ghazi, and "ARA Santa Fe," at http://en.wikipedia.org/wiki/ARA_Santa_Fe_(S-21).

43. D. Lague, "Chinese Submarine Threat Is Growing, Analysts Say," *New York Times*, 25.2.2008, at http://www.nytimes.com/2008/02/25/world/asia/25submarine.html.

44. See M. McGwire, "The Tomahawk and General Purpose Naval Forces," in Betts, ed., *Cruise Missiles*, pp. 241–47, and J. Jones, "'Oscar': A Change in Soviet Naval Policy," *Jane's Defense Weekly*, 24.5.1986, pp. 942–47.

14. FROM KOREA TO THE SINAI

1. Morozov and Uskov, "On Guard for Peace and Labor," p. 2.

2. Ibid., p. 4.

3. See Xiaoming Zhang, "China and the Air War in Korea, 1950–1953," *Journal of Military History*, 62, April 1998, pp. 340–44, 368.

4. See, for this episode, I. Rendall, *Rolling Thunder: Jet Combat from World War II to the Gulf War*, New York, Free Press, 1999, p. 93.

5. See, for a detailed comparison between the two aircraft, "Mikoyan-Gurevich MiG-15," at http://en.wikipedia.org/wiki/MiG-15.

6. See, on Boyd's idea of the OODA loop, R. Coram, *Boyd: The Fighter Pilot Who Changed the Art of War*, New York, Little, Brown, 2002, pp. 336–37.

7. Xiaoming Zhang, "China and the Air War in Korea," p. 367.

8. Early U.S. figures from "USAF Col John Boyd," at http://www.sci.fi/~fta/JohnBoyd.htm; subsequent U.S. figures from Bruning, *Crimson Sky*, p. 206; see also Sandler, *The Korean War*, pp. 189–90. Communist figures from Morozov and Uskov, "On Guard for Peace and Labor," p. 4.

9. Figures from R. F. Futrell, *The United States Air Force in Korea*, Maxwell AFB, AL, 1983, pp. 644–66, as well as W. Cagle and F. A. Manson, *The Sea War in Korea*, Annapolis, MD, U.S. Naval Institute, 1957, appendix X.

10. C. E. LeMay and M. Kantor, *Mission with LeMay*, Garden City, NY, Doubleday, 1960, p. 382; C. A. MacDonald, *Korea: The War Before Vietnam*, New York, Free Press, 1986, pp. 235–36.

11. Futrell, *The United States Air Force in Korea*, p. 227.

12. Broughton, *Rupert Red Two*, p. 145.

13. See MacDonald, *Korea*, p. 228.

14. Groehler, *Geschichte des Luftkrieges*, p. 546.

15. See, for the way the repair teams were organized, ibid.

16. See, for the details, "F-84 Thunderjet," at http://en.wikipedia.org/wiki/F-84_Thunderjet.

17. Futrell, *The United States Air Force in Korea*, p. 581.

18. Korean figure from ibid., p. 122; American one from J. Houston, *The Sinews of War*, Washington, D.C., GPO, 1966, p. 530.

19. O. P. Weyland, "The Air Campaign in Korea," originally published in *Air University Quarterly Review*, 6, 3, fall 1953, and quoted in Emme, ed., *The Impact of Air Power*, p. 396.

20. Xiaoming Zhang, "The Sixty-Years Endeavors of Chinese Airpower," in J. Olsen ed., *Global Airpower*, pp. 377–378.

21. See, on these factors, pp. 144–146 above.

22. See, for the British and French airborne operations, Hickey, *Out of the Sky*, pp. 188–91.

23. "Chronological Listing of Israel Defense Force/Air Force," n.d., at http://www.ejection-history.org.uk/Aircraft_by_Type/ISRAEL/Dassault%20Mystere%20IV.htm.

24. According to B. Whaley, *Stratagem: Deception and Surprise in War*, Cambridge, MA, MIT Press, 1969, vol. 2, pp. 547–48.

25. See Pakdef.info, "Claims and Counter Claims," n.d., at http://www.pakdef.info/pakmilitary/airforce/war/claims.html.

26. S. Peres, *The Next Stage*, Tel Aviv, Am Hasefer, 1965 [Hebrew], p. 125.

27. Cobleigh, *War for the Hell of It*, p. 101.

28. See, for a blow-by-blow description of some such missions, R. Pecker, *Hawk in the Sky*, Tel Aviv, Yediot, 2002 [Hebrew], pp. 121–48.

29. D. Shalom, *Like Thunder on a Clear Day: The Destruction of the Arab Air Forces*, Rishon Lezion, Pirsumei Teufa, 2002 [Hebrew], p. 63.

30. Both figures from Y. Stigman, *From the War of Independence to Operation Kadesh*, Tel Aviv, Ministry of Defense, 1990 [Hebrew], p. 206.

31. I. Spector, *Loud and Clear: The Memoir of an Israeli Fighter Pilot*, New York, Zenith, 2009, p. 125.

32. Quoted in Oren, *Six Days of War*, p. 176.

33. E. Weizman, *On Eagles' Wings*, Tel Aviv, Steimatzky's, 1979, p. 216.

34. S. Golan, *A War on Three Fronts*, Tel Aviv, Maarachot, 2007 [Hebrew], p. 201.

35. Ibid., p. 198.

36. See G. W. Gawrych, *Key to the Sinai: The Battles of Abu Ageila in the 1956 and 1967 Arab-Israeli Wars*, Fort Leavenworth, KS, IS Army C&GS College, 1990.

37. Hallion, *Storm over Iraq*, p. 2.

38. See on this M. van Creveld, *Nuclear Proliferation and the Future of Conflict*, New York, Free Press, 1993, pp. 97–122.

39. See, on this aspect of the war, M. van Creveld, *The Sword and the Olive: A Critical History of the Israel Defense Force*, New York, PublicAffairs, 2003, pp. 159–61.

15. FROM THE SINAI TO TEHRAN

1. D. Shalom, *Phantoms over Cairo: Israeli Air Force in the War of Attrition, 1967–1970*, Rishon Lezion, Bavir, 2007 [Hebrew], vol. 1, p. 482. Though it is strongly biased in favor of the Israeli Air Force, so much more detailed is this account compared to all other published ones that I have used it as my main one for the War of Attrition.

2. Ibid., p. 491.

3. S. Gordon, "Air Superiority in the Arab-Israeli Wars, 1967–1982," in J. Olsen, ed., *A History of Air Warfare*, Washington, D.C., Potomac, 2010, p. 131.

4. Shalom, *Phantoms over Cairo*, vol. 1, pp. 184, 250.

5. See, for a contemporary account of these developments, E. O'Ballance, *The Electronic War in the Middle East, 1968–1970*, London, Faber & Faber, 1974, pp. 102–3, 110–11, 113–14, 116–17, 120–22, 123–24.

6. See R. Higham, "The Arab Air Forces," in Higham and Harris, eds., *Why Air Forces Fail*, pp. 90–91.

7. Quoted in Shalom, *Phantoms over Cairo*, vol. 1, p. 582.

8. One of those who promoted the idea was Yitzhak Rabin, serving as ambassador to Washington; see his *A Service Record*, Tel Aviv, Maariv, 1978 [Hebrew], vol. i, pp. 261–63. The views of other Israeli decision makers on this subject are recorded in D. Shueftan, *Attrition: Nasser Egypt's Political Strategy Following the 1967 War*, Tel Aviv, Maarachot, 1989 [Hebrew], pp. 120–25.

9. See on this Y. Bar Siman Tov, "The Myth of Strategic Bombing: Israeli Deep-Penetration Air Raids in the War of Attrition, 1969–70," *Journal of Contemporary History*, 19, 3, July 1984, pp. 549–70.

10. Shalom, *Phantoms over Cairo*, vol. 1, pp. 571–72.

11. See Cobleigh, *War for the Hell of It*, pp. 194–205.

12. Shalom, *Phantoms over Cairo*, vol. 1, p. 405.

13. Ibid., vol. 2, pp. 1104, 1105, 1146.

14. Indian Air Force, "The War of December 1971," n.d., at http://indianairforce.nic.in/show_page.php?pg_id=71; Rahim Khan, "Airscene," *Air Enthusiast*, 2, 3, March 1972, p. 111.

15. See, e.g., J. M. Janhimneadki, *The Flawed Architect: Henry Kissinger and American Foreign Policy*, Oxford, Oxford University Press, 2004, pp. 155–57.

16. See Federation of American Scientists, "Pakistan Nuclear Weapons," 2002, at http://www.fas.org/nuke/guide/pakistan/nuke/.

17. See, on this episode, D. N. Ganesh, "Indian Air Force in Action," in J. Singh, ed., *Kargil 1999: Pakistan's Fourth War for Kashmir*, New Delhi, KW, 1999, pp. 178–88.

18. Frost & Sullivan, "India to Modernize Armed Forces, Develops UAV Market," OCB/2007, 27.9.2007, at http://www.pcb007.com/pages/zone.cgi?a=16239&z=4&v=; *SAWF News*, 27.8.2009, at http://kuku.sawf.org/Articles/59694.aspx.

19. S. Gordon, *Thirty Hours in October*, Tel Aviv, Maariv, 2008, p. 225.

20. D. Asher, *The Syrians on the Borders: The IDF Northern Command in the Yom Kippur War*, Tel Aviv, Maarachot, 2008 [Hebrew], pp. 354, 264.

21. Pekker, *Hawk in the Sky*, pp. 336–38.

22. Gordon, *Thirty Hours in October*, p. 390.

23. A. Adan, *On the Banks of the Suez*, San Rafael, CA, Presidio, 1980, pp. 119, 122.

24. Gordon, *Thirty Hours in October*, pp. 482, 484, 490, 491, tables 17, 18, 20, 27, 30.

25. Details concerning the American airlift to Israel are available in C. J. Krisinger, "Operation Nickel Grass: Airlift in Support of National Policy," *Airpower Journal*, 3, spring 1989.

26. S. Hersch, *The Samson Option: Israel's Nuclear Arsenal and American Foreign Policy*, New York, Vintage, 1993, pp. 17, 40, 66, 174–75, 177, 216, 220, 223–31. Apparently Hersch was used by M. Zeyada and A. Abul Eneen, "Nuclear Blackmail Spared Israel Complete Route in 1973," Islam Online, 6.10.2003, at http://www.islamonline.net/English/News/2003-10/06/article04.shtml.

27. According to S. Shazly, *The Crossing of the Suez: The October War 1973,* London, Third World Centre for Research, 1980, pp. 234–35.

28. See, on this aircraft "C-5 Galaxy," at http://en.wikipedia.org/wiki/C-5_Galaxy.

29. See pp. 230–231 above and 410–412 below.

30. W. O. Staudenmaier, "A Strategic Analysis," in S. Tahir-Kheli and S. Ayubi, eds., *The Iran Iraq War,* New York, Praeger, 1982, p. 30, table 2.1 For the history and state of the Iraqi and Iranian air forces during this period see also R. E. Bergquist, *The Role of Airpower in the Iran-Iraq War,* Maxwell AFB, AL, Air University Press, 1988, pp. 19–28.

31. "MiG-23 Draws Iraqi Complaints," *Strategy Week,* 6, 41, 13–9.10.1980, p. 4.

32. S. Chubin, *Iran's National Security Policy,* New York, Carnegie Foundation, 1994, p. 36, table. 3.

33. B. Mossavar-Rahmani, "Economic Implications for Iran and Iraq," in Tahir-Kheli and S. Ayubi, eds., *The Iran Iraq War,* p. 53, table 3.3.

34. J. Bulloch and H. Morris, *The Gulf War: Its Origins, History and Consequences,* London, Methuen, 1989, p. 175.

35. See, for oil prices during this period, the graph in "Iran-Iraq War," Global Security.org, n.d., at http://www.globalsecurity.org/military/world/war/Iran-Iraq.htm.

36. See, for the details, "Al Hussein Missile," at http://en.wikipedia.org/wiki/Al_Hussein_(missile).

37. According to the *International Herald Tribune,* 20.7.1987.

38. "Iran-Iraq War," Global Security.org, n.d., at http://www.globalsecurity.org/military/world/war/Iran-Iraq.htm.

39. D. Middleton, "Iran-Iraq War Impasse," *New York Times,* 6.10.1981.

40. See, for a very good summary, "Operation Entebbe," at http://en.wikipedia.org/wiki/Operation_Entebbe.

41. See A. Perlmutter and others, *Two Minutes over Baghdad,* New York, Corgi, 1982, especially pp. 109, 115, 117, 118, 123, 134, 135–37.

42. See, for the details, "Operation Eagle Claw," at http://en.wikipedia.org/wiki/Operation_Eagle_Claw.

16. SPURIOUS VICTORIES?

1. See, for the link between birthrates and postmodern warfare, E. N. Luttwak, "Where Are the Great Powers? At Home with the Kids," *Foreign Affairs,* 73, 1994, pp. 23–29. For the reasons why, after millennia during which armed forces were practically all male, women are suddenly joining see M. van Creveld, *Men, Women and War,* London, Cassell, 2001, pp. 210–21.

2. See on all this the excellent work by C. Coker, *Humane Warfare,* London, Routledge, 2005.

3. See, on the possibilities and limitations of technological superiority, van Creveld, *Technology and War,* pp. 225–30.

4. Data from Encyclopaedia Britannica, *1993 Yearbook,* pp. 794 and 796.

5. See on this R. M. Stein and T. A. Postol, "Patriot Experience During the Gulf War," *International Security,* 17, 1, 1992, pp. 199–240.

6. See, out of the huge literature, T. Benbow, *Magic Bullet: Understanding the Revolution in Military Affairs*, London, Brassey's, 2004, especially pp. 13–54.

7. Hallion, *Storm over Iraq*, p. 185.

8. Ibid., p. 227.

9. See W. C. Pagonis, *Moving Mountains: Lessons in Leadership and Logistics from the Gulf War*, Boston, Harvard Business School, 1992, p. 7, table 1-1, and p. 146.

10. See Hallion, *Storm over Iraq*, pp. 162–66.

11. Olsen, *John Warden*, pp. 144–82.

12. Plan "Instant Thunder," as it was called, is well described in E. N. Luttwak, "The Renaissance of Strategic Air Power," Washington D.C., CSIS, 1999, appendix 1.

13. See The Lucky Devils, "The Gulf War with the 401FTW," n.d., at http://www.lucky-devils.net/baghdad.html.

14. Chubin, *Iran's National Security Policy*, p. 38, table 3.

15. Figures from Hallion, *Storm over Iraq*, pp. 147, 153.

16. "Middle East Carrier War," *The Hook*, 19, 1, spring 1991, p. 50.

17. Hallion, *Storm over Iraq*, p. 181; H. N. Schwarzkopf, *It Doesn't Take a Hero*, New York, Bantam, 1992, p. 486.

18. According to S. Biddle, *Military Power: Explaining Victory and Defeat in Modern Battle*, Princeton, Princeton University Press, 2004, p. 142.

19. Hallion, *Storm over Iraq*, p. 236.

20. Biddle, *Military Power*, pp. 1–2, 148–49.

21. E.g., E. H. Arnett, "Welcome to Hyperwar," *Bulletin of the Atomic Scientists*, 48, September 1992, pp. 14–21.

22. See Hallion, *Storm over Iraq*, p. 151.

23. Quoted in H. C. Mann, *Thunder and Lightning: Desert Storm and the Airpower Debates*, Maxwell AFB, AL, Air University Press, 1995, p. 25.

24. For troop-per-mile figures see A. Cordesman and A. Wagner, *Lessons of Modern War*, Boulder, CO, Westview, 1996, vol. 4, pp. 17 and 118; for the effect of cluster bombs, Luttwak, "The Renaissance of Strategic Airpower," p. 13.

25. B. Lambeth, *NATO's Air War over Kosovo*, Santa Monica, CA, RAND, 2001, p. 17.

26. P. Richter, "US Pilots Face Perilous Task, Pentagon Says," *Los Angeles Times*, 20.3.1999.

27. Quoted in W. K. Clark, *Waging Modern War*, New York, PublicAffairs, 2001, p. 208.

28. Calculated on the base of Lambeth, *NATO's Air War over Kosovo*, pp. 27–28.

29. Ibid., p. 36.

30. See, on the targeting difficulties, Clark, *Waging Modern War*, pp. 201–2, 215–16, 219, 236, 241.

31. See M. Jackson, *Soldier*, London, Transworld, 2007, pp. 295–301.

32. See, for the process whereby the numbers were cut and cut, Lambeth, *NATO's Air War over Kosovo*, pp. 61, 129, 131–32.

33. J. Barry and E. Thomas, "The Kosovo Cover-Up," *Newsweek*, 15.5.2000.

34. See Lambeth, *NATO's Air War for Kosovo*, pp. 77–82.

35. G. T. Hammond, "Myths of the Air War over Serbia," winter 2000, at http://www.airpower,maxwell.af.mil/airchronicles/apj.apj100/win00.hammond.htm, p. 8.

36. Quoted in ibid., p. 6.

37. S. Rayment, "US Fears Iraq Radar Can See Stealth Plane," *The Telegraph*, 1.6.2002.

38. See C. Hellman, "Lessons of Kosovo: More B-2 Bombers?" *Weekly Defense Monitor*, 24.6.1999, at http://www.cdi.org/weekly/1999/issue24.html.

39. See ibid.

40. See, for these problems as far as they affected the U.S. Air Force, Hallion, *Storm over Iraq*, pp. 1–120.

41. A. H. Cordesman, *The Iraq War: Strategy, Tactics, and Military Lessons*, Washington, D.C., CSIS, 2003, p. 544.

42. Ibid., pp. 35–36.

43. All figures from ibid., pp. 24–25.

44. BBC News, "Iraqi Aircraft Buried in Desert," 1.8.2003, at Cordesman, *The Iraq War.*

45. Cordesman, *The Iraq War*, p. 27.

46. See G. Graham, "US Moved Early to Obtain Air Supremacy," *Washington Post*, 20.7.2003; M. R. Gordon, "US Air Raids in 2002 Prepared for War in Iraq," *New York Times*, 20.7.2003.

47. Personal communication, Highland Forum, August 2004.

48. S. Biddle and others, *Toppling Saddam: Iraq and Military Transformation*, Carlisle, PA, U.S. Army War College, 2004, p. v.

49. Clausewitz, *On War*, p. 204.

50. CNN.com, 2.5.2003, at http://www.cnn.com/2003/WORLD/meast/05/01/sprj.irq.main/.

51. E. Margolis, "The US Air Force Rules the Skies," LewRockwell.com, 31.7.2007, at http:www.lewrockwell.com/margolis/margolis85.html.

52. The term coined by Rupert Smith in *The Utility of Force: The Art of War in the Modern World*, New York, Vintage, 2008.

Part V: War Amongst the People, 1898–2010

1. Van Creveld, *The Transformation of War*, pp. 33–42, 49–62.

2. See on this J. Corum, "The Myth of Air Control," 14, 4, *Aerospace Power Journal*, winter 2000, at http://scholar.google.co.il/scholar?q=%22myth+of+air+control%22&hl=iw&btnG=%D7%97%D7%99%D7%A4%D7%95%D7%A9.

17. THE FIRST FOUR DECADES

1. Lt. Col. J. E. Maxfield, "War Ballooning in Cuba," *Aeronautical Journal*, iii, 12, October 1899, p. 86.

2. Th. A. Keaney, "Aircraft and Air Doctrinal Development in Great Britain, 1912–1914," Diss., University of Michigan, 1975, p. 221.

3. "Vickers Victoria," at http://en.wikipedia.org/wiki/Vickers_Victoria.

4. Smith, *British Air Strategy Between the Wars*, p. 29.

5. Quoted in ibid., p. 30, and Budiansky, *Air Power*, p. 144.

6. Quoted in A. Boyle, *Trenchard*, New York, Norton, 1962, p. 383.

7. Anon, "The Fiends of the Air," *Naval Review*, 11, 1, February 1923, p. 90.

8. According to B. Hoffman, *British Air Power in Peripheral Conflict, 1919–1976*, Santa Monica, CA, Rand, 1989, pp. 32–33.

9. See on this P. Satiya, "The Defense of Inhumanity: Air Control and the British Idea of Arabia," *American Historical Review*, 111, 1, 2006, pp. 16–51.

10. Much of what follows is based on R. Yermiash, "Wings of the Empire: The Royal Air Force in Palestine and Transjordan, 1919–1939," Diss. submitted to Hebrew University, Jerusalem, 2008 [Hebrew].

11. Satiya, "The Defense of Inhumanity," footnote 51, has a whole list of sources dealing with this subject. See also Lawrence to Liddell Hart in D. Garnett, ed., *Letters of T. E. Lawrence*, London, Cape, 1938, p. 323.

12. See on this M. van Creveld, *The Sword and the Olive*, pp. 19–24.

13. Yermiash, "Wings of Empire," pp. 87–98.

14. See, on this episode, D. Sayer, "British Reactions to the Amritsar Massacre, 1919–20," *Past and Present*, 131, May 1991, pp. 130–64.

15. Yermiash, "Wings of Empire," p. 127.

16. Ibid., pp. 129–30.

17. Ibid., p. 230.

18. Lecture at the Royal United Services Institute, 12.2.1937, reprinted in Emme, ed., *The Impact of Air Power*, p. 352.

19. J. Corum and W. Johnson, *Airpower in Small Wars: Fighting Insurgents and Terrorists*, Lawrence, University Press of Kansas, 2003, pp. 34–37.

20. See H. Stimson, *On Active Service in War and Peace*, New York, Harper, 1948, pp. 110–16.

21. See on these operations C. Christienne and P. Lissarague, *A History of French Military Aviation*, Washington, D.C., Smithsonian, 1986, pp. 231–33.

22. T. J. Schulte, *The German Army and Nazi Policies in Occupied Russia*, Oxford, Berg, 1989, p. 69.

23. V. Redelis, *Partisanenkrieg*, Heidelberg, Vowinckel, 1958.

24. C. D. Heaton, *German Anti-Partisan Warfare in Europe, 1939–1945*, Atglen, PA, Schiffer, 2001, pp. 148–49.

25. See on this K. Schneider, *Partisanenkrieg in Jugoslawien, 1941–1945*, Hamburg, Mittler, 2002, pp. 253–54.

26. F. W. Seidler, *Die Wehrmacht im Partisanenkrieg*, Selent, Pour le Mérite, 1999, p. 113.

27. Ibid., p. 110.

28. Schneider, *Partisanenkrieg in Jugoslawien*, pp. 323 and 381.

29. Ibid., pp. 381–88.

30. Ibid., pp. 413–17.

31. See, on the German retreat, K. Hnilicka, *Das Ende auf dem Balkan 1944/45: Die militaerische Raeumung Jugoslaviens durch die deutsche Wehrmacht*, Goettingen, Muesterschmidt, 1970, pp. 47–149.

18. LOSE AND LEAVE

1. See T. Jones, "The British Army and Counter-Guerrilla Warfare in Greece, 1945–1949," *Small Wars and Insurgencies*, 8, 1, spring 1997, p. 93.

2. Ibid., pp. 100, 101.

3. "SB2C Helldiver," at http://en.wikipedia.org/wiki/SB2C_Helldiver.

4. *Peak Organized Strength of Guerrilla and Government Forces in Algeria, Nagaland, Ireland, Indochina, South Vietnam, Malaya, Philippines, and Greece*, Washington, D.C., Special Operations Research Office, American University, 7.6.1965, p. 18.

5. G. G. Barnett, "The Role of the Royal Air Force in the Preservation of Peace," *RUSI Journal*, 103, 8, August 1958, p. 383.

6. Corum and Johnson, *Airpower in Small Wars*, pp. 190–95.

7. See L. James, *Imperial Rearguard: Wars of Empire, 1919–85*, London, Brassey's, 1988, pp. 153–54.

8. See, for this aircraft, Wikipedia, "De Havilland Hornet," at http://en.wikipedia.org/wiki/De_Havilland_Hornet.

9. James, *Imperial Rearguard*, p. 146; R. Thompson, *Defeating Communist Insurgency: The Lessons from Malaya and Vietnam*, New York, Praeger, 1966, p. 106.

10. Figures from J. Prados, "Assessing Dien Bien Phu," in A. Lawrence and F. Logevall, eds., *The First Vietnam War: Colonial Conflict and Cold War Crisis*, Cambridge, MA, Harvard University Press, 2007, p. 221.

11. According to P. Davidson, *Vietnam at War*, Oxford, Oxford University Press, 1988, p. 217.

12. Department of State, *Foreign Relations of the United States* (FRUS), *1950: East Asia and the Pacific*, Washington, D.C., GPO, 1953, vol. 6, pp. 890–93.

13. L. Cesari, "The Declining Value of Indochina: France and the Economics of Empire, 1950–1955," in Lawrence and Logevall, eds., *The First Vietnam War*, p. 182.

14. D. G. Marr, "Creating Defense Capability," in Lawrence and Logevall, eds., *The First Vietnam War*, p. 103.

15. Quoted in R. H. Spector, *Advice and Support: The Early Years of the United States Army in Vietnam, 1941–1960*, New York, Free Press, 1983, p. 125.

16. See, on Viet Minh methods of camouflage, J. Roy, *The Battle of Dienbienphu*, New York, Carroll & Graf, 2002, p. 110.

17. From Staff Sgt. Barry Sadler's "The Ballad of the Green Berets."

18. See on this episode N. Stone, *Dien Bien Phu*, London, Brassey's, 2004, p. 109.

19. Quoted in Spector, *Advice and Support*, p. 161.

20. B. Fall, *Hell in a Very Small Place: The Siege of Dien Bien Phu*, Philadelphia, Lippincott, 1967, p. 372.

21. Quoted in Spector, *Advice and Support*, 206.

22. D. D. Eisenhower, *The White House Years: Mandate for Change*, New York, Doubleday, 1963, p. 345.

23. Davidson, *Vietnam at War*, pp. 584–85.

24. See Spector, *Advice and Support*, p. 114.

25. The most detailed account is R. Vetillard, *Setif, Mai 1945, Massacres en Algérie*, Paris, Édition de Paris, 2008.

26. See A. Horne, *A Savage War for Peace: Algeria 1954–1962*, London, Macmillan, 1977, pp. 119–24.

27. C. R. Shrader, *The First Helicopter War: Logistics and Mobility in Algeria, 1954–1962*, Westport, CT, Praeger, 1999, p. 77.

28. Figure from P. Vial and P. Tanchoux, "Les Archives d'Algérie: De l'Armée de l'air," *Revue Historique des Armées*, 187, June 1992, p. 68.

29. Shrader, *The First Helicopter War*, p. 116.

30. Ibid., p. 90.

31. See, for this and the following paragraph, M.-C. Villatoux and P. Villatoux, "Aerial Intelligence During the Algerian War," in M. S. Alexander and J. F. V. Keiger, eds., *France and the Algerian War, 1954–62*, London, Cass, 2002, pp. 74–75.

32. See on this J. J. Tolson, *Vietnam Studies: Airmobility*, Washington, D.C., GPO, 1973, pp. 128, 200.

33. According to A. Horne, *A Savage War for Peace*, pp. 249–50.

34. See, on all this, B. Estival, "The French Navy and the Algerian War," in Alexander and Keiger, eds., *France and the Algerian War, 1954–62*, pp. 81–84.

35. Redelis, *Partisanenkrieg*, pp. 118–20.

36. See for the various types Shrader, *The First Helicopter War*, p. 77.

37. P. Leulliette, *The War in Algeria: Memoirs of a Paratrooper*, New York, Bantam, 1964.

38. See, for a description of the "battle," P. Miquel, *La Guerre d'Algérie*, Paris, Fayard, 1993, pp. 267–85.

39. See on this A. Marlowe, "Forgotten Founder," *Weekly Standard*, 19.10.2009, at http://theweeklystandard.com/Content/Public/Articles/000/000/017/054kkhvp.asp?pg=2.

40. B. Hoffman, preface to D. Galula, *Pacification in Algeria, 1956–58*, Santa Monica, CA, RAND, 2006, p. iv.

41. Galula, *Pacification in Algeria*, p. 243.

42. Ibid., p. 23.

19. A WAR TOO FAR

1. "The Korean War Speaks to the Indo-Chinese War: A Quarterly Review Staff Study," *Air University Quarterly Review*, 7, 1, spring 1954, p. 60.

2. See, for his views, F. Smith, "Nuclear Weapons and Limited War," *Air University Quarterly Review*, 3, spring 1960, pp. 3–27.

3. See Corum and Johnson, *Airpower in Small Wars*, pp. 233–36.

4. See J. Slater, "The Domino Theory and International Politics: The Case of Vietnam," *Security Studies*, 3, 2, 1993, pp. 186–207.

5. See Spector, *Advice and Support*, pp. 21–54.

6. See, for a list of South Vietnamese Air Force aircraft, "South Vietnam Air Force, 1951–1975," at http://vnaf.net/.

7. Lt. Gen. Lionel McGarr, quoted in E. H. Tilford, *Setup: What the Air Force Did in Vietnam and Why*, Maxwell AFB, AL, Air University Press, 1991, p. 62.

8. Gravel, ed., *The Pentagon Papers*, vol. 1, p. 337.

9. V. H. Demma, "The U.S. Army in Vietnam," *American Military History* (1989), the official history of the United States Army, at http://www.ibiblio.org/pub/academic/history/marshall/military/vietnam/short.history/chap_28.txt.

10. See D. J. Anderson, *Trapped by Success: The Eisenhower Administration and Vietnam, 1953–61*, New York, Columbia University Press, 1991, especially pp. 175–91.

11. Corum and Johnson, *Airpower in Small Wars*, p. 252.

12. See, on the creation of the air commandos, C. H. Hildreth, *USAF Counter-Insurgency Doctrines and Capabilities, 1961–1962*, Washington, D.C., Office of Air Force History, 1962, pp. 8–9.

13. This and subsequent figures from Corum and Johnson, *Airpower in Small Wars*, pp. 262 and 263.

14. See W. A. Buckingham, "Operation Ranch Hand: Herbicides in Southeast Asia," *Air University Review*, 34, 5, July–August 1983, pp. 42–53.

15. According to T. C. Thayer, *War Without Fronts: The American Experience in Vietnam*, Boulder, CO, Westview, 1985, pp. 26, 37.

16. Figures from M. Clodfelter, *The Limits of Air Power: The American Bombing of North Vietnam*, New York, Free Press, 1989, p. 129.

17. See D. Kinnard, *The War Managers*, Annapolis, MD, Naval Institute Press, 2007 [1977], pp. 55–56.

18. For a discussion of the various helicopter types see G. L. Rottman and A. Hook, *Vietnam Airmobile Warfare Tactics*, Oxford, Osprey, 2007, pp. 5–11.

19. Dayan, *Vietnam Diary*, pp. 65, 77, 83.

20. See, on Viet Cong and North Vietnamese anti-helicopter tactics, C. B. Currey, *Victory at Any Cost: The Genius of Vietnam's General Vo Nguyen Giap*, Washington, D.C., Potomac, 1999, pp. 237–38.

21. G. Roush, "Helicopter Losses During the Vietnam War," Vietnam Helicopter Pilots' Association, n.d., at http://www.vhpa.org/heliloss.pdf.; Rottman and Hook, *Vietnam Airmobile Warfare*, p. 11.

22. See on this W. C. Westmoreland, *A Soldier Reports*, New York, Dell, 1976, pp. 252–74.

23. See, above all, Schelling, *Arms and Influence*.

24. Broughton, *Rupert Red Two*, p. 317.

25. See on this J. Broughton, *Going Downtown: The Air War Against Hanoi and Washington*, New York, Orion Books, 1988, p. 28, as well as J. Record, *The Wrong War: Why We Lost in Vietnam*, Annapolis, MD, Naval Institute Press, 1998, p. 111.

26. See on all this Tilford, *Setup*, pp. 172–210.

27. Cobleigh, *War for the Hell of It*, p. 108.

28. Tilford, *Setup*, p. 108.

29. Quoted in A. M. Schlesinger, *The Imperial Presidency*, Boston, Houghton Mifflin, 1973, p. 32.

30. Hammond, *The Mind of War*, p. 61.

31. Cobleigh, *War for the Hell of It*, pp. 146–49.

32. Figures from C. Hobson, *Vietnam Air Losses*, Hinkley, UK, Midland Press, 2001, pp. 15–166, and J. Van Staaveren, *Gradual Failure*, Washington, D.C., Air Force Museums and History Program, 2002, p. 316.

33. See on this J. Schlight, *A War Too Long: The USAF in Southeast Asia, 1961–1975*, Washington, D.C., Air Force History and Museums Program, 1996, p. 48.

34. W. Thompson, *To Hanoi and Back*, Washington, D.C., Smithsonian, 2002, p. 303.

35. According to R. Littauer and N. Uphoff, eds., *The Air War in Indochina*, Boston, Beacon, 1971, p. 281.

36. Cobleigh, *War for the Hell of It*, pp. 139–40.

37. According to Armitage and Mason, *Airpower in the Nuclear Age*, p. 100.

38. According to R. M. Nixon, *The Memoirs of Richard Nixon*, New York, Grosset & Dunlap, 1978, p. 606.

39. Clodfelter, *The Limits of Airpower*, p. 254.

40. W. P. Head, *War from Above the Clouds: B-52 Operations During the Second Indochina War and the Effects of the Air War on Theory and Doctrine*, Maxwell AFB, AL, Air University Press, 2002, p. 173.

41. According to G. Lewy, *America in Vietnam*, New York, Oxford University Press, 1978, p. 478.

42. F. R. Futrell, *U.S. Air Force in Southeast Asia: Aces and Aerial Victories, 1965–1973*, Maxwell AFB, AL, Air University Press, 1976, pp. 95–102.

43. A. C. Enthoven and K. Wayne Smith, *How Much Is Enough: Shaping the Defense Program, 1961–1969*, New York, Harper & Row, 1971, p. 304.

44. W. Thompson, "Operations over North Vietnam, 1965–1973," in J. Olsen, ed., *A History of Air Warfare*, p. 134.

45. Ibid., p. 107.

46. Figures from Thayer, *War Without Fronts*, p. 80, table 8.1, and I. Rendall, *Rolling Thunder: Jet Combat from World War II to the Gulf War*, New York, Free Press, 1997, p. 168.

47. There is even an entry in Wikipedia: "Than Hoa Bridge," at http://en.wikipedia.org/wiki/Thanh_Hoa_Bridge.

48. J. L. Frisbee, "The Air War in Vietnam," *Air Force Magazine*, 55, 9, September 1972, p. 48; see, too, Davidson, *Vietnam at War*, pp. 708–10.

49. Pape, *Bombing to Win*, pp. 174–210.

50. See, on the battle, Westmoreland, *A Soldier Reports*, pp. 440–58, as well as Currey, *Victory at Any Cost*, pp. 265–66.

51. T. C. Thayer, "The Impact of the Air Effort Probably Outweighed Many of Its Benefits," in W. Scott Thompson and D. D. Frizzell, eds., *The Lessons of Vietnam*, New York, Russak, 1977, pp. 145–50.

20. AFTER VIETNAM

1. Figures and other details from J. Y. Henkin, "Like Fish in the Bush: Insurgents and Counterinsurgency in Rhodesia, 1965–1980," Diss. submitted to the Hebrew Uni-

versity, Jerusalem, 2009 [Hebrew], pp. 28–29. This dissertation makes extensive use of Rhodesian Army records and I have used it extensively.

2. See, for the Rhodesian Air Force, J. R. T. Wood, *Counter-Strike from the Sky: The Rhodesian All-Arms Fireforce in the War in the Bush, 1974–1980*, Johannesburg, 30 South Publishing, 2009, pp. 32–33.

3. Composition, training, equipment, and tactics of the unit in question are explained in "Rhodesian Light Infantry," at http://en.wikipedia.org/wiki/Rhodesian_Light_Infantry.

4. Henkin, "Like Fish in the Bush," pp. 129–49, 221–22, has some very detailed descriptions of the operations and their results.

5. See, on the largest of these operations, Wood, *Counter-Strike from the Sky*, pp. 123–202.

6. See Russian General Staff, *The Soviet-Afghan War: How a Superpower Fought and Lost*, Lawrence, University Press of Kansas, 2002, pp. 15–20, 197–200.

7. "The Red Army's New Look," *Newsweek*, 11.2.1980.

8. See D. Isby, *Weapons and Tactics of the Soviet Army*, London, Jane's, 1981, pp. 7–13.

9. See for these tactics Russian General Staff, *The Soviet-Afghan War*, pp. 58–79.

10. Ibid., editors' preface, p. xix.

11. Ibid., pp. 199–200.

12. See "BMD-1," at http://en.wikipedia.org/wiki/BMD-1.

13. See "FIM-92 Stinger," at http://en.wikipedia.org/wiki/FIM-92_Stinger.

14. Russian General Staff, *The Soviet-Afghan War*, p. 213.

15. "List of Soviet Aircraft Losses in Afghanistan," at http://en.wikipedia.org/wiki/List_of_Soviet_aircraft_crashes_in_Afghanistan.

16. See Corum and Johnson, *Airpower in Small Wars*, pp. 340–51.

17. Ibid.

18. See, for this aircraft, "IAI Kfir," at http://en.wikipedia.org/wiki/IAI_Kfir.

19. M. Heller, ed., *The Middle East Strategic Balance, 1984*, Jerusalem, Jerusalem Post, 1984, p. 114.

20. Spector, *Loud and Clear*, p. 283

21. A. Benn, "Report: IAF Wiped Out 59 Iranian Missile Launchers in 34 Minutes," *Haaretz* [Hebrew], 24.10.2006.

22. Quoted by Brigadier General R. Shmueli, chief of Air Force Intelligence, Israel, *Israel Air Force Gazette* [Hebrew], 173, February 2007, at http://www.iaf.org.il/Templates/Journal/Journal.In.aspx?lang=HE&folderID=1856&subfolderID=1857&docfolderID=1859&lobbyID=50&docID=26491.

23. Rubin, "The Rocket Campaign," p. 20, quoting former Israeli Air Force chief of staff Giora Rom. For a general description of Hezbollah's arsenal of rockets and the effects they had on the fighting see A. H. Cordesman and others, *Lessons of the 2006 Israeli-Hezbollah War*, Washington, D.C., CSIS, 2007, pp. 99–107.

24. I. Brun, "The Second Lebanon War, 2006," in Olsen, ed., *A History of Air Power*, p. 298.

25. O. Shelah and Y. Limor, *Captives of Lebanon*, Tel Aviv, Yediot, 2007 [Hebrew], pp. 241, 246.

26. See, for the confused decision-making process, ibid., pp. 177–204.

27. D. R. Herspring, *Rumsfeld's Wars: The Arrogance of Power*, Lawrence, University Press of Kansas, 2008, p. 83.

28. See H. K. Ullman and J. P. Wade, *Shock and Awe: Achieving Rapid Dominance*, Washington, D.C., National Defense University Press, 1996.

29. See U.S. Army, *Operation Enduring Freedom—October 2001–March 2002*, 2003, pp. 7–10, at http://www.history.army.mil/brochures/Afghanistan/Operation%20 Enduring%20Freedom.htm#p8.

30. "Senate Report: Bin Laden Was Within Our Grasp," 29.11.2009, at http:// xxnews/yahoo.com/s/ap/20091129/ap_on_go_co/us_tora_bora_bin_laden.

31. AFP, "Stinger Missiles in Afghanistan a Threat to US," 21.3.2006, at http:// www.spacewar.com/reports/Stinger_Missiles_In_Afghanistan_A_Threat_US.html.

32. As the Bundeswehr, e.g., does; E. Chauvistre, *Wir Gutkrieger: Warum die Bundeswehr im Ausland Scheitern Wird*, Frankfurt/Main, Campus, 2009, pp. 69–70.

33. E. MacAskil, "U.S. Commander in Afghanistan to Order Limits on Air Strikes," *Guardian*, 22.6.2009, at http://www.guardian.co.uk/world/2009/jun/22/mcchrystal -usa-afghanistan-air-attacks.

34. J. S. Landay and H. Bernton, "Taliban Strength Nears Military Proportion," McClatchy, 15.10.2009, at http://news.yahoo.com/s/mcclatchy/20091015/wl_mcclatchy/ 3333450.

35. See D. Wood, "Afghanistan: The Obama-Bush Exit Strategy," *Politics Daily*, 3.12.2009, at http://www.politicsdaily.com/2009/12/03/afghanistan-the-obama-bush -exit-strategy/.

36. See on this Herspring, *Rumsfeld's Wars*, pp. 103–5.

37. See on this K. Beebe, "The Air Force's Missing Doctrine," *Air and Space Journal*, April 2006, pp. 1–2.

38. See pages F1-4 of FM 3-24, Counterinsurgency, at http://www.fas.org/irp/ doddir/army/fm3-24fd.pdf.

39. M. Weisberger, "King Airs Take on USAF Surveillance Role in Iraq and Afghanistan," Flight International, 9.9.2009, at http://www.flightglobal.com/articles/ 2008/09/09/315696/king-airs-take-on-usaf-surveillance-role-in-iraq-and.html.

40. See, e.g., S. Waterman, "Analysis: USAF Counterinsurgency," UPI.com, part 1, 17.6.2008, p. 2, at http://www.spacewar.com/reports/Analysis_USAF_counterinsurgency _Part_1_999.html.

41. Th. Baker, "At Odds with Air Force, Army Adds Its Own Aviation Unit," *New York Times*, 22.6.2008, at http://www.nytimes.com/2008/06/22/washington/22 military.html.

42. R. H. Holmes and others, "The Air Forces' New Ground War," *Air and Space Power Journal*, October 2006, pp. 2 and 8.

43. "US Casualties in Iraq," GlobalSecurity.Org, November 2009, at http://www .globalsecurity.org/military/ops/iraq_casualties.htm; AP, "US Military Deaths in Iraq

War at 4,367," 30.11.2009, at http://news.yahoo.com/s/ap/20091201/ap_on_re_us/us_iraq_us_deaths_1.

44. R. Farley, "Abolish the Air Force," *American Prospect*, November 2007, at http://www.prospect.org/cs/articles?article=abolish_the_air_force.

CONCLUSIONS: GOING DOWN, 1945–?

1. Pape, *Bombing to Win*, pp. 314–31.

2. See, for country-by-country, figures, p. 114, 115, and 118 above.

3. Unless otherwise indicated, all figures are taken from Wikipedia.

4. L. B. Thompson, "The Slow Death of American Air Power," *Defense Aerospace*, 16.1.2007, at http://harpgamer.com/harpforum/lofiversion/index.php?t1133.html; as well as S. Deitchmann, "Exploiting the Revolution in Conventional Weapons," *Aerospace America*, June 1987, pp. 34–37.

5. Data from "F-22 Raptor," at http://en.wikipedia.org/wiki/F-22_Raptor.

6. "Italian Eurofighter Typhoons Providing Air Cover for Turin Winter Olympics," *Eurofighter Typhoon*, 14.2.2006, at http://www.eurofighter.com/news/article232.asp.

7. See above, p. 267.

8. Figures from M. J. Armitage, *Unmanned Aircraft*, Washington, D.C., Potomac, 1988, p. 99.

9. Armitage and Mason, *Airpower in the Nuclear Age*, pp. 252–53; personal communication by Dr. Grant Hammond, 3.1.2010.

10. See P. Sprey as quoted in J. Fallows, *The National Defense*, New York, Vintage, 1982, p. 100.

11. H. Redemann, *Innovations in Aircraft Construction*, West Chester, PA, Schiffer, 1991, pp. 28–31.

12. Broughton, *Red Rupert Two*, pp. 229–30.

13. See the figures in Budiansky, *Air Power*, p. 421.

14. D. A. Deptula, "Air and Space Power, Lead Turning, the Future," *Orbis*, 52, 4, fall 2008, pp. 585–86; also Builder, *The Icarus Syndrome*, p. 156.

15. Se. J. Freedberg, "Wear and Tear Adds Up on Military Aircraft," *National Journal*, March 2008, at http://www.govexec.com/dailyfed/0308/032108nj1.htm.

16. "HMS Victory," at http://en.wikipedia.org/wiki/HMS_Victory.

17. The most recent case is that of the USAF in Afghanistan; see N. Shachtman, "How the Afghanistan Air War Got Stuck in the Sky," *Wired Magazine*, 8.12.2009, at http://www.wired.com/magazine/2009/12/ff_end_air_war/2/.

18. See, e.g., Hallion, *Storm over Iraq*, p. 283, table 2.

19. See, e.g., U.S. Air Force, "Airborne Network to Link Sensors, Shooters, Decision Makers," 3.2.2005, at http://www.af.mil/news/story.asp?storyID=123009935.

20. S. Shuger, "Outgunned: What the Crusader Cancellation Really Means to the Army," *Slate*, 23.5.2002, at http://slate.msn.com/id/2066158/.

21. Pierce Report, 15.10.1936, unpublished, kindly put at my disposal by Ms. Yermiash. Commander Richard Pierce was the officer commanding, RAF, in Palestine during this period.

22. See, for the details, B. B. Mike Cannon, "PEO Tactical Missiles Sensor to Shooter Timeline Equation," at http://www.dtic.mil/ndia/2004precision_strike/CANNON TimelineEquation.pdf.

23. "Israeli Tech Improved Response Time Against Rockets to 30 Seconds," World-Tribune.com, 21.1.2009, at http://www.worldtribune.com/worldtribune/WTARC/2009/me_israel0061_01_21.asp.

24. See van M. Creveld, *Command in War*, Cambridge, MA, Harvard University Press, 1985, pp. 232–57.

25. Quoted in Hallion, *Storm over Iraq*, p. 267.

26. See on this van Creveld, *Technology and War*, pp. 265–96.

27. See Ph. de Souza, "Naval Forces," in Ph. Sabin and others, eds., *The Cambridge History of Greek and Roman Warfare*, Volume 1: *Greece, the Hellenistic World and the Rise of Rome*, Cambridge, Cambridge University Press, 2008, p. 358, and J. S. Morrison," Hellenistic Oared Warships, 399–31 BC," in R. Gardiner, ed., *Age of the Galley: Mediterranean Oared Vessels Since pre-Classical Times*, Conway Maritime Press, 2004, pp. 73–74.

28. See, in general, B. Brodie, *Naval Strategy*, Princeton, Princeton University Press, 1943.

29. See on this E. A. Cohen, "The Meaning and Future of Air Power," *Orbis*, 39, 2, spring 1995, pp. 189–201.

30. For the pros and cons of President Bush's policy in this matter see A. Krepinevich, "Skipping 'Skipping a Generation of Weapon Systems,'" CSBA release, 1.5.2002, at http://www.csbaonline.org/4Publications/Archive/B.20020501.Skipping_Skipping/B.20020501.Skipping_Skipping.htm.

31. See, for a discussion of the pros and cons, B. Deblois, "Ascendant Realms: Characteristics of Airpower and Space Power," in Meilinger, ed., *The Paths of Heaven*, pp. 563–78; also, for a contrary view, T. A. Burdine, "The Army's 'Organic' Unmanned Aircraft Systems," *Air and Space Power Journal*, summer 2009, at http://www.airpower.maxwell.af.mil/airchronicles/apj/apj09/sum09/burdine.html.

32. F. Kaplan, "Attack of the Drones: Death of the F-22 Fighter Plane," *Newsweek*, 28.9.2009, pp. 54–57.

33. W. B. Yeats, "An Irish Airman Foresees His Death," in W. B. Yeats, *The Poems*, New York, Macmillan, 1989, p. 135.

34. Quoted in Kennett, *The First Air War*, p. 225.

35. Thompson, "Air Operations over North Vietnam," p. 123.

36. C. Jaeger, "Flying High," in Lewis, ed., *Mammoth Book*, p. 436.

37. Quoted in Builder, *The Icarus Syndrome*, p. 184.

38. See on these processes van Creveld, *Men, Women and War*, *passim*.

39. Probert, *Bomber Harris*, p. 121.

40. Van Creveld, *Men, Women and War*, pp. 143–47; also, and above all, A. Noggle, *A Dance with Death: Soviet Airwomen in World War II*, College Station, Texas University Press, 1994.

41. See M. van Creveld, *Das Bevorzugte Geschlecht*, Munich, Gerling Akademie, 2003, pp. 54–55.

42. J. Holm, *Women in the Military: An Unfinished Revolution*, Novato, CA, Presidio, 1992, p. 181; and W. Breuer, *War and the American Woman: Heroism, Deeds and Controversy*, Westport, CT, Praeger, 1997, pp. 70–71.

43. See, for the evidence, K. O'Beirne, "The War Machine as Child Minder," in G. Frost, ed., *Not Fit to Fight: The Cultural Subversion of the Armed Forces*, London, Social Affairs, 1998, p. 36; L. Miller, *Feminism and the Exclusion of Army Women from Combat*, Harvard University, John M. Olin Institute for Strategic Studies, n.d., p. 19; J. Stiehm, *Arms and the Enlisted Woman*, Philadelphia, Temple University Press, 1989, p. 100.

44. See Hammond, *The Mind of War*, pp. 39, 49.

45. See M. McMichael and C. Moskos, *The Mother of All Hooks: The Story of the U.S. Navy Tailhook Scandal*, Oxford, Transaction, 1997.

46. See, for this story and the relevant references, "Ernest King," http://en.wikipedia.org/wiki/Admiral_King.

INDEX

Martin van Creveld is an internationally recognized authority on military history and strategy. The author of twenty-two books which were translated into twenty languages, he has lectured or taught at virtually every strategic institute, military or civilian, in the Western world, including the U.S. Naval War College. He used to be the only non-American author on the U.S. Army's required reading list for officers, and the only person—foreign or American—to have had two books on that list. Born in the Netherlands, he holds degrees from the Hebrew University of Jerusalem and the London School of Economics. He lives near Jerusalem.